HUMAN EMPIRE

Arguing that demographic thought begins not with quantification but in attempts to control the qualities of people, *Human Empire* traces two transformations spanning the early modern period. First was the emergence of population as an object of governance through a series of engagements in sixteenth- and seventeenth-century England, Ireland and colonial North America, influenced by humanist policy, reason of state and natural philosophy, and culminating in the creation of political arithmetic. Second was the debate during the long eighteenth century over the locus and limits of demographic agency, as church, civil society and private projects sought to mobilize and manipulate different marginalized and racialized groups – and as American colonists offered their own visions of imperial demography. This innovative, engaging study examines the emergence of population as an object of knowledge and governance and connects the history of demographic ideas with their early modern intellectual, political and colonial contexts.

TED McCORMICK is Associate Professor of History at Concordia University in Montreal. His first book, *William Petty and the Ambitions of Political Arithmetic* (2009), won the 2010 John Ben Snow Prize, awarded by the North American Conference on British Studies for the best book on any aspect of British history before 1800. He is a Fellow of the Royal Historical Society.

IDEAS IN CONTEXT

Edited by DAVID ARMITAGE, RICHARD BOURKE and JENNIFER
PITTS

The books in this series will discuss the emergence of intellectual traditions and of related new disciplines. The procedures, aims and vocabularies that were generated will be set in the context of the alternatives available within the contemporary frameworks of ideas and institutions. Through detailed studies of the evolution of such traditions, and their modification by different audiences, it is hoped that a new picture will form of the development of ideas in their concrete contexts. By this means, artificial distinctions between the history of philosophy, of the various sciences, of society and politics, and of literature may be seen to dissolve.

A full list of titles in the series can be found at: www.cambridge.org/IdeasContext

HUMAN EMPIRE

Mobility and Demographic Thought in the
British Atlantic World, 1500–1800

TED McCORMICK

Concordia University, Montréal

CAMBRIDGE
UNIVERSITY PRESS

CAMBRIDGE
UNIVERSITY PRESS

University Printing House, Cambridge CB2 8BS, United Kingdom

One Liberty Plaza, 20th Floor, New York, NY 10006, USA

477 Williamstown Road, Port Melbourne, VIC 3207, Australia

314–321, 3rd Floor, Plot 3, Splendor Forum, Jasola District Centre,
New Delhi – 110025, India

103 Penang Road, #05–06/07, Visioncrest Commercial, Singapore 238467

Cambridge University Press is part of the University of Cambridge.

It furthers the University's mission by disseminating knowledge in the pursuit of
education, learning, and research at the highest international levels of excellence.

www.cambridge.org
Information on this title: www.cambridge.org/9781009123266
DOI: 10.1017/9781009128834

© Ted McCormick 2022

First published 2022

A catalogue record for this publication is available from the British Library.

Library of Congress Cataloging-in-Publication Data
NAMES: McCormick, Ted, author.
TITLE: Human empire : mobility and demographic thought in the British
Atlantic world, 1500–1800 / Ted McCormick.
DESCRIPTION: Cambridge ; New York, NY : Cambridge University Press, 2022. |
Includes bibliographical references and index.
IDENTIFIERS: LCCN 2021970029 | ISBN 9781009123266 (hardback) |
ISBN 9781009128834 (ebook)
SUBJECTS: LCSH: Demography – Political aspects – Great Britain – History. |
Great Britain – Colonies – Population. | Great Britain – Politics and government – 1485– |
Great Britain – Intellectual life. | BISAC: POLITICAL SCIENCE / History & Theory
CLASSIFICATION: LCC HB3583.A3 M33 2022 | DDC 304.60941–dc23/eng/20220105
LC record available at https://lccn.loc.gov/2021970029

ISBN 978-1-009-12326-6 Hardback

For my daughters, Vivian and Audrey

Contents

Acknowledgments

I began thinking about this book before my last one was published and before I started my job as Assistant Professor at Concordia, in 2008. In the course of working on this study of demographic thinking, I married, became a father to two children and lost my own father – demographic events that are, as all demographic events are, more than statistics. Like its author, the book has grown and changed beyond recognition in the years since its inception. Some of those thanked here may wonder why their names appear; others may have given up waiting. Still, it could not have been done without them.

My biggest debts of gratitude are still owed to my doctoral and post-doctoral mentors, David Armitage and Nicholas Canny; neither supervised this project, but both did more than anyone else to help me find the professional footing necessary to carry it out. Conversations with Carl Wennerlind, particularly in the early years, and with Vera Keller throughout helped me to pinpoint my subject and think about its significance; it would be fair to say that they have also helped me to define the kind of historian I am. Theresa Ventura has been with me at every stage of this project, listened to and questioned successive iterations of it over the years, read more drafts than I can remember writing, traveled across the globe to enable me to pursue related opportunities and sacrificed her time to help secure mine. No thanks can cover that.

A shockingly large number of scholars, some friends and some email acquaintances have given me the opportunity to collaborate with them in the conference panels, seminars, symposia, journal special issues or edited volumes that have done so much to shape and reshape this project. (I have said no to very little, and the book is richer for it.) Special thanks in this regard are due to Roy Ritchie, my host at the Henry E. Huntington Library during 2010–11; Alison Bashford, who brought me to the Sydney Centre for the Foundations of Science at University of Sydney in early 2013; Philip Stern, who, along with Carl Wennerlind, invited me to contribute a chapter to their volume on *Mercantilism Reimagined* (2013); Robert Mayhew, whose invitation to write about pre-Malthusians for his volume *New Perspectives on Malthus* (2016) did more than anything else to clarify the argument of this book in its final form; and Emma Spary and my Concordia colleague Anya Zilberstein, whose invitation to write on population and food-related projects – coinciding with Christine Zabel's suggestion that I think, write and talk about the history of self-interest – sent me deeper into the Hartlib Papers than I had ever planned to go.

For invitations to share my research in person or in writing and to talk about the questions involved, I thank David Armitage, Nigel Smith, Owen Williams and the Folger Institute Center for the History of British Political Thought; Pascal Bastien and the Groupe de recherche en histoire des sociabilités at the Université de Québec à Montréal; Dan Carey, Eileen Gillooly and the Heyman Center for the Humanities at Columbia University; Janet Clare; Jeff Collins and the Department of History at Queen's University; Elizabeth Cook, Tayler Meredith and participants in the Green Britain conference at the Birmingham Centre for Reformation and Early Modern Studies; Kevin Gilmartin and the Humanities Seminar at Caltech; Brian Lewis and the Montreal British History Seminar at McGill University; Vanessa Harding, Kris Heitman and participants in the London Bills of Mortality symposium at the Folger Shakespeare Library; Peter Mancall and the University of Southern California-Huntington Library Early Modern Studies Institute; John Marshall and the Department of History at the Johns Hopkins University; Allyson May and participants in the Law and Governance in Britain Conference at the University of Western Ontario; Jane Ohlmeyer; Lindsay O'Neill and the Seminar in Early Modern British History at the Huntington; Akos Sivado and the Research Centre for the Humanities in Budapest; Scott Sowerby and the British Studies Graduate Cluster at Northwestern University; Rachel Weil and the few but proud participants in our roundtable on population at the North American Conference on British Studies in Providence; and Christine Zabel and participants in the Knowledge(s) of Self-Interest workshop at the Kulturwissenschaftliches Institut, Essen.

In and around these occasions, the book has benefited from conversations, comments, readings and exchanges with many others. I am sorry for any omissions, but let me at least record my gratitude to Fredrik Albritton Jonsson, Donna Andrew, Eric Ash, Moya Bailey, Bill Bulman, Will Cavert, Joyce Chaplin, Hal Cook, Brian Cowan, David Cressy, Will Deringer, Barbara Donagan, Molly Farrell, Moti Feingold, Mary Fissell, Jeremy Fradkin, Robert Frank, John Gagne, Stephen Gaukroger, Hugh

Goodacre, Elsbeth Heaman, Amanda Herbert, David Hitchcock, Joanna Innes (who warned me that my subject was boundless), Mark Jenner, Phil Kreager, Karen Kupperman, Rhodri Lewis, Bruce Moran, Matthew Neufeld, Tara Nummedal, Maggie Pelling, Keith Pluymers, Nick Popper, Chanda Prescod-Weinstein, Andrea Rusnock, Barbara Shapiro, Kenny Sheppard, Brent Sirota, Paul Slack, Abby Swingen, Bob Tittler and Andrew Wear. My Concordia colleagues Sarah Ghabrial, Norman Ingram, Andy Ivaska, Wilson Jacob, Shannon McSheffrey and Elena Razlogova have broadened my perspectives, as have chats over several years now with my former student, James Leduc. My research assistants, Sólveig Hanson and Hannah Sparwasser Soroka, went above and beyond in help-ing me make the manuscript neater and clearer than it would otherwise be. Warm thanks to Liz Friend-Smith at Cambridge University Press, the series editors and the two anonymous reviewers, for their encouragement and advice.

Research involved sojourns to a range of institutions. Not all are evident in the final product, but each played a role in its completion. My thanks go to the archivists, librarians and staff of the American Philosophical Society Library, the British Library, the Carlisle Library, the Cheshire Record Office, the East Sussex Record Office, the Folger Shakespeare Library, the Henry E. Huntington Library, the Library of Congress, the London Metropolitan Archive, the McGill University Library, the National Archives (UK), the New York Public Library, the Royal Society Library and the Concordia University Library. Nor could the book have been written without extensive use of digital resources, including the Corpus of Electronic Texts, Early English Books Online, Eighteenth-Century Collections Online, the Hartlib Papers Online and the Holinshed Project. Funding for the original project – conceived very differently than the book before you – came from a Seed Grant from Concordia in 2009–10 and from a 2010–14 Standard Research Grant from the Social Science and Humanities Research Council of Canada, improved by a Mellon Fellowship at the Huntington in 2010–11 and a Visiting Fellowship at the Sydney Centre for the Foundations of Science in 2013.

Introduction: Transformations in Demographic Thought

This book traces two transformations in early modern English thinking about the governance of populations. The first, spanning the Tudor and early Stuart eras, was a shift in emphasis in defining the real object of demographic knowledge and intervention. While sixteenth-century engagements with what we would consider demographic entities and processes tended to identify particular, qualitatively defined groups (referred to here as "multitudes" to distinguish them from "population" as a quantity) as their units of analysis, by the middle decades of the seventeenth century something much closer to the national population, as a total and knowable number of people, had come to the fore.[1] Underlying this shift, I argue, was not primarily a new spirit of quantification but rather new attitudes to the state and to the natural world.[2] While a new reason of state embracing commercial and colonial expansion stretched the traditional metaphor of the body politic past the breaking point, a growing appreciation of the importance of the nation's natural environment and geographical situation – and of policies that exploited these in the service of the nation's interest – directed attention both

---

[1] Early modern authors used "multitude" to describe myriad collectivities, including groups we now call populations. Its analytical use here draws attention to the way such groups were defined in qualitative terms for purposes of governance. To speak of a "multitude" either generally or in some delimited way (the multitude of vagrants, for instance) was to identify a collectivity with certain qualities, whose size was not necessarily subject to precise measurement. By contrast, "populations," in modern social scientific discourse, are inherently quantifiable; in common parlance they *are* numbers. The distinction differentiates tendencies but is not absolute; for multitudes as objects of calculation in the Middle Ages, see Peter Biller, *The Measure of Multitude: Population in Medieval Thought* (Oxford: Oxford University Press, 2000).

[2] On the "quantifying spirit," see Daniel Headrick, *When Information Came of Age: Technologies of Knowledge in the Age of Reason and Revolution, 1700–1850* (Oxford: Oxford University Press, 2000), pp. vi, 65, 88; Tore Frängsmyr, J. L. Heilbron and Robin E. Rider (eds.), *The Quantifying Spirit in the Eighteenth Century* (Berkeley: University of California Press, 1990). For a similar argument about the prior impact of "quantitative perception," see Alfred W. Crosby, *The Measure of Reality: Quantification and Western Society, 1250–1600* (Cambridge: Cambridge University Press, 1997).

to the balance between numbers and resources and to the plasticity of the population as a whole.[3] The problem that organized demographic thinking ceased to be that of maintaining a healthy body politic. It became instead a question of transforming – not merely increasing or mobilizing, but changing and improving – populations, in an ever-growing variety of ways.

The second transformation began in the mid-seventeenth century and was completed with Malthus's *Essay on the Principle of Population*, the sixth and fullest edition of which appeared in 1826.[4] This was a shift in the locus of what we might call demographic agency: The power, and thus the responsibility, to determine the course of demographic growth and related processes, as well as to shape the qualities of populations. Riding a wave of neo-Baconian rhetoric about the transformative powers of human science, and participating in the creation of a fiscal-military and imperial state, seventeenth-century "projectors" proposed schemes for manipulating the size, distribution and composition of the national population in the interests of productivity, security and stability.[5] In later decades, however, initiative moved increasingly to the public sphere, in the guise of philanthropic efforts, drives for moral reform and discourses of public health. The constraints of nature, including a human nature bound by the impulses of passion and the calculus of individual interest, girded skepticism about the effectiveness and legitimacy of royal, state

---

[3] On the reorientation of reason-of-state discourse and the role of interest, see Vera Keller, *Knowledge and the Public Interest, 1575–1725* (Cambridge: Cambridge University Press, 2015). On the attenuation of the body politic as a governing metaphor in early modern economic thought, see Andrea Finkelstein, *Harmony and the Balance: An Intellectual History of Seventeenth-Century Economic Thought* (Ann Arbor: University of Michigan Press, 2000).

[4] Thomas Robert Malthus, *An Essay on the Principle of Population, as It Affects the Future Improvement of Society. With Remarks on the Speculations of Mr. Godwin, M. Condorcet, and Others* (London: Printed for J. Johnson, 1798) [hereafter cited as Malthus, *Essay* (1798)]; *Thomas Robert Malthus An Essay on the Principle of Population, Or, A View of Its Past and Present Effects on Human Happiness, with an Inquiry into Our Prospects Respecting the Future Removal or Mitigation of the Evils which It Occasions* (London: John Murray, 1826).

[5] Ted McCormick, *William Petty and the Ambitions of Political Arithmetic* (Oxford: Oxford University Press, 2009); Colin Brooks, "Projecting, Political Arithmetic, and the Act of 1695," *English Historical Review* 97:382 (1982), 31–53. On the wider context of "improvement" in England, see Paul Slack, *The Invention of Improvement: Information and Material Progress in Seventeenth-Century England* (Oxford: Oxford University Press, 2015). Outside Britain, similar developments often originated within the state, and took shape as policies rather than projects. See, for example, Carol Blum, *Strength in Numbers: Population, Reproduction, and Power in Eighteenth-Century France* (Baltimore, MD: Johns Hopkins University Press, 2002); Leslie Tuttle, *Conceiving the Old Regime: Pronatalism and the Politics of Reproduction in Early Modern France* (Oxford: Oxford University Press, 2010).

or imperial intervention.[6] By the time Malthus penned his *Essay*, both the effective power and the moral responsibility of demographic decision-making resided first and foremost with the sovereign individual. Once a privileged *arcanum imperii*, demographic agency – not merely the power to reproduce, but the responsibility to make reproduction a conscious and morally freighted economic calculation – had become a mode of individual subjectivity.

Straddling and linking these two transformations, in the later decades of the seventeenth century, was "political arithmetic," the creation of the polymathic Sir William Petty (1623–87).[7] Petty was an intellectual innovator of a very particular kind. Neither a great thinker on the order of his patron Thomas Hobbes nor a scientist on the level of his colleague Robert Boyle, he offered not a philosophy but rather a way of thinking about political and social problems – including what we would consider economic questions, but also matters of colonial policy and the management of religious fissures within and between Britain and Ireland – that placed an empirical, quantitative grasp of population at the center. The intermediate level of Petty's intellectual engagement, linking theory and practice but reducible to neither, foreshadowed the uneasy tie between the later social sciences, which he and others like him supplied with concepts,

---

[6] For later projects, see Sarah Lloyd, *Charity and Poverty in England, c. 1680–1820: Wild and Visionary Schemes* (Manchester: Manchester University Press, 2009); Joanna Innes, *Inferior Politics: Social Problems and Social Policies in Eighteenth-Century Britain* (Oxford: Oxford University Press, 2009), pp. 109–75. Charlotte Sussman's emphasis on "peopling" rather than "population" fuels a related analysis of migration for the period after 1660; see Sussman, *Peopling the World: Representing Human Mobility from Milton to Malthus* (Philadelphia: University of Pennsylvania Press, 2020), pp. 1–16. On criticism of projecting see also Charlotte Sussman, "The Colonial Afterlife of Political Arithmetic: Swift, Demography, and Mobile Populations," *Cultural Critique* 56 (2004), 96–126, and Peter Buck, "People Who Counted: Political Arithmetic in the Eighteenth Century," *Isis* 73:1 (1982), 28–45. See also Donald Winch, *Riches and Poverty: An Intellectual History of Political Economy in Britain, 1750–1834* (Cambridge: Cambridge University Press, 1996), pp. 80–1, 91; Peter Miller, *Defining the Common Good: Empire, Religion, and Philosophy in Eighteenth-Century Britain* (Cambridge: Cambridge University Press, 1994), pp. 349–412.

[7] On political arithmetic, see Paul Slack, "Government and Information in Seventeenth-Century England," *Past and Present* 184 (2004), 33–68; Julian Hoppit, "Political Arithmetic in Eighteenth-Century England," *Economic History Review* 49:3 (1996), 516–40; John A. Taylor, *British Empiricism and Early Political Economy: Gregory King's 1696 Estimates of National Wealth and Population* (Westport, CT: Praeger, 2005); William Peter Deringer, "Calculated Values: The Politics and Epistemology of Economic Numbers in Britain, 1688–1738," unpublished PhD dissertation, Princeton University (2012), and William Deringer, *Calculated Values: Finance, Politics, and the Quantitative Age* (Cambridge, MA: Harvard University Press, 2018). On Petty, see McCormick, *William Petty*; Sabine Reungoat, *William Petty: Observateur des Îles Britanniques* (Paris: Institut National d'Études Démographiques [INED], 2004).

and modern social engineering, which echoed his aspirations. In the seventeenth century, it characterized the figure of the "projector," forerunner of the modern expert: A man with a new way of doing things, willing to use his knowledge to solve the world's problems – for a price.[8] As this implies, the knowledge Petty offered his royal and vice-regal patrons was not discovered but created. Population was a project.

Its formulation and articulation in the context of Restoration-era international economic and imperial competition, the Irish land settlement and the politics of religion have been studied. Less understood is the source of its novelty. Like all projectors, Petty worked to differentiate his offerings from the competition, and the slogan he chose was a portentous one: "number, weight, and measure."[9] Combining biblical authority with the rhetoric of Baconian philosophy, this triad justified Petty's materials and methods (extrapolation of numbers from the partial evidence of parish registers of births, marriages and burials, London mortality bills and tax returns) while underlining the precision, practicality and impartiality of his conclusions.[10] Much as Petty intended, political arithmetic became synonymous with quantification; to praise one, in the eighteenth century, was to praise the other. The converse was also true: When Adam Smith, in the *Wealth of Nations*, or David Hume, in his *Essays*, wished to cast doubt on the reliability of demographic figures, it was political arithmetic that they criticized.[11] Modern commentators have followed suit, seeing in political arithmetic the fountainhead, or at least the precursor, of a modern, statistical worldview.

Yet, what was most radical about Petty's political arithmetic was not its rhetoric of quantification or its instrumental use of numbers, but its

---

[8] On projecting and the projector, see Vera Keller and Ted McCormick, "Towards a History of Projects," *Early Science and Medicine* 21:5 (2016), 423–44; Koji Yamamoto, "Reformation and the Distrust of the Projector in the Hartlib Circle," *The Historical Journal* 55:2 (2012), 375–97.

[9] See, for example, William Petty, *Political Arithmetick* (London: Printed for Robert Clavel and Henry Mortlock, 1690), sig. A3v, sig. A4v, p. 21. The triad originated in the apocryphal Wisdom of Solomon, 11:20: "thou hast ordered all things in measure and number and weight" (KJV); in his *Novum Organum*, Francis Bacon had advised "that all things in both natural bodies and natural powers be (so far as is possible) numbered, weighed, measured, and determined." Francis Bacon, *The New Organon*, edited and translated by Lisa Jardine and Michael Silverthorne (Cambridge: Cambridge University Press, 2000), p. 229.

[10] On the legitimating role of number, see Mary Poovey, *A History of the Modern Fact: Problems of Knowledge in the Sciences of Wealth and Society* (Chicago: University of Chicago Press, 1998), pp. 120–38; Deringer, "Calculated Values," 1–46.

[11] See Adam Smith, *An Inquiry into the Nature and Causes of the Wealth of Nations*, 2 vols., ed. R. H. Campbell, A. S. Skinner and W. B. Todd (Oxford: Oxford University Press, 1979), vol. I, pp. 534–5; David Hume, "On the Populousness of Ancient Nations," in David Hume (ed. Eugene F. Miller), *Essays Moral, Political, and Literary*, revised ed. (Indianapolis, IN: Liberty Fund, 1987), pp. 377–464, at p. 381.

purpose, which Petty distinguished by an equally telling but less modern term: "transmutation."[12] In the first instance, this meant "the transmutation of the Irish into English" by means of large-scale, forced "transplantations" of socially marginal English women. Mobilizing these women as gendered subjects much as naval impressment mobilized men (a comparison Petty made), political arithmetic applied to Ireland promised to exploit women's customary household roles and natural reproductive capacities to effect the transformation of the Irish population into one with English language, manners, habits and allegiances. Applied to England, the same instrument might be used to manipulate the relative sizes of different religious constituencies or to adjust balances between different trades, transforming confessional and economic demography. Extended across the Atlantic, it might dictate the transformation of Indigenous girls into English housewives, while sparing England's own "teeming" (marriageable) women for service at home. Political arithmetic should not be seen as a new mode of analysis; it was, rather, a new kind of governance. Its object was a knowable, measurable and above all manipulable population. Its essence was not quantification but a new kind of demographic agency, initially intended for the use of the state, but soon subject to appropriation and contestation from other quarters.

How might we investigate the history of this power, and of the conception of population that it required? To do so is not the same as investigating the history of demographic quantification, or of statistics, both of which have rich historiographies.[13] The practice of gathering information about numbers of people and their property is ancient, while the modern census, in Britain, dates only from 1801; local or otherwise highly specific enumerations – urban censuses of the poor, lists of householders, militia musters and

---

[12] This is examined in McCormick, *William Petty*, pp. 168–258. On the role of alchemical metaphor in the formation of imperial ideology, see Ralph Bauer, *The Alchemy of Conquest: Science, Religion, and the Secrets of the New World* (Charlottesville, VA: University of Virginia Press, 2019). Bauer's work, which came to my attention during revisions, argues persuasively for the influence of medieval alchemy and eschatology on European thinking about the New World, but leaves the subjection of Old World groups to "transmutative" projects out of account.

[13] On the history of demographic quantification, see D. V. Glass, *Numbering the People: The Eighteenth-Century Population Controversy and the Development of Census and Vital Statistics in Britain* (Farnborough: D. C. Heath, 1973); Jacques Dupâquier and Michel Dupâquier, *Histoire de la démographie: la statistique de la population des origines à 1914* (Paris, Librarie Académique Perrin, 1985). On probability, see Lorraine Daston, *Classical Probability in the Enlightenment* (Princeton, NJ: Princeton University Press, 1985); Ian Hacking, *The Emergence of Probability: A Philosophical Study of Early Ideas about Probability, Induction, and Statistical Inference*, 2nd ed. (Cambridge: Cambridge University Press, 2006).

registers of congregants – were common in the sixteenth century.[14] These were hardly unrelated to governance, but they were rarely framed with a view to transmuting the people they counted in any fundamental sense. That is to say, such enumerations neither required any notion of population as an object of transformative intervention nor implied the existence of any agent capable of transforming it. Unless and until political arithmeticians appropriated them, indeed, such lists and registers scarcely even implied the existence of such a unit as a national population. Quantification came to be crucial to the conceptualization and exercise of demographic agency in the later seventeenth century, but nothing in the prior history of demographic figures made this outcome inevitable. To the contrary, the manipulability of human populations was conceived largely without reference to anything resembling empirical statistics. Its history lies elsewhere.

Approaching the question of power over population from the other end, we might look for answers in the development of the state apparatus. This has chronological and historiographical appeal: The formation of the "fiscal-military state" in Britain coincided with the "golden age of political arithmetic" that historians of economic thought have found between 1660 or 1688 and 1714; indeed, observers linked them at the time.[15] Historians, however, have doubted the practical effect of political arithmetic on government, and although recent work suggests closer connections between them than once thought, other developments muddy the waters.[16] The most important of these is the rethinking of the state itself, as narratives of secularization, bureaucratization and centralization have given way to studies emphasizing the diversity of initiatives and motivations, the importance

[14] See Rebecca Jean Emigh, Dylan Riley and Patricia Ahmed, *Antecedents of Censuses from Medieval to Nation States: How Societies and States Count* (Basingstoke: Palgrave Macmillan, 2016). On the history of the national census in Britain, see Glass, *Numbering the People*; Kathrin Levitan, *A Cultural History of the British Census: Envisioning the Multitude in the Nineteenth Century* (New York: Palgrave Macmillan, 2011). For earlier enumerations in Britain and Ireland, see Colin R. Chapman, *Pre-1841 Censuses and Population Listings in the British Isles*, 5th ed. (Baltimore, MD: Genealogical Publishing, 2012); Jeremy Gibson and Mervyn Medlycott, *Local Census Listings, 1522–1930: Holdings in the British Isles*, 3rd ed. (Bury: Federation of Family History Societies, 1992).

[15] On the "golden age," see Hoppit, "Political Arithmetic," 516–17. On political arithmetic, demographic information and the state, see Edward Higgs, *The Information State in England: The Central Collection of Information on Citizens since 1500* (Basingstoke: Palgrave Macmillan, 2004); John Brewer, *The Sinews of Power: War, Money and the English State, 1688–1788* (Cambridge, MA: Harvard University Press, 1988), pp. 221–49.

[16] A compelling recent case for political arithmetic's effectiveness is Deringer, "Calculated Values"; see also William Deringer, "Finding the Money: Public Accounting, Political Arithmetic, and Probability in the 1690s," *Journal of British Studies* 52:3 (2013), 638–68. John Brewer, by contrast, has suggested that "political arithmetic promised much more than it could deliver"; Brewer, *Sinews of Power*, p. 224.

of local, low-level officials as well as of popular politics and the diffusion of governmental functions among a variety of institutions, not least the church.[17] Approaching population as a state concern, then, raises as many questions as it answers – for who constituted the state and what were its boundaries? Nor can such an approach account for an idea of population before there was a fiscal-military state to speak of, or for its later appropriation by nonstate actors. As odd as a history of demographic power would be without the state, it would not quite be *Hamlet* without the prince. Their coincidence was contingent and their relationship was unstable.

If histories of statistics and the state miss the mark, that of biopolitical governmentality – Michel Foucault's name for a complex of discourses and practices geared to the government of life through a combination of institutional authority and self-regulation – comes closer.[18] Not only is governmentality distinguished from earlier modes of power by its distinctive focus on population; not only is population itself grasped as a historically contingent concept, distinct from older notions of multitude; but this idea is also understood in such a way as to illuminate the rise of quantification and that of the state without collapsing into either. Each of these points informs the present study. Yet, problems hamper a biopolitical approach to early modern population thought. Locating the origins of modern governmentality in the later eighteenth century, Foucault treated political arithmetic as a "virtual" anticipation of something that only became "operational" a century later.[19] Scholars of Britain and Ireland have addressed this by arguing for the chronological priority of English developments or by questioning the causal linkages Foucault presumed.[20] But this skirts deeper problems. First,

---

[17] See especially Michael Braddick, *State Formation in Early Modern England, c. 1550–1700* (Cambridge: Cambridge University Press, 2000), and Steve Hindle, *The State and Social Change in Early Modern England, 1550–1640* (Basingstoke: Palgrave, 2002).

[18] See, especially, Michel Foucault *Security, Territory, Population: Lectures at the Collège de France, 1977–1978*, edited by Michel Senellart and translated by Graham Burchell (Basingstoke: Palgrave Macmillan, 2007); Michel Foucault "Governmentality," in Graham Burchell, Colin Gordon and Peter Miller (eds.), *The Foucault Effect: Studies in Governmentality* (Chicago: University of Chicago Press, 1991), pp. 87–104; Michel Foucault *The Will to Knowledge: The History of Sexuality Volume 1*, translated by Robert Hurley (London: Penguin, 1978), especially pp. 135–9.

[19] Foucault, *Security, Territory, Population*, pp. 277–8.

[20] See Steve Pincus, "From Holy Cause to Economic Interest: The Study of Population and the Invention of the State," in Alan Houston and Steve Pincus (eds.), *A Nation Transformed: England After the Restoration* (Cambridge: Cambridge University Press, 2001), pp. 272–98, at pp. 273–4; Andrea A. Rusnock, "Biopolitics: Political Arithmetic in the Enlightenment," in William Clark, Jan Golinski and Simon Schaffer (eds.), *The Sciences in Enlightened Europe* (Chicago: University of Chicago Press, 1999), pp. 49–68, and Andrea A. Rusnock, *Vital Accounts: Quantifying Health and Population in Eighteenth-Century England and France* (Cambridge: Cambridge University Press, 2002), pp. 3–4; Nessa Cronin, "Writing the 'New Geography': Cartographic Discourse and Colonial Governmentality in William Petty's *The Political Anatomy of Ireland* (1672)," *Historical Geography* 42 (2014), 58–71.

by distinguishing modern governmentality sharply from both the preceding regime of princely sovereignty and from the pastoral power of the church, Foucault segregated two major loci of early modern demographic agency from the emergence of population.[21] Second, by locating the distinctiveness of population, as an object of *bio*politics, in its biological character, Foucault made its historical emergence as a concept dependent on the prior existence of "life" sciences and its analytical perspicacity dependent on linkages between governance and biological knowledge.[22] Not only is empirical evidence of such connections sparse before the later eighteenth century – with the partial exception of "medical arithmetic," which linked political arithmetic to questions of public health from the early 1720s – but focusing on them also means ignoring what other contexts for demographic thought might tell us about how populations and demographic agency came to be conceptualized.[23] To the extent that population is construed as a manifestation of biopolitical governmentality, it cannot describe what sixteenth- and seventeenth-century vernacular commentators, addressing populations in most metropolitan and colonial contexts, had in mind.

However, Foucault surfaces here in a second way. If ideas about the governance of populations and the locus of demographic agency have no obvious historiographical home, it is because they hover – as their early modern promoters and projectors did – at the margins or in the interstices of institutional and disciplinary life. They are neither methods of demographic analysis in the statistical sense nor doctrines in the sense given to "doctrines of population" as reasoned preferences for maximal or optimal numbers of people relative to resources; both mercantilist "pronatalism" and "Malthusianism" involve ideas about how populations work and where control over them is vested, but neither is defined by them.[24]

---

[21] On pastoral power, see Michel Foucault, "Omnes et Singulatim: Towards a Criticism of Political Reason," The Tanner Lectures on Human Values, Stanford University, 10 and 16 October 1979, reprinted in Jeremy R. Carrette (ed.), *Religion and Culture: Michel Foucault* (New York: Routledge, 1999), pp. 134–52.

[22] Foucault, *Security, Territory, Population*, pp. 11, 21–22; see also Michel Foucault, *The Order of Things: An Archaeology of the Human Sciences* (New York: Random House, 1994), pp. 250–302. On the limits of biopolitics as an analytical category, see Patrick Carroll, *Science, Culture, and Modern State Formation* (Berkeley: University of California Press, 2006), pp. 113–42, and Aaron James Henry, "William Petty, the Down Survey, Territory and Population in the Seventeenth Century," *Territory, Politics, Governance* 2:2 (2014), 1–20.

[23] On medical arithmetic, see Rusnock, *Vital Accounts*; Innes, *Inferior Politics*, pp. 131, 153–4.

[24] On methods of analysis, see, for example, Karl Pearson and E. S. Pearson, *The History of Statistics in the Seventeenth and Eighteenth Centuries: Against the Changing Background of Intellectual, Scientific, and Religious Thought* (High Wycombe: Charles Griffin, 1978). On "doctrines" or "theories" of population expressed as preferences for maximal or optimal numbers see Charles Emil Strangeland, *Pre-Malthusian Doctrines of Population: A Study in the History of Economic*

(Nor, for the same reason, can ideas about demographic governance and agency usefully be characterized as attitudes to population, pro- or contra.) They neither rise to the level of theories nor descend to the details of policies – though they inform both. They are more like models or logics of demographic thought, tacit rules or conditions for seeing, thinking about and engaging with populations in a coherent way. They are epistemic structures. Unearthing them, sketching their shape and dimensions and tracing their implications for and connections to their historical contexts means digging beneath the history of disciplines, institutions or ideologies. It resembles what Foucault described as archaeology.[25]

Yet, these ideas were not expressions of some all-embracing *episteme* or succession of *epistemes* that shaped the perception and cognition of an age or sequence of ages.[26] The ways of thinking about population traced here were subject to contestation even at the height of their influence, and unlike Foucauldian *epistemes* and Kuhnian paradigms, they changed slowly and subtly rather than suffering revolutionary ruptures.[27] Though they linked different areas of intellectual and practical activity, moreover, they were in important respects local. What this means is, admittedly, a matter of degree and of perspective. Trained as an intellectual historian to study individuals, texts and events, I am predisposed to understand the objects of my investigation in terms of specific political and intellectual contexts: The struggle over the Irish land settlement in the 1650s and 1660s; the impact of biblical criticism on sacred historiography in the 1670s, 1680s and 1690s.[28] A subject such as this, which both persists and

Theory (New York: Augustus M. Kelley, 1904); James Bonar, *Theories of Population from Raleigh to Arthur Young* (London: George Allen and Unwin, 1982); Joseph J. Spengler, *French Predecessors of Malthus: A Study in Eighteenth-Century Wage and Population Theory* (Durham, NC: Duke University Press, 1942); E. P. Hutchinson, *The Population Debate: The Development of Conflicting Theories up to 1900* (New York: Houghton Mifflin, 1967); Johannes Overbeek, *History of Population Theories* (Rotterdam: Rotterdam University Press, 1974).

[25] See especially Foucault, *Order of Things*, pp. xxi–xxii.

[26] As is implied in Foucault, *Order of Things*, pp. xxii–xxiii.

[27] On paradigms see Thomas S. Kuhn, *The Structure of Scientific Revolutions*, 3rd ed. (Chicago: University of Chicago Press, 1996). On developments in historical epistemology before Kuhn and since, see Hans-Jörg Rheinberger, *On Historicizing Epistemology: An Essay* (Stanford, CA: Stanford University Press, 2010).

[28] Political contexts of comparatively tight geographical and temporal specificity – and texts of an elite intellectual caliber – have marked the "Cambridge School" of intellectual history since the early methodological work of Quentin Skinner; see Quentin Skinner, *Visions of Politics I: Regarding Method* (Cambridge: Cambridge University Press, 2002), especially pp. 57–89; see also Elizabeth A. Clark, *History, Theory, Text: Historians and the Linguistic Turn* (Cambridge, MA: Harvard University Press, 2004), pp. 130–55. A concern with the reception, appropriation and tradition has, however, expanded the temporal scope of some studies; the paradigmatic example is J. G. A. Pocock, *The Machiavellian Moment: Florentine Political Thought and the Atlantic Republican Tradition* (Princeton, NJ: Princeton University Press, 2003).

changes over the course of centuries, and which intersects with a large number of other historical questions (economic and social policy, gender and sexuality, poverty and deviance, racism and slavery, colonialism and empire, communication and information, to name just the most obvious) affronts this habit. There is no single context for the development, articulation, appropriation or modification of ideas about how and by whom populations can be governed, any more than there is a single disciplinary tradition to which these phenomena belong.[29] A comprehensive study tying each iteration of these ideas over three centuries to a particular set of contingencies – a global account told as the sum of all local histories – would soon become incoherent.

My solution to the problem of making a big argument about durable ideas without losing all sense of context has been to pursue the subject episodically, and to narrow my principles of selection and angles of analysis for the episodes I examine. The most obvious contractions of focus are geographical and linguistic: With few exceptions, this book deals with English-language works and with works produced in England or by authors and presses in English colonial settlements in Ireland or North America. This decision is not just a matter of logistical necessity, however; there are positive reasons for treating Anglophone discussions of population as a category. The first is their richness and diversity – which is not to say originality, priority or uniqueness – throughout the period. Historians of early demographic thought concerned with doctrine or theory credit Jean Bodin and, especially, Giovanni Botero with setting discussions of population and its relationship to resources on a new course.[30] Historians of demographic or social policy have examined pro-natalist, poor relief, public health and data-gathering projects in France, Italy, Germany, the

---

[29] Historians of demographic ideas can draw as usefully on strands of constructivist history of science – notably its openness to multiple and heterogeneous contexts, and its attentiveness to the construction of putatively natural objects of knowledge – as on the histories of political or economic thought. On constructivism see Jan Golinski, *Making Natural Knowledge: Constructivism and the History of Science* (Chicago: University of Chicago Press, 2005); Steven Shapin, *A Social History of Truth* (Chicago: University of Chicago Press, 1994). The persistent linkage of demographic ideas to statistics and to bureaucratic institutions means that works taking this approach are mostly modern in focus: See Theodore M. Porter, *Trust in Numbers: The Pursuit of Objectivity in Science and Public Life* (Princeton, NJ: Princeton University Press, 1995); Geoffrey C. Bowker and Susan Leigh Star, *Sorting Things Out: Classification and Its Consequences* (Cambridge, MA: MIT Press, 1999); Libby Schweber, *Disciplining Statistics: Demography and Vital Statistics in France and England, 1830–1885* (Durham, NC: Duke University Press, 2006).

[30] Strangeland, *Pre-Malthusian Doctrines of Population*, pp. 99–107; Bonar, *Theories of Population from Raleigh to Arthur Young*, p. 16; Overbeek, *History of Population Theories*, pp. 31–2; Yves Charbit, *The Classical Foundations of Population Thought* (Dordrecht: Springer, 2011), pp. 43–62.

Low Countries and beyond.[31] Historians of slavery and the slave trade have put the control of large numbers of forced migrants and laborers in a polyglot Atlantic and global context.[32] Ideas, texts and people cross borders; practices and policies provoke imitation. What can justify such a category as Anglophone demographic thought?

One paradoxical answer begins where the idea for this book did: with the political arithmetic of the Restoration period. The paradox is suggested by comparing the two figures who, together, invented political arithmetic. While John Graunt was an apparently little-traveled and most probably monolingual London tradesman, William Petty studied in Utrecht, Leiden, Amsterdam and Paris and spent most of his later life shuttling between London, Dublin and his Irish estates. We can think of their political arithmetic as having local as well as global faces. Petty pitched projects of national and geopolitical import, bound up with international commercial competition, military conflict and the growth of colonial empire; Graunt's chief object of interest, meanwhile, looks parochial by contrast: the management of social problems – poverty and disease – in his own city. The truth is more complicated. When a review of Graunt's *Natural and Political Observations ... upon the Bills of Mortality* appeared in the pioneering Parisian *Journal des Sçavans*, the reviewer noted that an interest in mortality bills was peculiarly English.[33] Does the appearance of the review in a French academic journal place Graunt in a Continental context, or does the reviewer's reading of Graunt establish political arithmetic as an English peculiarity? Does our answer to the question change if, as is suspected, the author of the review was William Petty himself?[34]

---

[31] A useful survey is Robert Jütte, *Poverty and Deviance in Early Modern Europe* (Cambridge: Cambridge University Press, 1994). See also, Justin Stagl, *A History of Curiosity: The Theory of Travel, 1550–1800* (London: Routledge, 1995); Philip S. Gorski, *The Disciplinary Revolution: Calvinism and the Rise of the State in Early Modern Europe* (Chicago: University of Chicago Press, 2003); Ulrike Strasser, *State of Virginity: Gender, Religion, and Politics in an Early Modern Catholic State* (Ann Arbor: University of Michigan Press, 2004); Valentin Groebner, *Who Are You? Identification, Deception, and Surveillance in Early Modern Europe* (New York: Zone Books, 2007); Jacob Soll, *The Information Master: Jean-Baptiste Colbert's Secret State Intelligence System* (Ann Arbor: University of Michigan Press, 2009).

[32] Robin Blackburn, *The Making of New World Slavery: From the Baroque to the Modern, 1492–1800* (London: Verso, 1997); John Thornton, *Africa and Africans in the Making of the Atlantic World* (Cambridge: Cambridge University Press, 1998); Emma Christopher, Cassandra Pybus and Markus Rediker (eds.), *Many Middle Passages: Forced Migration and the Making of the Modern World* (Berkeley: University of California Press, 2007).

[33] *Journal des Sçavans* 31 (1666), 359–70; John Graunt, *Natural and Political Observations, Mentioned in a Following Index, and Made upon the Bills of Mortality* (London: Printed by Thomas Roycroft for John Martin, James Allestry and Thomas Dicas, 1662).

[34] Hacking, *Emergence of Probability*, p. 102.

What about the rapid spread of the same interest to English colonies in North America?[35]

The European – which principally, in the later seventeenth century, meant the French – reaction to English political arithmetic suggests some interest in its analytical and comparative uses but no special concern with its conceptual origins or political implications.[36] The former aspect is, of course, important to the intellectual and political history of quantification. Petty and his various English successors embroiled themselves in debates with counterparts in Paris over the relative sizes of their countries and capital cities; by the end of the century, Graunt's claims about life expectancy had sparked appropriations and critiques from Leibniz and a number of lesser lights.[37] Well before the mid-eighteenth century, overlapping European and transatlantic networks of natural philosophers, physicians, clerics and learned amateurs exchanged mortality bills, descriptions of epidemics, assessments of inoculation, accounts of remarkable longevity and fertility and estimates of urban, national and even global population, past and present.[38] It is arguable that by the early 1760s, political arithmetic's two greatest exponents were the Prussian cleric Johann Peter Süssmilch and the American preacher Ezra Stiles.[39] Not only was eighteenth-century political arithmetic a "broad church," as Julian Hoppit has put it, but also it was a transnational evangelical enterprise.[40] In under a century, demographic statistics went from curiosity to currency across

[35] On American bills of mortality, see Patricia Cline Cohen, *A Calculating People: The Spread of Numeracy in Early America* (Chicago: University of Chicago Press, 1982), pp. 86–91; Susan E. Klepp, *"The Swift Progress of Population": A Documentary Study of Philadelphia's Growth, 1642–1859* (Philadelphia, PA: American Philosophical Society, 1991).

[36] On differences between French and English demographic discourse, see Hervé Le Bras, "Introduction: peuples et populations," in Hervé Le Bras and Sandrine Bertaux (eds.), *L'Invention des populations: biologie, idéologie et politique* (Paris: Éditions Odile Jacob, 2000), pp. 9–54, at pp. 18–21.

[37] Petty translated his work, or had it translated, into French: See William Petty, *Five Essays in Political Arithmetick* (London: Printed for Henry Mortlock, 1687), with parallel French and English text. On political arithmetic in France and elsewhere, see Jean-Marc Rohrbasser and Jacques Véron, *Leibniz et les raisonnements sur la vie humaine* (Paris: INED, 2001); Thierry Martin (ed.), *Arithmétique politique dans la France du 18e siècle* (Paris: INED, 2003).

[38] See Chapter 4.

[39] On Süssmilch, see Justus Nipperdey, "Johann Peter Süssmilch: From Divine Law to Human Intervention," *Population* 66:3 (2011), 611–36. On Stiles, discussed in Chapter 5, see James H. Cassedy, *Demography in America: Beginnings of the Statistical Mind, 1600–1800* (Cambridge, MA: Harvard University Press, 1969), pp. 110–15, 172–8; Cohen, *A Calculating People*, pp. 85, 110–12.

[40] Hoppit, "Political Arithmetic," 517; Ted McCormick, "Statistics in the Hands of an Angry God? John Graunt's *Observations* in Cotton Mather's New England," *The William and Mary Quarterly* 72:4 (2015), 563–86.

Europe and the colonial world, part of the toolkit of Enlightened policy and of reasoned public critique.[41]

Yet, both the clerical and the colonial dimensions of eighteenth-century political arithmetic hint that "numbering the people" was more than a merely statistical matter: Population remained much more than a number even after it had at last *become* a number. They point, too, to the potential salience of political and confessional boundaries and to the persistence of distinctly "pre-Enlightenment" concerns. Among the most enthusiastic early adopters of Graunt and Petty's brand of demographic quantification were Church of England clergymen and lay religious authors: pastoral interpreters of Providence, learned apologists for scriptural history and chronology, orthodox opponents of pre-Adamism, deism and atheism.[42] Colonial readers, meanwhile, turned Petty's instrument first to the assessment of their natural environments and later, particularly from mid-century, to the criticism of their metropolitan rulers. Both sets of appropriations disclose agendas for the use and modification of demographic ideas that must be understood in terms of national or imperial politics and institutions rather than as mere variations on a transcendent, global theme. Indeed, both sets of discussions linked writers in England with others in the English colonies, particularly New England. Most importantly, both explicitly involved the question of how populations were, could, or should be qualitatively transformed, and by what – or whose – agency. In short, there is a meaningfully English and Anglo-American history of thinking about demographic governance in the era of political arithmetic.

If this is the prospect looking forward from *c.* 1660, equally compelling reasons for an English focus can be found in the earlier Tudor and Stuart past. Probably the most important pertain to the contexts in which demographic agency was first problematized. Long before Bodin and Botero were translated into English (and in some instances even before their works had been written), debates around the enclosure of commons

---

[41] On the study of population in the Enlightenment, see Mark Raeff, "The Well-Ordered Police State and the Development of Modernity in Seventeenth- and Eighteenth-Century Europe: An Attempt at a Comparative Approach," *American Historical Review* 80:5 (1975), 1221–43; Sylvana Tomaselli, "Moral Philosophy and Population Questions in Eighteenth-Century Europe," *Population and Development Review* 14: Supplement (1988), 7–29; John Robertson, *The Case for Enlightenment: Scotland and Naples 1680–1760* (Cambridge: Cambridge University Press, 2005), pp. 325–76; Charles W. J. Withers, *Placing the Enlightenment: Thinking Geographically about the Age of Reason* (Chicago: University of Chicago Press, 2007), pp. 161, 198–201; Alan Houston, *Benjamin Franklin and the Politics of Improvement* (New Haven, CT: Yale University Press, 2008), pp. 106–46.

[42] Ted McCormick, "Political Arithmetic and Sacred History: Population Thought in the English Enlightenment, 1660–1750," *Journal of British Studies* 52:4 (2013), 829–57.

and the conversion of arable land to pasture, the emergence of poverty and vagrancy as symptoms of a diseased body politic, and the elaboration in English as well as colonial settings of concepts of idleness and degeneration prompted English writers, projectors, legislators and governors to envision multitudes of people as movable, mutable and perhaps manipulable entities.[43] A major point of this book is the importance of what we might think of collectively as marginal groups – the displaced, the impoverished, the criminalized and the colonized – to the formation of ideas about what sort of things populations were, particularly in the 130–150 years before the English Civil War. What we see as marginality, however, contemporaries identified as threats to the body politic emanating from particular locations within it – internal not only metaphorically but also, often, territorially.[44] The process of enclosing the commons can be discussed in general terms; but from any given author's (or legislator's) perspective, it was a set of actions undertaken by landowners in this or that county or region: Norfolk in the run-up to Kett's Rebellion in 1549, for example.[45] We can think of colonization as a process replicated in a series of settings over five centuries or more; but anxieties about its failure – and assessments of the prospects and the means for its success – attached to specific locales and groups at particular moments: the "Old English" in late Elizabethan Ireland, for instance.[46] The power of marginal populations to

---

[43] On enclosure debates, see Andrew McRae, *God Speed the Plough: The Representation of Agrarian England, 1500–1660* (Cambridge: Cambridge University Press, 1996); Joan Thirsk, "Enclosing and Engrossing, 1500–1640," in Joan Thirsk (ed.), *Agricultural Change: Policy and Practice, 1500–1750 (Chapters from the Agrarian History of England and Wales, 1500–1750*, vol. III) (Cambridge: Cambridge University Press, 1990), pp. 54–109. On vagrancy and mobility, see Paul Slack, *Poverty and Policy in Tudor and Stuart England* (Harlow: Longman, 1988); Steve Hindle, *On the Parish? The Micro-Politics of Poor Relief in Rural England, 1550–1750* (Oxford: Oxford University Press, 2004); Patricia Fumerton, *Unsettled: The Culture of Mobility and the Working Poor in Early Modern England* (Chicago: University of Chicago Press, 2006). For the persistence of vagrancy after the Civil War, see David Hitchcock, *Vagrancy in English Culture and Society, 1650–1750* (London: Bloomsbury Academic, 2016).

[44] Jonathan Gil Harris suggests that, under Paracelsian influence, the metaphor of the body politic constructed threats to the commonwealth as exogenous; see Jonathan Gil Harris, *Foreign Bodies and the Body Politic: Discourses of Social Pathology in Early Modern England* (Cambridge: Cambridge University Press, 1998). See Chapters 1 and 2. Yet the scalability of corporate language meant that the boundary between internal and external was ambiguous; the metaphor seems to have been sufficiently flexible for endogenous threats to remain important well into the seventeenth century. See Phil Withington, *The Politics of Commonwealth: Citizens and Freemen in Early Modern England* (Cambridge: Cambridge University Press, 2005); Finkelstein, *Harmony and the Balance*, pp. 15–25.

[45] See Andy Wood, *The 1549 Rebellions and the Making of Early Modern England* (Cambridge: Cambridge University Press, 2007), pp. 37–50.

[46] See Nicholas Canny, *Making Ireland British, 1580–1650* (Oxford: Oxford University Press, 2001), pp. 59–120; David Glimp, *Increase and Multiply: Governing Cultural Reproduction in Early Modern England* (Minneapolis: University of Minnesota Press, 2003), pp. 87–90.

spur demographic thought, and the drift of the thinking they provoked, reflected their location.

A second reason for an English focus relates to the material forms of demographic knowledge. Even if Petty was behind the *Journal des Sçavans* review, the suggestion of a peculiarly English fascination with mortality figures has a basis in fact. The keeping of parish registers of baptisms, marriages and burials was by no means unique to England, but it was an explicit component of the reformation of the English church, having been enjoined by Thomas Cromwell in 1538; looking backward, Petty envisioned the national church and its parish constituents as, among other things, a massive data-gathering apparatus with systematic and unparalleled access to the lives of the people and the closest of ties to the monarchical state.[47] Similarly, by the time Graunt turned his "shop-arithmetique" on them, the London bills of mortality had been collected regularly for nearly seventy years.[48] Beyond registers and bills, further, lay all manner of more or less local censuses of the poor, listings of householders, tax or tithing records and so on. There was no national census before 1801, but there was nevertheless a plethora of numbers from the sixteenth century onward, and around it a culture of political information was expanding rapidly by the dawn of the seventeenth.[49] Yet it would be unwise to put too much stress on the mere existence of this information. In the first place, other European cities and states collected much the same kinds of material, if less extensively or on a more ad hoc basis. (The mortality bills themselves had initially been gathered during plague epidemics; even in Petty's day, they were restricted to London.) More to the point, as Graunt and Petty recognized, the mere existence of such figures had not, by itself, determined or even especially encouraged their calculated use. Quantification alone changed little.

More consequential than the collection of numbers was their publication – in particular, the printing, posting, reprinting and recontextualization through print of the bills of mortality. Here was a distinctively English, or rather a distinctively London, phenomenon. Numbers of the

[47] See Simon Szreter, "Registration of Identities in Early Modern English Parishes and amongst the English Overseas," in Keith Breckinridge and Simon Szreter (eds.), *Registration and Recognition: Documenting the Person in World History: Proceedings of the British Academy* 182 (2012), pp. 67–92, at pp. 67–70; on the wider European context, see also Peter Burke, *A Social History of Knowledge: From Gutenberg to Diderot* (Cambridge: Polity Press, 2000), pp. 116–48.

[48] Graunt, *Natural and Political Observations*, sig. A4r, pp. 1–11.

[49] See Barbara J. Shapiro, "Empiricism and English Political Thought, 1550–1720," *Eighteenth-Century Thought* 1 (2003), 3–35; Barbara J. Shapiro, *Political Communication and Political Culture in England, 1588–1688* (Stanford, CA: Stanford University Press, 2012).

dead were not just a matter of municipal administration, as they were throughout Europe, but of public discourse and private conversation.[50] Graunt hinted at this, obliquely, in describing his resolution to engage scientifically with numbers that had hitherto been merely the stuff of idle banter. Readers of Samuel Pepys's diary can observe his habit of tracking the progress of the 1665 epidemic, and charting his own reactions to it, by constant reference to the weekly bills.[51] (They may also note his anger at a parish clerk who admitted to falsifying the numbers of the dead.) Well before this, as Mark S. R. Jenner has shown, mortality statistics reached a reading public through the medium of "Lord Have Mercy Upon Us" broadsides, which juxtaposed casualty tables with providential commentary on plague outbreaks and stark visual reminders of the death and judgment they brought.[52] Plague was a recurring feature of life throughout late medieval and early modern Europe, and both cultural and administrative responses to it – the *danse macabre*, the quarantine – crossed borders and lost all trace of national distinction.[53] From the late sixteenth through the early eighteenth century, however, the embedment in public discourse about plague of precise, ostensibly accurate and routinely updated numbers of the dead remained an English peculiarity, as did the increasing publication of mortality and other demographic figures in newspapers and almanacs around the English Atlantic world.[54] Still other kinds of demographic numbers found use in earlier debates, as we shall see. Suffice it to say that in England and its colonies, demographic numbers of several kinds had a public profile and a complex set of meanings bound up with the proliferation of print, with changes in rural and urban life and with the evolution of the national church and state, all from an early date.

Another implication of focusing on English texts is linguistic rather than strictly geographical: this is a study concerned especially with discussions of population in the vernacular. The idea of the vernacular has

---

[50] See J. C. Robertson, "Reckoning with London: Interpreting the Bills of Mortality before John Graunt," *Urban History* 23:3 (1996), 325–50; C. John Sommerville, *The News Revolution in England* (Oxford: Oxford University Press, 1996), p. 66.

[51] John Warrington (ed.), *The Diary of Samuel Pepys*, 3 vols. (London: J. M. Dent and Sons, 1953), vol. II, pp. 116–65.

[52] Mark S. R. Jenner, "Plague on a Page: *Lord Have Mercy Upon Us* in Early Modern London," *The Seventeenth Century* 27:3 (2012), 255–86.

[53] See Paul Slack, *The Impact of Plague in Tudor and Stuart England* (Oxford: Oxford University Press, 1985), pp. 53–78, 199–226. John Stow describes the spread of the image of the *danse macabre* from Paris to London under Henry VI; John Stow, *A Survey of London Written in the Year 1598* (Stroud: Sutton, 1994), pp. 309–10.

[54] Cassedy, *Demography in America*, pp. 117–47; Cohen, *Calculating People*, p. 83; Klepp, "*The Swift Progress of Population,*" pp. 7–8.

gained new currency during the last generation, enriching our sense of the complexity of intellectual, cultural and social developments, but losing some of its clarity in the process. The rise of the "vernacular" once described the liberation of both Scripture and learning from the Latin of the universal church – lending itself to grand narratives of Enlightenment, the emergence of national literatures and the creation of a secular modernity in Europe and beyond.[55] These accounts are now harder to sustain, and the vernacular turn in more recent scholarship (particularly in the history of science) complicates the idea of a neat and decisive shift in the linguistic realm and, in looking beyond the traditional questions of canon formation and national sensibility, casts the vernacular as more a matter of class or status than of language. We now speak not only of vernacular literature or liturgy, but also "vernacular empiricism" in contrast to Latinate natural philosophy, "vernacular conceptions of the cosmos" as against "elite modes of knowing nature," and "vernacular science," differentiated from "the high-culture natural philosophy and intellectual pretensions of the university and the court" less by its choice of language than by its emphasis on observation, experiment and critical debate.[56] The vernacular now refers not chiefly to the distinction between Latin and English, but rather to the distance and the linkages between high and low, learned and popular, theoretical and practical across all areas of cultural and intellectual life.

This accounts for its pertinence here. Though there is no direct analogy between the social positions of the "artisan/practitioners" highlighted in recent histories of science and technology and the heterogeneous set of authors examined in this book – many of whom belonged to political, professional, intellectual or clerical elites – seeing the governance of populations as a project located between the realms of high theory and ground-level practice locates it in a vernacular space.[57] In the first place, relatively few of the elite commentators on population drew any claim to demographic expertise from their elite status. The most apparent

[55] See for instance Peter Gay, *The Enlightenment: An Interpretation*, vol. I, *The Rise of Modern Paganism* (New York: W. W. Norton, 1966), p. 95; Dorinda Outram, *The Enlightenment*, second ed. (Cambridge: Cambridge University Press, 2005), p. 18; Headrick, *When Information Came of Age*, pp. 11, 18–20.

[56] William Eamon, *Science and the Secrets of Nature: Books of Secrets in Medieval and Early Modern Culture* (Princeton, NJ: Princeton University Press, 1994), p. 95; Pamela H. Smith, "Science on the Move: Recent Trends in the History of Early Modern Science," *Renaissance Quarterly* 62 (2009), 345–75, at 348 and 364–7; Deborah E. Harkness, *The Jewel House: Elizabethan London and the Scientific Revolution* (New Haven, CT: Yale University Press, 2007), p. xvii.

[57] On artisan/practitioners, see Pamela O. Long, *Artisan/Practitioners and the Rise of the New Sciences, 1400–1600* (Corvallis: Oregon State University Press, 2011).

exceptions come in the eighteenth century and concern physicians con-
tributing to the genre of "medical arithmetic," whose claims to authority
involved appeals to professional status, but still more to practical experience and observation.[58] Political arithmetic became a matter of expertise,
but not a learned pursuit in itself. Second, even in the sixteenth century, the learned most often put their thoughts on population – at least
as a present-tense problem of governance – into the vernacular. More's
Utopia was written in Latin, and translated into the vernacular only in
1551; but Starkey's *Dialogue between Pole and Lupset*, Smith's *Discourse
of the Common Weal of this Realm of England* and Spenser's *View of the
Present State of Ireland* were English texts.[59] Even the "learned lumber" of
sacred history – a genre long given to speculation about the past population of the earth – was increasingly written in English by the time
empirical observations of population influenced it.[60] So too, of course,
were the many polemical pamphlets intended to sway opinion and spur
action around issues of the moment, and so were the founding works of
political arithmetic. Neither Graunt, who lacked the capacity, nor Petty,
who lacked the incentive, composed any demographic work in Latin.
Neither man took the learned as his principal audience, scientific pretensions notwithstanding. (Graunt's double dedication of his *Natural and
Political Observations* to the President of the Royal Society and to the
Lord Privy Seal captures his dual aims.)[61] Political arithmetic, the main
Enlightenment-era vehicle for thought about demographic agency, was
a vernacular enterprise from the start, in the linguistic sense and in the
sense of being beneath the cognizance of learned philosophical discourse.
It was the stuff of projectors and pamphleteers – and, by the time of Defoe
and Swift, of essays and satire. It remained so long enough for Adam
Smith, Professor of Moral Philosophy at the University of Glasgow, to
sneer at it much as Petty's critics had.

The second set of constraints governing this study pertains to its two
interrelated subjects: how populations were conceived as objects of knowledge and manipulation, and where the power to transform them was
understood to lie. As these questions indicate, this is not a demographic

---

[58] The best current study of medical arithmetic is Rusnock, *Vital Accounts*.

[59] On Raphe Robinson's translation of More, which appeared at the same time as a series of other "commonwealth" texts on governance, see Wood, *The 1549 Rebellions*, p. 37.

[60] R. J. Arnold, "'Learned Lumber': The Unlikely Survival of Sacred History in the Eighteenth Century," *English Historical Review* 125:516 (2010), 1139–72; Jed Z. Buchwald and Mordechai Feingold, *Newton and the Origin of Civilization* (Princeton, NJ: Princeton University Press, 2013), pp. 164–94.

[61] Graunt, *Natural and Political Observations*, sigs. A2r–A4v.

history. It is true that awareness of demographic change formed part of the context in which knowledge of and power over populations were problematized. It is much less clear, however, how precise this awareness was at any point, at least before the late seventeenth century. This is not simply because of the absence of a national census; enumerations of different sorts of people proliferated, so that both the fact and the recording of demographic events of all kinds would have been familiar to a wide swath of observers. But with the qualified exception of the London bills, empirical records, even when reliably kept, were overwhelmingly local and small-scale. Only a handful of officials had access even in principle to records from different parts of the country, and there is no sign that they made any systematic use of the information in practice. (The English figure nearest in aspiration to the French "information master" Colbert was probably Petty, a projector excluded from significant office.)[62] There was, in other words, little ground on which to base any accurate and empirically responsive sense of national population or demographic trends, and not much more evidence of attempts to do so before the Restoration. Rather than granting national population actor-category status and reading contemporary sources in the borrowed light of our own estimates, then, it seems safer to presume – bearing in mind the extant forms of enumeration and commentary – that most people who thought about, observed or consciously experienced population or demographic change did so in local terms. Even in cases where commentary seems in retrospect to respond to national trends, we should not assume, in the absence of evidence, that it did so without mediation.

Nor is it always easy to tell whether, how or why observers isolated the purely demographic aspects of the various phenomena to which they reacted – even after political arithmeticians created a quantitative idiom for doing so. Thus, the present book is not a history or even a "prehistory" of demography as a discipline. To the contrary: the impetus for it came from a sense of frustration with the shape of the disciplinary historiography and the ahistorical notion of population it often takes for granted. As Yves Charbit perceptively notes in his contribution to the field, "Whereas the history of demography as a social science has been amply explored, the construction of the concept of population has been neglected."[63] Yet, even as he historicizes the different ideas of population he finds in Plato, Bodin and the Physiocrats, Charbit carries

---

[62] Compare Soll, *Information Master*, and McCormick, *William Petty*, pp. 276–84.
[63] Charbit, *Classical Foundations of Population Thought*, p. vii.

with him the yardstick of the concept of population as demographers know it today. What begins as an exercise in contextualization ends up reproducing salient features of traditional disciplinary historiography, including its teleological structure, if not its internalist account of intellectual change. Avoiding the ahistorical application of "population" but retaining the telos and characteristic obsessions (notably, quantification) of this literature results in a series of apparently incommensurable notions of demography that are nevertheless presented as steps – or leaps – toward the modern concept. I have thought it best to focus on themes that emerged in the course of research on political arithmetic and its origins, and to leave the concerns of modern demographers and their historians to one side while pursuing early modern engagements with these themes. If my subjects throw light on what was for them an unanticipated future, so much the better if they can do it from so great a distance.

In the first instance, however, the transformations traced in this book reflect specific and interrelated intellectual, cultural, social and political changes of the early modern period. Isolating these from among the myriad issues that involve ideas of population in one way or another is no easy task; the range of historiographies touched on, from political to religious to environmental to gender to intellectual history and beyond, is some indication. Cutting across most of these bodies of scholarship, further, are a number of "grand narratives" in which population thought plays a role – and which, *pari passu*, have done much to shape historians' interest in demographic ideas: the formation of the state; the secularization of society; the ascension of the individual over the collective; the reification of the natural world; the rise of capitalism, of liberalism, of the public sphere. Did the emergence of an idea of population as a quantifiable and manipulable object of science and policy enable or reflect the creation of a pool of free labor? Was it an extension to society of an exploitative view of nature as a bundle of resources and processes to be mastered? Did it lay the foundations of the modern, liberal welfare state? Or does attention to the details and the nuances, the twists and turns and ambiguities of population as it came to be understood and used over the course of three centuries force us to question the neat distinctions and clear polarities on which these stories of our world depend?

Trying to take on all of these questions would be foolish. Yet avoiding them completely is impossible within the framework of the "early modern," a period that has been defined since its inception in the mid-twentieth century by the large-scale transformations it witnessed rather than by its more elusive continuities.[64] It may be that the centrality of transformation to early modernity points a way through the difficulty of specifying the continuities that underpin the subject. To a great extent the problem of population, as it came to command the attention of thinkers and writers from the sixteenth century through the eighteenth, *was* a problem of transformations: in the first instance, alterations of landscape, unwonted displacements, perilous mixtures and frightening degenerations; but also, and increasingly by the early seventeenth century, planned and directed manipulations of groups of bodies designed to produce changes not only of place but also of character, of nature. The advent of demographic quantification, part of the transformation of science institutionalized in England halfway through our period, enabled projectors, politicians, pamphleteers and professionals to put this endlessly ramifying set of transmutative operations on an empirical footing, to ground it more securely in the ascendant epistemology of "number, weight and measure," to ensconce it in the bureaucratic functions of an imperial state, to publish it in academic journals, lampoon it in utopian fiction and debate it in the periodical press – but also to subject it to the constraints of ever-more-confidently asserted natural and social laws, which ultimately, in Malthus, came to undermine the possibilities of transformation that had generated the idea of population in the first place.

From this perspective, what gives the early modern period coherence is that it was during these centuries that the conceptualization of population as the object of a particular knowledge was bound up with the possibility of transforming people not only as a matter of policy but also in line with widely held ideas of the common good and, later, of boundless improvement in society and economy. Prior to the early modern period, populations were certainly targeted by policy; they were enumerated, moved around, mixed, segregated, settled in colonies and expelled from kingdoms. Medieval history witnessed, moreover, a series of epoch-making transformations in which such policies, to say nothing of unplanned demographic changes, played central roles.[65] Yet, none of this required or provoked discussion of populations or the processes shaping them – as distinct from nations and their genealogies – as particular kinds of thing, whose salience necessitated the addition of new kinds of knowledge to the political repertoire. Nor was it justified with reference to the progressive improvement of life on Earth.

---

[64] See Phil Withington, *Society in Early Modern England: the Vernacular Origins of Some Powerful Ideas* (Cambridge: Polity Press, 2010), pp. 45–70.

[65] See Robert Bartlett, *The Making of Europe: Conquest, Colonization and Cultural Change, 950–1350* (London: Penguin, 1994).

Both of these things changed in the sixteenth and seventeenth centuries. Medieval "population politics" were comprehensible within the framework either of classical political philosophy (in particular, Aristotle's *Politics*) or of Scripture. Political arithmetic – posited as a new instrument of government, employing new kinds of information and new modes of analysis, and holding the key not only to stable rule but also to economic and social transformation – was not.

After Malthus's *Essay*, on the other hand, the distinct importance and scientific credentials of demographic enquiry were established; population was *the* fundamental social reality, and its status was soon shored up by a nineteenth-century "avalanche of numbers" in the form of censuses and surveys of all kinds.[66] This new body of knowledge, however, was divorced from the transformative aspirations of the political arithmeticians – and those of their more philosophically optimistic and politically radical Enlightenment successors, Malthus's immediate targets. For Graunt and Petty, demographic quantification and analysis was a tool for the advancement of what Bacon had called "human empire," the power of art and policy to channel and manipulate natural processes.[67] For Malthus's followers, to the contrary, demographic knowledge demonstrated the incapacity of art to challenge the iron laws of an inhuman, and inhumane, nature. The law of population – shown, with a grander flourish of statistical data in each new edition, to be at work alike in primitive and developed societies; in monarchies, republics and despotisms; in cold climates and hot; in the Old World and the New – obliterated any chance of significant changes in the human condition and guaranteed the futility of projects designed to improve humankind's lot. This view of the relationship between nature and human agency did not triumph uncontested, and the twentieth century saw the resurgence not only of progressive ideas of social change but also of large-scale projects of social engineering – much of it carried on, ironically, by neo-Malthusians.[68] Nevertheless, in the liberal exaltation of the individual over the collective, in the belief that the spontaneous order of nature invariably trumps the clumsiness of human interference, and in the persistent association of natural demographic behavior with the inevitability of inequality within and between nations, the paleo-Malthusian view endures.

---

[66] Ian Hacking, *The Taming of Chance* (Cambridge: Cambridge University Press, 1990), p. 118.

[67] Francis Bacon, *The New Atlantis*, in Brian Vickers (ed.), *Francis Bacon: The Major Works* (Oxford: Oxford University Press, 2008), p. 480.

[68] See Matthew Connelly, *Fatal Misconception: The Struggle to Control World Population* (Cambridge, MA: Harvard University Press, 2008); James C. Scott, *Seeing Like a State: How Certain Schemes to Improve the Human Condition Have Failed* (New Haven, CT: Yale University Press, 1998).

This book traces one arc of thought about how populations could be known and governed from the early Tudor era to the cusp of the Victorian age. The account offered is "teleological" only in the restricted sense that elements of the content, structure and claims to authority of demographic ideas articulated at the end of the story will look more familiar than those with which we begin. This much is inevitable. We remember Malthus because he wrote a book, pioneered views and came to be regarded as the founder of a discipline, all of which exert influence today. Yet, the state of play in 1798 or 1826 was neither the inevitable consequence of intellectual progress nor the distillation of the "best" or most "modern" ideas of the three preceding centuries. Early modern demographic thought is not the prehistory of Malthus. Nor, on the other hand, did Malthus escape the past by dint either of his thought-experiment or of the statistics he rallied in its support. Even the most striking novelties of the *Essay* reveal the persistence of early modern questions: the balance between numbers of people and numbers of acres; the speed at which populations have grown through history; the relative influence of art and nature over the conditions of human existence; and the providential significance of demographic patterns and the moral import of demographic agency. Surveying the whole period, the story is better seen as a series of contingent and open-ended adaptations of a persistent framework of ideas to various kinds of social, cultural and political change, rather than as a linear progress, fueled by cumulative advances in data and analysis, toward a radically new worldview. To put it another way: there is much in Malthus's *Essay* with which William Petty or Thomas More would have disagreed; there is nothing they would have failed to understand.

Nevertheless, the ways demographic knowledge and agency were thought about changed significantly in the time that separated these figures, and it is to these changes, and the contexts within which they made sense, that we now turn. This main body of the book is composed of five chapters. The first half, Chapters 1–3, examines the formation, through a series of engagements with particular local, problematic or marginal subpopulations (referred to as "multitudes"), of conditions that promoted engagement with population as something knowable principally by empirical and quantitative means, and as preeminently subject to the manipulation of the state, over a period stretching from before the Henrician Reformation of the 1530s through the Cromwellian Protectorate of the 1650s. Chapter 4 examines the climax of these tendencies in the political arithmetic of the Restoration and Augustan periods, which promised "a new instrument of government" predicated on "number, weight and

24   Introduction: Transformations in Demographic Thought

measure" that would enable the programmatic "transmutation" of entire populations across the Three Kingdoms and the nascent British Empire. Chapter 5 traces the diffusion of demographic agency among an increasing variety of public and private agents – the proliferating initiatives of Enlightenment-era civil society in Britain and beyond – and, paradoxically, the simultaneous loss of confidence, in some quarters, in the efficacy and the legitimacy of political and other artificial attempts to overcome the constraints of environment (often part of a complex labeled "situation") or the operations of nature in the shaping of population. The conclusion looks again at Malthus's *Essay on the Principle of Population*. This work, designed by its author to terminate a philosophical discussion and remembered today as initiating a social-scientific discipline, marked both a closure and a culmination of the early modern problematic of population since 1500. Raising the providential operation of natural law above the reach of human art or policy, and restricting meaningful demographic agency to the rational but weak moral individual, Malthus left the task of purposive demographic transformation suspended between illegitimacy and impossibility – where, in the by turns nefarious and utopian guise of social engineering, it remains.

CHAPTER I

Mobility and Mutability in the Early Tudor Body Politic

Multitude before "Population"

Before there was population, there were multitudes. Before the precise numbers of people inhabiting specific territories – or the global sum of such numbers – became familiar objects of knowledge and policy, the problem of knowing and governing the multiplicity of people was thought about, experienced, and engaged with in ways so unlike our own that they may fail to register with us as pertaining to population at all. This is not to deny pre-modern manifestations of interest in numbers of people. Long before the coming of demographic statistics, anyone familiar with Scripture knew not only the divine injunction to "be fruitful, and multiply" but also about the practice of "numbering the people" – although the latter had constituted a serious and consequential sin, in King David's case.[1] More learned exegetes explored in greater depth the peopling of the earth by Adam's troubled progeny, its repopulation after the Great Flood by Noah's three sons and their wives and the rapid multiplication of the Israelites during their captivity in Egypt. The work of the great sixteenth- and early seventeenth-century chronologists – and that of their less learned but better informed successors in the later seventeenth and eighteenth centuries – involved many calculations of the world's past population and a great deal of agonizing over rates of growth (or doubling), the incidence of twins, the probable effects of the patriarchs' superlative longevity and the antediluvian environment on fertility, gestation periods, nursing habits and much else.[2] Sophisticated

---

[1] Genesis 1:28 (addressing Adam and Eve) and 9:1 (addressing Noah and his sons); 2 Samuel 24 (KJV).
[2] Buchwald and Feingold, *Newton and the Origin of Civilization*, pp. 164–94; see also Paolo Rossi, *The Dark Abyss of Time: The History of the Earth and the History of Nations from Hooke to Vico*, translated by Lydia G. Cochrane (Chicago: University of Chicago Press, 1984), pp. 121–92; Anthony T. Grafton, "Joseph Scaliger and Historical Chronology: The Rise and Fall of a Discipline," *History and Theory* 14:2 (1975), 156–85; Frank N. Egerton III, "The Longevity of the Patriarchs: A Topic in the History of Demography," *Journal of the History of Ideas* 27:4 (1966), 575–84. On the later use of political arithmetic in this context, see McCormick, "Political Arithmetic and Sacred History."

demographic thought was not lacking in the sixteenth century. Moreover, the heirs of this tradition would number among the earliest and most enthusiastic users of political arithmetic.

Yet, certain features of the exegetical and sacred-historical discourse of population differentiate it from modern modes of demography, on the one hand, and from other early modern engagements with the knowledge and governance of multitudes, on the other. First, it was concerned with the multiplication of mankind not as an object of present or future political concern but rather as a historical and hermeneutical problem with religious implications – which became sharper as challenges to biblical chronology and history mounted in the context of deepening confessional schism.[3] This implied, second, a global sense of scale. In this regard, modern historians are wrong to see the idea of "world population" as an innovation of our self-proclaimed global era. To the contrary, the history of the world's population as revealed or implied by Scripture received attention from late antiquity and had attained a high degree of elaboration by the later sixteenth century, for reasons of faith and as a matter of Counter-Reformation geopolitics.[4] Third, and related, this discourse vested demographic agency – the power behind changes in population – not in earthly powers or human passions but in Providence, acting directly or through the mechanisms of the natural world. The successive population, extinction and repopulation of the earth around the Flood, along with the dramatic reduction in human lifespan, were, like the confusion of tongues and division of nations that followed Babel, divine judgments. This left little space for any notion of effectual human policy in the demographic realm. It also imbued demographic events, individual or collective, with profound

---

[3] On some of these challenges, see Don Cameron Allen, *The Legend of Noah: Renaissance Rationalism in Art, Science, and Letters* (Urbana: University of Illinois Press, 1963); Richard H. Popkin, *Isaac La Peyrère (1596–1676): His Life, Work, and Influence* (Leiden: E. J. Brill, 1987); David N. Livingstone, *Adam's Ancestors: Race, Religion, and the Politics of Human Origins* (Baltimore, MD: Johns Hopkins University Press, 2008); William Poole, *The World Makers: Scientists of the Restoration and the Search for the Origins of the Earth* (Oxford: Peter Lang, 2010).

[4] Johannes Temporarius (Jean du Temps) even included a prototypical bar graph of postdiluvian world population in his *Chronologicarum demonstrationum libri tres* (1596); see Daniel Rosenberg and Anthony Grafton, *Cartographies of Time: A History of the Timeline* (Princeton, NJ: Princeton University Press, 2010), pp. 70–1. For earlier comments see Clarence W. Glacken, *Traces on the Rhodian Shore: Nature and Culture in Western Thought from Ancient Times to the End of the Eighteenth Century* (Berkeley: University of California Press, 1967), pp. 200, 216–17, 259–60; Biller, *Measure of Multitude*. For Catholic and Protestant concerns about the global balance of confessional populations, see Romain Descendre, *L'État du Monde: Giovanni Botero entre raison d'État et géopolitique* (Geneva: Librairie Droz S. A., 2009), pp. 248–9; Peter Harrison, *'Religion' and the Religions in the English Enlightenment* (Cambridge: Cambridge University Press, 1990), pp. 99–104.

moral and religious significance in learned and pastoral settings: particular deaths and general plagues, instances of remarkable fertility and large-scale changes in lifespans all indicated the hand of God and the operations of his judgment.[5] Finally, in contrast to many of the practical approaches to multitude discussed later, exegetical discussions of population reveled in quantitative calculations; yet these calculations, which fit demographic history to scriptural chronology on a global scale, lacked empirical foundation. Certain of these features would recur in other engagements with multitude and later in political arithmetic, but these engagements began elsewhere.

The Bible and sacred history were not the only sources for ideas about population. Educated readers could also consult Aristotle's *Politics* for the role of numbers in the ancient *polis*.[6] Here, particularly in Book VII, population was fundamental to politics: "A state … only begins to exist when it has attained a population sufficient for a good life in the political community."[7] The quantity and quality of inhabitants were elements of the city's constitution, matters for the legislator from the beginning: "First among the materials required by the statesman is population: he will consider what should be the number and character of the citizens, and then what should be the size and character of the country."[8] Not only the viability of the state, but also its form of government, mechanisms of administration and share of particular types of people depended in part on the number of its inhabitants – which in turn depended on the extent and quality of territory.[9] Yet number alone was no measure of greatness. For one thing, not all inhabitants counted alike. Besides crucial distinctions between citizens, slaves and foreigners, there was the question of balance between occupations:

> [E]ven if we reckon greatness by numbers, we ought not to include everybody, for there must always be in cities a multitude of slaves and resident aliens and foreigners; but we should include those only who are members of the state.… The number of the latter is a proof of the greatness of a

[5] See Alexandra Walsham, *Providence in Early Modern England* (Oxford: Oxford University Press, 1999), especially pp. 65–166; Glacken, *Traces on the Rhodian Shore*, pp. 150–68, 375–428; Slack, *The Impact of Plague in Tudor and Stuart England*, pp. 227–54; Jenner, "Plague on a Page." On the Augustinian origins of these connections, see Genevieve Lloyd, *Providence Lost* (Cambridge, MA: Harvard University Press, 2008), pp. 129–59.

[6] On the influence of the *Politics* on medieval population thought, see Biller, *The Measure of Multitude*, pp. 296–382.

[7] Jonathan Barnes (ed.), *The Complete Works of Aristotle: The Revised Oxford Translation*, 2 vols. (Oxford: Oxford University Press), vol. II, p. 2254.

[8] Barnes (ed.), *Complete Works of Aristotle*, vol. II, p. 2254.

[9] Barnes (ed.), *Complete Works of Aristotle*, vol. II, pp. 2194, 2210. On the role of environment in constraining population, and on environmental change over time, see "Meteorology," I:14, in Barnes (ed.), *Complete Works of Aristotle*, vol. I, p. 622.

city; but a city which produces numerous artisans and comparatively few soldiers cannot be great, for a great city is not the same as a populous one.[10]

At a still more basic level, excess was as harmful as deficiency to the welfare of the community. Here, as elsewhere, virtue lay in mediocrity – a *via media* between opposite extremes achieved by means of restraint.[11] Beneath a certain number, a community could not sustain itself; beyond an upper limit, a population became ungovernable – literally unreachable by the voice of command: "For who can be the general of such a vast multitude, or who the herald, unless he have the voice of a Stentor?" In too populous a state, the population, the state's essential membership, was diluted as foreigners gained citizenship. There was thus a natural limit to the size of a state, determined by experience and circumstance but guided by a vision of economic and aesthetic sufficiency. Aristotle described this as "the largest number which suffices for the purposes of life, and can be taken in at a single view."[12]

If population was conceived here as a problem of government, its quality and effects were envisioned by drawing an analogy between the state and the person, whose beauty and health similarly inhered in the maintenance of balance and proportion between the essential parts of an organic and naturally bounded whole.[13] The goal of statecraft with respect to population was not greatness in a quantitative sense. It was instead a kind of beauty, "and the state which combines magnitude with good order must necessarily be the most beautiful."[14] The knowledge needed to establish an optimal multitude, moreover, involved individual health, fertility and mortality directly:

> [T]he limit should be fixed by calculating the chances of mortality in the children, and of sterility in married persons. The neglect of this subject, which in existing states is so common, is a never-failing cause of poverty among the citizens; and poverty is the parent of revolution and crime.[15]

---

[10] Barnes (ed.), *Complete Works of Aristotle*, vol. II, p. 2254.
[11] Ethan Shagan's argument that the early modern English pursuit of the *via media* implied and legitimated external coercion also applies to the pursuit of a moderate population through the denial of citizenship or residency (and, *a fortiori*, to restrictions on marriage or procreation) – constraints that would render the multitude moderate both in the quantitative sense and in the sense of being governable, and that would at the same time demonstrate the moderation of the legislator. See Ethan Shagan, *The Rule of Moderation: Violence, Religion, and the Politics of Restraint in Early Modern England* (Cambridge: Cambridge University Press, 2011), pp. 7–8, 15, 48, 64–5.
[12] Barnes (ed.) *Complete Works of Aristotle*, vol. II, p. 2254.
[13] On the role of an Aristotelian idea of the body politic in early modern English economic thought, see Finkelstein, *Harmony and the Balance*, pp. 15–25, 37.
[14] Barnes (ed.), *Complete Works of Aristotle*, vol. II, p. 2254.
[15] Barnes (ed.), *Complete Works of Aristotle*, vol. II, p. 2151.

Aristotle thus presented population not just as a measurable number of inhabitants but also, more saliently, as the living material of the city-state. Its size would be constrained by the territory it occupied. It should be limited, too, by the counterpoised imperatives of magnitude and order in the context of a polity conceived as an organic unit – a body politic – with a constitution. More significant than absolute size was the relative proportion of the body's parts: The balance between citizens, slaves and foreigners, and between soldiers, husbandmen and artisans.

Aristotelian preoccupations with the quality of the population, in addition or in preference to its quantity, informed sixteenth-century European engagements with population, from Niccolò Machiavelli through Jean Bodin.[16] These preoccupations also surfaced in English demographic thinking from the mid-sixteenth century, as it absorbed the influence and adopted the vocabulary of Italian and Continental humanism.[17] But the Tudor engagement with knowing and governing multitudes of people predates this. It began not with global, national or urban *populations* as given objects, but rather on the process of rural *depopulation*, linked in the first instance with enclosure and with the conversion of arable land to pasture. It dwelt less on the decline of numbers – though this played a distinct rhetorical role – than on the loss of a particular type of person with a vital economic and social function: the ploughman. This discourse of depopulation dealt with changes in the land that might spread from place to place over time but that were experienced primarily at the local or regional level rather than national level. It vested both the responsibility for depopulation and the power to reverse it in human hands. Lordly greed for the profits of the expanding wool trade drove ploughs from the land; the restraining hand of the king might forestall further damage and restore the vanished multitude to its rightful place. In the meantime, however, the effects of depopulation risked spiraling out of anyone's control as displaced husbandmen and their dependents took to the roads to seek a livelihood, swarming the city and turning, in their idleness, to crime.

Key features of this discourse, originating in the literature of "agrarian complaint," set the tone for engagements with demography in other contexts and established the position from which later changes – addressing new problems or opportunities and absorbing new intellectual influences – would

---

[16] On Machiavelli's view of population, see Pocock, *Machiavellian Moment*, p. 207. On Bodin, see Charbit, *Classical Foundations of Population Thought*, pp. 43–62.

[17] See Thomas F. Mayer, *Thomas Starkey and the Commonweal: Humanist Politics and Religion in the Reign of Henry VIII* (Cambridge: Cambridge University Press, 1989); Withington, *Politics of Commonwealth*, pp. 51–84.

take place.[18] First, the object of concern was not a "population" in the sense of a number of people or a collection of unspecified or interchangeable individuals. It was, rather, a "multitude" with a specific place – a natural and normative location – and a specific role, as well as characteristic moral qualities. The ploughman belonged in the depopulated village just as the plough that employed him belonged on the land. This should remind us of the *local* – communal, parochial and corporate – nature of demographic phenomena in the experience of early modern people and in their thought. Second, while number was not irrelevant to multitude, numbers did not define multitude or underpin discussions of it. Exaggerated or emblematic figures or ratios served instead to emphasize the qualitative aspects of a group; to emblematize its links to the land, to the other multitudes constitutive of the community and to the fate of the realm and, later, the commonwealth; and to dramatize – but not in any exact sense to measure – its growth or decline. Third, analysis of depopulation's negative effects, both on the displaced multitude of ploughmen and on the realm, pathologized mobility in the context of a community or commonwealth conceived of as a closed and organic whole.[19] The mobility of a multitude implied change: change of place and, therefore, change of nature. Ploughmen denied land ceased to be ploughmen; loose on the roads, they became vagrants. Having lost their place and function, they lost their virtues. Industry turned to idleness, idleness begot crime. Mobility was thus an agent of transmutation (here, degeneration) in that it turned one kind of multitude into another. Fourth, inasmuch as the crown or the nobility had the power to prevent or control this mobility – whether by restraining the passions that produced it or by imposing order on the multitudes it produced – doing so was a political, moral and even religious imperative. Demographic agency rested with the human lawgiver. Its object or target was the marginalized, mobile and degenerate multitude. Its goal was to restore damaged communities by replacing their displaced members.

Denunciations of depopulating landlords were a feature of the literary landscape for over a century. In another genre, however, the governance of multitudes turned much more quickly from an ad hoc, local response to a central component of political rule. Between the late 1520s and the late 1540s – a period that saw Henry VIII's break with Rome, the dissolution of the monasteries and the sale of their extensive lands – the humanist

---

[18] See McRae, *God Speed the Plough*, pp. 23–57. On the broader context of economic and social change, see Thirsk, "Enclosing and Engrossing"; Keith Wrightson, *Earthly Necessities: Economic Lives in Early Modern Britain* (New Haven, CT: Yale University Press, 2000).

[19] These ideas are discussed in Fumerton, *Unsettled*, pp. 1–59.

political writing of Thomas Starkey and Thomas Smith, and the anonymous "Polices to Reduce this Realme of Englande vnto a Prosperus Wealthe and Estate," offered analyses of the commonwealth that set the challenge of mobile multitudes in a less local and more abstract light. Turning the metaphor of the body politic into a complex social model, Starkey and Smith – the former writing in the context of the Henrician Reformation, the latter in the wake of the 1549 rebellions under Edward VI – treated multitudes not as concrete elements of local communities but rather as functional elements of a national, organic or mechanical whole.[20] Here, anxieties about the degenerative and disruptive effects of mobile multitudes went hand in glove with a new vision of policy, conceived in terms of the ongoing maintenance of proper balance, proportion and relation between different multitudes. The "Polices" went still further, intimating an atomistic view of human multitudes and a view of the constraints imposed by nature, foreshadowing crucial features of seventeenth-century population thought. Demographic agency remained with the lawgiver; indeed, inasmuch as the health of the commonwealth depended on the concatenation of multitudes, it became constitutive of his office. At the same time, questions about the scope and limitations of this power, themes that marked the path from multitudes to population, were beginning to emerge.

Mobile Multitudes: Enclosure and Depopulation

The earliest extant English use of "population," according to the *Oxford English Dictionary*, was in 1544, and it carried the now-obsolete sense of "a populated or inhabited place." Its more familiar sense of "the collection of inhabitants" of a given area, or "a body of inhabitants," in general, entered print only in 1612.[21] In sharp contrast to the sluggish uptake of

---

[20] On the impact of "Erasmian" humanism, see James Kelsey McConica, *English Humanists and Reformation Politics under Henry VIII and Edward VI* (Oxford: Oxford University Press, 1965); for doubts about its political impact and about the utility of the "Erasmian" label, see Alistair Fox, "English Humanism and the Body Politic," in Alistair Fox and John Guy (eds.), *Reassessing the Henrician Age: Humanism, Politics, and Reform, 1500–1550* (Oxford: Blackwell, 1986), pp. 34–51. For Starkey and Smith, see Thomas F. Mayer, *Thomas Starkey and the Commonweal: Humanist Politics and Religion in the Reign of Henry VIII* (Cambridge: Cambridge University Press, 1989); Harris, *Foreign Bodies*, pp. 30–40; Neal Wood, *Foundations of Political Economy: Some Early Tudor View on State and Society* (Berkeley: University of California Press, 1994), pp. 124–54 and 191–235.

[21] "population, n.1," *OED Online*, Oxford University Press, 2016 (accessed July 15, 2016). A search of the Early English Books Online Corpus, however, turns up one occurrence of "population" in the second sense from 1578: http://earlyprint.wustl.edu/toolwebgrok.html?corpus=plaintext&searchPattern=population&startYear=1578&endYear=1578&authors=&titles=&page=1.

"population," "depopulation" – meaning both the "reduction of population" and, less familiar to us, "the action of depopulating" – appeared as
early as the 1460s, and was in common usage during the sixteenth century.[22] If nothing else, this peculiar chronology might caution us against
applying statistical ideas of population to the early modern world – for
how can the word for a number's decline have predated the word for the
number itself? On the other hand, the prominence of both place and process – the *location* of population, and the *action* of depopulation – should
alert us to aspects of these ideas that are now lost or muted. A population
was, or existed in, a particular place: perhaps a kingdom, but most likely a
town or village. It was not a quantum floating in the abstract space of
a statistical census but a group of people occupying the concrete place of
a parish church, market or guildhall, or a metaphorical limb of the body
politic. Depopulation, rather than merely denoting a decrease in numbers, was the hindrance or destruction of this occupation: the forcing of
a specific group of people out of a specific place. Its signs were not entries
in a ledger but vacant churches, decayed houses and empty villages. And,
notwithstanding the pertinence of commercial networks and processes of
religious reform, depopulation was not a neutral effect of impersonal economic or social forces but an act – a calculated and callous act – fraught
with moral and political implications.

In the earlier part of the sixteenth century, depopulation usually
referred to a specific process of rural change. Its victims were ploughmen (often rendered, metonymically, as "ploughs"), a multitude with an
essential role that tied its members, families and households to a specific part of the landscape. Contemporary rhetoric blamed depopulation
on the "enclosure" of common land – so much so that "enclosure" and
"depopulation" sometimes worked as synonyms. As agricultural historians have pointed out, however, this can be misleading. In national
terms, enclosure was neither a new nor a single, continuous process.
According to Mark Overton, 45 percent of English land had already
been enclosed by 1500; the fastest rates of enclosure, however, would
occur only in the seventeenth century, during which 24 percent of the
country was enclosed – as opposed to a meager 2 percent in the sixteenth
century, the high point of antienclosure complaint.[23] What made acts

[22] "depopulation, n.1," *OED Online* (accessed July 15, 2016).
[23] Mark Overton, *Agricultural Revolution in England: The Transformation of the Agrarian Economy 1500–1850* (Cambridge: Cambridge University Press, 1996), p. 148. On complaints about enclosure, see McRae, *God Speed the Plough*; Wood, *Foundations of Political Economy*, pp. 7–29.

of enclosure significant with respect to depopulation was the change in land use that they often marked or enabled. Specifically, enclosure permitted the conversion of arable land (in tillage or under the plough) to pasture for the grazing of cattle and, in the early sixteenth century especially, sheep.[24] Rather than a loss of population in the absolute sense, depopulation was a community-, county- or shire-level process by which the creation of pasture for sheep meant the displacement of ploughs and the people who depended upon them.

Perhaps the most famous contemporary comment on this process came in Thomas More's *Utopia*. In Book I, Raphael Hythlodaye complained that "Your sheep ... that commonly are so meek and eat so little; now, as I hear, they have become so greedy and fierce that they devour men themselves."[25] Hythlodaye went on to identify the human agents of depopulation, their character and motivations and the effects of their actions:

> For in whatever parts of the land sheep yield the finest and thus the most expensive wool, there the nobility and the gentry, yes, and even some abbots ... are not content with the old rents.... Living in idleness and luxury without doing society any good no longer satisfies them; they have to do positive evil. For they leave no land free for the plough; they enclose every acre for pasture; they destroy houses and abolish towns, keeping only the churches — and those for sheep-barns. And as if enough of your land were not already wasted on forests and game preserves, these worthy men turn all human habitations and cultivated fields back to wilderness.[26]

More's denunciation was unusual in its eloquence but not in its substance or passion. At the other end of the century, *Bastard's Epigrams on Enclosures* (1598) captured the same alteration with similar imagery and pith:

> Sheepe haue eate vp our medows and our downes,
> Our corne, our wood, whole villages and townes.
> Yea, they haue eate vp many wealthy men,
> Besides widowes and Orphane childeren:
> Besides our statutes and iron lawes
> Which they haue swallowed down into their maws.[27]

[24] On enclosure and the conversion of land, see Thirsk, "Enclosing and Engrossing"; Ann Kussmaul, *A General View of the Rural Economy of England, 1538–1840* (Cambridge: Cambridge University Press, 1990), pp. 76–102.

[25] Thomas More, *Utopia*, edited by George M. Logan and Robert M. Adams (Cambridge: Cambridge University Press, 1989), pp. 18–19.

[26] More, *Utopia*, pp. 18–19.

[27] Printed in R. H. Tawney and Eileen Power (eds.), *Tudor Economic Documents: Being Select Documents Illustrating the Economic and Social History of Tudor England*, 3 vols. (London: Longmans, Green and Co., 1951) [hereafter *TED*], vol. III, p. 81.

Yet, although they often wrought similar changes in different parts of England over the course of the early modern period, acts of enclosure and the conversion of land from one use to another – with its attendant effects on the shape of rural labor and community – were local events at any given time. As Joan Thirsk has noted, More's broad indictment "in fact castigates a regional phenomenon only, the increase of sheep in those areas which were already dedicated to sheep-keeping."[28]

Enclosure brought moral, as much as economic, transformations. The monstrous hunger of sheep for land ventriloquized the monstrous greed of landowners for profit. Rather than simply responding rationally to rising wool prices, landlords were choosing their own good over the common weal; instead of a predictable adjustment in the labor market, the result was the destruction of communities and the return of settled habitations to wilderness. But, as More's Hythlodaye went on to describe, the effects did not stop here. On the one hand, the reduction of arable hurt grain production and drove up the price of bread, while an expansion of sheep-rearing raised the prices of other livestock products. On the other hand, the displaced – the ploughmen and families driven from their land, homes and communities – suffered moral degeneration as well as social dislocation. Belonging nowhere, they wandered the country, turning to theft and ending on the gallows.[29] Not only had their former habitations been depopulated; they themselves had been transformed, through enforced mobility, into vagrants and criminals. Private actions borne of moral failure, in the absence of legal restraint, removed a useful multitude from its natural place, destroying it and leaving its putrefying remnants to infect the common weal. This was depopulation.

If Book I treated unregulated mobility as a cause of degeneration, however, Book II – Hythlodaye's account of Utopia – suggested that controlled mobility could sustain order. At first glance, the Utopian population was marked by homogeneity: "Farming is the one job at which everyone works, men and women, with no exception."[30] Although each Utopian was bred to farming, however, each was also trained in "a particular trade of his own, such as wool-working, linen-making, masonry, metal-work, or carpentry"; and, though expected to follow his father's business, he could be "transferred by adoption into a family practising the trade he prefers."[31] Rather than belonging to a functional multitude as if by nature, leaving only to degenerate, Utopians could change place without becoming

---

[28] Thirsk, "Enclosing and Engrossing," p. 32.
[29] More, *Utopia*, p. 17.
[30] More, *Utopia*, p. 50.
[31] More, *Utopia*, p. 50.

*dis*placed. While a system of adoption tamed mobility, the homogeniza-
tion of Utopian labor – that is, the elimination of qualitatively distinct
multitudes with different relationships to work – ensured industry.

> Their working hours are ample to provide not only enough but more than
> enough of the necessities and even the conveniences of life. You will easily
> appreciate this if you consider how large a part of the population in other
> countries exists without doing any work at all. In the first place, hardly
> any of the women, who are a full half of the population, work; or, if they
> do, then as a rule their husbands lie snoring in bed. Then there is a great
> lazy gang of priests and so-called religious men. Add to them all the rich,
> especially the landlords, who are commonly called gentlemen and nobility.
> Include with them the retainers, that mob of swaggering bullies. Finally,
> reckon in with these the sturdy and lusty beggars who go about feigning
> some disease as an excuse for their idleness.[32]

In an Aristotelian vein, More identified an optimal number of households
(6,000) for each *polis*; anticipating Botero and later theorists of empire,
as we shall see, he had his Utopians argue that the colonization of nearby
"waste" land was justifiable when numbers grew too large.[33] Yet, this was
a means of keeping stable order in Utopia rather than a route to boundless expansion; the overarching goal was an optimum population and a
healthy commonwealth, not a sprawling empire. In this sense, More's
goals were traditional. His means – especially his instrumentalization of
mobility and mutability in the service of order – were radical.

More's utopian vision was remarkable, and his heterotopic domestication of mobility foreshadowed late Elizabethan developments. But his
description of England itself indicated more typically early Tudor attitudes toward mobility and mutability, as well toward the religious basis of
community before the Reformation. A quarter of a century before *Utopia*,
the 1489 "Act Agaynst Pullyng Doun of Tounes" (4 Henry 7, *c.* 19) had
denounced the "desolacion and pulling down and wilfull waste of houses
and Townes within this realme, and leyeng to pasture londes which cus-
tumeably have ben used in tilthe." With a flourish of symbolic ratios, the
statute described the decimation of communal life, estimating that "where
in somme Townes two hundred persones were occupied and lived by their
laufull labours, nowe ben there occupied two or three herdemen." (Here it
is worth noting not only the use of ratio, but also the emphasis on the
replacement of one type of person by another.) As for More later on, the

---

[32] More, *Utopia*, p. 52.
[33] More, *Utopia*, pp. 55–6.

harm done by depopulation was moral as well as practical. Husbandry was "one of the grettest commodities of this realme," and manpower crucial to "the defence of this land ageyn oure ennemyes outwarde"; at the same time, the idleness depopulation brought was "the ground and begynnyng of all myschefes." Its harm extended into the spiritual realm: "churches destroied, the service of God withdrawen, the bodies there buried not praied for, the patrone and Curates wronged."[34]

From this perspective, the Reformation exacerbated (and, through the sale of church lands, further fueled) disruptions to parish life and spiritual community that were already linked to enclosure. Writing of the fifteenth century, Eamon Duffy discusses inclusion on the bede-roll (a list of persons to be prayed for) as the basis of inclusion in "the cult of intercession for the dead" – and thus "as a means of prolonging the presence of the dead within the community of the living."[35] The destruction of churches decried in the 1489 Act severed links of intercessory prayer that bound living and dead in an economy of salvation oriented to Purgatory and the saints, long before these beliefs came under direct attack by reformers. Indeed, legislation and official views from Henry VIII's reign echo this lament. The 1517 "Act Avoiding Pulling Down of Towns" (7 Henry 8, *c.* 1), directed against the encroachment of enclosures of pasture for sheep as well as of parkland for hunting, repeated much of the 1489 statute almost verbatim. It paid the same attention to moral and spiritual effects, denouncing the introduction of "idleness" and the interruption of prayers for the dead. The emblematic reference to numbers of essential types of people lost also reappeared: "in some town 200 persons ... living by sowing corn and grains, breeding of cattle, and other necessary for man's sustenance ... now the said persons and their progenies be minished and decreased."[36] Two years later, a Commission of Inquiry assailed those who "have enclosed with hedges and dykes ... towns, hamlets and other places ... where many of our subjects dwelt ... and exercised tillage and husbandry," turning arable to pasture "for the sake of their private gain and profit"; as a result, "our subjects ... are now brought to idleness, which is the step-mother of virtues ... and the memory of souls of Christians buried there utterly and wholly perished." This was the "undoing of our realm and diminution of our subjects."[37]

---

[34] *TED*, vol. I, pp. 4–6.
[35] Eamon Duffy, *The Stripping of the Altars: Traditional Religion in England, c. 1400–c. 1580* (New Haven, CT: Yale University Press, 1992), pp. 303, 334–5.
[36] Alfred E. Bland, Philip A. Brown and Richard H. Tawney (eds.), *English Economic History: Select Documents* (London: G. Bell and Sons, 1914) [hereafter *EEH*], p. 260.
[37] *EEH*, p. 263.

This last phrase suggests that laments for local multitudes were sometimes linked to concern for the total number of subjects in the realm. As a political idea, this was rooted in the scriptural proverb that states: "In the multitude of people is the king's honor: but in the want of people is the destruction of the prince."[38] Strength in multitude was a truism of early modern political commentary. A 1549 set of "Polices to reduce the Realme of Englande vnto a Prosperus Wealthe and Estate," for example, repeated the biblical adage that "in the multitude of people Is the state of a kinge: and in the Fewnes of Subiectes is the princes dishonour" before adding the purportedly Pythagorean dictum that "subiectes ar to a kinge as a winde is to a fyer."[39] Indeed, numbers of sailors and fighting men were of obvious practical concern in an era of frequent wars and domestic ructions. The central administration kept musters in Elizabeth's time; Francis Bacon highlighted their potential as demographic guides in 1612, and John Rickman would later cite them in arguing for a national census.[40] Yet, as these examples indicate, the centralization of records and the leap from mustering soldiers to numbering the people were less obvious and longer in coming than might seem logical in retrospect. Before the advent of standing national armies, numbering troops neither required nor implied quantifying the population as such.

It appears that the quantitative impact of enclosure was expressed most clearly when depopulation threatened England's security – as in 1489, when the Tudor hold on the throne was not yet assured, or in 1548, when William Forrest's "Pleasaunt Poesye of Princelie Practise" blamed "this Royalmys great depopulation" on lords' disregard of the yeomanry essential to defense.[41] The disastrous year of 1549 saw rebellions in Norfolk and the West Country against enclosure and accelerating religious Reformation, respectively. Though the rebellions themselves were distinct, the two issues were connected in complex ways – not only as threats to communal relationships and ideals, but also in material terms. The dissolution of the monasteries during the later 1530s had meant the transfer of as much as a quarter of English land from church to private hands, as well as the displacement (and transformation) of former monks and nuns.[42] While the suppression of monasteries, convents, chantries and other

---

[38] Proverbs 14:28 (KJV).
[39] *TED*, vol. III, p. 314.
[40] See Slack, *Invention of Improvement*, p. 46; Glass, *Numbering the People*, p. 111.
[41] *TED*, vol. III, pp. 41–5. On numbers of fighting men as a concern, see Higgs, *Information State in England*, pp. 50–3.
[42] Wood, *The 1549 Rebellions*, p. 13; Leonard Cantor, *The Changing English Countryside, 1400–1700* (London: Routledge and Kegan Paul, 1987), p. 36.

local sites of veneration desacralized the landscape, the rapid theological reforms of Edward's brief reign (codified in the "King's" Prayer Book of 1549) dispensed with the doctrine of Purgatory, which had helped tie the living inhabitants of a place to their forebears through piety and prayer.[43] If groups of people were becoming mutable and mobile, local landscapes were also, arguably, losing their distinctive spiritual functions. Enclosure both fed on and fueled these alterations.

Inner discord weakened outward strength. John Coke's *Le Débat des Hérauts d'armes de France et d'Angleterre* (modeled on an earlier debate written in the wake of the Hundred Years War) pointed up enclosure's implications for international rivalry. The French herald asserted "the great nombre of people beyng in Fraunce," contrasting its many "cyties, townes and vyllages" with the "forests, chases, parks, and enclosures" that covered England, where farms of "vi or viii persons" had given way to "oonly a shepparde or wretched heardman and his wife." Perhaps "you have as many dere in England as we have people in France," he allowed; "But for men, women and children, there is in France a c. for i. [i.e., 100 for 1]" in England. Yet, ratios gave way to absolute numbers only for specific, functional or elite groups, relating more to the kingdom's status than to any statistical idea of its population. The herald boasted that "there is in France lxxxv bysshops, and in England there is only xiiii," and similarly touted the size of the French nobility.[44] If such figures were meant as proxies for total population, they would have been extremely imprecise. The English herald, in any case, did not dispute figures but instead replied in a qualitative register, deriding "the great nombre of people you have" as "caytives and wretches, lyvyng in lyke thraldom as they dyd to the Romaynes"; 500 of "such ribaldry" weren't worth "a c. good yomen of England." Even when discussed in national terms, populations were defined more by the "maner of people" than by the number of people that they comprised.[45]

One intriguing exception to this was an anonymous tract printed in 1552, entitled *Certayne Causes Gathered Together, Wherin Is Shewed the Decaye of England, Only by the Great Multitude of Shepe.*[46] This began with "syxe olde

---

[43] Alexandra Walsham, *The Reformation of the Landscape: Religion, Identity, and Memory in Early Modern Britain and Ireland* (Oxford: Oxford University Press, 2011), pp. 123, 275; Diarmaid MacCulloch, *The Boy King: Edward VI and the Protestant Reformation* (Berkeley: University of California Press, 2002), p. 81.

[44] *TED*, vol. III, pp. 4–5.

[45] *TED*, vol. III, pp. 5–6.

[46] *Certayne Causes Gathered Together, Wherin Is Shewed the Decaye of England, Only by the Great Multitude of Shepe, to the Utter Decay of Houshold Keping, Mayntenance of Men, Dearth of Corne, and Other Notable Dyscommodityes Approued by Syxe Olde Prouerbes* (London: Printed by Heugh Syngelton, 1552). See also *TED*, vol. III, pp. 51–7, which apparently reproduces a version of the same tract, dated *c.* 1550–3.

Prouerbes" declaring that increasing numbers of sheep raised the prices or hurt the supply of wool (due to price-fixing by great landowners in Oxfordshire, Buckinghamshire and Northamptonshire), mutton and beef (due to the shift from cattle to sheep), corn (due to the expansion of pasture at the expense of tillage) and "white meat" and eggs (due to the destruction of cottages that kept pigs and poultry, resulting also in declining rural hospitality).[47] The author then spelled out further effects of these changes in more detail. The first was that "there is not so many plowes used, occupied, and mainteyned" in the affected locales. Much as More had pointed out, displaced ploughmen were "for lacke of masters, by compulsion driven some of them to begge, and some to steale."[48] Another loss, linking enclosure to security, was "the great decay to artyllery: for that we do reken that shepeherdes be but yll artchers."[49] Once again, as in the 1489 statute and subsequent commentary, depopulation was a national concern by virtue of its military implications. Remarkably, however, *Certayne Causes* attempted to quantify it.

To do so, the author took the same course that political arithmeticians would employ over a century later, stipulating a household multiplier – a notional number of people (six, in this case) each plough supported. The author then applied this to the number of ploughs destroyed by the expansion of sheep farming, estimated by supposing the number of towns and villages in England to be 50,000 and assuming that one plough, on average, had disappeared from each since 1485. The computation and commentary are worth quoting at length:

> [T]here is in England townes and villages to the number of fifty thousand & upward, & for every towne and vyllage take them one with another throughout all, there is one plowe decayed sens the first yeare of the raigne of kynge Henry the seuenth. And … yf there be for euery towne and village one plough decayed … Then is there decayed. l. thousand plowes and upwarde. The whiche. l. thousande plowes, euery ploughe were able to mainteine. vi. persons. That is to saye: the man, the wyfe and fower other in his house lesse and more. l. thousand plowes, syx persons to euery plough, draweth to the number of thre hundred thousand persons were wonte to haue meate, drynke and rayment, uprysing and downe lyinge, paying skot and lot to God, & to the kyng. And now they haue nothynge, but goeth about in England from dore to dore, and are theyr almose for Goddes sake. And because they will not begge, some of them doeth steale, and then they be hanged, and thus the Realme doeth decay[.][50]

---

[47] *Certayne Causes*, sigs. A3v–A6r.
[48] *Certayne Causes*, sigs. A6r–A7r.
[49] *Certayne Causes*, sig. B1v.
[50] *Certayne Causes*, sigs. B3r–B3v.

Perhaps for the first time, depopulation was made a national number: 300,000 people displaced by enclosure since the accession of Henry VII. Yet, it is easy to exaggerate the departure that this calculation represented. However impressive, the figure was the fruit of speculation. It may have reflected knowledge of real farming households and communities, even if the number of those communities looks like a wild guess. But there was nothing rigorously empirical about it. Nor, in contrast to seventeenth-century calculators, did the author suggest otherwise. He neither justified his assumptions by appealing to logic, personal knowledge or common experience, nor called for further data gathering to improve calculations. The "300,000" mattered in terms of a moral economy of mutable multitudes. What counted was not its statistical meaning – without other statistics with which to compare it, it had none – but the degeneration of the realm for which it stood. Even an absolute number was less a demographic fact than an emblem of decay.[51]

This remained so even when Bacon, looking back in his 1621 *History of the Reign of King Henry VII*, linked enclosure and security. His analysis of the 1489 Act began by distinguishing carefully between profitable and "depopulating" enclosures. To forbid all enclosure, he argued, "had been to forbid the improvement of the patrimony of the kingdom.... But they took a course to take away depopulating enclosures and depopulating pasturage and yet not by that name ... but by consequence." Yet, his reading of the act's goals and mechanism rings true to earlier comment:

> [T]he houses being kept up did of necessity enforce a dweller, and the proportion of land for occupation being kept up, did of necessity enforce that dweller not to be a beggar or a cottager, but a man of some substance.... This did wonderfully concern the might and mannerhood of the kingdom, to have farms as it were of a standard sufficient to maintain an able body out of penury.... For ... the principal strength of an army consists in the infantry or foot. And to make good infantry, it requires men not bred in servile fashion, but in some free and plentiful manner.[52]

The key point was not to sustain numbers but to maintain conditions for the support and reproduction of a functionally defined and organically situated type:

> Therefore if a state run most to noblemen and gentlemen, and that the husbandmen and ploughmen be but as their workfolks or labourers, or else mere cottagers (which are but housed beggars), you may have a good

---

[51] Poovey, *History of the Modern Fact*, links quantification with facticity. The emblematic use of numbers suggests a wider range of meanings for quantification.

[52] Francis Bacon, *The History of the Reign of King Henry VII* (London: Hesperus Press, 2007), p. 54.

cavalry, but never good stable bands of foot, like to coppice woods, that if you leave them in staddles too thick, they will run to bushes and briars, and have little clean underwood.[53]

We shall see that Bacon's emphasis on "improvement" and his anxiety about degeneration were more characteristic of the late sixteenth and seventeenth centuries than of the fifteenth or early sixteenth century. But for him, as for Coke, depopulation was a national concern principally because of the role and location of depopulated multitudes, not their number.

In contrast to the deep appreciation of its local and domestic, moral and social effects, depopulation's military and strategic implications – and, with these, its total quantitative impact – remained an occasional and undeveloped feature of anti-enclosure literature. With the exception of *Certayne Causes*, there were hardly any serious attempts at demographic quantification on a national scale in the sixteenth century, and few for a long time thereafter. (Bacon's commentary, though suggestive of the informational value of musters, included no numbers.) Stress fell instead on relative proportions, such as the 10:1 ratio between households that ploughed and those that kept sheep, the 100:1 ratio between French and English subjects, or the 5:1 ratio between the value of English yeomen and that of French caitiffs. Where specific numbers of people did appear, they most often emblematized the devastation that the conversion of arable to pasture and the ensuing displacement of people wrought on specific localities. In this vein, for instance, the returns to the 1517 enclosure commission included an account of an Essex farm belonging to Sir Robert Cotton, "the M[a]ner plase therof ys decaid and pulled dounby the said Sir Robert and non Inabytacyon wher Ther was wont to be kept on yt a good howseeld and ferm lond plowid." As a result of enclosure and conversion, "wher ther was wont to be kept in yt a fermer and his wyfe and xviij or xxii personys ... now ... the tenaunt and his wyfe kepyth" alone.[54] Good land was unploughed, a thriving household decimated. Place and proportion: These were the terms in which people thought about depopulation, while church and commonwealth alike were conceived as politic bodies.[55]

Such views persisted well into the seventeenth century, even as local causes were increasingly credited with national political and moral import. In 1604, for example, Lincolnshire clergyman Francis Trigge charged

---

[53] Bacon, *History of the Reign of King Henry VII*, pp. 54–5.

[54] I. S. Leadam (ed.), *The Domesday of Enclosures, 1517–1518* (London: Longmans, Green and Co., 1897), p. 217.

[55] On the church as a body politic, see Alexandra Walsham, *Charitable Hatred: Tolerance and Intolerance in England, 1500–1700* (Manchester: Manchester University Press, 2006), pp. 41–2, 73–5.

enclosure of the commons with "rooting out" husbandmen as well as eliminating "a multitude of servants," "depopulating" or "dispeopling" towns and "diminishing the people"; he echoed the scriptural equation of the "multitude of people" with the "honor" of a king, and even asserted that landlords beguiled by "improvement" – that keyword of seventeenth-century projects – would be cursed with barrenness.[56] Tillage supported not only ploughs, but also "a multitude of valiant souldiers" whose loss endangered the kingdom.[57] For Trigge as for Tudor observers, further, the process was degenerative. Enclosure did not simply remove husbandmen and soldiers; "it makes beggers, and ... theeves" of them.[58] A generation later, Robert Powell's *Depopulation Arraigned* (1636) took the moral condemnation of enclosing landlords to new rhetorical heights and expanded its frame of reference without radically altering the analytical framework that sustained it. A lawyer, Powell emphasized the economic and military costs of enclosure, which, by "translating culture into pasture," spread idleness, weakened the state – replacing villages of 200 or 300 with handfuls of shepherds – and angered God.[59] "Tillage," by contrast, "is the occasion of multiplying of people, both for service in the wars, and time of peace"; it promoted virtue and industry, enabling the nation to "stand upon it selfe."[60] Lest this sound merely pragmatic, the tone of Powell's "arraignment" of "depopulators" was severe:

> But if, to shut up and close up the wombe of the earth, *communis reipublicae matricis* [the common womb of the state] ... bee a worse sinne than the hiding and hoarding up of her fruits after its birth; then is the one more pernitious and intolerable then the other.... And if the curse be denounced against that, *Qui abscondit frumentum maledicitur in populo, Pro.* 11.26. [Proverbs, 11:26: "He that withholdeth corn, the people shall curse him"] it must needs fall heavier upon this. *Depopulation* is *praefocatio matricis*, a strangling or choaking of the womb, and causing an utter sterility.[61]

The depopulator was a "man of bloud," a "*matricide*" who "choakes up the earth our common mother, from yeelding her ... increase unto her

[56] Francis Trigge, *The Humble Petition of Two Sisters; the Church and Common-Wealth: For the Restoring of their Ancient Commons and Liberties, Which Late Inclosure with Depopulation Hath Uncharitably Taken Away* (London: Printed by George Bishop, 1604), sigs. A3v–A4r, A5r, A6r, B6v, C4r, E2r. See McRae, *God Speed the Plough*, pp. 71–2.

[57] Trigge, *Humble Petition*, sig. B5r.

[58] Trigge, *Humble Petition*, sig. F7v.

[59] Robert Powell, *Depopulation Arraigned, Convicted and Condemned, by the Lawes of God and Man* (London: Printed by R. B., 1636), pp. 31–2, 54–5, 79.

[60] Powell, *Depopulation Arraigned*, pp. 35–6.

[61] Powell, *Depopulation Arraigned*, p. 4.

offspring."[62] He "robbes and pilles the people of their due meanes and maintenance," hindering "their service and leige obedience, immediately to their Prince, and mediately to the Common-weale."[63] The essence of depopulation was not loss but mutation, the decay of a vital multitude into a troublesome counter-population. Yet, beyond displacing and debasing the multitude, depopulation *alienated* it. For this reason, its degenerative impact was national: "it alters the quality of the people; from good Husbands, it makes them houseless and thriftlesse, puts them in a course of idleness.... So as they become aliens and strangers to their nationall government, and the kingdome ... dispeopled and desolated."[64] The discourse of depopulation had been absorbed into a larger vision of commonwealth.

Ordering Multitudes: The Commonwealth and the Body Politic

Though More's *Utopia* offered an early and celebrated statement of it, the discourse of depopulation was rooted in opposition to enclosure and the expansion of pasturage that had begun in the later fifteenth century. Agrarian complaint, then, fostered English thinking about the governance of a human multitude independently of specifically humanist influence. Still, it was in humanist writing that the task of government more broadly came to be cast in terms of managing the relationships, balance and flows between a series of functionally interdependent multitudes, conceived of in more and more detailed terms as limbs or vital organs of a living polity. As this suggests, a key metaphor in this writing was the familiar one of the body politic. But this was now linked to, and elaborated through, the idea of a "commonwealth" that required active government – or reformation – through some mixture of education, the cultivation of reason and (in more self-consciously Christian and, later, Reformed renderings) conscience, and "policy" or "police" geared to promoting the common weal and fostering "civility" by material as well as moral means.[65] Having first emerged as local problems in the context of specific rural transformations, the governance of qualitative multitudes was recast as a problem of political knowledge and a privileged object of coordinated and sustained

---

[62] Powell, *Depopulation Arraigned*, p. 51.
[63] Powell, *Depopulation Arraigned*, p. 6.
[64] Powell, *Depopulation Arraigned*, pp. 6–7.
[65] Withington, *Politics of Commonwealth*, pp. 51–84; Mayer, *Thomas Starkey and the Commonweal*, especially pp. 106–38; Paul Slack, *From Reformation to Improvement* (Oxford: Oxford University Press, 1999), pp. 5–28. On Christian humanism and its influence on Calvinist social and political thought, see also Margo Todd, *Christian Humanism and the Puritan Social Order* (Cambridge: Cambridge University Press, 1987), pp. 22–52; Gorski, *Disciplinary Revolution*, p. 22.

intervention. By Elizabeth's reign, the lenses of the mobility, mutability and mixture of multitudes brought a variety of social and political challenges into focus.

This section examines the mid-Tudor political uptake of multitude through three works. Two are canonical examples of English humanist social thought: Thomas Starkey's *Dialogue between Pole and Lupset* (completed between 1532 and 1535, in the wake of Henry VIII's divorce of Catherine of Aragon, but not printed in the period) and Sir Thomas Smith's *Discourse of the Common Weal of this Realm of England* (completed *c.* 1549, during the troubled reign of Edward VI, but printed only in 1581).[66] Emerging from different historical contexts and intellectual milieus, Starkey and Smith's works vary in the details of their analysis, as well as in their political and religious outlooks. Nor were they the first or only English humanist works to take up the question of governing multitudes – as witness the specter of More, who was executed in 1535 and whose *Utopia* was printed in English for the first time in 1551. Yet, they evince similar ideas about the nature of the multitudes that constituted the body politic. The third, an anonymous tract written in 1549 and addressed to the Lord Protector, the Duke of Somerset – entitled "Polices to reduce this Realme of Englande vnto a Prosperus Wealthe and Estate" – departs from these ideas in significant and prescient ways.[67] Yet, all three works employ an analytical and normative vocabulary centered on the possibilities of policy and the imperatives of civility, inflected particularly in the last by religious reform. This vocabulary facilitated the transfer to new contexts, in England, Ireland and beyond, of ideas first voiced in relation to rural depopulation. Long before Bodin and Botero, the governance of multitude was the object of a new and self-conscious politics.

In terms both of chronology and depth of engagement, Thomas Starkey claims pride of place in this change. A humanist, Padua-trained lawyer and sometime associate of cardinal Reginald Pole – splitting with him over the royal divorce – Starkey has long been credited with a major role in the development of English humanism. Exactly what this consisted of, however, is debated. For James K. McConica, Starkey was less an "original mind" than an able exponent of reform and moderation as preached by Erasmus of Rotterdam. On this account, Starkey's work inspired the

---

[66] Thomas Starkey, *A Dialogue Between Pole and Lupset*, edited by T. F. Mayer, Camden Fourth Series (London: Royal Historical Society, 1989); [Thomas Smith], *A Discourse of the Common Weal of This Realm of England*, edited by Elizabeth Lamond (Cambridge: Cambridge University Press, 1954).

[67] *TED*, vol. III, pp. 311–45; the original is in Goldsmiths Library, MS 10.

Cromwellian injunctions of 1536 and 1538 (the latter of which enjoined the keeping of parish registers), designed to make England an "Erasmian polity" capable of accommodating a range of religious views by means of the conceptual device of *adiaphora*, or "things indifferent" – matters of religious belief or practice on which Scripture was silent.[68] This view has been undermined, however, both by Alistair Fox's criticism of "Erasmianism" as a misleading label for Tudor humanists, and by Alexandra Walsham's and Ethan Shagan's arguments that the concept of *adiaphora* – and the ideal of "moderation" for which it stood – implied not the toleration of different views but their suppression in the interest of social harmony.[69] While McConica's Erasmian moderation was bound to a vision of the church that vanished with Henry VIII only to resurface under Elizabeth, Shagan's was a flexible language, appropriated successively by conservative reformers, Puritans and separatists alike. Its exaltation of civil, and civilized, power was thus unhindered by changes of regime.[70]

In another vein, Neal Wood has seen Starkey, together with Sir Thomas Smith and the author of the "Polices," as skilled "publicists" for the "social environmentalism" of Erasmus and More. This treated the state as a "mechanism" for the reconciliation of conflicting economic interests, and it presumed a kind of human malleability that made specific multitudes the logical objects of political reform.[71] To this view, Phil Withington's work on the discourse of commonwealth adds an important nuance. Rather than imagining the polity in terms of a traditionally fixed set of estates or corporate bodies, Starkey's and Smith's work emerged from and reflected "a process of structural and behavioral urbanisation" that envisioned social interaction itself through a corporatist and moral lens of "enclosed city commonwealths" or bodies politic.[72] To this civic vision of nested polities subject to scalable applications of corporatist language, Withington contrasts the different strain of humanism behind Francis Bacon's more court-oriented opposition of national subject populations to putatively omnipotent governors.[73] While Chapter 2 will suggest that this contrast is overdrawn, at least with respect to the question of demographic governance, both the fungible nature of corporatist discourse and the

---

[68] McConica, *English Humanists*, pp. 194–9.
[69] Fox, "English Humanism and the Body Politic"; Walsham, *Charitable Hatred*, pp. 241–3; Shagan, *Rule of Moderation*, pp. 73–110.
[70] Shagan, *Rule of Moderation*, passim; on the conceptual link between civil authority and civilization, see p. 212.
[71] Wood, *Foundations of Political Economy*, pp. 1–2, 124–235.
[72] Withington, *Politics of Commonwealth*, pp. 48, 51–84.
[73] Withington, *Politics of Commonwealth*, pp. 54–5.

links between moderation and the expansion of the state are important to grasping humanist approaches to multitude.

At the core of Starkey's *Dialogue between Pole and Lupset* is a humanist construction of the body politic, influenced by Aristotle but written at a moment of unprecedented royal assertiveness.[74] The goal of "polytyke rule," for Starkey, is "to enduce the multytud to vertuse [i.e. virtuous] lyvyng."[75] This depends upon the calibrated function of the body politic's parts, "that the hole body of the commynalty may lyve in quytenes <& tranquyllyte> every parte dowyng hys offyce & duty."[76] At the most basic level, much as in Aristotle's *Politics*, the polity requires not merely sufficient numbers of people to perform essential duties, but also that this loose substrate, the unspecified "multytude," be reduced to "gud ordur & cyvylyte" through the "pollycy" or "grete wyse & polytyke men."[77] Policy, in short, is the artful ordering of multitudes in the shapes, sizes and positions essential to civil life. What makes this possible – what gives human art power over multitudes – is God's creation of humankind in his image. Man is an "erthely god ... lord of al other bestys & creaturys ... for al be un to hym subjecte, al by pollycy and brought to his obedyence"; indeed, the earth itself "by the dylygent labur & pollycy of man ys brought to marvelous culture & fortylite [i.e. fertility]."[78] Starkey enthuses over human "memory & wyte," art and policy, as over the human creation of customs designed to promote virtue and civil laws calculated to reconcile humanity to the immutable "law of nature" – denial of which is a "corrupt opynyon" to be overcome, like all human frailty, by education.[79]

If the flesh of the body politic is bare multitude civilized by policy, the civil order is an organic one. Starkey repeatedly draws direct and detailed analogies between political and medical health.[80] Both consist not just in the "necessyte, strength & beuty" of the individual parts concerned, but also, most importantly, in their mutual proportion.[81] In this schema, that is, functionally defined multitudes are thought of as more or less necessary, strong, beautiful and above all "proporcynabul" limbs and organs. To the extent that any idea of the total population or the overall scale of

---

[74] See Harris, *Foreign Bodies*, pp. 30–40.
[75] Starkey, *Dialogue Between Pole and Lupset*, p. 36.
[76] Starkey, *Dialogue Between Pole and Lupset*, p. 4.
[77] Starkey, *Dialogue Between Pole and Lupset*, p. 7.
[78] Starkey, *Dialogue Between Pole and Lupset*, p. 8.
[79] Starkey, *Dialogue Between Pole and Lupset*, pp. 9–12.
[80] Harris suggests that Starkey's use of corporate metaphor effects a novel substitution of the nation for the body of the universal church; see Harris, *Foreign Bodies*, pp. 32–4.
[81] Starkey, *Dialogue Between Pole and Lupset*, pp. 23–4.

the bare multitude figures in this discussion, it is under the Aristotelian rubric of "necessity," the number of people required for the "felycyte" of the whole.[82] What matters is not that this number be large, but that it strike a balance between the constraints of necessity and the demands of discipline – between hands, one might say, and mouths:

> For where as ther be other [i.e. either] to many pepul in the cuntrey, in so much that the cuntrey by no dylygence nor labur of man <may> be suf-fycyent to nurysch them & mynyster them foe ther wythout dowte can be no commyn wele, but ever myserabul penury & wrechyd poverty, lyke as yf ther be of pepul over few in so much that <the> cuntrey may not be well tyllyd & occupyd, nor craftys wel & dylygently exercysed, ther schal also sprynge therof grete penury & scasenes [i.e. scarcity] of a thynges necessary for man's lyfe, & so then cyvyle lyfe & true commyn wele can in no case be <ther> maynteynyd[.][83]

The organic civil polity required not a large population but a "convenyent multitude."

In practice, the strength and beauty of the "polytyke body" depended more directly on the order and proportion of constituent submultitudes than on their cumulative size. As it was with "every mannys body," wherein "the hart ... as the fountayn of al natural powarys, mynystryth them with dew ordur to al other ... as the ye [i.e. eye] to se the yere to here the fote to go & hand to hold & rech," so with the commonwealth: the prince and his officers were as the heart and sensory organs, craftsmen and soldiers the hands and ploughmen and tillers the feet.[84] Strength depended on the transfer of power from the former to the latter "accordyng to the order of nature," beauty on the proportion between the parts:

> <So> that one parte <ever> be agreabul to a nother, <in forme & fastyon quantyte & nombur as craftys men and plow men in dew nombur <& pro-portyon with other partys accordyng to the place cyty or <towne>>, for yf ther be to many or to few of one or of the other ther ys in the commynalty a grete deformyte[.][85]

The idea of "nombur" – as distinct from actual numbers – functioned here as a component of relative proportion rather than a measure of absolute size. The proportions at issue were those of qualitatively distinct, function-ally defined, interdependent multitudes: ploughmen, artisans, tillers of the soil; rulers and their counselors; and denizens of towns and cities. Ordered

[82] Starkey, *Dialogue Between Pole and Lupset*, pp. 28–9.
[83] Starkey, *Dialogue Between Pole and Lupset*, p. 32.
[84] Starkey, *Dialogue Between Pole and Lupset*, pp. 32–3.
[85] Starkey, *Dialogue Between Pole and Lupset*, p. 33.

by policy in accordance with nature, these composed, through their local functions and mutual interactions, a living political community:

> When al thes partys thys couplyd togyddur, exercyse wyth dylygence theyr offyce & duty, as the plowmen & laburerys of the ground dylygently tyl the same for the gettyng of fode, & necessary sustenance to the rest of the body, & craftys men worke al thynges mete for mayntenance of rhe same, ye and they hedys & rularys <by just pollycy> maynteyne they state <stablyshyd in the cuntrey> ever lokyng to the profyte of they hole body, then that commyn wele must nedys florysch[.][86]

Relocating particular multitudes from their geographical locales into the metaphorical space of the body politic, Starkey articulated them both to one another and to the general idea not of a kingdom headed by a monarch but of a state ruling by policy. The government of multitudes, in their operations and relations, was an explicit object of political art.

The metaphor of the body politic implied analogies not only between good order and good health but also between social disorder and physical decay or disease. Starkey's rendition of the latter was especially detailed.[87] As it had been for writers on enclosure, so for Starkey, discussion began with depopulation, the "great dekey" felt in "our cytes castellys & townes of late days."[88] Going beyond most of them, however, Starkey clearly suggested an absolute decline in population – that is, he apparently construed depopulation in national (or perhaps generically rural) rather than local terms: "the cuntrey hath byn more populos then hyt is now."[89] Though he likened this "lake [i.e. lack] of pepul" to "a consumptyon or grete sklendurnes of mannes body," however, there was "a nother dysease & syknes more grevus than thys," namely, idleness.[90] Counterpoised to the requirements of a flourishing commonweal, the essence of idleness was not mere unemployment or inactivity in the abstract but more specifically the neglect, through lassitude or "yl" occupation, of the "offyce & duty" dictated by one's place in the "polytyke body."[91] Idlers high and low came in for criticism: "yf you aftur thys maner examyn the multytude in every ordur & degre, you schal fynd … the thryd parte of our pepul lyvyng in idulnes as personys to the commyn wele utturly unprofytabul."[92] More

---

[86] Starkey, *Dialogue Between Pole and Lupset*, pp. 39–40.
[87] See Harris, *Foreign Bodies*, p. 35.
[88] Starkey, *Dialogue Between Pole and Lupset*, p. 47. See Wood, *Foundations of Political Economy*, p. 139.
[89] Starkey, *Dialogue Between Pole and Lupset*, p. 50.
[90] Starkey, *Dialogue Between Pole and Lupset*, pp. 51–2.
[91] Starkey, *Dialogue Between Pole and Lupset*, p. 52.
[92] Starkey, *Dialogue Between Pole and Lupset*, p. 52.

dangerous than the number of idlers, as the use of ratio reflects, was the disproportion they caused. Starkey likened this to a "palsy" borne of "dyscord & debate" between the idle and the dutyful in every quarter.[93]

> [T]he partys of the body be not proporcyonabul one to a nother, one parte ys to grete, a nother to lytyl, one parte hath in hyt over many pepul a nother over few, as prestys are to many & yet gud clerkys to few … monkys frerys & chanonys are to many & yet gud relygyouse men to few, procturys & brokarys of both laws … are to many, & yet gud mynystrys of justyce are to few, marchantes caryng out thyngys necessary for our owne pepul are over many & yet they wych schold bryng necessarys are to few, craftys men & makers of tryfullys are to many <& yet gud artyfycerys be to few>, and occupyarys & tyllarys of the grounds are to few servantes in mennys houses are to many[.]

As this catalog of functionally (but no longer geographically) localized imbalances indicates, harmony and proportion within and between the parts of a closed system were uppermost in Starkey's mind. In this context, numbers – more often implied than stated, and stated more often as fractions than as absolute figures – were symbols of political deformity, not forms of demographic data.

England's infirmities affected particular parts of the body politic – particular, functionally defined multitudes. Political medicine thus meant policies targeting the relative size, composition and quality of these groups. To be sure, Starkey did address the "grete lake of pepul, the multytude wherof ys as hyt were the ground & fundatyon of thys our commyn wele"; just as "batyl & pestylens hyngur & darth" were to be feared, so means "to allure man to thys natural procreatyon" should be found.[94] But these must be consistent with "a cyvyle ordur," for while man had the same inborn propensity to increase as other beasts, as the sole creature "borne to cyvylyte … he may not, wythout ordur or respecte study to the satysfactyon of thys natural affecte." Legitimate increase, in civil conditions, could only be through "lauful matrymony," and promoting this meant engaging with the corporate characteristics and relative sizes of the multitudes whose orderly articulation composed the polity.[95] Thus, one "let" on marriage (a fraught one, when Starkey wrote) was clerical and scholarly celibacy. Offering a pragmatic argument for a contentious religious reform, Starkey thought it best to "admyt all secular prestys to

---

[93] Starkey, *Dialogue Between Pole and Lupset*, pp. 55–6. On Starkey's vocabulary of pathology, see Harris, *Foreign Bodies*, p. 35; see also Wood, *Foundations of Political Economy*, p. 138.

[94] Starkey, *Dialogue Between Pole and Lupset*, pp. 96–7.

[95] Starkey, *Dialogue Between Pole and Lupset*, p. 97.

mary ... consideryng now the grete multytude & nowmbur of them." A similar but secular problem was "the grete multytude of servyng men" unable to form households. To remedy this, Starkey suggested a sumptuary restriction by which noblemen might retain no more servants than they could "set forward" to marriage; this done, "the multytude of them should be mynysched [i.e. diminished] gretely."[96] Bachelors were also to be taxed. [97] By such means were marriage and the formation of households to be enjoined, and the "convenyent multitude" required for civil life assured.

Other measures targeted particular multitudes in the interests of the strength and beauty of the polity, ecclesiastical and civil. Among these were reducing those "occupy'd ... <<in> vayn> craftys"; making clergy "fewar <in nombur> ... but better <in lyfe>"; restricting "the multytude of ... <advocatys>"; and so on.[98] More than most critics of enclosure, Starkey concerned himself not just with the qualities and relative proportions of such particular groups but also with the causal and generative or degenerative links between them, as well as with the actual flows of people from one multitude to another. As More and others had, for example, Starkey connected the multitude of servants to the multiplication of beggars and thieves.[99] His strictures against excessively large aristocratic households, as we have seen, were designed to channel would-be servants into more productive, and reproductive, places. A hierarchy of productive employments legitimated constraints on the growth of "vayn" professions. The general goal of a healthy, strong and beautiful body politic, free of "deformyte & yl proportion," was imagined and pursued through the augmentation or diminution, restriction or reformation, isolation or association of specific multitudes.[100]

Compared to the moralistic Starkey, Sir Thomas Smith has been called "the first political economist, indeed the founder of that science."[101] Accepting the egoistic passions of individuals, Smith is seen as having based his analysis on the operations of self-interested, profit-seeking economic agents, and abandoned both the cultivation of virtue that had justified policy in the mirror-of-princes tradition and the customary assumptions and nostrums of agrarian complaint literature.[102] Where

[96] Starkey, *Dialogue Between Pole and Lupset*, pp. 98–9.
[97] Starkey, *Dialogue Between Pole and Lupset*, p. 100.
[98] Starkey, *Dialogue Between Pole and Lupset*, pp. 103–6, 127.
[99] Starkey, *Dialogue Between Pole and Lupset*, p. 117.
[100] Starkey, *Dialogue Between Pole and Lupset*, p. 106.
[101] Wood, *Foundations of Political Economy*, p. 191.
[102] McRae, *God Speed the Plough*, pp. 52–5.

Starkey viewed the polity as a body, one might say, Smith pictured the state as a household. More than this: by means of a mechanical analogy he moved toward an understanding of a sphere of economic relations distinct from state and society, in which individual selfishness defied education and legislation but might nevertheless be reconciled to the common good by political means. Smith's abstraction, naturalistic interpretation and political deployment of specifically economic phenomena in his *Discourse of the Common Weal* arguably anticipated William Petty's essays in economic policy, and Bernard Mandeville's programmatic embrace of human desires, if not Adam Smith's Invisible Hand.[103] These thinkers are associated with a shift away from corporatist thinking and microcosmic metaphor – the nexus of moral, religious, social and political imperatives in which pre-modern economic ideas were embedded – toward a world of self-owning individuals propelled by natural appetites, deflected slightly if at all by the regulatory powers of the state.

Without denying the novelty of Smith's analysis, however, one can see similarities between his demographic ideas and those that have been examined here. There are several bases for this continuity. First, the dialogue that carried the substantive "discourse" began as a commentary on enclosure, penned by a royal administrator in the midst of Kett's Rebellion, and presented as a response to Somerset's earlier appointment of a commission, under Edward VI's aegis, to investigate the progress of depopulation since Henry VII's time.[104] The *Discourse* thus addressed a familiar problem in familiar moral terms – to which Somerset's own response to the rebellion seems to have been peculiarly, and for his own career fatally, sympathetic.[105] Second, the form of a conversation between stylized *personae* – a landowning knight, a husbandman, a merchant, an artificer and a scholar ("members of everue state that find theim selves greved now a days") – enabled Smith to represent received views of the body politic and the interdependent and morally charged types of people it comprised.[106] It is noticeable that as Smith's analysis departed from convention in the text, the three laboring figures dropped out of the conversation, leaving the scholar to present his views to the landowner unopposed. Even so, the structuring role of qualitative multitudes persisted.

---

[103] Wood, *Foundations of Political Economy*, pp. 191–235.
[104] Smith, *Discourse of the Common Weal*, p. 13; See "Instructions to the Enclosure Commissioners Appointed June, 1548, and Hale's 'Charge to the Juries Impanelled to Present Enclosures'," in *TED*, vol. I, pp. 39–44.
[105] See MacCulloch, *The Boy King*, pp. 44–9.
[106] Smith, *Discourse of the Common Weal*, p. 12.

Smith divided the *Discourse* into three dialogues, which dealt in turn with the problems of dearth and disorder facing the commonwealth, their causes and their solutions. The first dialogue began with complaints about enclosure, including familiar estimates of its depopulating effects and social consequences. Fittingly, the husbandman expounded on these:

> I haue knowen of late a docen plowes with in lesse compasse then 6 myles aboute me laide downe with in theise [vij] yeares; and wheare xl persons had theire lyvings, nowe one man and his shepard hathe all. Which thing is not the least cause of theise vprors, for by theise inclosures men doe lacke livinges and be idle[.][107]

The tradesman and merchant confirmed the resulting depopulation of both countryside and towns, "London excepted." The husbandman then went on to catalog the troubles of each estate in a manner suggestive not only of their comprehensiveness but also of their interconnections:

> Euerie man findethe him selfe greved at this time … the gentleman, that he can not live on his landes onely, as his father did before. The artificer can not set so manie on worke, by reason all manner of victualles is so deare. The husbandman, by reason of his londe, is dearer rated then before hathe bene. Then we that be merchauntes paye dearer for euerie thinge that comethe ouer the sea[.][108]

The gentleman's problems had become the husbandmen's and the artificer's, and all of theirs the merchant's. While the knight himself denied that enclosure caused the dearth either of corn (which, he argued, remained cheap) or of cattle (which enclosure itself helped to supply), he too invoked an organic vision of the polity in his own recommendation that, like physicians, the interlocutors move from symptoms through diagnosis to cure.[109]

In the second dialogue, discussion turned to the causes of dearth. The husbandman again blamed the knight for raising rents, while the capper reasserted the depopulating and destabilizing effects of enclosure, complete with emblematic proportions: "in stead of some C. or CC. parsons [i.e., persons], that had their livinges theron, now be theare but thre or foure sheppards, and the maister only."[110] The scholar demurred on the role of enclosure, though he agreed that should it continue for another twenty years at the rate of the twenty years previous, "the people still encreasinge and theire Liuinges deminished, yt must nedes cume to passe that a

---

107 Smith, *Discourse of the Common Weal*, p. 13.
108 Smith, *Discourse of the Common Weal*, p. 32.
109 Smith, *Discourse of the Common Weal*, pp. 17, 35–6.
110 Smith, *Discourse of the Common Weal*, pp. 38, 48.

greate parte of the people shalbe Idle."[111] The knight replied – citing the experiences of Essex, Kent and Devonshire – that enclosure had proven to be profitable. Common land, in contrast, was commonly neglected. The scholar's response was to differentiate the effects of enclosure as such from the conversion of land from arable to pasture; as far as yields went, he argued, landlords "maie not purchace them selues profit by that may be hurtfull to others."[112] Nor, however, could they be expected to act against their own interest. The problem was how "To make the profitt of the plow to be as good, rate for rate, as the profitt of the graisiers and shep-masters" – how, that is, to align the interest of each member with the common weal.[113]

Historians of economic thought have argued that Smith's dialogue introduced individual economic interest into social thought. "For euerie man will seke wheare most advautage is," he reasoned, "And so longe [as] it is" more profitable to graze sheep than raise corn, so long shall "pasture … encroche vpon the tillage, for all the laws that euer can be made to the contrarie."[114] From a different perspective, however, this analysis implied a precocious deployment of human nature as a fundamental constraint on policy. This would in time become a distinguishing feature of Restoration-era political arithmetic. Yet if decisions were driven by individual perceptions of advantage fed through mechanisms of calculation common to all mankind, still the politically salient effects of these decisions were felt and addressed in terms of the relative waxing and waning of subordinate multitudes and the resultant disproportion between members of the social body. Thus, the reduction of lordly hospitality in the countryside created a mass of servants whose idleness and appetite for consumption were markers of degeneracy; declining cloth exports similarly turned domestic clothiers restless and troublesome to the polity.[115] Perhaps, the knight suggested, disorderly groups might be transformed into more useful kinds of people. Better not, the doctor cautioned, if this risked making imbalances worse.[116]

Even the doctor's explanation of "the imporishment of this realme" in terms of the debasement of the coinage partook of a similar logic – debasement was, after all, a kind of degeneration.[117] Gold and silver

---

[111] Smith, *Discourse of the Common Weal*, pp. 48–9.
[112] Smith, *Discourse of the Common Weal*, pp. 49–50.
[113] Smith, *Discourse of the Common Weal*, p. 53.
[114] Smith, *Discourse of the Common Weal*, p. 53.
[115] Smith, *Discourse of the Common Weal*, pp. 81–3, 88.
[116] Smith, *Discourse of the Common Weal*, pp. 89–90.
[117] Smith, *Discourse of the Common Weal*, p. 69.

had a natural function as "Instruments of exchange." The specific qualities with which nature had endowed them – the capacity to be divided and recombined, stamped and handled "with out perishinge of the substance," as well as their "lightnes of cariage" – conduced to their employment as currency, as the "common consent" of the civilized world attested.[118] Because of this, they knit together the different nations of the world and the different orders of the commonweal. Much as dress distinguished each estate, so royal marks indicated the weight and worth of each coin. Debasement, the "corruptinge of our coine and treasure," severed the link between external sign and internal value in the same way that mobility and mutability cut multitudes off from their distinctive roles and places. By a perverse alchemy, it turned bullion to "brasse" and made "our chiefe commodities" worthless, just as displacement and indolence turned ploughmen into vagrants.[119] This is not the place to explore the ties Smith invoked between appearance, credit and dissimulation – a theme later taken up by Elizabethan commentators on consumption and the social order – except to note that this nexus informed ideas around the debasement of people and currency alike.[120] The point here is that for Smith, these two processes were not only formally similar but also causally connected. A degenerate coinage distorted the exchange relationships that kept each multitude in its place and relation to the whole.[121]

The same logic of degeneration in the context of corporeal analogy ran through the third dialogue, concerning "remidies" for the "deseases" already described. As with the restoration of balance in the body natural, so the aim of physic in the body politic was a restoration of "auncient wealthe" and social equilibrium; the commonwealth's ills did not require a radical change of regimen but were to be "redressed … with lest daunger or alteration of thinges."[122] Debasement had set off a chain reaction, pulling one group after another into hardship:

[118] Smith, *Discourse of the Common Weal*, pp. 72–3.
[119] Smith, *Discourse of the Common Weal*, p. 69; see also pp. 116–17.
[120] On this theme in relation to early modern political thought, see Jon Snyder, *Dissimulation and the Culture of Secrecy in Early Modern Europe* (Berkeley: University of California Press, 2009); in relation to identity, Valentin Groebner, *Who Are You? Identification, Deception, and Surveillance in Early Modern Europe* (New York: Zone Books, 2007); in relation to consumption, Ann Rosalind Jones and Peter Stallybrass, *Renaissance Clothing and the Materials of Memory* (Cambridge: Cambridge University Press, 2000) and Jean-Christophe Agnew, *Worlds Apart: The Market and the Theater in Anglo-American Thought, 1550–1750* (Cambridge: Cambridge University Press, 1986).
[121] See Smith, *Discourse of the Common Weal*, p. 104.
[122] Smith, *Discourse of the Common Weal*, pp. 97, 131.

> [S]traungers first selles their wares dearer to vs; and that makes all fermors
> and tennauntes, that rerethe any commoditie, agayne to sell the same dear-
> er; the dearthe therof makes the gentlemen to rayse their rentes, and to take
> farmes into theire handes … and consequently to inclose more groundes.[123]

Smith's audience would have known that these changes in what we consider economic behavior – which implied not merely new stresses on established relationships, but also dramatic and consequential changes in the
land itself – inflicted new kinds of mobility, mixture and degeneration on
the groups involved. Debasing the currency that bound estates together
compromised relations between labor and land, country and town,
deforming and displacing essential multitudes whose remnants recombined as cancerous excrescences in the city and on the roads. Smith's grasp
of individual economic motivations may have given him new purchase on
the mechanisms by which debasement ramified through English society.
But the structure through which the poison spread was still envisioned in
organic and corporate rather than mechanical or atomistic terms.

Policy was a kind of restorative medicine, an "arte" that worked by grasping "the chiefe and efficient causes" at work, and then redressing, revers-
ing or redirecting their effects as far as nature and Providence allowed.[124]
Counterfeiters had done with the prince's "treasure house, which is the
Realme … as the Alcmistes weare wounte to doe with private men, promising them to multiplie, when of truethe they did minishe."[125] Undoing
the damage meant restoring the "iust and dwe proportion" between coin
and content that the nature of the metals and the exigencies of human
trust and calculation demanded.[126] On the other hand, the dearth debasement produced, to the extent that it originated in human "Avarice" rather
than divine judgment, must be addressed by other means.[127] Getting rid
of "covetousness" was no more feasible than "making men to be without Ire, without gladnes, withoute feare, and without all affections."[128]
Policy should seek instead to remove the "occasion" for greed's expression,
namely the "exceading lucre" that made enclosure desirable.[129] To this
end, Smith proposed a combination of legislative and demographic interventions: Legal restraints on enclosure, import restrictions to stimulate

---

[123] Smith, *Discourse of the Common Weal*, p. 104.
[124] Smith, *Discourse of the Common Weal*, p. 105.
[125] Smith, *Discourse of the Common Weal*, pp. 116–17.
[126] Smith, *Discourse of the Common Weal*, p. 107.
[127] Smith, *Discourse of the Common Weal*, p. 121.
[128] Smith, *Discourse of the Common Weal*, pp. 121–2.
[129] Smith, *Discourse of the Common Weal*, p. 122.

domestic industry ("20000 persons might be set a-worke with in this Realme" through import substitution projects), incentives for craftsmen to return to towns and the targeted settlement of "strange artificers" from overseas.[130] Foreshadowing later schemes, he suggested fostering export trades and exerting greater corporate control over the function, location and preponderance of different classes of artificer.[131] These were dramatic interventions in the body politic, extending even to transplanting foreign bodies into it where vital organs would not regenerate themselves. Even here, however, the aim was to supply a missing part or address a handicap rather than alter the dynamics of social relations and economic activity. Smith's overarching vision was one of holistic reform, restraint and restoration, geared toward the maintenance of order and proportion between functionally interdependent multitudes of people.

Smith's analysis was sophisticated in its grasp of economic relations, but in conceptual terms, the anonymous "Polices to Reduce this Realme of Englande vnto a Prosperus Wealthe and Estate" advanced a more radical program "fore the redresse and amendment of the Publicke Weal."[132] Part of its boldness derived from the author's overt linkage of political reform and the reformation of the church, which became more programmatic (and more Calvinist in orientation) under Edward VI than it had been in his father's time. With "the trew worshepping of god" established, the tract expressed the hope that God would at last make king and council "his ministres in plauking vppe by the rottes al the Cawses" of national decay.[133] Despite this providential strain, the author coupled the usual invocation of Proverbs 14:28 with an appeal to "the wise Phillosopher Pithagoras," whose purported dictum had a naturalist slant: "the subiectes ar to a kinge as a winde is to a fyer: For the grosher that the winde is the greatter is the Fier."[134] Alone among the texts so far considered, too, the "Polices" advocated maximizing numbers of people in the realm outright, almost without regard to their qualities or location. As the author put it, its purpose was "to declare how this realme ... may be made Populus, the people wealthie the king riche the Realme withoute Cyvill Discorde: vitall plenty."[135]

---

[130] Smith, *Discourse of the Common Weal*, pp. 124–9. As the figure of "20000" is offered without any further quantitative context, it may indicate the significance rather than the precise scale of the projects envisioned. On import substitution as a focus of projecting, see Joan Thirsk, *Economic Policy and Projects: The Development of a Consumer Society in Early Modern England* (Oxford: Oxford University Press, 1978).

[131] Smith, *Discourse of the Common Weal*, p. 130.

[132] *TED*, vol. III, p. 312.

[133] *TED*, vol. III, p. 313.

[134] *TED*, vol. III, p. 314.

[135] *TED*, vol. III, p. 314.

As with most of the references to national numbers we have encountered, the immediate context for concern with them in "Polices" was the security of the realm. This was conceived in military and economic terms: "thinvasion of eneymies," "cyvile warres" and especially "penury of victualles" leading to "famyne" all threatened.[136] The "Polices" offered a well-worn and simplistic causal analysis of England's internal problems, trafficking in broader categories and blunter mechanisms than Smith had used. Husbandry was "the Naturall mother of Victuall," and victual "the very Norse [i.e., nurse] of all Sciences and Artifficers"; idleness created dearth and thereby raised the price of all "that is wroughte or made by mans hande or labour."[137] Unlike earlier treatments, however, "Polices" organized its discussion of multitude around a quantitative conception of national strength that owed less to corporeal analogy than to a Christian humanist ideal of stewardship.[138] Idleness was less a matter of individual or collective moral degeneracy than of ill apportioned numbers, days and acres:

> [W]hat a great nombre of people is now in this realme which working a litell in Somer be more then halfe Idell all the residew of the yere: besides theme which be alwayes Idell: considering thother side, what a great quantitie of grounde in this realme lieth waste and ouergroine bering nowe nothing wherof commith eney proufit, which being manuride might be causide to encrease yerly an numerable quantitie of Corne.[139]

Numbers here were not divorced from local contexts and events, much less from moral or spiritual questions. As already noted, "Polices" set its call for political reform in the context of religious reformation. It went on to connect them still more directly: the cultivation of idle land it demanded was also bound up with the suppression of a Catholic ritual calendar that robbed the realm of working days, the elimination of idolatrous practices that wasted time and money, and the suppression of monastic institutions that had harbored an idle multitude of clerics:

> Let it be also consideride what a great nombre of Monkes, Channons, Friers and Chauntrye pristes with ther Servantes were mentaned in Idelnes: when the Abbeyes did stande: besides the tyme when the residew of the realme did also bestowe them in Idelnes and Idell workes in gooing of pilgramagis: keping of Idell hollidayes ... and yet neuerthelese, the artifficers and laborers in those dayes dyd all the worke and labour for the tilling and

---

[136] *TED*, vol. III, p. 313.
[137] *TED*, vol. III, p. 320.
[138] See Todd, *Christian Humanism*, pp. 118–75.
[139] *TED*, vol. III, p. 322.

manuring of the gronde: and for the victualing and clothing of all the
people in the hole realme[.][140]

Yet, the problem that monks, canons, friars and chantry priests posed was
not that they had degenerated from some more useful type. Nor, despite
the author's evangelical leanings, was it simply that they harmed the spiritual health or temporal peace of the body politic. The problem was that
they did no work. Like waste land and idle hours, they served no profitable purpose. Unlike displaced husbandmen, they had never done so.
Against such a spare construction of the problem of idleness, elaborate
corporeal and medical metaphors had little power.

On the other hand, precisely because this negative concept of idleness
sidestepped narratives of degeneration and distinctions of place and function, number took on new practical importance. (That this should have
happened at a time when calculations remained inescapably speculative
indicates how complex a process the advent of quantification was.) For
what the "Polices" proposed was the fullest exploitation of *numbers* of
people, acres and days alike:

> If euery laborer, and artifficer, and all other the common people of this
> realme wer well sett at worke and the residew of our superfluus hollid-
> ais pute done: we might be able, besides the prouision of Corne victuall
> and clothe for saruing our owne realme, [to] sende ouer the Sees yerly
> xij C. thowsande poundes-worth of Corne, Lede, tyne, Clothe and other
> marchauntdice. For ther is yet standing beside the Sondayes xxxvth hol-
> lidayes, wherof xxiiijth or xxvth may well be putt downe.... For ther is in
> this realme ... Fiftene thowsande parishes: and admitt ther is as meney
> artifficers and Laborers Reckening bothe men and women with ther ser-
> vauntes and prentices in euery one parishe: as may gayne to ther selfes in
> one working daye xl. *s.* toward ther meate and drunke.... [T]his amount-
> ithe in all englande in one daye to thirtye thowsande pounde, so that by
> putting done of xxth hollidayes this realme maye be enrichede euery yere
> Six hundreth thousande pounde[.][141]

For Starkey, Smith and other writers concerned with enclosure, the logic
of the body politic directed attention to the qualities, roles and locations
of specific kinds of people. The author of the "Polices," by contrast, intimated a view of numbers of bodies as interchangeable laboring units, oper-
ating on similarly convertible land – effectively just space – and bound
only by the limits of work-time. An ailing body politic needed repair, with
the aim of restoration to a former, flourishing state. Idle numbers called

---

[140] *TED*, vol. III, p. 322.
[141] *TED*, vol. III, p. 323.

instead for maximal exploitation, conjuring visions not of healthy equilibrium but rather of mounting surpluses quantified through the projection of abstract calculations onto land and people. "Polices" was not representative of Tudor or early Stuart views in these respects, but in expanding the spatial and temporal boundaries of demographic governance beyond the confines of bodily metaphor it would turn out to be prescient.

It was prescient, too, in looking to nature for an alternative to the more usual account of idleness as the result of historically specific social dislocations and the consequent degeneration of distinct groups. Having made idleness the attribute not of local types but of national numbers, the "Polices" offered an appropriately general explanation in the landscape these numbers inhabited – what later authors would term the "situation" of England as a whole: "mary even the great fructfulnes of our gronde."[142] This was an unusual move for English authors before the seventeenth century, so it is perhaps not surprising that this author cited an Italian source. His authority on environmental influence was the Sienese humanist Francesco Patrizi:

> For as Patricius Senensis boke *de regno [et] institucione regis* sayeth. That country which of hime selfe is so frutefull that it bringeth forth plenty of vitall and all other things necessary for mans life and sustinance, bringeth vppe also solouthefull and Idell people. And contrary wise, those people which inhabit the Barren contries, be muche more Diligent and Industrius.[143]

Similar references to the dynamic, adaptive interaction between land and people – whether praising the hardscrabble industry of the Dutch in overcoming the limitations of their flat and flooded strip of earth, or in scolding the lazy denizens of lush colonial landscapes – would become a staple

---

[142] *TED*, vol. III, p. 328. Rather than an iteration of the social "environmentalism" of the sort attributed to More and others, "situation" as a national attribute and a factor in political calculation characterized new genres of "empirical" political, economic and natural-historical writing from the Elizabethan period on. See Shapiro, "Empiricism and English Political Thought," 6; and Chapter 2 here.

[143] *TED*, vol. III, p. 328. The text referred to is Francesco Patrizi's mirror for princes, *De regno et regis institutione* (1482). See Nicolai Rubinstein, "Italian Political Thought, 1450–1530," in J. H. Burns and Mark Goldie (eds.), *The Cambridge History of Political Thought, 1450–1700* (Cambridge: Cambridge University Press, 1991), pp. 30–65, at 33; Leslie F. Smith, "Francesco Patrizi: Forgotten Political Scientist and Humanist," *Proceedings of the Oklahoma Academy of Science* 47 (1966), 348–51. Quentin Skinner interprets the similarities between Patrizi's and English humanists' handling of the virtues as evidence of shared conventions rather than of influence; the same may apply to the "environmentalism" noted here. The latter was nevertheless unusual in Tudor discussions of multitude. See Quentin Skinner, *The Foundations of Modern Political Thought*, 2 vols. (Cambridge: Cambridge University Press, 1978), vol. I, p. 229 n.1.

of later Stuart economic and political commentary. By then, the language of nature was part of a more elaborate framework for differentiating mutable and immutable constraints on policy. The "Polices" did not anticipate this framework. It would have kept poor company with the author's confident expectation – characteristic of the age – that divinely approved acts of "the Rulers" could right the wrongs of human vice.[144] It would also have implied a clearer sense of human nature unmediated by the corporate identities and forms of association to which even the "Polices" ultimately appealed in proposing "brotherhedes" or "fraternities" for different tradesmen. But for the time being, such bodies remained the most visible and tractable manifestations of multitude. They, rather than the numbers that loomed behind them, were still the real objects of governance.

[144] *TED*, vol. III, p. 336.

CHAPTER 2

Marginality, Incivility and Degeneration in Elizabethan England and Ireland

Limits of the Body Politic

The long reign of Queen Elizabeth witnessed subtle but significant changes in approaches to marginal multitudes. Discussions of demographic governance developed along the lines suggested by mid-Tudor intellectual developments, in particular the humanist-inflected articulation of the body politic as a system of interacting members whose relative proportions and locations were the proper objects of policy. In an economic, social and political world constituted by corporate bodies of all kinds and at all levels, the interdependency of functionally or qualitatively distinguished collectivities was a comfortable and flexible ideological template. Transferring this template from one context to another might extend the scope and content of the discourse of multitudes without much changing its intellectual basis or political logic. In this way, a discourse of demographic governance rooted in late fifteenth-century responses to agrarian change and rural depopulation expanded over the course of a century to address the ramifying effects of depopulation on the social body and to define approaches to different types of problem set in different kinds of space.

For all the continuities in the discourse of multitudes throughout the Tudor period, however – and complaints about depopulation persisted far into the seventeenth century – new contexts for its application reflected new circumstances confronting Elizabethan observers and legislators, and brought new implications. Though neither precise nor universally shared, an awareness of real and nationwide demographic change colored commentary on the problems of poverty, mobility and the growth of the metropolis. England's population had numbered approximately 2.58 million in 1500, climbing to around 2.77 million in 1541; by 1601, it was perhaps 4.11 million, and migration had doubled London's share of this over the same period.[1] Against this

---

[1] On English population, see Edward Anthony Wrigley and Roger Snowden Schofield, *The Population History of England, 1541–1871: A Reconstruction* (Cambridge: Cambridge University

backdrop, attention turned from rural depopulation to overpopulation, urban crowding and the governance of vagrants and the idle poor. Literary and political engagements with vagabond masses spawned a variety of ideas about the challenge they posed not only by virtue of their mobility and degeneration but also through their capacity to reproduce and to spread corruption. Rather than restoring a displaced multitude to its proper place, demographic governance came to mean reforming or transforming one sort of multitude into another by more invasive and open-ended means – confinement, forced labor and education; in effect, the civilization of the "wild" progeny of a multitude whose use to the body politic was no longer given.

Meanwhile, similar themes and changes marked English thinking about a different problem. Thanks to a combination of local political shifts, constitutional and social alterations and fluctuating initiatives from England, later sixteenth-century Ireland – a long-standing marchland, a recent kingdom and a new site of colonial plantation – was torn by conflict between national and confessional groups.[2] As the medieval tradition of indirect rule through local magnates gave way to an English administration pursuing political and fiscal reform from Dublin, the task of governing the island's divided populations came to resemble that of managing troublesome multitudes in England. Yet Ireland differed from England in ways that heightened anxiety about the mobility of multitudes and undermined their connection to a single, organic and closed body politic. On one hand, English portrayals of the Gaelic Irish both in England and among the English-descended settler population in Ireland increasingly evoked an ingrained barbarism that had no conceivable civic function and that only radical measures could civilize. On the other, English Protestant wariness of the "Old English" – Anglo-Irish landed families who had stayed Catholic and, seemingly, turned Irish – gave degeneration an ethnic aspect, linking it not merely to mobility but also to the mixture of different groups.[3] By the seventeenth century, projects

---

Press, 1989), pp. 209–10; but compare Robert Allan Houston, *The Population History of Britain and Ireland 1500–1700* (Cambridge: Cambridge University Press, 1992), p. 16, which suggests that the English population had reached 3.02 million by 1541. On London, see Houston, *The Population History of Britain and Ireland*, p. 20.

[2] The chronology and causes of the change have been subject to debate; compare the drawn-out shift described by Ciaran Brady, *The Chief Governors: The Rise and Fall of Reform Government in Tudor Ireland, 1536–1588* (Cambridge: Cambridge University Press, 1994) with Brendan Bradshaw, *The Irish Constitutional Revolution of the Sixteenth Century* (Cambridge: Cambridge University Press, 1979), which gives Thomas Cromwell a revolutionary role. For a survey, see Steven G. Ellis, *Ireland in the Age of the Tudors, 1447–1603: English Expansion and the End of Gaelic Rule* (London: Longman, 1998), pp. 119–351.

[3] See Canny, *Making Ireland British*, pp. 1–120.

for subduing Ireland by force or persuasion instrumentalized processes earlier commentators had feared, turning planned mobility and the mixture of multitudes into tools of colonial plantation. A mode of population thought that had begun with agrarian complaint in rural England was thus poised for use in a transatlantic empire.

In different ways, Elizabethan literary and legislative engagements with vagrants and Elizabethan and early Jacobean thinking about the government of Ireland both stretched the metaphor of the body politic, elaborated by humanists into a framework for the governance of marginal or problematic multitudes, to the breaking point. No longer dealing simply with groups whose place and function in a healthy polity were clearly understood – no longer confined within the bounds of a single contiguous polity at all – the governance of multitudes now embraced, as practical problems, the reclamation of wild and degenerate masses, the assimilation to English rule of alien or alienated subjects, the fitting for civil life of presumed barbarians, and the projection, settlement and maintenance of colonies in new and putatively vacant spaces in the Old World and the New. Though the language of the body politic persisted, such transformations and projections of human material made nonsense of the fixed positions and settled roles it ascribed to its component parts. The established, qualitative conception of multitude lost some of its purchase, and as new attitudes toward and new practices of demographic quantification developed, space opened up between the early and mid-seventeenth century for substantially new approaches to the nature and governance of population.

Extraneous Multitudes: Vagrants and the Poor

The metaphor of the body politic that organized Henrician and Edwardian thinking about the commonwealth as a plexus of multitudes was common currency in political thought across much of Europe. So, in a different register, were some of the key concepts from which the discourse of vagrancy issued: the distinction between the deserving and the undeserving poor, and the concept of "idleness" that came to characterize and even supplant poverty itself as an object of concern. The evolution of these ideas has been linked to both Renaissance humanism and the Reformation.[4] Humanist critiques of medieval charitable practices and other aspects of the theology

---

[4] Paul Slack's work on England emphasizes humanism rather than reformation as the inspiration for new thinking about the poor, but the impact of religious change on the institutional context of poor relief is evident. See Paul Slack, *The English Poor Law, 1531–1782* (Cambridge: Cambridge University Press, 1995), pp. 6–7; Jütte, *Poverty and Deviance in Early Modern Europe*, pp. 100–42.

of works reimagined poverty as a corrigible moral failing or a solvable social problem rather than a necessary feature of human existence.[5] Fear of the mobility and disorderly nature of the poor – their masterlessness, and the corruption they represented and propagated – made confinement and compulsory labor schemes preferable to unregulated alms and "outdoor" relief. Thus Erasmus advocated charity "with discrimination" between the aged or infirm and the "able-bodied"; he also thought that, like soldiering and domestic service, "monastic life too is a kind of idleness" in need of restraint.[6] Juan Luis Vives's *De subventione pauperum* of 1526 – which compared the governor's role in a city to the mind's over a body – decried "vagabond beggars with no fixed abode who are able-bodied" and qualified Proverbs 14:28 by noting that "The absence of beggars is an immense credit to a city. A multitude of them implies callousness in individuals and neglect in the rulers."[7] Martin Luther's *Liber vagatorum*, first appearing *c.* 1509 and reissued in 1528, distinguished (as did Huldreich Zwingli) between a community's duty to "their own paupers" and the fraudulent claims of "outlandish and strange beggars," which he itemized in a sort of bestiary, complete with a lexicon of "Beggars Cant" and handling instructions for each kind: "stabeylers" dragging families from place to place; "lossners" pretending to have escaped captivity; "klenckners" missing hands or feet; and a motley gathering of fake friars, vagrant scholars, false pilgrims and so on.[8]

Problematizing poverty in the early modern period meant engaging intellectually as well as administratively with the quantities and qualities of human groups, as the retrenchment or reorganization of the church's worldly functions created space for state and corporate initiatives in poor relief, education and other services.[9] In England, too, ideological and institutional changes shaped the construction of poverty, vagrancy and idleness

---

[5] See Todd, *Christian Humanism*, pp. 118–75. On medieval ideas about poverty, see Diana Wood, *Medieval Economic Thought* (Cambridge: Cambridge University Press, 2002), pp. 42–68.

[6] Desiderius Erasmus, *Ten Colloquies*, translated by Craig R. Thompson (Indianapolis, IN: Bobbs-Merrill, 1957), p. 163; Desiderius Erasmus, *The Education of a Christian Prince*, edited by L. Jardine and translated by N. M. Cheshire and M. J. Heath (Cambridge: Cambridge University Press, 1997), p. 83.

[7] Frank R. Salter (ed.), *Some Early Tracts on Poor Relief* (London: Methuen, 1926), pp. 6, 12, 30.

[8] Martin Luther, *The Book of Vagabonds and Beggars with a Vocabulary of Their Language and a Preface by Martin Luther*, edited by D. B. Thomas and translated by J. C. Hotten (London: Penguin, 1932), pp. 65, 71–93, 136–43. See also Huldreich Zwingli, "Ordinance and Articles Touching Almsgiving," in Salter (ed.), *Early Tracts on Poor Relief*, pp. 97–103.

[9] Jütte, *Poverty and Deviance*, pp. 100–42. On relief as an aspect of state-formation in Protestant areas, see Gorski, *Disciplinary Revolution*, pp. 39–77, 114–55, which links Calvinist theology to an emphasis on social discipline; but compare Strasser, *State of Virginity*, which suggests that the cooptation of theological imperatives served state-formation in Catholic Europe equally well.

as social and political problems. The suppression of monasteries removed major centers of hospitality and charitable activity, including many hospitals.[10] In filling this gap, neighboring countries and regions provided models for emulation, or at least reflection. One example was the system of poor relief used in the Flemish city of Ypres from 1525. Starkey may have observed this in person, and William Marshal translated a description of it, the *Forma subventionis pauperum*, into English in 1535.[11] While Ypres allowed that "beggynge is a kynde of polycye and wysdome" for the truly needy, no such liberty could be granted "valyaunt beggers" and "wyld wanderers." Prefects or overseers of the poor, aided by "subprefectes and vnder offycers," were to ensure "that poore men shall kepe at home and natte ronne wanderinge aboute," both to compel them to work and to prevent their "yvell example" from corrupting the youth.[12] While restraining mobility and degeneration by rendering the poor sedentary, Ypres policy drew a clear line between "strangers and wanderers" from without and "our citizens," the preferred objects of support "bycause they be membres with vs of one politicall body."[13] As English Protestants agreed, due attention to the health of the body politic – its protection against corruption by strange or idle "multitudes" – was "a gyde towardes godlynesse."[14]

If Tudor views of the poor differed little from those across the Channel, however, the challenges of depopulation, economic dislocation, poverty and vagrancy were to be observed and confronted in the space between parish and kingdom. Even as humanist ideas and reforming imperatives crossed borders, that is, they elevated princely authority and state policy – which in turn depended upon local coordination and will for their implementation.[15] Writing to Thomas Cromwell from Yorkshire in the wake of the Pilgrimage of Grace, the Duke of Norfolk complained of "vacabonds" that "I neuer sawe so many as be in thiese cuntrees," and blamed their numbers on "the almes that they haue in religious houses … and also the slackenes of the Justice of pease" in enforcing the law.[16] The law in question was Cromwell's poor law of 1536, by which vagrants were to be returned to

---

[10] John Stow's celebrated *Survey of London* listed hospitals in the City of London and its suburbs, including at least fourteen that were "suppressed," mostly under Henry VII; Stow, *Survey of London*, pp. 434–7. See Slack, *English Poor Law*, pp. 6–8.

[11] Marshal's translation is reproduced in Salter (ed.), *Early Tracts on Poor Relief*, pp. 32–79. On Starkey's knowledge of the scheme, see Mayer, *Thomas Starkey*, p. 81.

[12] Salter (ed.), *Early Tracts on Poor Relief*, pp. 42, 45, 50–2, 55–7.

[13] Salter (ed.), *Early Tracts on Poor Relief*, pp. 63–4.

[14] Salter (ed.), *Early Tracts on Poor Relief*, pp. 72–3.

[15] On central and local agency in state formation and social policy, see Braddick, *State Formation in Early Modern England*; Hindle, *State and Social Change*, pp. 1–65, 146–75.

[16] *TED*, vol. II, p. 301.

their home parishes (as stipulated in earlier laws of 1495 and 1531) and set on work once there; poor children were to be put out to service and the impotent poor supported by weekly collections. Casual almsgiving and begging were suppressed.[17] As in humanist and Protestant criticisms of charitable practice, the stress fell on immobilizing, containing and forcing to work a wandering multitude, whatever its origins. But mobility and mutability proved slippery targets for legislation. As John Bayker – an artificer who "haythe travyled and gone thorowe the most payrt of your Reallme to gett and erne my lyvynge" – lamented to Henry VIII, "god [i.e., good] and holsome statutes and lawes" did not stop vagrants running "from towne to towne or place to place withoute a lawfull lysynys"; indeed "the multitude of thayme dothe dayly encreace more and more," bringing fornication, robbery and murder in their train.[18] For Bayker, an economic migrant himself, the greed of landlords produced vagrants faster than the law could subdue them.[19] From Norfolk's elite perspective, the failure was a problem of enforcement. Meanwhile, the vagrant multitude swarmed.

Municipal initiatives led the way in practice. Even as the divergent measures of individual parishes were brought into line with statutory norms and mechanisms, the experience of vagrancy as a problem and the job of dealing with it remained in local hands.[20] So it was with the erection of "hospitals" for putting the idle to work, and with the policing of mobility: A 1552 petition from the Citizens of London to the Privy Council called for Bridewell to be used as "an house of occupations" for containing "the froward, strong, and sturdy vagabond" and compelling him "to live profitably in the commonwealth"; in 1554, the merchant tailor Henry Machyn noted in his diary a "proclamasyon that all vacabonds ... boyth Englys men and all maner of strangers ... shuld avoyd the cete [i.e., city] and the subarbes."[21] So it was, too, with the first dedicated collection of data on the numbers of the poor. Much as Cromwell's Injunctions of 1538 had required parish registers of baptisms, marriages and burials, so a bill of 1552 required "surveys of the poor in every parish."[22] In the long run, these demands helped create the conditions for demographic quantification. But in their Tudor context,

---

[17] Slack, *English Poor Law*, p. 9.
[18] *TED*, vol. II, pp. 302–3.
[19] Bayker captured the transformation of "howsess and habytatyons" to "bayre walls" by appeal to ratio: what "one man" now has "dyd suffyse ij or iij men" before enclosure; *TED*, vol. II, pp. 303–4.
[20] See Hindle, *On the Parish?*, pp. 7–8, 1945.
[21] *TED*, vol. II, pp. 307–8; J. G. Nichols (ed.), *The Diary of Henry Machyn, Citizen and Merchant-Taylor of London, 1550–1563* (London: Camden Society, 1848), p. 69.
[22] Slack, *The English Poor Law*, p. 10.

while parishes across the nation were enjoined to enumerate the poor, the numbers remained local: focused on a particular type, with significance in a particular place, for purposes of local administration.

This was the setting for the Elizabethan war on idleness and vagrancy that initiated a transformation in the role of numbers – or, more precisely, added a new use to their existing repertoire. The symbolic import of figures and ratios, the power of high numbers or striking proportions to emblematize a social problem, continued to mark discussions of poverty and crime much as they had those of enclosure and depopulation. But the creation of parish-level overseers tasked with counting, classifying and reporting numbers of the poor implied a more immediate purpose for empirical census-taking – as did the later elaboration of tools such as *An Ease for Overseers of the Poore* (1601), which included "an easie and readie table for recording then number, names, ages, exercises and defects of the poore," the better to place them in actionable categories.[23] Here, it would seem, was a clearly instrumental use of quantification tailored to the surveillance needs and carceral imperatives of a burgeoning bureaucratic state.[24] Yet by the early seventeenth century, demographic numbers were becoming familiar in a variety of other ways, for example in the weekly bills of mortality kept in London first during outbreaks of plague and eventually on a regular basis, gathered and printed by parish and collected for the city as a whole, and reused and recontextualized in the genre of "Lord Have Mercy Upon Us" broadsides.[25] In such cases, empirical data collection served no single policy but worked on the minds of citizens as motivation to take flight or quake at the judgments of Providence. Rather than increasing empirical precision driving a shift from symbolic or ideological to practical, governmental uses, quantification became an increasingly multifaceted cultural practice, with a range of possible meanings that mapped only imperfectly onto the various methods of ground-level enumeration, educated guessing and speculative arithmetic through which specific numbers of people were produced.

---

[23] *An Ease for Overseers of the Poore Abstracted from the Statutes, Allowed by Practise, and Now Reduced into Forme, as a Necessarie Directorie for Imploying, Releeuing, and Ordering of the Poore* (London: Printed by Iohn Legat, 1601).

[24] On surveillance in decentralized early modern states, see Higgs, *Information State in England*, pp. 28–63. On the state's resort to the institutional confinement of troublesome subpopulations, see Pieter Spierenburg, *The Prison Experience: Disciplinary Institutions and Their Inmates in Early Modern Europe* (Amsterdam: Amsterdam University Press, 2007), pp. 1–38. On disciplinary institutions as elements of modern social control, Michel Foucault's work – though justly criticized for overlooking sixteenth- and seventeenth-century developments – has been vital; see for example Michel Foucault, *Discipline and Punish: The Birth of the Prison*, translated by Alan Sheridan (New York: Vintage, 1995).

[25] See Jenner, "Plague on a Page."

Two different kinds of late Tudor source show how uses of number remained embedded in local and qualitative constructs of multitude, even as the problems they targeted became objects of national policy: literary representations of vagrants and censuses of the poor. "Rogue literature" has a checkered historiographical reputation, especially among social historians wary of naïve readings. Works such as Gilbert Walker's *Manifest Detection of Diceplay* (1552), John Awdeley's *Fraternitie of Vagabonds* (1561), Thomas Harman's *Caveat for Common Cursitors Vulgarly Called Vagabonds* (1566) and Robert Greene's *Notable Discovery of Cozenage* (1591) are distinguished by their simultaneously revelatory and utilitarian framing, claims to empiricism, taxonomic, nomenclatural and linguistic obsessions and gazetteer-like presentation.[26] Harman, for instance, claimed to have based his typology of vagabonds on laborious interviews "with these wily wanderers," who only reluctantly gave up "their scelerous secrets," and he listed many of his sources by name in an appendix.[27] As Stephen Greenblatt has argued, this betrayal of real-life informants established the validity of Harman's observations and added to his book's appeal.[28] Such verisimilitude facilitated – and was vindicated by – the incorporation of Harman's accounts into empirical commentary in other genres, including William Harrison's *Description of England*, published as part of Holinshed's *Chronicles* in 1577.[29] Yet Harman's subjects were but distantly connected to social reality.[30] Patricia Fumerton argues that his colorful portrait of a vagrant counter-culture "assuaged fears of displaced labor by transforming the fact of an unsettled economy grounded on a shifting mass of itinerant labor into the fiction of role-playing rogues."[31] We should not take ideological romance for empirical reportage. Yet the boundaries between the two were porous, and both played a role in constituting populations as objects of thought and intervention.[32]

---

[26] All four are reprinted, with other examples of the genre, in Arthur F. Kinney (ed.), *Rogues, Vagabonds, and Sturdy Beggars: A New Gallery* (Amherst: University of Massachusetts Press, 1990); see also Gamini Salgādo (ed.), *Cony-Catchers and Bawdy Baskets: An Anthology of Elizabethan Low Life* (Harmondsworth: Penguin, 1972).

[27] Kinney (ed.), *Rogues, Vagabonds, and Sturdy Beggars*, pp. 110, 146–8.

[28] Stephen Greenblatt, *Shakespearean Negotiations: The Circulation of Social Energy in Renaissance England* (Berkeley, CA: University of California Press, 1988), p. 50.

[29] Reprinted as William Harrison, *The Description of England: The Classic Contemporary Account of Tudor Social Life*, edited by George Edelen (New York: Dover, 1968); for the use of Harman's observations see pp. 183–4. See Henry Summerson (comp.), "Catalogue of Additional Sources Mentioned in Passing in Holinshed's *Chronicles*," The Holinshed Project.

[30] Greenblatt, *Shakespearean Negotiations*, p. 50; Slack, *Poverty and Policy*, pp. 23–7.

[31] Fumerton, *Unsettled*, p. 36.

[32] Roger Chartier labels contemporaneous French descriptions of the poor "des fantasmes des élites," but as he also notes, "Le discours sur les marginaux est un moyen indirect de tester les

In this sense, and in light of later manifestations of concern with mobile and mutable multitudes, Awdeley's *Fraternitie of Vagabonds* and Harman's *Caveat for Common Cursitors* are especially informative. In a manner reminiscent of Luther's *Liber vagatorum*, Awdeley listed outlandish or ironic names for different vagrant types – "Abraham Man," "Ruffler," "Prigman," "Whipjack," "Frater" and so on – and sketched their characteristic features and pretenses (the ruffler, for instance, "goeth with a weapon to seek service").[33] Awdeley also, like Luther, gave examples of beggars' "canting" dialect. But he went beyond taxonomy in describing political relations, captured in the canting lexicon, between and within the several orders of vagabonds. The "upright man," he wrote, "is of so much authority that meeting with any of his profession he may call them to account, and command a share or 'snap' ... of all that they have gained by their trade in one month." An upright man's wife was a "doxy"; beneath him in terms of authority was a "curtal"; his children were called "Kintchin Co" and "Kintchin Mort" – male and female, respectively.[34] Awdeley constituted vagrants as a kind of antisocial corporation, separated from legitimate society by their inversion of its moral and sexual norms and seriocomic perversion of its rituals (couples could divorce by shaking hands over a dead horse: thus "death depart the married folk"), yet parallel to it in the fact of their political, fiscal, gendered and reproductive organization.[35] Indeed, Awdeley repeatedly used the language of the body politic not to locate vagrancy within the English commonwealth but to describe the vagabonds' own social world, laying out twenty-five "Orders of Knaves" and describing "Wild Rogues" as a "corporation."[36] The political body here was the multitude of vagrants itself.

Harman developed the idea of vagrants as a polity in greater detail. He began with the common distinction between the "needy, impotent and miserable" poor and "vagrants and sturdy vagabonds," who were

---

consensus sociaux." Roger Chartier, "Les élites et les gueux. Quelques représentations (XVIe-XVIIe siècles)," *Revue d'histoire moderne et contemporaine* 21:3 (1974), 378. Even official perceptions of reality sometimes display picaresque tendencies, as in a 1585 report submitted to Burghley of a "schole howse" for cutpurses in Billingsgate; Fleetwood to Burghley, 7 July 1585, reprinted in *TED*, vol. II, pp. 306–11.

[33] Kinney (ed.), *Rogues, Vagabonds, and Sturdy Beggars*, pp. 91–8.

[34] Kinney (ed.), *Rogues, Vagabonds, and Sturdy Beggars*, pp. 92–4.

[35] Kinney (ed.), *Rogues, Vagabonds, and Sturdy Beggars*, p. 94.

[36] Kinney (ed.), *Rogues, Vagabonds, and Sturdy Beggars*, pp. 93, 98. For later French figurations of the marginalized as corporations (but also, from the mid-fifteenth century, as a monarchy), and for interest in their categorization and linguistic difference, see Chartier, "Les élites et les gueux," 380–8. Chartier emphasizes sixteenth- and seventeenth-century French constructions of the poor as *monstrous*; Tudor comment does not appear to pursue this line of thinking.

distinguished principally by their mobility – they "passeth through and by all parts of the famous isle" – and who required "extreme punishment."[37] Putting a twist on earlier discussions of depopulation, Harman portrayed vagrants as the degenerate residue of various more useful types of people, deformed by mobility – but made mobile in the first place, paradoxically, not by lordly greed but by their own inherent idleness. "Of these ranging rabblement of rascals," he wrote, "some be serving-men, artificers, and laboring men, traded up [i.e., trained] in husbandry. These not minding to get their living with the sweat of their face, but casting off all pain, will wander."[38] Harman paid even more attention to the inner structure and dynamics of this multitude, which had not only characteristic mysteries – the fake passports, feigned illnesses, self-inflicted injuries and other tricks listed since Luther, and the "politic" habit of maintaining a second, legitimate profile where needed – but also distinctive procedures of recruitment and advancement as well as forms of regulation.[39] Within a year or two of entering the trade, a "ruffler" (former soldier or servant) might become an "upright man"; together, the upright men imposed a kind of "licensing" or training system, complete with oaths, on apprentice criminals not yet "stalled to the rogue."[40] Lines of authority, special skills and rites of passage bounded and linked various groups, each with its exotic, canting name: "Priggers of Prancers" (horse thieves), "Fresh-Water Mariners" (who claimed losses from shipwreck or piracy), "Demanders for Glimmer" (pretended victims of fire); among women, "bawdy-baskets" (procurers of stolen food), "Doxies" (made prostitutes by intercourse with upright men) and "Dells" (girls of reproductive age "yet not known or broken").[41] As in other trades, family ties secured membership and standing. The purest specimen was the "wild rogue" (among girls, the "wild Dell") or "beggar by inheritance," "born a Rogue" and "from his infancy traded up in treachery."[42]

Focusing exclusively on the grotesque, titillating or sensational aspects of Harman's work risks missing that the vision he offered was also a demographic one. This was clearest where the text touched on themes familiar from the discourse of depopulation. Like the roving criminals enclosure produced, the "wily wandering" of Harman's "rascal rabblement"

---

[37] Kinney (ed.), *Rogues, Vagabonds, and Sturdy Beggars*, p. 109.
[38] Kinney (ed.), *Rogues, Vagabonds, and Sturdy Beggars*, p. 116.
[39] Kinney (ed.), *Rogues, Vagabonds, and Sturdy Beggars*, p. 118.
[40] Kinney (ed.), *Rogues, Vagabonds, and Sturdy Beggars*, pp. 115–16, 118.
[41] Kinney (ed.), *Rogues, Vagabonds, and Sturdy Beggars*, pp. 124–9, 137–44.
[42] Kinney (ed.), *Rogues, Vagabonds, and Sturdy Beggars*, pp. 123–4, 144.

represented a displacement and a loss of useful people through degeneration and mobility.[43] As earlier commentators had treated depopulation
as historically specific, Harman stressed that the existence of vagrants as
an estranged, almost foreign anti-polity within the commonwealth was a
recent phenomenon: "their language, which they term peddler's French
or canting, began but within these thirty years, little above." That is to
say, they were products of the upheavals of the 1530s, the first decade of
the Henrician Reformation, persisting thanks to the failures of policy and
the flagging vigilance of "Justices and shrieves" in the intervening years.[44]

Though More and Harman alike traced social upheaval to moral
failings, however, Harman blamed not the rapacious greed of enclosing landlords but the native lassitude or inbred criminality of vagrants
themselves. Rather than an atrophied limb, vagrants were a pathological
presence, indeed a virtually foreign – and yet not exogenous – body.[45]
Its members had distinctive features, habits and language, and even a
typical lifespan and form of death: hanging, Harman wrote, "is the final
end of them all, or else to die of some filthy and horrible diseases. But
much harm is done in the meanspace by their continuance, as some
ten, twelve, and sixteen years before they be consumed."[46] Finally, as
the account of wild rogues and wild dells ("beastly begotten in barn
or bushes, and from … infancy traded up in treachery") made clear,
this multitude not only recruited degenerates from other orders but
also reproduced itself independently, vagrant children of these casually
formed and dissolved households inheriting their parents' appetites and
practices.[47] Indeed, it was this two-track multiplication of vagrants, who
spread the contagion of idleness by ranging over the country even as
they birthed criminals through promiscuous intercourse, that raised the

---

[43] Kinney (ed.), *Rogues, Vagabonds, and Sturdy Beggars*, p. 110.
[44] Kinney (ed.), *Rogues, Vagabonds, and Sturdy Beggars*, pp. 110–12.
[45] Harris, *Foreign Bodies and the Body Politic*, describes a tendency in the late sixteenth and early seventeenth centuries toward seeing marginal groups as both pathological *and* exogenous, reflecting
a shift in medical analogies from humoral to iatrochemical theory. By contrast, this book treats
endogenous degeneration (loss from within the body politic, rather than invasion from without)
and the potential for troublesome multitudes to be reassimilated through policy as important to
Tudor and Stuart engagements with marginal groups.
[46] Kinney (ed.), *Rogues, Vagabonds, and Sturdy Beggars*, p. 111.
[47] Kinney (ed.), *Rogues, Vagabonds, and Sturdy Beggars*, pp. 123–4. Harman's definition of "wild
Dells" as (fleetingly) virginal girls of childbearing age foreshadows the "teeming women" or
"breeders" that later seventeenth- and early eighteenth-century political arithmeticians enthused
over; see Chapter 5. In both cases, a focus on reproductive capacity and a presumption of sexual
availability reflected the social marginalization of the group concerned. But, as we shall see, the
political meaning of multiplication differed widely between the two cases as ideas about the
state's demographic agency and the nature of population changed.

issue of quantification: for despite their brief lifespan, "the number of them doth daily renew."[48] Joining empirical pretensions and speculative projection, Harman followed his list of "the most notorious and wickedest walkers" with the observation that in addition, "above an hundredth of Irishmen and women" had come to wander English roads in the last two years. "All these above written," he concluded, "for the most part walk about in Essex, Middlesex, Sussex, Surrey, and Kent. The let the reader judge what number walks in other Shires. I fear me too great a number."[49] Numbers, loosely extrapolated from local observation, had gone from capturing past depopulation to projecting harmful multiplication in the present and future.

Yet these numbers, presented alongside exoticizing accounts of qualitative difference, remained emblematic expressions of a problem for the body politic rather than disembodied statistics or empirical evidence of demographic laws. For Harman and those who used his work, round numbers, geographical mobility and cultural mutability fit together in a picture of poverty and vagrancy as linked threats to the commonweal. William Harrison juxtaposed images of the "the thriftless poor ... the vagabond that will abide nowhere but runneth up and down from place to place ... and the rogue and strumpet [that] run to and fro all over the realm" with a more gradated sketch of the "orders and degrees of vagabonds" that owed much to Harman and other pamphleteers.[50] Without giving numbers, he dismissed the idea that "the great increase of people in these days" was "a superfluous augmentation of mankind," believing that "a wall of men is far better than stacks of corn and bags of money" for repelling invasion.[51] Vagrant numbers, on the other hand, were scarcely separable from the strange qualities of the people they represented:

> It is not yet full threescore years since this trade began, but how it hath prospered since that time it is easy to judge, for they are now supposed, of one sex and another, to amount unto above 10,000 persons, as I have heard reported. Moreover, in counterfeiting the Egyptian rogues, they have devised a language among themselves which they name 'canting' ... [such] as none but themselves are able to understand.[52]

[48] Kinney (ed.), *Rogues, Vagabonds, and Sturdy Beggars*, p. 111.
[49] Kinney (ed.), *Rogues, Vagabonds, and Sturdy Beggars*, pp. 146–8.
[50] Harrison, *Description of England*, pp. 181, 184.
[51] Harrison, *Description of England*, p. 182. The contemporaneous perception of English overpopulation to which Harrison refers is discussed in Chapter 3.
[52] Harrison, *Description of England*, pp. 183–4. My thanks to David Cressy for drawing my attention to this passage.

By Harrison's time, centrally directed or corporately regulated mobility (especially in the form of overseas colonization) was coming to be seen as having potentially positive domestic effects – a foretaste of the more ambitious policy schemes of the following century. But there is nothing in discussions of vagrancy, concerned though they were with the size and growth of demographic groups, to suggest that any ineluctable or progressive adoption of quantification caused this change. Numbers in this context were still signs rather than objects.

That distinction is harder to maintain with respect to urban censuses of the poor. As we have seen, various kinds of enumeration predated the Elizabethan concern with vagrancy, while the act of enumeration had been an object of theological and political concern throughout the medieval period: Jacques Le Goff describes anxiety about the "sin of David" in numbering the people as wearing off in the thirteenth century, ushering in an era of "calculation" in everything from the determination of penance for sin to logistical preparations for the Church Council of Lyons in 1274.[53] More anticipatory of Tudor efforts, perhaps, are town and village headcounts in fifteenth-century Florence and Holland.[54] In bringing quantification to bear on concerns about the qualities of specific multitudes, rather than surveying people or property for simple fiscal or military purposes, however, the late sixteenth-century censuses of the urban poor appear to have been unusual, at least in comparison with contemporaneous European experience.[55] Moreover, the municipal measures these enumerations facilitated – particularly in the celebrated case of Norwich, where a census was undertaken in 1570, with new poor relief measures following in 1571 – soon served not just as models for other towns but also as the basis for the national Poor Law of 1572.[56] The figures presented in agrarian complaint and rogue literature dramatized the social consequences of moral deformation; census data appear by contrast as direct objects of government, building blocks of an "information state."[57]

If the case of the Norwich census suggests the national significance of local measures over the long term, it also indicates the local embedment of national developments. This local context was legislative, political and demographic. In the wake of Kett's Rebellion in 1549, Norwich had been

---

[53] Jacques Le Goff, *The Medieval Imagination*, translated by Arthur Goldhammer (Chicago: University of Chicago Press, 1988), pp. 60–6. On medieval concern with demographic growth and ratios – often separate from empirical data-gathering – see Biller, *Measure of Multitude*.

[54] Burke, *Social History of Knowledge*, pp. 135–6.

[55] Jütte, *Poverty and Deviance*, pp. 54–6. Strasbourg (1523) is the one exception noted.

[56] Slack, *Poverty and Policy*, p. 149.

[57] On the concept and its use in this period, see Higgs, *Information State in England*, pp. 1–63.

among the first English cities to mandate payments for poor relief; another
rebellion – directed against Dutch and Walloon refugees from the Spanish
Netherlands, blamed for filling the city with "disease-ridden" and foreign
poor – followed the Revolt of the Northern Earls in 1569.[58] Though part of
a wider war on vagrancy, as a local practice the census was house-by-house
search for the idle or disorderly, "harlottes" or "gresse wenches" and patho-
genic strangers – including non-Norwich-born English – who might be
compelled "to go away" individually or *en famille*. Census entries reflect this,
separating those that "dwelt here ever" or for many years from recent arrivals:

> Thomas Matheu, laborer, gone from his wyke, of 40 yeris, from whom she
> hath no helpe, & Margaret, his wyf, of 32 yeris, & no shylderne. She spyn
> white warpe & have dwelt here ever, & she know not wher his husbond
> is, & hav not dwelt here 3 yer. [to go away].
>
> ...
>
> Thomas Fraunces of 30 yere, a smyth & boteman, with Margaret, his wyfe,
> of 28 yeren who spyn white warpe. They hav dwelt here aboue a yere &
> befor in Yermothe, & now they dwell to gether; & 1 son of 1 moneth olde.
> [to go away].
>
> ...
>
> Herri Mydelton of 54 yeris, laborer, veri syk & without worke, & Alyce, his
> wyf, of 52 yeris, that spyn towe; & a daughter of 12 yeris that spyn towe,
> & 3 yonge chyldren, & hav dwelt here 2 yere & a half, & came out of the
> contry fom place to place, & not abov a yere. [to depart].
>
> ...
>
> Robert Blyth, of 60 yeris, a laborer, that work nott, & Katherine, his wyf of
> that age, that spyn hempe, & hath dwelt here 2 yere & syns mydsomer, &
> cam from the furder part of Trouse. [to departe].
>
> ...
>
> Jone Plomer, wedow, of 34 yers, that spyn, & ys a diseased woman, & hav
> dwelt her 2 yer, & cam from Spyxfor [to depart][.][59]

Such information was used in orders reorganizing Norwich's handling
of poor relief from late June 1571. Citizens were "agreed that the cittie
was so replenysshed with great nombres" of poor ("to the nombre of ii[m]
and ccc [i.e. 2300] persons"); these went "from dore to dore counterfeat-
tinge a kinde of worke" and, worse, "were soffred and nourished at everue

---

[58] John F. Pound (ed.), *The Norwich Census of the Poor 1570* (Norwich: Norfolk Record Society,
1971), pp. 8–12. Pound asserts Norwich's primacy in instituting compulsory poor relief in 1549,
but compare *TED*, vol. III, pp. 305–6, which identifies the London rate of 1547 as the first.

[59] Examples quoted from Pound (ed.), *Norwich Census of the Poor*, pp. 23–42. Deletions in the original text have been omitted; insertions are enclosed within square brackets.

mans dore without inquerínge from wheare they came."[60] The result of such "foolyshe pittie" and indiscriminate charity was that "they encreased to suche nombre as the strangers ... surcharged the cittie above cc [200] pounds by yere."[61] But this was not all: "So cared they not for apparrell," the ordinance continued, "that what with diseases and want of shyftenge their Flesh was eaton with vermyn and corrupte diseases that grewe upon them so faste and so grevouslye as they were paste remedye." Not content with drinking themselves senseless, "they abused the holy name of God" and "defiled ther bodies with filthines" and contagion: "one so corrupteth another that the charge to heale them is verie greate."[62] A multiplying mass of mobile, idle strangers spread physical rot and moral decay through the body politic. Numbers were subsumed into a bodily language of mutation and disease.

Yet the solutions proposed to the problem of vagrancy from the 1570s diverged from the laments for Christian rectitude that marked earlier complaints about enclosure. Where the latter had sought to suspend or reverse the process that had created the problem – appealing either to the king as Christian shepherd or to the virtues of the commonwealth's landed elite – the Norwich ordinance took the vagrant multitude itself as the object of government. Further, the ordinance subjected this multitude to forms of confinement and coercive regulation that, while implying its reintegration into the body politic, were compatible with its indefinite isolation. Thus, door-to-door begging and indiscriminate private charity were outlawed and the former punished with the whip. Instead of outdoor relief, a "working place" for batches of the able-bodied was set up, wardens appointed and work schedules established that combined a seasonal and ritual calendar with the daily rhythms of clock time: five in the morning to eight at night in summer (from Lady Day to Michaelmas) and six in the morning to seven or half-past seven in winter – "with the alowance of one halfe hower or more to eate and a quarter of an hower to spende in prayer."[63] Refusal of labor met with redoubled confinement, this time in Bridewell. The effects of this policy were measured in numbers employed and pounds earned:

---

[60] *TED*, vol. II, p. 316.

[61] *TED*, vol. II, pp. 316, 318.

[62] *TED*, vol. II, pp. 317–18.

[63] *TED*, vol. II, pp. 319–20. There was municipal-level precedent for some of this, for example, in the 1539 regulations for beggars at Chester, which besides ordering the "the number and names of all indigent and needy mendicant people" to be gathered (but for control of licensed begging, not its abolition) also commanded the able-bodied idle to assemble at the city's high cross to offer their services for hire at every weekday morning at six o'clock in winter and four o'clock in summer. See *EEH*, pp. 366–7.

of ix^cl [950] children which daielie was ydle and did nothinge butt begge, the same now kepte in worke may earne one with another vj *d.* a weke, which a mownte in the yere to j^m. ii^c xxv *li.* [£1225] which the comon wealth doth reape benefyte therbye.

Also that iij^xx iiij [64] men which dayelie did begge and lyved ydely and now are hable and do earne xij *d.* a weke at the least....

Also that j^c iiij^xx [180] women which dayelie did begge and lived idely and nowe are hable to earne at lest some xij *d.* and some xx *d.*, and some ij *s.* vj *d.* a weke[.][64]

Vagrants were now to be managed not only as displaced corporations in need of restitution or restoration but also as an agglomeration of individual laboring bodies.[65] Contingent, multivalent and local as such changes initially were, this step away from the conceptual framework of qualitative multitudes implied an alternative: the quantitatively defined population.

Neither the abruptness nor the intentionality of this shift should be exaggerated. On one hand, the coherent articulation of a new idea of population lay far in the future. On the other, the Norwich census and orders of 1570–1 merely put in practice measures outlined in earlier pieces of actual or proposed national legislation: the 1495 and 1531 laws against vagrants, the 1536 law empowering local authorities to put vagabonds to work, bind out their children and collect funds; the 1552 bill calling for surveys of the poor. What the last three decades of the sixteenth century saw was less a fundamental or systematic change in outlook than a practical manifestation, through the enforcement and elaboration of existing law and policy concerning troublesome multitudes, of quantitative tendencies and governmental aspirations that would come to distinguish engagements with population in the next century. This included the re-evaluation and even instrumentalization of regulated, controlled or coerced mobility, generation and mutability in specific spheres of legislative or corporate action. It also involved the creation of a national context of *practical* political engagement with ever more abstractly conceived multitudes, most saliently via countrywide poor and vagrancy laws that drew on local experience and relied on local agency for their effect.[66]

---

[64] *TED*, vol. II, p. 323.

[65] As Steve Hindle has shown, the revision of poor relief that began in cities like Norwich and then became national gave parish officers the power "to fracture and reconstitute the households of the poor," unmaking as well as remaking families by splitting them into their component parts and inflicting various forms of mobility as well as labor upon them. This atomization of multitudes into individual bodies was a practical as much as a conceptual development. See Hindle, *On the Parish?*, p. 57.

[66] Paul Slack has noted the "creative" power of the poor laws: "The system made paupers and delinquents by labelling them." Slack, *Poverty and Policy*, p. 107. This "invention" of the dangerous

Between them, the 1572 "Acte for the Punishement of Vacabondes" (14 Elizabeth, *c.* 5) and the 1576 "Acte for Setting of the Poore on Worke" (18 Elizabeth, *c.* 3) envisioned a mass of intact, individual, adult bodies – displaced, masterless and unskilled – and assigned them spaces and materials in and on which to labor. The laws subjected them to the oversight of a new class of managerial official, punished deviations from the program and sought to forestall the degeneration of poor children through early assimilation into the same regime. By the 1572 act, the residual category of "all and everye persone and persones beyng whole and mightye in Body and able to labour, havinge not Land or Maister, nor ... any lawfull Marchaundize Crafte or Mysterye" absorbed the heterogeneous mass of marginal wanderers, merging migrant workers and the indigent with the kinds of rogue that stalked pamphlets like Harman's, dissolving them all into a pool of labor: "Fencers Bearewardes Comon Players ... and Minstrels," "Juglers Pedlars Tynkers and Petye Chapmen," "Comon Labourers" refusing work for set rates, "[counterfeiters] of Lycenses [and] Passeports," "Scollers of the Universityes ... that goe about begging," "Shipmen pretendinge Losses by Sea," "persones delivered out of Gaoles."[67] Likewise, by the act of 1576, poor "Yowthe" were to be "accustomed and brought up in Laboure and Worke," lest they "growe to bee ydle Rogues" by the force of their natural parents' example. Cities and corporate towns were to lay up "a competent Store and Stocke of Woole Hempe Flaxe Iron or other Stufe" for the poor to work upon and create houses of correction where they could be confined and forced to labor.[68]

New legislation in 1597 strengthened enforcement while entrenching the ideas behind earlier laws. The "Acte for the Releife of the Poore" (39 Elizabeth, *c.* 3) charged Overseers of the Poor with "settinge to worke of the Children" of indigent or otherwise unfit parents, and JPs with committing the willfully unemployed to the "Howse of Correccion" – and negligent Overseers to prison. Any who wandered or begged "in any place whatsoever, by Licence or withowte," were henceforth "to be esteamed taken and punyshed as [rogues]."[69] The accompanying "Acte for Punyshment of Rogues, Vagabondes and Sturdy Beggars" (39 Elizabeth, *c.* 4) reaffirmed

---

poor, in particular, can be seen as an unintended consequence of policy. But it is argued here that both in regard of the poor and other types of people the generative capacity of legislation and other interventions was more and more consciously appreciated over time, becoming an explicit premise of seventeenth-century projects.

[67] *TED*, vol. II, pp. 328–9.

[68] *TED*, vol. II, pp. 331–4.

[69] *TED*, vol. II, pp. 346–50.

the reduction of phony scholars, pretended victims of shipwreck, quack astrologers, dice-players, minstrels, tinkers, peddlers and other idle wanderers to the catchall category of "Rogues Vagabondes and Sturdy Beggars" subject to one or another form of "sedentarization" and compulsory labor. All would be returned to their home parishes, confined to houses of correction, or jailed.[70] Both the national dimensions of this taxonomy and the alien nature of its targets were confirmed by a prohibition on conveying "in any Vessell or Boate from and out of the ... Realme of Irelande, Scotlande or Isle of Mann into the Realme of England or Wales" of "such as shalbe forced or very like to lyve by begging." In 1601, the *Ease for Overseers of the Poore* appeared, complete with blank forms for use in the observation, classification and government of the poor. From the age of seven onward, those without a fixed abode, trade or master were in principle placed, by that fact alone, at the disposal of the state. Policy would give them shape.

Vagrancy had provoked comment, and royal as well as parliamentary responses, for a century. Only toward the end of Elizabeth's reign, however, did the multitude of vagrants come to be defined in terms of physical capacity (sturdiness), moral incapacity (idleness) and social marginality (wandering), increasingly without geographical reference (beyond a putative foreignness) or historical provenance, and set over against the commonwealth (as a body politic unto itself, marked by perverted social and sexual norms) rather than understood as a degenerate product of the commonwealth's failings. Instead of signaling their contingent origins in local histories of displacement, the qualities of mobility, mutability and idleness that defined vagrants now segregated them from the legitimate social body. Mobility made vagrants foreign wherever they went. Recorder of London William Fleetwood noted that of "above a C. lewed people" arrested in a January 1582 search for masterless men, "we had not of London, Westminster, nor Southwarke nor yet Middlesex nor Surrey above twelve"; and of the rest "fewe or none of theym had ben abowt London above iij or iiij mownthes."[71] Idleness itself was increasingly described as an inherited characteristic,

[70] *TED*, vol. II, pp. 354–5. By the same act, the "diseased or ympotente poor" were also forbidden (358–9) to "resorte or repayre from their dwellinge Places" to the medical spas of Bath or Buxton without a license. James Scott defines the "sedentarization" of mobile populations as "a state's attempt to make a society legible, to arrange the population in ways that simplified" its operations; Scott, *Seeing Like a State*, p. 2. Apt as the term is for the vagrancy laws, it fails to capture the state's concomitant interest in planned and coerced mobility, often of the same populations targeted for "settlement."
[71] *TED*, vol. II, pp. 335–7.

something to be bred out by separating the children of the idle from their feckless parents and inuring them to labor before their very sinews became (as Edward Hext, a Somerset JP, put it in 1596) "so benumed and styff throwghe Idleness" as to render their sturdy bodies incapable of physical work.[72] Morally and socially as well as physically, the idle and wandering poor were abnormal.

Another paradoxical implication of this stigmatization of the minds and bodies of the mobile poor was that even as the countercultural connotations of vagrancy reached their most elaborate expression, discussions of the *multitude* of vagrants came to dwell on their *quantity*, distinguished from the complex assemblage of their qualities, origins and relation to the body politic. Their qualities having been set out in statute and elaborated in pamphlets, their growing numbers required vigilant but separate attention. This new focus on quantity did not always imply statistical precision, and numbers never shed their rhetorical force. To the contrary: Hext, writing to Burghley, complained of the "Infinytt numbers of the wicked wandrynge Idell people of the land," "such numbers as are abroade," "the Infynyte numbers of the Idle" and so on, which "multiplye dayle" at the expense of "the poore Cuntryman" and "noble men and gentlemen" alike.[73] Still, even Hext's fear of limitless increase was a far cry from the ratios deployed against depopulation a generation before, and not only because of the visibility of demographic growth.[74] Mid-Tudor authors decried the destruction of ploughs and villages and the replacement of farming families by lonely shepherds. These were the real problems that purely notional fractions and ratios symbolized. For late Elizabethan JPs and Overseers of the Poor, by contrast, the numbers of vagrants *were* the problem. Solving it required quantitative knowledge: censuses of the poor for cities, overseers' accounts at the ward or parish level. Success, too, would be quantifiable. Once "they weare reduced to good subieccion" by policy – immobilized and inured to industry – no vagrants would remain.[75]

---

[72] *TED*, vol. II, p. 340. Material responsibility for care of the poor was left as far as possible to their progenitors and offspring. As the April 1598 orders to Essex JPs put it, "It is expounded that the great grandfather, grandfather, Father and sonne upward and downeward in lyneall descent or degree shall releive one an other as occasion shall require." *TED*, vol. II, p. 364.

[73] *TED*, vol. II, pp. 339–42.

[74] Compare the empirical enumeration of vagrants required by the Elizabethan poor laws with the symbolically resonant numbers of poor or infirm catered to by the medieval hospitals listed in Stow's *Survey of London*: "thirteen poor men" at St. Anthony's; "one hundred poor" at St. John at the Savoy; "a hundred blind people" at St. Mary within Cripplegate; "thirteen poor men" at God's House, Whittington College. Stow, *Survey of London*, pp. 434–6.

[75] *TED*, vol. II, p. 344.

Ambiguous Instruments: Mobility, Mixture and Civility in Ireland

The power of corporeal metaphor in Tudor commentary reflected in part the extent to which England was believed by privileged observers really to be one political, economic and social body. Compared to other European kingdoms, it was unified, networked and centralized to a high degree.[76] Ireland's experience, and still more its construction in the English political imagination, was very different. Legally divided until 1541 between English areas whose inhabitants were recognized as subjects and Irish areas populated by foreign "enemies," the island was further divided in practice into numerous Gaelic lordships, whose dominant families wielded effective power over most of the country, and whose relations with each other, with the English lineages descended from the Anglo-Norman invaders of the twelfth century, and with the English administration in Dublin and the "Pale" around it, shaped Irish politics in ways beyond the capacity of English monarchs or ministers to control.[77] Even after 1541 – when the Irish parliamentary "Act for the Kingly Title" (33 Henry 8, *c.* 1) constituted Ireland as a Tudor kingdom, extending subject status to the entire population as a step toward legal and administrative unification – the division between "mere" or "wild" Irish and English persisted, reinforced by a series of military conflicts and complicated by a deepening distinction between "Old" English (Catholic) families and "New" English (Protestant) planters and office-seekers, as well as by a growing Scottish population in Ulster.[78] To speak of a "body politic" in Tudor Ireland was, more evidently than in England, to voice an aspiration.

The parallels between the treatment of vagrants as England's internal others and that of different kinds of problematic Irish people – whose heterogeneity or degeneration from English blood and civilization was stressed later in the sixteenth century, notwithstanding their status as Tudor subjects – should, therefore, to be seen in this distinctive

---

[76] This is not to exaggerate the power of the Tudor monarchy, or to deny social polarization. Political integration involved a network of relationships through which a common but equivocal vocabulary could secure the consent of the governed to the initiatives of their governors, and by means of which elites could translate social into political power; see Wood, *1549 Rebellions*, pp. 195–201; compare Geoffrey R. Elton, *The Tudor Revolution in Government: Administrative Changes in the Reign of Henry VIII* (Cambridge: Cambridge University Press, 1962).

[77] Christopher Maginn, *William Cecil, Ireland, and the Tudor State* (Oxford: Oxford University Press, 2012), pp. 16–17, 25, 33–4; Ellis, *Ireland in the Age of the Tudors*, pp. 11–17, 98–160.

[78] See Bradshaw, *The Irish Constitutional Revolution*, pp. 193–257; Brady, *The Chief Governors*, pp. 13–44. Group labels are helpfully discussed in Maginn, *William Cecil*, p. 146.

context.[79] Impediments to subjecting the whole of Ireland to an English civil administration were understood in terms of the mobility, mutability and mixture of specific groups: the "wild" Irish and the Old English. As in discussions of English vagrants, so in treatments of Ireland mobility was linked to idleness, idleness to poverty and poverty to crime. Yet the roots of this mobility did not lie, as in England, in the enclosure or conversion of arable. They were instead traced to a variety of sources: the customary use of transhumance in animal husbandry, flight from the tyrannical exactions of Gaelic lords, the chronic instability of native political mechanisms or – in the virulent work of Edmund Spenser, among others – the ethnic inheritance of Scythian barbarism.[80] This last point suggests another contrast between English and Irish multitudes. Although both canting vagrants and Irish-speaking Gaels were in some sense alien (late Elizabethan legislation connected the two), the Irish were distinguished not merely by language, dress or custom but by genealogy and history.[81] Ireland's populace might be subject to Tudor rule, but Ireland was another country and the Irish multitude was a body – or several bodies – apart.

As a putatively debased elite, the Old English present still another set of parallels and contrasts with England's marginal multitudes, as well as with the Irish.[82] If enforced mobility had turned ploughmen to vagrants in England, it was the contaminating mixture of Irish people, blood, language and habits with English that had degraded and alienated the Old English from their national origins and, it was suggested, their due allegiance.[83] Even as "New" English arrivals began to displace Old English families

[79] On Elizabethan constructions of Irish difference, see Canny, *Making Ireland British*, pp. 1–120; on earlier Tudor ideas compare John Patrick Montaño, *The Roots of English Colonialism in Ireland* (Cambridge: Cambridge University Press, 2011).

[80] See Nicholas Canny, "The Ideology of English Colonization: From Ireland to America," *The William and Mary Quarterly* 30:4 (1973), 575–98, at 587; Andrew Hadfield, "Briton and Scythian: Tudor Representations of Irish Origins," *Irish Historical Studies* 28:112 (1993), 390–408.

[81] The 1597 "Acte for Punyshment of Rogues, Vagabonds, and Sturdy Beggars" (39 Elizabeth, *c.* 4) forbade anyone "having charge in any Viage" to "bringe or conveye … in any Vessell or Boate from and out of the said Realme of Irelande, Scotlande or Isle of Mann into the Realme of England or Wales … any Vagabonde Rogue or Begger, or any such as shalbe forced or very like to lyve by begging"; *TED*, vol. II, pp. 354–64, at p. 358.

[82] On the marginalization of the Old English aristocracy, see Brady, *The Chief Governors*; Jane Ohlmeyer, *Making Ireland English: The Irish Aristocracy in the Seventeenth Century* (New Haven, CT: Yale University Press, 2012), pp. 25–207; Aidan Clarke, *The Old English in Ireland, 1625–1642* (Dublin: MacGibbon and Kee, 1966); Francis G. James, *Lords of the Ascendancy: The Irish House of Lords and Its Members, 1600–1800* (Washington, DC: Catholic University of America Press, 1995), pp. 11–39.

[83] Ciaran Brady identifies degeneration with the abandonment of English law; see Ciaran Brady, "From Policy to Power: The Evolution of Tudor Reform Strategies in Sixteenth-century Ireland," in Brian Mac Cuarta (ed.), *Reshaping Ireland, 1550–1700: Colonisation and Its Consequences*

from their traditional political roles in the administration of the Pale, however, the social standing and education of many of the latter enabled them to address powerful and learned counterarguments to English as well as Irish and European audiences – defending their own Englishness and civility (and even advocating further plantation) to the first, while articulating a shared history and a commitment to Catholicism to the latter two.[84] Thus, while the language of degeneration and alienation likened the Old English to the vagrant poor, and while this implied structural similarities between the two challenges, the problems were fundamentally different. Different parties, further, had a stake in solving them. The multiplication of idlers was a threat to social order and, thus, to the welfare and security of the kingdom. But the degeneration of the Old English into Irish was an immediate political and military threat: In a context of repeated rebellion in Ireland and simmering conflict with Spain, it imperiled English rule in Ireland and beckoned the invasion through Ireland of England itself.

The obverse of this Irish threat was English opportunity. Tudor dissatisfaction with rule through established Old English proxies – particularly the Fitzgerald earls of Kildare, whose rebellion in 1534 set in train Ireland's creation as a kingdom – led to the imposition of a succession of English viceroys tasked incongruously with imposing order and cutting costs. By the latter part of the century, mistrust between these and their local subordinates in the Pale had encouraged an influx of New English office-seekers. At the same time, the failure of the "surrender and regrant" scheme (designed to turn Irish lords into English nobles by a voluntary exchange of allegiance for title), the creeping militarization of Irish government in response to the resistance this provoked and the concomitant escalation of violence between English armies and Irish septs prevented the Old English from serving their self-proclaimed role as "civilizers" of the Irish and cast doubt, in English Protestant minds,

(Dublin: Four Courts Press, 2011), pp. 21–42, at p. 27. However, concerns with language, dress and custom – and with blood and religion in addition to law – are evident in late Tudor criticisms of the Old English. See Canny, *Making Ireland British*; Ellis, *Ireland in the Age of the Tudors*, pp. 325–6; Glimp, *Increase and Multiply*, p. 88.

[84] For examples, see Nicholas Canny, "Rowland White's 'Discors Touching Ireland' *c.* 1569," *Irish Historical Studies* 20:80 (1977), 439–63; Colm Lennon, *The Life of Richard Stanihurst the Dubliner, 1547–1618* (Dublin: Irish Academic Press, 1981); Bernadette Cunningham, "Representations of King, Parliament and the Irish People in Geoffrey Keating's *Foras Feasa Ar Eirinn* and John Lynch's *Cambrensis Eversus* (1662)," in Jane H. Ohlmeyer (ed.), *Political Thought in Seventeenth-Century Ireland* (Cambridge: Cambridge University Press, 2000), pp. 131–54; Brendan Kane, "Domesticating the Counter-Reformation: Bridging the Bardic and Catholic Traditions in Geoffrey Keating's 'The Three Shafts of Death,'" *The Sixteenth-Century Journal* 40:4 (2009), 1029–44.

on their capacity for it.[85] Each new wave of rebellion brought in its wake new executions, attainders, confiscations of land and attempts to "plant" more reliable landowners and tenants in the supposedly vacated territories: the failed plantation of King's and Queen's county in Leinster in the 1550s and 1560s, the short-lived colonization by Sir Thomas Smith (by then a member of the Privy Council) of the Ards Peninsula in Ulster in the early 1570s, the appropriation of a scattering of tracts in Munster in the 1580s and 1590s, and finally, the plantation of much of Ulster following the "Flight of the Earls" – the sudden departure of Gaelic leaders Aodh Mór Ó Néill (Hugh O'Neill), Earl of Tyrone, Rudhraighe Ó Domhnaill (Rory O'Donnell), Earl of Tyrconell and numerous followers to Spain in 1607.[86] Having gone from tenuous lordship to marginal kingdom under Henry VIII, Elizabethan Ireland became a space for colonial projecting.

One way that the cross-cultural and colonial aspects of late Tudor English engagements with Ireland reshaped approaches to the governance of multitudes is visible in Smith's colonial project in the Ards, as justified in a 1572 invitation to would-be planters. Representing conversations with Smith's son and collaborator Thomas Smith – who died in the course of the enterprise – the pamphlet, entitled *A Letter sent by I.B. Gentlemen to his very frende Mayster R.C. Esquire*, laid out the rationale for private plantation as an engine of civilization and order over against both Irish barbarism and Old English degeneration.[87] Smith's picture of Ireland was a curious one. It was not in any clear sense *terra*

---

[85] Ellis, *Ireland in the Age of the Tudors*, pp. 161–89, 265–351; Brady, *The Chief Governors*, pp. 159–66. On violence see also David Edwards, "The Escalation of Violence in Sixteenth-Century Ireland," in David Edwards, Pádraig Lenihan and Clodagh Tait (eds.), *Age of Atrocity: Violence and Political Conflict in Early Modern Ireland* (Dublin: Four Courts Press, 2007), pp. 34–78.

[86] On the changing pattern of plantation see Audrey Horning, *Ireland in the Virginian Sea: Colonialism in the British Atlantic* (Chapel Hill: University of North Carolina Press, 2013), pp. 17–100; compare William J. Smyth, *Map-Making, Landscapes and Memory: A Geography of Colonial and Early Modern Ireland c. 1530–1750* (Cork: Cork University Press, 2006), pp. 166–97, pp. 54–102, and Nicholas Canny, "The Marginal Kingdom: Ireland as a Problem in the First British Empire," in B. Bailyn and P. D. Morgan (eds.), *Strangers within the Realm: Cultural Margins of the First British Empire* (Chapel Hill: University of North Carolina Press, 1991), pp. 35–66. On the Munster plantation, see also Michael McCarthy Morrogh, "The English Presence in Early Seventeenth Century Munster," in Ciaran Brady and Raymond Gillespie (eds.), *Natives and Newcomers: Essays in the Making of Irish Colonial Society, 1534–1641* (Dublin: Irish Academic Press, 1986), pp. 171–90; on Ulster, Philip Robinson, *The Plantation of Ulster: British Settlement in an Irish Landscape, 1600–1670* (Belfast: Ulster Historical Foundation, 1994), pp. 9–65.

[87] *A Letter sent by I.B. Gentleman vnto his very frende Mayster R.C. Esquire, vvherein is conteined a large discourse of the peopling & inhabiting the Cuntrie called the Ardes, and other adiacent in the North of Ireland* (London: Printed by Henry Bonneman for Anthony Kitson, 1572). The text is reprinted in George Hill, *An Historical Account of the MacDonnells of Antrim* (Belfast: Archer and Sons, 1873), pp. 405–15; the latter version is used here.

nullius, open for the taking, as later theorists drawing on More and later still on John Locke would argue the New World to be.[88] To the contrary, "the Kings of England haue had footing and continuall gouernement [in Ireland] these foure hundred yeeres and more." And yet, like later targets of English colonial expansion, the north of Ireland was bounteous enough to guarantee a return on investment ("a large Cuntrie, commended wonderfully for fertilenesse and commodious site therof"), "barbarous" enough to require plantation (having never been "fully subdued" but subject to "often rebellion") and "desolate" enough for space to be plentiful and future settlements secure.[89] One need not reduce Ireland to a "testing-ground" for transatlantic empire, or forget the long history of English involvement in the country or its status as a Tudor kingdom, to see in Smith's plans a set of assumptions and arguments that marked the island out as a colonial space.[90]

Smith, who had visited Ireland as part of the current Lord Deputy Sir William Fitzwilliam's commission in 1569, traced the failure of English government there neither to "the impossibilitie thereof" nor, happily, "to the evil gouernment of Deputies." Instead, he blamed a lack of commitment from the crown, which, distracted by Continental and domestic politics, had diverted funds from needy viceroys, inhibiting effective rule and creating incentives for rebellion. Rather than securing real control, "Princes contented themselues if they myght only preserue a footyng" in the country as cheaply as possible.[91] Centuries of distraction and neglect had created a political and legal vacuum; the need to fill this had driven the Old English to seek native alliances, setting in train their own degeneration:

> The Englishe race overrunne and daily spoiled, seeing no punishment of malefactors did buy their owe peace, allied and fostred themselves with the Irishe, perceiving their immunitie from law and punishemente degenerated, choosing rather to maintain themselves in the Irish mans beastly liberty tha[n] to submit themselves and to lieue there alone, and not the Irish in the goodly awe of the lawes of England.[92]

---

[88] See Anthony Pagden, *Lords of All the World: Ideologies of Empire in Spain, Britain, and France, c. 1500–c. 1800* (New Haven, CT: Yale University Press, 1995), pp. 76–9.

[89] I.B., *Letter*, pp. 405, 411.

[90] Audrey Horning argues against treating Irish plantation as a model for simultaneous or subsequent colonial settlements in Virginia; see Horning, *Ireland in the Virginian Sea*, pp. 17–18, 355. But the idea that Ireland was subject to colonization in this period does not depend upon what Horning calls the "'testing-ground' theory" of its relationship to Virginia or other New World colonies; comparison of Irish with *metropolitan* policies and projects supports it.

[91] I.B., *Letter*, pp. 405–6.

[92] I.B., *Letter*, p. 406.

Combined with the barbarism and rebelliousness of the native Irish, this "degenerating and daily decay of the English manners by little and little" through mixture with them made Ireland a daunting landscape for settlement. Yet Smith was sanguine about salvaging Ireland and convinced that he could do so at minimal charge to the state, generating civilization and profit at the same time. The potential value of the land was unquestionable:

> [F]or there cannot be (sayeth he) a more fertile soile throwoe out the world for that climate … a more pleasant, healthful, full of springs, rivers, great fresh lakes, fishe, and foule, and of most commodious herbers [i.e. harbors] … it lacketh only inhabitants, manurance, and pollicie.

In short, "Irelande once inhabited with Englishe men, and polliced with Englishe lawes, would be as great commoditie to the Prince as the realme of England."[93] In the absence of a royal army, however, some "invention" would be needed to bring this bright future about.

This invention was private plantation. As with other projects in this period, its credibility depended on a combination of enticement and rigorous defense. Smith's justification came in the form of an appeal to history, and *pari passu* of the mechanisms of degeneration. Denying that "it is not possible to inhabite in any Cuntrie there" without "the Princes pay," Smith emphasized that the Old English had done just that: "many parcels have been wonne by the English men therein without the King's forces, whiche eyther by the occasions afore rehersed were lost, or els for lack of inward policy degenerated"; he instanced the Fitzgeralds and Butlers in Munster, the Burkes in Connacht, the Nugents in Meath and the de Lacys and Mortimers in Ulster. The problem was not conquest but the pattern of settlement:

> Moste of those that haue taken in hand before this to winne and inabite in Ireland, have, after the place once possessed, deuided themselves eche to dwell uppon his owne land, and to fortify himself therein. But this made not the enemy afrayed…. So they degenerated as is aforesayd, and in time all was frustrate[.][94]

Smith's plantation would avoid these mistakes. Taking "a place so neere as wee can that is naturallye strong," the settlers "would not suffer the souldiers too be dispersed," keeping the frontier of the compact plantation constantly manned against "divers inconveniencies." The Ards Peninsula was ideal for the purpose: "the neerest part of all Ireland to Lancashire," it was

---

[93] I.B., *Letter*, p. 406.
[94] I.B., *Letter*, p. 407.

"easie to be wonne, inhabited, safely kepte, and defended."[95] Moreover, the time was ripe. Just as Alexander the Great defeated a Persian Empire that would have vanquished his forebears, so Elizabethan planters could promise what the Old English had failed to deliver.

To explain why this was so, the younger Smith blended his father's mid-Tudor brand of social analysis with what was to become a standard trope in Elizabethan and Jacobean propaganda for colonial settlement projects: overpopulation. As Smith wrote,

> England was neuer that can be heard of, fuller of people than it is at this day, and the dissolution of Abbayes hath done two things of importance heerin. It hath doubled the number of gentlemen and marriages, whereby commeth daily more increase of people, and suche younger brothers as were wonte to be thruste into Abbayes, there to liue (an idle life), sith that is taken away from them must nowe seeke some other place to liue in. By this meanes there are many lacke abode, and few dwellings emptie.[96]

In contrast to later ideas of colonial settlement as an outlet for surplus numbers, however, the overpopulation Smith described resulted from the kinds of mechanisms that shaped accounts of depopulation. The Reformation, in particular, removed both clerical celibacy and monastic storage facilities for the younger sons of landed families. Coupled with primogeniture and the rising price of "diet and apparel," this inhibited "men which haue but small portions" from maintaining "them selves in the emulation of this world with like countenance as the grounded riche can do."[97] Overpopulation consisted not in numbers outrunning space but in an increasing proportion of gentry unable support themselves in the style to which they were by status accustomed, and for whom there was no place "at home." In outline, this was not very different from the degeneration of husbandmen into vagrants that explained depopulation. It was less about quantity per se than about the displacement or marginalization of a specific social type.

Accordingly, Smith did not envision Ireland as a dumping-ground for surplus Englishmen, but rather as a suitable field in which a displaced multitude might cultivate its defining martial and civilizing qualities and enjoy their just rewards. The English body politic had, in effect, produced an organ that needed transplantation to serve its purpose. For geographical, political, legal and civilizational reasons, Ireland was the safest and the

---

[95] I.B., *Letter*, p. 408.
[96] I.B., *Letter*, p. 409.
[97] I.B., *Letter*, p. 409.

most appropriate host: "Then went I," the author wrote, "to examine the estate of Countreis abrode, and found that all the Countries adiacent ... were as wel peopled, or better than we be, or else more barren, so that, except we might master and expel the inhabitants, it would not availe." Even "barren" Scotland was "ruled by a frend King, and peopled sufficiently." But "Ireland is the Queenes inheritaunce," and parts "lye almoste desolate" of settlers. "To inhabite and reforme so barbarous a nation as that is, and to bring them to the knowledge and law," he argued, "were bothe a godly and commendable deede and a sufficient worke for our age." Providence linked the excess growth of a domestic multitude with the settlement of wasted land and the civilization of savage people; what was superfluous to the English body politic might make the Irish one whole. Colonization continued the divinely sanctioned settlement and civilization of the Earth that had begun in biblical times: "let us ... vse the persuasions which Moses vsed to Israel ... and tell them that they shall goe to possesse a lande that floweth with milke and hony, a fertile soile truly if there be any in Europe."[98]

It is significant in this regard that Smith's private plantation in the Ards did not – as later colonial projects in Ireland and elsewhere would attempt – exclude the native Irish or the Old English from participation. In part this was a matter of labor supply; Smith anticipated that Irish husbandmen (or "churls") would flock to a plantation run along English rather than Gaelic lines:

> So soone as we ... have proclaymed that all such of the Irishe as will liue quyetly and manure the ground vnder vs shal be welcome ... and haue no coine, liverie, nor cesse [dues exacted by Irish and many Old English landlords] layd upon them ... There is no doubt but ther will great numbers of the Husbandmen which they call Churles, come and offer to liue vnder vs, and to ferme our grounds both such as are of the cuntry birth, and the Englyshe pale[.]

Beyond creating private profits for the English planter, involving the Irish and Old English in the labor and rhythms of settled agriculture would also discipline and civilize a mobile multitude. Tillage "settleth the occupier and what with tending his fallowe, reaptyde, seede time, and thrashing, it bindeth always the occupier to the Lande, and is a continuall occupaton of a great number of persons, a helper and mainteyner of ciuilitie."[99] Just as the "peculiar gaine" of individual planters (ten times their investment, the

---

[98] I.B., *Letter*, p. 409.
[99] I.B., *Letter*, p. 410.

author suggested) would conduce to the "common profite" of the nation, so "keeping men in Tyllage" rather than "the idle followyng of heards, as the Tartarians, Arabians, and Irishe men doo" would generate commercial and cultural transformation.[100] The author invoked More in marveling at the genius of the scheme: "How say you now, have I not set forth to you another Eutopia?"

The simultaneous exaltation of and apology for novelty was part and parcel of projecting in the later sixteenth and seventeenth centuries. This engagement with change, as Vera Keller has argued, was part of a shift in the temporal and geographical orientation of political thought that reflected and proposed to coordinate the recovery of ancient learning, technological innovation, commercial growth and territorial expansion.[101] Though later thinkers such as Giovanni Botero and Francis Bacon (considered in Chapter 3) articulated these ideas in the languages of reason of state and mastery of nature, I.B.'s *A Letter* suggests similar connections. The younger Smith presented the "invention" of private plantation as an advancement of political learning:

> his proceedings are others than hathe bene heretofore vsed, and other mennes errors haue taught him to take this order, to marke and consider them well is the onely way to perfectnesse, (sayth he) and nothing hath bene so well done, and if it were to do againe might be better done, for time is it that in the moste aduised gouernementes discouereth faults which while we patch and mende by little and little, the first order is altered, and become another thing, the very vanitie of the world[.][102]

This sense that policy by its nature not only adapted to change but, in the framing of new settlements, also actively assimilated the lessons of past failures in other settings – that dynamic policy rather than mere stable rule was the task of government, and that policy could more easily shape "a cuntrie almost desolate" than mend the flaws time exposed in settled kingdoms – brings out the significance of the colonial context for the handling of multitudes.[103]

Rather than repairing a broken body politic, private plantation in Ireland would synthesize a new one by combining surplus parts from England with regenerated Old English and freshly civilized Irish multitudes. Success depended not, as in English agrarian complaint literature, upon the reconstitution of local communities or relationships, but on their absence or

[100] I.B., *Letter*, pp. 409–11.
[101] Keller, *Knowledge and the Public Interest*.
[102] I.B., *Letter*, p. 413.
[103] I.B., *Letter*, p. 411.

abrogation: on the prior desolation of the landscape and on the willingness of the Irish to abandon their present economic and social relationships. The salient qualities of the territory (again, in contrast to those of depopulated regions in England) were few, broad and chiefly strategic, relative to the location, power and economy of the mother country. The human desiderata were somewhat more precise – soldiers, husbandmen and artisans were all needed – as were their numbers. Smith sought at least "sixe or seaven hundred" Englishmen to settle the area. But these specifications reflected no positive ideal of beauty or proportion; they were the minimal requirements for the survival of a new colony in a hostile space; "sixe thousande of them [i.e. the Irish] dare not set uppon seaven hundred Englishe men," Smith thought, provided the latter had the advantage of a defensible situation.[104] There was no maximum number, no fixed proportions between the parts represented and no idea that the growth of the plantation as a whole would be limited by any endogenous principle of cohesion or political health. Self-contained, it was, nevertheless, justified by its limitless potential and transformative effects on the alien society and uncivilized people beyond its walls.

The organization of the colony, as Audrey Horning has argued, reflected the elder Smith's knowledge and admiration of Roman models. It was not a blueprint for transatlantic empire. Yet in the context of the Tudor engagements with degenerated multitudes in England examined above, it, nevertheless, marked a significant departure from established modes of demographic governance.[105] The colonial setting – the need to sedentarize and civilize a barbarian populace and to plant the colony as a seed of longer-term transformation in the country around it – made this difference. Like contemporaneous and subsequent English commentary on colonial sites, *A Letter* served promotional purposes, and the scene it painted was a fantasy. Smith's Ards plantation fizzled by 1575, against a wider backdrop of ever more costly cycles of reform, resistance and brutalizing conflict that mocked projectors' promises and claimed mounting numbers of lives. Yet even as doubts about the efficacy of reform strategies multiplied, the civilizing imperative behind Smith's and other projects gained strength. The distinction between English civility, Old English degeneration and Irish barbarism cast the task of governing Irish multitudes as an essay in controlled transformation. Even where the means proposed were less

---

[104] I.B., *Letter*, p. 411. The implied ratio of 10:1 may be symbolic of the strength of English civilization over Irish barbarism, rather than empirically determined. The author did, however, allege several instances of small English forces overcoming larger Irish numbers.

[105] See Horning, *Ireland in the Virginian Sea*, pp. 65–8. Keller emphasizes the close relationship between innovation and the recovery of ancient knowledge; see Keller, *Knowledge and the Public Interest*.

innovative than Smith's, the problem was seen in terms that favored either novelty or, at any rate, new severity.

In this respect even the conservative recommendations submitted in 1577–8, near the end of Sir Henry Sidney's second viceroyalty, by Sidney's critic and Lord Chancellor, William Gerrard, are revealing.[106] Gerrard sought "to woorke reformacion" in what he considered to be a "ruynated state."[107] For over a century after the initial conquest, Gerrard wrote, "that lande rested well governed under English justice." But in the fourteenth century "two sortes of people firste brake that quiet": "Irishe enymies" and "Englishe rebells." These posed different challenges. English authority notwithstanding, the native Irish were foreign – distinguished "by name, speache, habitt, feadinge, order, rule, and conversacion" as well as by their predatory mode of government, "supplyinge … their wantes by prayinge and spoylinge of other countryes adioyninge." They accepted "noe superior" in the country, and "mortally hateth the Englishe," living in the 1570s just "as the Irishe lyved … before the conqueste." There were two ways to deal with them: either to make conquest good by force of arms, reducing the Irish to obedience, or else "by … pollecye to keepe them quiett" and the English population safe – in short, either assimilation or segregation.[108] Given past failures and fiscal constraints, the latter seemed the likeliest course.

Gerrard spent more time on the other problematic multitude, the English in Ireland, "people of our owne nacion." These fell into two sorts. Those who had taken the field "in open hostilitie and actuall rebellion" required forcible suppression, no less than rebels against the crown in England. "Thother sorte of Englishe rebells," however, "are suche as refuzinge Englishe nature growe Irishe in soche sorte as (otherwise then in name) [they are] not to be discerned from the Irishe." That is to say, a segment of the English community in Ireland were rebels simply by virtue of their degeneration from English into Irish:

> Theye … speake Irishe, use Irishe habitt, feadinge, rydinge, spendinge, coyshering, coyninge; they exacte, oppresse, extorte praye, spoyle, and take pledgies and distressies as doe the Irishe. They marry and foster with the Irishe, and, to conclude, they imbrace rather Irishe braghan lawes then sweete goverement by justice.[109]

---

[106] William Gerrard, "Lord Chancellor Gerrard's Notes of His Report on Ireland," *Analecta Hibernica* 2 (1931), 93–291. On Gerrard's criticism of Sidney, see Brady, *The Chief Governors*, pp. 154–5.
[107] Gerrard, "Lord Chancellor Gerrard's Notes," 93–4.
[108] Gerrard, "Lord Chancellor Gerrard's Notes," 95.
[109] Gerrard, "Lord Chancellor Gerrard's Notes," 96.

Against such denatured rebels, force was of no avail: "For can the swoord teache them to speake Englishe, to use Englishe apparell, to restrayne them from Irishe exaccions and extorcions, and to shonne all the manners & orders of the Irishe"? No, Gerrard answered, "it is the rodd of justice" that must be applied. This was not new; fourteenth-century parliaments had grasped and sought to counteract the degenerative effects of coyne and livery, fostering and intermarriage, Irish dress and brehon law, the keeping of kern, and all other "soche evells as Irishe infeccion poysoned them with."[110] They had seen that "Irishe customes, exaccions & imposicions destroyed the Englishe subiecte and, therefore, forbad them," in the Statutes of Kilkenny and since.[111]

These laws had failed. For all the prohibitions "restrayninge the Englishe from the Irishe," the English of the Pale "were in everye forbidden respecte growen more Irishe then before." Indeed, it appeared doubtful whether there was still an English community in Ireland to speak of; "if Irishe speache, habit and conditions made the man Irishe, the most parte of the Englishe were Irishe." Where Smith had treated degeneration as a consequence of royal neglect, however, Gerrard (a royal officer, not a private planter) suggested a greater degree of Old English responsibility and of Irish agency, even policy, in the process. The Irish, he wrote, "have gotten still ground over" the English "by fosteringe and mariage."[112] The Old English, meanwhile, had willingly abrogated law and natural allegiance in resorting to Irish alliances and customs. Their rebellion, indeed, consisted in their having shed their English qualities and taken on those of the enemy. Gerrard implied that rebellion and Irishness were one, opposed to Englishness and order: "those termed Englishe rebells were such as were transformed into the Irishemen and ioyned with them in all Irishe disorders, and being of the race of Englishe degenerated from Englishe order were termed rebells."[113] More than just linking Irishness and rebellion, Gerrard's framing of degeneration couched the process of transformation as a political act in itself – a desertion or dereliction of duty, in the context of colonial or marchland settlement, and a usurpation of sovereignty over the complex of qualities that defined a multitude as loyal subjects rather than rebels or foreign foes.

[110] Gerrard, "Lord Chancellor Gerrard's Notes," 96, 120–3.
[111] Gerrard, "Lord Chancellor Gerrard's Notes," 97, 121.
[112] Gerrard, "Lord Chancellor Gerrard's Notes," 122.
[113] Gerrard, "Lord Chancellor Gerrard's Notes," 122.

Gerrard fought shy of conscious innovation in treating the problem he diagnosed. Notwithstanding past failures, his preferred remedy was to enforce and extend existing law:

> [T]he waye firste to be taken to bringe the Englishe so subiecte to Englishe orders, habitt, usages & customs as in the years and tymes aforesayd they remayned in were duely to execute those lawes alreadye made and to provide more sharpe to be made to purdge the Englishe of their Irish spottes and staynes which wroughte them altogether Irishe: and such as meete with all Irishe exactions, extorsions, coynnies and lyveries, abandoninge Kerne & idell followers.[114]

In common with other reformers, Gerrard also called for the extension of judicial circuits to make such laws good – a strategy that successive viceroys pursued up to the outbreak of the Nine Years' War.[115] Yet, however familiar the measures in question were, the manner in which Gerrard presented them treated law as a means of imposing – or, as needed, removing – a second nature. The Statutes of Kilkenny had aimed to forestall degeneration by outlawing mixture with the Irish and the appropriation of their qualities. Now, Gerrard argued, undoing degeneration required scouring the Old English to remove the "spottes and staynes" of Irishness. Such imagery might imply that a kernel of pure Englishness persisted beneath the surface, but Gerrard's account made it clear that any such kernel was politically insignificant. The Irishness of the Old English may have been "wrought" – that is, artificial – but it was no less real for that: through a process of "staining" they had *become* Irish, with all that that entailed for their loyalty and civility. Their Englishness would be restored just as artificially, and just as effectively. Not for the last time, the transformation of Irish multitudes was cast as the artful imposition of desirable qualities on human material.

Before the Nine Years' War, the Tudor project of extending and reforming an imperfectly established government depended on maintaining relations with English as well as Irish powerbrokers in the country. Indeed, Old English desire for reform had largely motivated the 1541 act, and – despite mounting frustrations with successive English viceroys – similar sentiment continued to support some central initiatives thereafter. This raises the question of Old English views of demographic governance. Unlike other multitudes we have examined, the Old English were not a marginalized group but vital agents – or, at least, facilitators – of effective English rule.

---

[114] Gerrard, "Lord Chancellor Gerrard's Notes," 123.
[115] See Maginn, *William Cecil*, pp. 191–212.

Unlike the "mere" Irish, they had influential defenders (such as the English Jesuit scholar Edmund Campion) and the capacity to represent themselves to elite audiences in England and beyond. Their position, however, was insecure: during the last three decades of Elizabeth's reign, confessional divisions in general and Counter-Reformation infiltration in particular became objects of Protestant concern in England, just as Old English power and territory became objects of New English envy in Ireland. These attentions provoked the Old English to more urgent protestations of their Englishness, loyalty and civility – set off against the barbarism and rebelliousness of their Irish coreligionists. The paradoxical effect was a striking similarity between Protestant and Old English views of the mere Irish, mitigated by different ideas about just where the Old English fit.

Both Campion and his protégé, the scholar and Palesman Richard Stanihurst (who contributed Irish material to Holinshed's influential *Chronicles*, before embracing Catholicism) drew clear lines between the "wild" Irish and "the citizens, townesmen, and inhabitants of the English pale," who "differ little or nothing from ... their progenitors, the English and Welsh men" of the twelfth century.[116] The Irish were wild, rural and subject to strange and backward customs; the Old English – at least, those of the Pale – were literate, civilized city-dwellers. Geography, custom, language, law and governance separated the two. At the same time, however, both authors emphasized the plasticity of the "wild Irish" and turned the degeneration of those Old English living outside the Pale to account. In his *Historie of Ireland* (existing in manuscript from 1571, though printed only in 1633), Campion agreed that "the simple Irish are utterly another people then our Englishe in Ireland," noting that Englishmen who were "conversant with the brutish sort of that pepel, become degenerate in short space, and are quite altered to the worst ranke of Irish Rogues, such a force hath education to make or marre."[117] Yet, the very fact that the Old English had so degenerated in parts of Ireland proved that the mere Irish might be civilized:

> The People are thus inclined; religious, franke, amorous, irefull, sufferable, of pain infinite, very glorious, many sorcerers, excellent horsemen, delighted with Warres, great almes-givers, passing in hospitality: the lewder

---

[116] Stanihurst, in Raphael Holinshed, *Chronicles of England, Scotland, and Ireland*, 6 vols. (London, 1587), vol. III, p. 44. On Stanihurst see Lennon, *The Life of Richard Stanihurst*; Florian Kläger, *Forgone Nations: Constructions of National Identity in Elizabethan Historiography and Literature: Stanihurst, Spenser, Shakespeare* (Trier: Wissenschaftlicher Verlag Trier, 2006), pp. 27–96.

[117] Edmund Campion, *A Historie of Ireland* [MS 1571] (London, 1633; New York: Scholars Facsimiles and Reprints, 1940), pp. 14–15.

sort both Clarkes and Lay-men, are sensuall and loose too leachery above measure. The same being virtuously bred up or reformed, are such mirrours of holinesse and austerity, that other Nations retaine but a shewe or shadow of devotion in comparison of them.[118]

Campion and Stanihurst, no less than Smith, intimated a need for a civilizing transformation in Ireland. Where Old English writers and their allies differed from English projectors was over the mechanism of transformation and over how far the degeneration of the Old English made them targets rather than agents of the civilizing effort.[119] The key, for Campion and Stanihurst, was not military conquest or colonial plantation but education through virtuous example, mutual commerce and proximity. Conversion, like degeneration, was a matter of conversation: one group, "by living neere [another], or by liking their trade are transformed into them."[120] Its proper agents, now as in the Middle Ages, were the English of the Pale.

The conservative hue of this vision does not mitigate its novel implications, which recall developments in the handling of English vagrants and anticipate aspects of much more radical English programs for Ireland. As Campion's and Stanihurst's histories showed, the mobility and the mixture of multitudes had an equivocal record in Ireland. Despite Old English degeneration, Campion noted that the Irish of his day lacked "the faults of their Auncestors" thanks to English incursions and settlement, "whereby many of these enormities were cured, and more might be."[121] On the other hand, describing Pictish attempts to settle in Ireland, Campion had the Irish turn their king, Roderick, away with the argument that "mingling of nacions in a Realme breedeth quarrels remedilesse" – a sentiment some Protestant planters would come to share.[122] What protected civilization from degeneration was not the segregation of sedentary communities but education, which if adequately backed by the state would channel the effects of Anglo-Irish mixture by institutionalizing exposure to English rather than Irish example. Campion called for grammar schools in every diocese, assuring his readers that "our unquiet neighbours would finde such sweetenesse in the taste [of learning], as it should be a ready way

---

[118] Campion, *Historie of Ireland*, p. 13.
[119] Here, it is worth noting with Kläger that Stanihurst differentiated sharply between Palesmen and degenerated Old English families elsewhere, while also denigrating the qualifications and commitment of "New" English agents; Kläger, *Forgone Nations*, pp. 51–2, 55.
[120] Campion, *Historie of Ireland*, pp. 14–15. On Stanihurst's emphasis on education, see Kläger, *Forgone Nations*, pp. 90–1.
[121] Campion, *Historie of Ireland*, p. 15.
[122] Campion, *Historie of Ireland*, p. 31.

to reclaime them."[123] In contrast to the English association of wandering scholars with vagrants, and to Protestant fears of Catholic movement, Campion saw the civilization of the Irish as a cultural uplift born of travel between learned institutions – a transnational phenomenon he hoped to domesticate:

> [O]ur Realme is at this day an halfe deale more civill then it was, since noble men and worshipfull, with others of ability, have used to send their sonnes into England to the Law, to Vniversities, or to Scholes. Now when the same Scholes shall be brought home to their doores, that all that will may repaire unto them, I doubt not, considering the numbers brought up beyond the Seas, and the good already done in those few places, where learning is professed, but this addition discreetly made, will foster a young frye, likely to proove good members of this commonwealth, and desirous to train their children the same way.[124]

Civilization was the opposite of degeneration: assimilation through mixture, channeled in an English rather than an Irish direction by the sluice of education. Where the Old English had turned Irish in the absence of such props, schools would ensure that "Babes from their Craddles" imbibed "a pure English tongue, habite, fashion, discipline," converting the Irish "by this example, or at the least wise [denying them] the opportunity … to infect others."[125] The task of policy was to create the conditions for a desirable transformation.

As royal parsimony, court faction and resistance turned ambitious reform programs into a scramble for quick results, English writers such as Philip Sidney – defending his father's record as Lord Deputy in 1565–71 and 1575–8 – questioned the capacity of the Old English to civilize their savage neighbors before the latter had discovered "the sweetenes of dew subjection" through military means.[126] Still, a belief in the power of education and example to drive mutability in productive directions persisted. Though he shared little else with the martyred Campion (executed by Elizabeth in 1581), the Jacobean writer Sir James Perrott – son of Sir John Perrott, Lord Deputy from 1584–8 (and himself convicted of treason in 1592) – viewed the problem of civilization in Ireland in similar terms. Despite the influence of "soyle and scituation" on the Irish "constitution," Perrott credited

[123] Campion, *Historie of Ireland*, p. 132.
[124] Campion, *Historie of Ireland*, p. 132.
[125] Campion, *Historie of Ireland*, p. 132.
[126] Philip Sidney, "A Discourse on Irish Affairs" [1577], in Philip Sidney (edited by Albert Feuillerat), *The Complete Works of Sir Philip Sidney*, 4 vols. (Cambridge: Cambridge University Press, 1923), vol. III, pp. 46–50, at p. 49.

"educasion," "conversation" and "the example of the contriemen where any persons have theyr birth" with the power to shape "the condition of theyr myndes." Indeed, "thoe nature hath either a sway, or at the least some sympathy to produce symilitude or anticipate in dissimilitude of manner and conditions, yet suerly education, example, and use bringes forth great effectes of perfection and imperfection in men."[127] In an age of expanding trade, Irish backwardness was the product of isolation; "theyr breedinge ... could be but meane," he wrote, since they "had little, and in a manner, noe commerce with forayne nacions, which is commonly the cheifest meane to begette civilitie."[128] Regardless of its accuracy, this assessment implied that mobility and mixture were not the cause of Ireland's problems, but – under the right conditions – the solution.

Sir Edmund Spenser's 1596 dialogue, *A View of the Present State of Ireland*, written as its New English author contemplated losing his substantial Munster estates to the fury of the Nine Years' War, is often regarded as a break with earlier, more moderate strains of English commentary – even as an incitement to genocide.[129] Yet while counseling conquest as a matter of policy, Spenser shared his predecessors' ambivalence about Irish mobility, mixture and mutability. His spokesman Irenius's diagnosis of Ireland's ills gave predictable weight to Old English failings: "the moste parte of them," he wrote, "are degenerated and growen almost mere Irishe." This was a disastrous loss not only of nation but also of civilization, as Irenius's English interlocutor Eudoxus intimated in his horrified wonder "that an Englishe man brought vpp naturallie in such sweete civillitie as England, affordes, could fynd such lykinge in that barbarous rudeness, that he should forget his own nature and forgoe his owne nacion."[130] The mere

[127] James Perrott, *The Chronicle of Ireland, 1584–1608* (Dublin: Irish Manuscripts Commission, 1933), pp. 14–15.

[128] Perrott, *Chronicle of Ireland*, p. 16. Looking back from 1619, Perrott (p. 100) thought the Dutch "example of industry" most promising, anticipating such later commentators as William Petty and William Temple.

[129] See, for instance, Elizabeth Fowler, "The Failure of Moral Philosophy in the Work of Edmund Spenser," *Representations* 51 (1995), 47–76, at 68; Ben Kiernan, *Blood and Soil: A World History of Genocide and Extermination from Sparta to Darfur* (New Haven, CT: Yale University Press, 2007), pp. 176–7.

[130] Edmund Spenser, *A View of the Present State of Ireland [A vewe of the present state of Ireland discoursed by way of a dialogue betwene Eudoxus and Irenius. 1596.] Edited, principally from MS Rawlinson B 478 in the Bodleian Library and MS 188.221 in Caius College, Cambridge*, edited by W. L. Renwick (London: Scholartis Press, 1934), p. 62. This is the edition – a composite based on manuscripts – used here. Spenser's *View* was first printed in 1633 in James Ware, *The Historie of Ireland, Collected by Three Learned Authors viz. Meredith Hanmer Doctor in Divinitie: Edmund Campion sometime fellow of St Iohns Colledge in Oxford: and Edmund Spenser Esq* (Dublin: Printed by the Society of Stationers, 1633). Ware's edition has been reprinted with scholarly commentary as Edmund Spenser, *A View of the Present State of Ireland*, eds. Andrew Hadfield and Willy Maley (Oxford: Blackwell, 1997).

Irish themselves were barbarians, the descendants and cultural heirs of the ancient Scythians. Their every habit – indeed, their very habit, the mantle ("a fitt house for an outlawe, a meete bedd for a rebel, and [an] apte cloake for a thief") – marked them as uncivilized. Unregulated mixture with such people could not end well.

Yet mixture itself was an indispensable engine of positive as well as negative transformation. Despite the perils of degeneration, Irenius described the "mingelinge of nations" as "a wonderfull providence," and it was in this historical context of progressive, additive demographic mixture that English colonization promised to be "the last and the greatest" chapter in the "impeoplinge" of Ireland.[131] Beyond the waves of migration that had underpinned this process of peopling, civility, too, was the product of regular "trade and enterdeale" between nations and subnational regions, a circulation of goods as well as people that brought "new fashions" from overseas to Ireland's shores and thence to "Inlande dwellers" through cultural contact and commercial exchange.[132] "For nothinge," Spenser wrote, "doth sooner cause Civillitie in any Countrie, then many market townes by reason that people reparinge often thither for theire needes will dalie see and learne Civill manners of the better sorte."[133] Change – whether in the direction of civilization or savagery – was a matter of social as well as territorial movement: "where the lords and chief men wax so barbarous and bastardlike, what shalbe hoped of the peasantes and base people?" Spenser elaborated a complex model of civilization in which education, conversation, commerce and emulation – each linking both English and Irish and elite and lower orders, and each involving different sorts of mobility and mixture in distinct kinds of space – were all important. The fact of degeneration was proof of their power to civilize.

That same fact underscored the importance of controlling the spaces, contexts and conditions in which mobility and mixture took place. What Eudoxus thought of as Ireland's capacity to "alter men's natures," Irenius put down to "the first evill ordynance and Institucion of that commonwealth" – a disastrous political failure to exploit the normal rights of conquest in the twelfth century, a failure abetted by Old English divisions along lines of private interest. The fruit and symbol of this failure was the "vnnatural" Old English adoption of Irish wives and nurses – and thereby, given the importance of early teaching and the power of example on children, of Irish

---

[131] Spenser, *View of the Present State of Ireland*, p. 62.
[132] Spenser, *View of the Present State of Ireland*, pp. 78–9.
[133] Spenser, *View of the Present State of Ireland*, pp. 212–13.

language and custom.[134] Ordinarily, "lawes ought to be fashioned vnto the manners and condycion of the people," as Bodin had suggested.[135] But the degenerate and barbarous condition of the people made this unthinkable; and "since wee cannot now applye lawes fytte to the people, as in the first instytucion of common wealthes yt ought to bee, wee will applye the people and fytte them to the lawes."[136] To be governed civilly, the people must first be civilized, and "yt is vaine to speake of plantinge of lawes and plotting of pollycies, till they be altogeather subdued" by military force.[137] Civilization required policy; policy required subjection; subjection required violence – up to and including massacre and mass starvation.

This appeal to the sword gives weight to Spenser's reputation as a geno-cidal apologist for English colonial domination. It should be borne in mind, however, that he advocated violence not as a way of clearing and claiming the land, but as a way of making mixture between English and Irish safe, with the goal not of replacing the Irish but of transforming them: "for evill people by good ordynance and gouerment, maye be made good."[138] Control of circumstances, not sheer force, made the difference between degeneration and civilization. Such control, moreover, was not a once-for-all achievement but the basis of an ongoing process of governance meant to maintain civilization among English and Irish alike.[139] Eudoxus feared that English planted among Irish "must runn with the streame," meaning "the greater will carrye away the lesse." Irenius responded with a paean to the transformative power of government: "where there is noe good staye of gouerment and strong Ordynances to hold them there indeed, the fewer will followe the more But where there is due order of decyplyne and good rule, there the better shall goe foremost, and the worse shall followe." Given the proportions between Ireland's different multitudes, the strength of numbers would have to be overcome by breaking down, redistributing and recombining elements of the two crucial multitudes:

> [S]ince Ireland is full of her owne nation, that maye not be rooted out and somewhat stored with englishe alreadye and more to be I thincke yt best by an vnion of manners and conformitie of myndes, to bring them to bee one people, and to putt awaye the dislikefull concepte but of the one and the other, which wilbe by no meanes better then by this entermingelinge of

---

[134] Spenser, *View of the Present State of Ireland*, pp. 62, 83, 87, 196.
[135] Spenser, *View of the Present State of Ireland*, p. 15. Spenser refers to Jean Bodin, *Six livres de la république*, livre V.I. (Paris, 1576).
[136] Spenser, *View of the Present State of Ireland*, p. 183.
[137] Spenser, *View of the Present State of Ireland*, p. 17; see pp. 124–7 for further details concerning military force.
[138] Spenser, *View of the Present State of Ireland*, p. 124.
[139] On the need to impose and maintain civility, see Kläger, *Forgone Nations*, p. 124.

them, that neyther all the Irishe maye dwell together, nor all the Englishe, but by translatinge of them, and scattringe them in small numbers, amongst the Englishe, not only to bring them by dalye conversaion vnto better lykinge of each other, but also to make both of them lesse able to hurte[.][140]

Conquest assumed, Spenser proposed a series of measures – distributing Irish land and Irish tenants among English planters; founding and fortifying ports and garrisons and reforming laws and taxation so as to break the power of the septs and reorient loyalties to the state.[141] Economic as well as geopolitical concerns played a role, but Spenser was very clear that the goal was civilization: "I [had] rather haue fewer Cowes kept and men better mannred" than the reverse.[142] The targeted use of mobility and mixture would transform Ireland's ethnically, culturally and confessionally divided peoples into what they had never before been: a single, civilized, subject population. This was a "body politic" of a new kind, however. Rather than a naturally coherent, bounded, self-sustaining assemblage of organically linked, functional multitudes, it was a body of subjects redefined in national (civil and religious) terms and reproduced through constant, active governance from without.[143]

Ireland's subjection to transformative projects did not end with Spenser. By seventeenth-century standards, as we shall see, it had scarcely begun. Nor did Spenser's instrumentalization of demographic mobility and mixture end debate about the perils of contact between English settlers and their descendants, on one hand, and Irish natives, on the other.[144] But his work, and the historical moment it addressed, marked important changes both in English thinking about Ireland and in English thinking about the government of populations. Writing in 1612, after the Nine Years' War and the Flight of the Earls had paved the way for new rounds of plantation, notably in Ulster, the Jacobean lawyer Sir John Davies echoed Spenser's *View* when he wrote that

> [A] barbarous Country must first be broken by a warre, before it will be capeable of good Gouernment; and when it is fully subdued and conquered, if it bee not well planted and gouerned after the Conquest, it wil eft-soones return to the former Barbarisme.[145]

---

[140] Spenser, *View of the Present State of Ireland*, pp. 196–7.
[141] Spenser, *View of the Present State of Ireland*, pp. 161, 165–6, 183, 189–90, 197–200.
[142] Spenser, *View of the Present State of Ireland*, p. 203.
[143] See Kläger, *Forgone Nations*, pp. 137–9, and on Spenser's *The Faerie Queene*, p. 167.
[144] See for example John Dymmok's denunciation of mixture in John Dymmok, *Treatice of Ireland* (c. 1600), in *Tracts Relating to Ireland* (Dublin: Irish Archaeological Society, 1843), pp. 1–90, at p. 6.
[145] John Davies, *A Discoverie of the Trve Cavses why Ireland Was Neuer Entirely Subdued, nor Brought vnder Obedience of the Crowne of England, vntill the Beginning of His Maiesties Happie Raigne* [1612], reprint (Shannon: Irish University Press, 1969), pp. 4–5.

But in Davies's view, Tyrone's defeat had brought just "an vniuersall and absolute conquest of all the Irishrie," reducing "all the people ... to the Condition of Subjects."[146] Gone was the pernicious legal distinction between the king's Irish "enemies" and his English subjects, gone the mistaken policy of "perpetuall separation and enmity" that had made this division the cause of degeneration, rebellion and war – not least by prohibiting contacts and mixtures that had proved inevitable.[147] Mixture was now not only safe but also essential. Only "Commerce with ... Ciuill men" could ameliorate the "wild and barbarous maner" of Irish life; only "a perfect Vnion betwixt the Nations" under "one King, one Allegiance, and one Law" could create a unitary body politic.[148] The Ulster plantation combined "Brittish" and Irish "that they might grow vp together in one Nation."[149] On a larger scale, conformity to English manners fostered "an hope, that the next generation, will in tongue & heart, and euery way else, becom English; so as there will bee no difference of distinction, but the Irish Sea betwixt us."[150] From one perspective, Davies's recommendations represented the second phase of Irish settlement, conquest having been the first. From another, they confirmed the agenda Spenser had outlined: the transformation of multitudes through policy.

There can be little doubt that the militarization of Irish politics from 1534 and what one might call its "colonialization" from 1570 or so changed the frame of reference for engaging with multitudes as objects of governance from what we have seen of early sixteenth-century English discussions. The multitudes in question were defined not functionally or locally but ethnically and on a national scale. They had no clearly defined place in any existing body politic, and indeed, their transformation was required for a recognizable body politic to be possible. It is not surprising that, in these conditions, transformative aspirations could be articulated more clearly and boldly than in the enclosed space of Tudor England. The creation of a civil multitude in a marginal and still half-foreign place was, inherently, a more open-ended enterprise than the restoration of a displaced multitude to its accustomed locale. Perhaps as much as the scattered plantations on the ground, this distinction substantiates the idea of later Tudor Ireland as a colonial site. Yet the drift of contemporaneous engagements with vagrancy in England was similar enough to suggest

---

[146] Davies, *Discoverie*, pp. 5–6.
[147] Davies, *Discoverie*, pp. 100–13.
[148] Davies, *Discoverie*, pp. 116–18, 121.
[149] Davies, *Discoverie*, p. 281.
[150] Davies, *Discoverie*, pp. 271–2.

a broader process of rethinking the nature of demographic governance. In both England and Ireland, marginal subpopulations came to be treated as national rather than local, and permanent rather than historically specific problems for government. At the same time, they became candidates for complex, transformative and increasingly routinized political and institutional interventions that deployed targeted and often coerced mobility and mixture with the overt aim of imposing a new and better nature on recalcitrant human material.

The routine exercise of transformative demographic agency extended the scope and altered the epistemological underpinnings and temporal orientation of governance. As the maintenance and periodic restoration of the body politic gave way to an open-ended manipulation of multitudes across metropolitan and expanding colonial spaces, Aristotelian concerns with harmony and proportion came first to include and then to be supplanted by interest in the possibility or necessity of progressive, lasting change as the goal of policy. This process has been examined before, in different ways and with different but overlapping chronologies: as the emergence of an idea of growth in seventeenth-century English economic thought, as the evolution of reason-of-state discourse from Machiavelli to Botero and beyond, or as the history of operationalism in science from the work of Renaissance "artisan/practitioners" to the aphoristic dictates of Baconian method.[151] Closed systems, fixed cycles and organic metaphors broke down before a new awareness of linear change and a new appreciation of the power of human agency – whether expressed as art, *virtù*, technology or policy – to conquer, exploit or at least deflect the operations of nature and the vagaries of fortune in time, and thereby not simply to maintain past or present states but to cast the future in another mold.[152]

In each of its guises – economic, political and scientific – this larger change implied new possibilities for the governance of populations. As we shall see in Chapter 3, its theorization in the decades around 1600 by the likes of Bodin, Botero and Francis Bacon set the stage for a plethora of self-consciously empirical engagements with populations, through private projects and state policies in England and across the Atlantic, against a backdrop of accelerating interest in quantitative data over the course of the seventeenth century. Here were the origins of political arithmetic. But well

---

[151] See Finkelstein, *Harmony and the Balance*; Keller, *Knowledge and the Public Interest*; Long, *Artisan/Practitioners and the Rise of the New Sciences*.

[152] Ralph Bauer has recently argued for the medieval alchemical and eschatological origins of similar ideas in the Spanish empire, and for their influence on Bacon, but with respect solely to the New World. See Bauer, *Alchemy of Conquest*.

before Bacon wrote or Botero was translated, the transformative ambitions they voiced, and many of the mechanisms their acolytes would employ in conjunction with empirical demographic numbers, had begun to take shape in qualitative Tudor engagements with marginal multitudes. Bacon would write in *The New Organon* that "The task and purpose of human Power is to generate and superinduce on a given body a new nature or new natures."[153] A mode of demographic governance that imposed civility and industry on wild rogues and the wild Irish had already embraced this task.

[153] Bacon, *New Organon*, p. 102.

CHAPTER 3

Beyond the Body Politic: Territory, Population and Colonial Projecting

From Depopulation to Overpopulation

Depopulation shaped early Tudor demographic ideas; overpopulation colored Elizabethan and Jacobean thinking. Between the two lay a change not only in perceptions of England's populousness but also in conceptions of multitudes as knowable and governable. We have seen this change manifest itself in engagements with specific groups over widening geographical and conceptual horizons – engagements in which the transformative power of policy and its instrumentalization of mobility and mutability eroded the idea of the stable body politic.[1] But another effect of the shift was the new prominence of quantity. Depopulation was a dislocation or degeneration within the body politic, expressible in symbolic ratios or figures but not essentially quantitative or even quantifiable. Overpopulation, though emblematized by poverty, idleness and crime, was at bottom a matter of numbers too great for the space they occupied. William Harrison, who thought it "an easy matter to prove that England was never less furnished with people than at this present" from manorial records, acknowledged fears "that we have already too great store of people in England."[2] Though he noted the qualitative effects of depopulation, Harrison treated groups as segments of an undifferentiated "store of people." And though he denied that this store was too large, his appeal to empirical counts suggests he thought it measurable and considered its precise measure – its number – significant. If depopulation touched

---

[1] Terence Ball argues that the idea of an organic body politic gave way during the seventeenth century to that of the polity as an artificial body. This is compatible with the view presented here, but the construction of policy as art is seen here as the key development, with the more flexible and loose use of the corporeal metaphor as a consequence. See Terence Ball, "Political Parties and the Legitimacy of Opposition," in Hans Erich Bödeker, Christina Donato and Hanns Peter Reill (eds.), *Discourses of Tolerance and Intolerance in the European Enlightenment* (Toronto: University of Toronto Press, 2009), pp. 73–99, at 77–8, 82–3.
[2] Harrison, *Description of England*, pp. 256–8.

multitudes as organs of a single body politic, overpopulation implied that the salient characteristics of groups were the numbers they represented and the area they covered. Quantification did not displace qualitative concerns, but it could reframe them.

Despite the paucity of data and disagreement about the direction of change in England at the time, complaints about overpopulation are usually read as responses to real demographic trends.[3] Concern with growth was also part of a wider European interest in empirical information and methodical observation as forms of practical knowledge and instruments of rule.[4] In a heroic age of natural history and the *ars apodemica*, even the fuzziest assessments of populousness helped describe and change the world in concrete, particular ways.[5] At the same time, the emergence of population as a measurable object suited a growing body of political thought centered on "reason of state." In emphasizing timely action, delineating a specifically political rationality and viewing history as a play of conflicting interests, this drew on Machiavelli.[6] In the half-century around 1600, however, attention moved from the cyclical struggle between princely *virtù* and fickle *fortuna* to the systematic exploitation of economic and military opportunity in the interests of indefinite if not unlimited growth.[7] Numbers of people, and knowledge of numbers, became central to assessing the past, navigating the present and shaping the future.

In healing the English body politic, mid-Tudor political theorists had drawn on continental experience and humanist ideas of policy. Later

[3] This is a theme in accounts of Elizabethan and early Stuart colonial expansion. See George Louis Beer, *The Origins of the British Colonial System, 1578–1660* (Gloucester, MA: Peter Smith, 1959), pp. 32–52; Mildred Campbell, "'Of People either Too Few or Too Many': The Conflict of Opinion on Population and Its Relation to Emigration," in William Appleton Aiken and Basil Duke Henning (eds.), *Conflict in Stuart England: Essays in Honour of Wallace Notestein* (London: Jonathan Cape, 1960), pp. 169–201; and, more recently, Horning, *Ireland in the Virginian Sea*, pp. 286–7.

[4] See Shapiro, "Empiricism and English Political Thought," 3–35; Stagl, *History of Curiosity*, pp. 95–153.

[5] Stagl, *History of Curiosity*, pp. 47–94; Harold J. Cook, *Matters of Exchange: Commerce, Medicine, and Science in the Dutch Golden Age* (New Haven, CT: Yale University Press, 2007), pp. 1–41. On the multiple sorts of "particulars" in natural history, see Brian W. Ogilvie, *The Science of Describing: Natural History in Renaissance Europe* (Chicago: University of Chicago Press, 2006), pp. 268–9. On the idea of "fact," see Barbara J. Shapiro, *A Culture of Fact: England, 1550–1720* (Ithaca, NY: Cornell University Press, 2000).

[6] See Jacob Soll, *Publishing the Prince: History, Reading, and the Birth of Political Criticism* (Ann Arbor: University of Michigan Press, 2005), pp. 22–40.

[7] Vera Keller argues persuasively for an "economic reorientation" of reason-of-state discourse in the work of Botero, Bacon and others; see Vera Keller, "Mining Tacitus: Secrets of Empire, Nature and Art in the Reason of State," *British Journal for the History of Science* 45:2 (2012), 189–212. On mercantilist (and pronatalist) ideas in reason-of-state thinking see Richard Tuck, *Philosophy and Government, 1572–1651* (Cambridge: Cambridge University Press, 1993), pp. 81–90. On *virtù* and *fortuna*, see Pocock, *The Machiavellian Moment*, pp. 156–82.

projects for instilling second natures in vagrants and the Irish had their own analogue in the theoretical literature of reason of state. Historians have long recognized the importance of this literature, and especially of Jean Bodin's and Giovanni Botero's contributions, in making population politically visible. Yet they have often isolated its quantitative and analytical side by focusing on its need for accurate numbers and concern over the potential for population to outstrip resources. Only recently have scholars come to explore Bodin's and Botero's more fundamental view of policy as a transformative art, and the corresponding construction of physical geography and the natural environment as the salient contexts in which this art improved or perfected nature. This understanding of art and nature gave meaning to numbers and theoretical expression to the transformative demographic governance that ad hoc engagements with troublesome groups implied. The body politic, once a template for the placement of multitudes, became a loose and flexible metaphor; territory, characterized by extent, location, climate, topography and commodities, became the arena for policy's work. The subject body was no longer a living assemblage of organs but a measurable stock of bodies and souls: a population.

Continental thinkers offer one perspective on the emergence of transformative demographic governance, colonial empire another. The body politic turned from model to metaphor just as the physical territory claimed by European powers expanded across the Atlantic. Botero argued for the viability of "scattered" empires in an era when these were ever more imposing realities for their rulers, subjects and rivals alike. Even before this, English authors and projectors – led by Richard Hakluyt and encompassing a range of speculative adventurers, empirical observers and colonial planters – advocated imperial expansion and colonial settlement as a matter of confessional duty, strategic necessity and economic advantage. Their proposals stirred familiar anxieties about the degenerative effects of mobility and mixture, while instrumentalizing mobility and mutability in the service of reform, improvement and security – including security from the corrupting political and moral effects of overpopulation at home. The New World setting of plantation, meanwhile, posed questions about the constraints and possibilities of new environments and new human neighbors, enemies and subjects. In this context, the conceptual shift from balancing multitudes in a body politic to distributing stocks of people across territory shaped by complex "situations" opened new horizons for political agency and created new needs for empirical knowledge.

Taken together, reason of state and colonial projection moved ideas about the governance of human groups away from a qualitative, organic and restorative mode toward a more open-ended, quantitative and expansive one. Bound up with this shift were changes in thinking about the nature and objects of political action and the geographical horizons and temporal scope of state power. These both drew upon and fed into developments on the ground, including the projection of English people, goods and claims across the Atlantic and around the globe, and their contact, conflict and fitful coexistence with non-European as well as European polities and populations. It is important not to overstate the case, however. On one hand, seventeenth-century discussions retained moral and religious as well as economic and political concerns with the degeneration of vagrants, idlers and other problematic multitudes. On the other, the regenerative uses of mobility that seventeenth-century colonial promoters touted had informed English and Irish projects for generations. Rather than a leap from a Tudor body politic governed by metaphor to a Stuart empire that ran on numbers, we can see changing political circumstances and vocabularies casting the management of human mutability as both a constant part of effective rule and a global task in which confessional, commercial and political survival might all be at stake. It was in this context that numbers and nature – key motifs of political arithmetic – emerged as objects of and constraints upon policy.

Policy and Situation in Reason of State

The equation of multitudes with kingly glory was enshrined in Proverbs 14:28. The idea of an optimum, located at the mean between insufficiency and ungovernable excess, originated in Aristotle's *Politics*. Both ideas were commonplace throughout the period, but neither implied any detailed account of population's political effects or the state's demographic agency. Writing in the context of a series of civil wars that divided the French subject body unevenly into religious factions, the humanist, historiographer and jurist Jean Bodin had cause to consider both matters.[8] Bodin's 1576 *Six livres de la république* (translated into English and printed in 1606) is best known for its articulation of unitary sovereignty as a precondition of order, and hence its contribution to the theory of absolute monarchy.[9]

---

[8] See Julian H. Franklin, *Jean Bodin and the Sixteenth-Century Revolution in the Methodology of Law and History* (New York: Columbia University Press, 1963); Anthony Grafton, *What Was History? The Art of History in Early Modern Europe* (Cambridge: Cambridge University Press, 2007), pp. 165–80, 218–20.

[9] Bodin, *Six livres*; Jean Bodin, *The Six Bookes of a Common-weale*, translated by Richard Knolles (London: [Printed by Adam Islip] and G. Bishop, 1606). I have used the modern facsimile edition: Jean Bodin, *The Six Bookes of a Commonweale*, translated by Richard Knolles and edited by Kenneth Douglas McRae (Cambridge, MA: Harvard University Press, 1962). See J. Russell Major,

Bodin has also garnered a reputation as a proto-mercantilist, pronatal-ist thinker, thanks to his pronouncement that "There are no riches other than men."[10] Yet while Bodin did identify numbers as sources of wealth and strength in Book V, call for a national census in Book VI and describe and dismiss ancient and modern efforts to curtail excess multiplication – insisting that "they erre much which doubt of [i.e., fear] scarcitie by the multitude of children and citizens" – sheer numbers were not the point.[11]

Bodin argued that human multiplication benefited "arts and disci-plines." Its more important effect, however – counterpoised to Aristotle's account of overpopulation – was forestalling faction:

> It is indeed lesse to feare that by reason of so great a multitude of citizens there will be deuisions, for that there is nothing that doth keepe a citie more free from mutinies and factions than the multitude of citizens, for that there are many which be as a meane betwixt the rich and the poore, the goode and the wicked, the wise and the simple, and artificers and noble-men, which may reconcile these extremes when they disagree[.][12]

The calming effect of a large population was not just a function of its size. Bodin argued that, barring attempts at "equalitie" like Lycurgus's in ancient Sparta and More's in *Utopia* (which hindered reproduction), great numbers would inevitably end up divided in multiple, crosscut ways by economic, intellectual and moral inequalities. If Bodin's idea of popu-lation here was not an undifferentiated mass of interchangeable units, however, neither was it an assemblage of qualitative, functional multi-tudes made coherent by the body politic metaphor. Complex social divi-sions, on this account, were an *effect* of large numbers, and Bodin was less concerned with maintaining a particular articulation of multitudes than with preventing their reduction to simple binaries.[13] The political effects of natural differentiation within a large subject body – the qualitative effects of quantity, one might say – justified its size.

This concern with establishing the quality, and the inequality, of the subject population informed Bodin's arguments for census-taking in the first chapter of Book VI. Here he surveyed ancient practices and figures. He also explained away the "sin of David," cited by "ignorant divines"

From Renaissance Monarchy to Absolute Monarchy: French Kings, Nobles, and Estates (Baltimore, MD: Johns Hopkins University Press, 1994), pp. 168–72.
[10] Quoted and discussed in Charbit, *Classical Foundations*, pp. 43–5; compare Strangeland, *Pre-Malthusian Doctrines*, pp. 102–3; Campbell, "Of People either Too Few or Too Many," p. 177.
[11] Bodin, *Six Bookes*, p. 571. See Charbit, *Classical Foundations*, pp. 43–62.
[12] Bodin, *Six Bookes*, p. 571.
[13] On Starkey as anticipating features of Bodin's thought, see Wood, *Foundations of Political Economy*, p. 238.

and opponents of the census, by arguing that David's mistake had not been to "number the people" but to neglect the collection of tribute and to number only those capable of bearing arms – "trusting more in the force of his legions, than in the power and helpe of the Almighty."[14] As for the usefulness of the census, Bodin wrote,

> The benefits which redounded to the publike by this numbring of the people, were infinite: for first they knew the number, age and qualitie of the persons, and what numbers they could draw foorth, either to go to the warres, or to remaine at home; either to bee sent abroad in colonies, or to bee imployed in publike works of reparations, and fortifications[.][15]

Besides its military applications, a census could prevent lawsuits over issues of "minoritie and maioritie," "forgerie & falshood," bastardy and legitimacy and so on. Finally, Bodin touched on a use that recalls English discussions of poverty and vagrancy:

> But one of the greatest and most necessary fruits that can bee gathered by this censuring and numbring of the subiects, is the discovery of euery mans estate and faculty, and whereby he gets his liuing, therby to expell all drones out of a commonweale, which sucke the hony from the Bees, and to banish vagabonds, idle persons, theeues, cooseners, & ruffians, which liue & conuerse among good men, as woolues do among sheepe[.][16]

The goal of the census was not to permit quantitative analysis but to clarify and codify qualitative distinctions between individuals and groups for the sake of peace, justice and security.

In this sense, the census was an instrument for shaping the qualities and relations of the population, and the state a demographic agent. This agency had limits, however. The most important of these derived from the physical environment. In Book V, Bodin treated both national character and human diversity (including skin color) in climatic terms.[17] Here he drew on an ancient tradition of thought that could be quite crude in its judgments. Yet Bodin's discussion of character was neither monocausal nor deterministic; nature was complicated, and different elements of it could work at cross-purposes. While he argued in general terms for the effects of fertile or hostile environments on human wit and industry,

---

[14] Bodin, *Six Bookes*, pp. 638–9.
[15] Bodin, *Six Bookes*, p. 640.
[16] Bodin, *Six Bookes*, p. 641.
[17] See Ivan Hannaford, *Race: The History of an Idea in the West* (Baltimore, MD: Johns Hopkins University Press, 1996), pp. 156, 326; Glacken, *Traces on the Rhodian Shore*, p. 439. Bodin attributed blackness to the sun's proximity, for example: Bodin, *Six Bookes*, p. 568.

for example – to such a degree that "The barrennesse and fruitfulnesse of places doth in some sort chaunge the naturall inclination of the heauens" – he also noted the particular effects of different topographies and relative locations, implying the possibility of change over time. Living by the sea made people "more subtill, politike, and cunning" than settlement in remote areas.[18] Barren soil "doth not onely make men more temperat, apt to labour, and of a more subtill spirit; but also it makes townes more populous" by minimizing the risk of invasion – "the inhabitants liuing in safetie doe multiplie, and are forced to traffique or to labour." The unearned bounty of rich soil made people "soft and slothfull."[19] A similar sense of complexity and dynamism in the links between regional climate, local geography and the qualities in settled populations, developed in colonial projecting, would be important to political arithmetic.

Among the factors shaping environment were various kinds of artifice. Anyone doubting "what force education, lawes, and customes, haue to change nature," Bodin advised, should consider how far Germans had come from the savagery Tacitus described to the "ciuill discipline" of the present – or how far the "warlike" Carthaginians had degenerated.[20] "The gouernment of euery Citie," too, "is of great force in the alteration of peoples natures and dispositions"; one must "not … obserue the climate alone" but consider "What may grow in the minds of men from the ayre, water, winds, hills and vallies, what from religion, lawes, customes, discipline, and from the state of euery commonweale."[21] People were mutable, and civilization was an artificial achievement; no less real for that, but fragile if neglected or moved:

> It is most certaine that if lawes and customes be not well maintained and kept, the people will soone returne to their naturall dispositions: and if they be transplanted into another countrey, they shall not be changed so soone, as plantes which draw their nourishment form the earth: yet in the end they shall be altered[.][22]

Disposed by climate to certain characters, people were further shaped by the location and features of their local environments, as well as by education, custom and law, by forms of government and the weight of history, in ways that could overcome inborn limitations. Both specific civil

---

[18] Bodin, *Six Bookes*, p. 564.
[19] Bodin, *Six Bookes*, p. 565.
[20] Bodin, *Six Bookes*, p. 565.
[21] Bodin, *Six Bookes*, pp. 567–8.
[22] Bodin, *Six Bookes*, p. 566. Bodin noted (p. 568) that "The transportation of Collonies works a great difference in men, but the nature of the heauens, winds, waters and earth, are of more force."

characters and civilization in general were the effects of art (including policy) applied, continually, to nature.

Much as English writers on vagrants and the Irish were coming to suggest at around the same time, Bodin described the governance of human groups as the management of mutability, the prevention of degeneration and the instillation of the elements of civility in flawed material.[23] What English authors suggested of specific multitudes, however, Bodin – concerned not with narrowly delimited, displaced groups, but with peace and sovereignty in a context of civil war – extended to the entire subject of population from the outset. Bodin also situated the task of controlling mutability (or the problem of instilling and maintaining civilization) in an equally broad temporal and spatial frame. In Book V of the *Six livres de la république*, he sketched the climatic, geographic and environmental constraints within which policy must operate; in his *Methodus ad facilem historiarum cognitionem* (1566), he had already, as Anthony Grafton puts it, "offered nothing less than a reevaluation and reconfiguration of time itself" predicated on "the possibility that human enterprise was changing and improving the world."[24] Bodin did not invent a way of thinking about the transformation of groups. Others, in England and elsewhere, did that independently. But unlike ad hoc and local engagements, Bodin indicated the general and relentless nature of the problem, its embedment in environmental and historical contexts, and its implications for the nature and horizons of governance.

Influential as Bodin was, the sixteenth-century author now most widely credited with innovative demographic thinking was the Tuscan-born Church diplomat Giovanni Botero. His major works appeared later than Bodin's: *Delle cause della gradezza delle città* in 1588 (translated into English in 1606 as *A Treatise, Concerning the Causes of the Magnificencie and Greatnes of Cities*), *Della ragion di stato* (*On the Reason of State*) the following year, and the *Relationi universali* in 1596 (a political gazetteer of which the first English translation, *The Trauellers Breuiat*, was printed in 1601).[25] If Bodin described broad connections, Botero was perhaps the first to give sustained attention to the specific mechanics of the relationship

---

[23] Spenser cited Bodin (*Six livres de la république*, V.i.17) on the need to fashion laws to the character of the people governed; see Spenser, *View*, p. 15.

[24] Grafton, *What Was History?*, p. 179.

[25] Giovanni Botero, *Delle cause della gradezza delle città libri III* (Rome: Appresso Giovanni Martinelli, 1588); Giovanni Botero, *A Treatise, concerning the Causes of the Magnificencie and Greatnes of Cities, Deuided into Three Bookes*, translated by Robert Peterson (London: Printed by T. P[urfoot] for Richard Ockould and Henry Tomes, 1606); Giovanni Botero, *Della ragion di stato libri dieci* (Venice: Appresso I. Gioliti, 1589); Giovanni Botero, *Le relationi universali* (Venice: Appresso Giorgio Angelieri, 1596); Giovanni Botero, *The Trauellers Breuiat, or, an*

between population, territory and the state. He is also often asserted to have been the first to express natural limits to demographic growth as functions of territory and resources, and (most significant from a theoretical perspective) the first to characterize the process of population in terms of inevitable conflict between the unlimited human capacity for multiplication and the limited power of territory and trade to supply food.[26] At the risk of prolepsis, one might say that Botero was the first to offer an analysis of demographic processes in terms Malthus would have recognized. Though the two may have worked from superficially similar premises, however, their purposes and conclusions were opposite.

As Romain Descendre has argued, *Della ragion di stato* and the Boterian trilogy of which it formed the core were directed against the *politiques*, Bodin especially, whose Machiavellian and Tacitist thinking had led them to compass the toleration of heresy.[27] Writing not from a divided French polity but rather in support of a centralizing, papalist Roman Church-state, and with an eye on the regional and global position of true religion, Botero disparaged their weakness and formulated a specifically Catholic reason of state as an alternative. As Descendre also indicates, the polemical thrust of Botero's work conditioned his treatment of population. Whereas Bodin conceived of the state in terms of rights, laws and norms, Botero's "non-juridical" or even "anti-juridical" vision reframed the question of political legitimacy as a matter of confessional identity, and concerned itself with political power as a matter of dominion over territory and population, constrained only by the limits of information and of the art of government.[28] For Botero just as for Bodin, empirical knowledge of land and people was vital to the operations of the state. But for Botero, the augmentation and manipulation of these resources was more clearly the essence of government, the task of policy as a perfective art.

Historicall Description of the Most Famous Kingdomes in the World Relating Their Situations, Manners, Customes, Ciuill Government, and Other Memorable Matters, translated by Robert Johnson (London: Printed by Edm. Bollifant for Iohn Iaggard, 1601). No English translation of *Della ragion di stato* was printed in the period, but a manuscript translation dated *c*. 1617–18 is in BL Sloane MS 1065; see Jamie Trace, "The Only Early English Translation of Giovanni Botero's *Della ragion di stato*: Richard Etherington and Sloane MS. 1065," *Electronic British Library Journal* (2016), article 4 [www.bl.uk/eblj/2016articles/pdf/ebljarticle42016.pdf]. I have used modern translations of the first two works: Giovanni Botero, *On the Causes of the Greatness and Magnificence of Cities*, translated by Geoffrey Symcox (Toronto: University of Toronto Press, 2012); Giovanni Botero, *The Reason of State*, translated by P. J. Waley and D. P. Waley (London: Routledge and Kegan Paul, 1956).

[26] On Botero's thought on population and territory, see Descendre, *L'État du Monde*.

[27] See for example the dedicatory epistle to Wolfgang Theoderic, Prince-Archbishop of Salzburg, in Botero, *Reason of State*, pp. xiii–xv; Descendre, *L'État du Monde*, pp. 57–87.

[28] Descendre, *L'État du Monde*, pp. 78–9.

Botero's most sustained arguments about population appeared in the first of the three works, *Delle cause della grandezza delle città*, and focused on the city as the locus of power. Besides its pertinence to Italian political circumstances, this frame threw Botero's break with Aristotelian thinking into bold relief. This was most explicit in Book III, where Botero contrasted Greek and Roman models of demographic governance:

> The ancient founders of cities, considering that it is not so easy to uphold law and civil order where there are large numbers of people, because multitudes engender confusion, set limits to the number of citizens, beyond which they believed the form and the constitution of their cities could not be maintained.... But the Romans, believing that strength, without which a city cannot long maintain itself, drives chiefly from a numerous population, did all they could to increase and populate their city[.]

While he admitted that stagnation and destruction had ultimately come to Rome and Greece alike, Botero made clear that "experience ... teaches us that the Romans' policy is to be preferred to that of the Greeks."[29] That is to say, greatness trumped order as a political goal. And, as Botero had noted at the beginning of Book I, "the greatness of a city does not consist in the extent of its site or the circumference of its walls, but in the number of its inhabitants and their strength."[30] Augmenting these should therefore be the overriding aim of policy. Books I and II explained how to do this.

Cain was "the first founder of cities," Botero wrote, but the civilizing effects of urban life appeared only when "authority" and "force" gave way to "pleasure" and, especially, "utility" (*utilità*, translated into English in 1606 as "profit") – that is, as incentives to concentrated settlement replaced compulsion and laid the basis for lasting growth.[31] Though its links to the benefits of "mutual exchange" within "a single body" recalled notions of the commonweal, "utility" in this context was an attribute of territory rather than of a healthy body politic. But, Botero cautioned, "utility is not a simple thing, of a single form."[32] It took in a mixture of natural and artificial considerations, combining factors Bodin might have treated under the separate headings of climate, environment, location, education, law, custom and so on. Botero emphasized geography both as providentially given and as modified by human settlement and technology: "the convenience of the site, the fertility of the Land, and the ease of communication" with

---

[29] Botero, *On the Causes*, p. 71.
[30] Botero, *On the Causes*, p. 9.
[31] Botero, *On the Causes*, p. 14. See Botero, *Delle cause*, p. 9; Botero, *Treatise*, p. 13.
[32] Botero, *On the Causes*, p. 17.

near neighbors and distant climes were all vital.[33] While the need for trade was ensured by God's distribution of natural commodities "in such a way that no single country received everything," and the medium provided by his creation of oceans and rivers, the shipping and the construction of harbors needed to exploit these divine gifts required the imitation and improvement of nature by human art.[34]

Book II took up the methods by which the Romans and others had drawn people to their cities.[35] Botero noted the "delights" and professional, administrative, judicial, educational and religious amenities cities possessed, but he focused on policy: sanctuary, citizenship and transplantation schemes – including the planned settlement of particular groups, as at Porto Ferraio and Livorno in Tuscany – as well as colonies.[36] These were not the New World plantations that were beginning to fire English imaginations as sources of exotic goods or dumping grounds for unwanted people; rather, they were local extensions of the ancient city, meant to moderate the temporary effects of poverty, conflict and disease in confined spaces:

> [J]ust as plants cannot grow and multiply as well in the nursery where they are sown as in the open ground where they are transplanted, in the same way human beings do not propagate as successfully when enclosed within the walls of the city where they are born, as they would in different places to which they are sent, because either the plague or some contagious disease devours them, or famine and hunger force them to seek another dwelling place, or foreign wars kill off the bravest among them while civil conflicts uproot the peaceful ones from their homes, and poverty and scarcity deprive many of the desire and the means to marry and have children.[37]

Colonies created breathing space for further growth. Within the city, the promotion of industry was paramount, more important even than agriculture inasmuch as "industry far outstrips nature" in the employment of

---

[33] Botero, *On the Causes*, pp. 17–20.

[34] Botero, *On the Causes*, pp. 20–1. Botero contrasted harbors "safe by their nature," including Messina and Marseille, with those constructed in imitation of nature, such as Genoa and Palermo. On the providential distribution of commodities, see Descendre, *L'État du Monde*, p. 210; for later instances, see Natasha Glaisyer, *The Culture of Commerce in England, 1660–1720* (Woodbridge: Boydell Press, 2006), p. 98.

[35] In a 1588 essay appended to some editions of *Delle cause*, Botero estimated that ancient Rome's population had been over 2 million at its height; Botero, *On the Causes*, p. 80.

[36] Botero, *On the Causes*, pp. 31–3. On Livorno (or Leghorn), see Corey Tazzara, *The Free Port of Livorno and the Transformation of the Mediterranean World, 1574–1790* (Oxford: Oxford University Press, 2017), pp. 21–47.

[37] Botero, *On the Causes*, pp. 33–4.

numbers and the production of wealth.[38] Industry, wealth and numbers grew together, expanding indefinitely outward.

At this point, some features of Botero's argument in *Delle cause* should be noted. The first is his identification of statecraft with art, both in the sense that the state should promote human industry and artisanship as sources of wealth, and in the sense that policy itself was an aspect of human ingenuity. The second is that policy, as an art, worked both upon human material and upon physical territory. Over time, the state's work on each of these things had implications for what could be done with the other. The idea of "utility" was crucial to this feedback. Early in Book I, Botero had contrasted authority and force with utility as centripetal forces: while the first two were unnatural or violent, and therefore of temporary effect, the third created natural incentives to lasting settlement.[39] Yet the composite nature of utility undermined this distinction. As Botero made clear in Book I, utility combined unalterable features of geography with aspects of environment that could be manipulated by art; as he added in Book II, "it will be very beneficial if the prince understands the natural advantages of the site, and works judiciously to improve it."[40] Acting upon nature to improve a site's utility by introducing new "conveniences" changed the context within which authority mobilized populations and assuaged the "violence" of transplantation. Rather than the state being at the mercy of geography, political interventions in territory and population could effect lasting change in both. Art surpassed nature by remaking it.

A last important aspect of the argument is the canvas on which the prince, as artist, painted. In comparison with the Tudor humanists examined in Chapter 1, Botero was eclectic and unsystematic in his use of metaphor. This is evident in the way he likened the colonial "transplantation" of men to that of plants. Both this image and policy rejected Aristotle's imposition of political limits on population: the point was no longer to maintain a balance between multitudes within a fixed corporeal frame, but to manage the effects of density by moving people around, facilitating further growth. Historians of economic thought have detected a similar bursting of Aristotelian bounds in the early seventeenth century.[41] Yet

[38] Botero, *On the Causes*, pp. 42, 43–4.
[39] Botero, *On the Causes*, p. 14.
[40] Botero, *On the Causes*, pp. 49–50.
[41] On the body politic in economic thought, see Finkelstein, *Harmony and the Balance*, pp. 13–97; on money and credit, Carl Wennerlind, *Casualties of Credit: The English Financial Revolution, 1620–1720* (Cambridge, MA: Harvard University Press, 2011), pp. 17–79.

Botero did not reject *all* limits. In Book III, he preferred Roman expansion to Greek restraint; but while Rome's glory had outshone Athens's, decline had still come. Asking why cities did not grow forever, Botero identified a providential clash between two forces: "the procreative power of human beings," which was constant, and "the cities' power to sustain them." The latter was a function of fertility and commerce, and thus amenable to improvement – but not infinitely. Sooner or later, the limits of territory and trade "become so many and so grave that they defeat all human effort."[42] No art could transcend nature altogether.

Della ragion di stato reiterated the idea of political rule as a perfective art, describing the prince as an "artificer" and the state as "his material."[43] It also carried some of Botero's points about the "utility" of cities into a discussion of "situation" (*sito*) in Book II.[44] Like utility, situation was complex. Botero first listed it alongside "age, fortune, and education" as a determinant of individual "nature, characteristics and temperament."[45] He then described "the situation of countries," including their latitude, topography and climate, as shaping national "qualities of mind and spirit," including capacity for government.[46] Like Bodin's reference to climate, this might evoke an ancient environmental determinism. Indeed, Botero celebrated an Aristotelian mean of temperature or topography as most desirable, while eschewing "novelty" and all but the subtlest changes in "policy" as imprudent.[47] Yet his argument was not that geography resisted political change, but rather that effective policy must imitate the gradualness of nature.[48] In Book III, he lauded such "great and noble achievements" as "the draining and improvement of marshy country ... also the corrivation of rivers for the benefit of navigation or agriculture" – work that altered the fertility, salubrity, physical features and thus the situation in which characters were formed and possibilities determined.[49]

Turning to the subject population, Book IV echoed Bodin on the importance of an intermediate class between rich and poor and reiterated the dangers of idleness. Book V dealt with the acquisition of subjects through conquest. Here the transformative role of policy was explicit: the prince's

---

[42] Botero, *On the Causes*, pp. 73–4.
[43] Botero, *Reason of State*, p. 3.
[44] See Botero, *Reason of State*, pp. 53–4.
[45] Botero, *Reason of State*, p. 38.
[46] Botero, *Reason of State*, p. 38.
[47] Botero, *Reason of State*, pp. 38, 49–52.
[48] Botero, *Reason of State*, p. 52.
[49] Botero, *Reason of State*, pp. 75–6.

task was "to make these new subjects ... become as like as possible to natural subjects."[50] The means to this end included the maintenance of "justice, peace and plenty" and the promotion of "religion, letters, and superior talents." Coming to education, however, Botero portrayed the goal of policy – as Tudor writers on "wild rogues" or the "wild Irish" had begun to do – as the imposition of "another nature" more governable than the original.[51] This was more than a matter of gradual assimilation by positive example or appeal to interest. New subjects were to learn the conquerors' language, use their law and adopt their faith.[52] Where these efforts failed, troublesome groups were to be segregated and divided, prevented from intermarrying and forced to move and resettle within the realm – or "dispersed and transplanted to other countries," as the Jews had repeatedly been, if need be.[53] There were, nevertheless, limits to what policy could do: "Kingdoms, and republics too, have their incurable diseases, and their mortal ones."[54]

Botero reiterated the view of colonies advanced in *Delle cause*, but Books VII–IX tempered the earlier work's emphasis on the quantity of people as a measure of wealth and strength.[55] Botero now treated "number" and "valour" as coequal "aspects of strength," arguing that while "it is the numerical strength of a people which makes the land fertile," valor (a focus of Book IX) counted for more on the battlefield.[56] Still, Book VIII dwelt on increasing numbers by means of "propagation" of the existing population and "acquisition" of people from other countries. Policy as a transformative art was central to both. Since "Agriculture is the basis of all propagation," for example, the prince must not only avoid waste but also "contrive to assist nature" by interventions in the landscape; all available labor, including that of "gypsies and strays and vagabonds," should be mobilized for improvement.[57] Acquisition, meanwhile, depended on industry:

> A prince ... who wishes to make his cities populous must introduce every kind of industry and craft by attracting good work-men from other countries ... by encouraging new techniques and singular and rare works,

[50] Botero, *Reason of State*, p. 95.
[51] Botero, *Reason of State*, pp. 95–7. Botero noted (p. 107) that the third-century emperor Probus had conscripted young Pamphylians and Isaurians "so that they should learn to be soldiers before they learnt to become thieves."
[52] Botero, *Reason of State*, p. 98.
[53] Botero, *Reason of State*, pp. 100–1, 105–6, 108, 110.
[54] Botero, *Reason of State*, p. 111.
[55] Botero, *Reason of State*, pp. 120–1; see also Book VIII, §5, at pp. 156–7.
[56] Botero, *Reason of State*, pp. 143–4, 153, 168.
[57] Botero, *Reason of State*, pp. 148–50.

and rewarding perfection and excellence. But above all he must not permit raw materials ... to leave his state, for with the materials will go the craftsmen.[58]

Botero has been seen as a proto-mercantilist, but he did not advance bullionist or balance-of-trade arguments, nor was he focused simply on maximizing the supply of cheap labor.[59] Control over the circulation of things was ancillary to control over the numbers and the kinds of people needed to make the state wealthy and secure.

Boterian demographic governance applied art to the transformation of nature in multiple ways: altering the landscape to sustain a larger population; fostering multiplication, immigration and colonization; improving the material conditions of human reproduction. The state was an improver, cultivating territory and population like a garden through policy, creating thereby something superior in quantity and quality to raw nature: "the diligence of man is more successful in multiplying lettuces and cabbages than is the fertility of nature with nettles and similar weeds."[60] The tools and techniques of this governance were complex, coming into play at different scales, levels of society and stages of life: "It is not sufficient ... for a prince to encourage marriages and fertility if he does not also assist the rearing and upkeep of the young."[61] Charity and education were part of this; so was the management of rural land and urban space; so were mobilizations of people within the kingdom or between it and colonial offshoots.[62] The numbers, fertility, health, sustenance and skills, as well as the religious and political commitments of the subject body, were all objects of demographic governance, addressed by interventions in the location, distribution and mobility of numbers of people.

How should this affect our view of English developments? There are obvious similarities between the frameworks of demographic governance articulated in Bodin and Botero and those implied by the handling of specific multitudes in England at roughly the same time. Neither Bodin's

---

[58] Botero, *Reason of State*, p. 153.
[59] As Vera Keller argues, the "mercantilist" label obscures the understanding of art and nature behind Botero's advocacy of particular policies; Keller, *Knowledge and the Public Interest*, p. 42. For mercantilism as a category of analysis, compare Eli F. Hecksher, *Mercantilism*, translated by Mendel Shapiro, 2 vols. (London: George Allen and Unwin, 1935); Donald Cuthbert Coleman (ed.), *Revisions in Mercantilism* (London: Methuen, 1969); Lars Magnusson, *Mercantilism: The Shaping of an Economic Language* (Abingdon: Routledge, 1994); Philip J. Stern and Carl Wennerlind (eds.), *Mercantilism Reimagined: Political Economy in Early Modern Britain and Its Empire* (Oxford: Oxford University Press, 2013).
[60] Botero, *Reason of State*, p. 154.
[61] Botero, *Reason of State*, p. 155.
[62] Botero, *Reason of State*, pp. 153–6.

Six livres de la république nor Botero's *Delle cause della grandezza della città* were translated until 1606, and *Della ragion di stato* did not appear in English except in a little-known manuscript, perhaps a dozen years later.[63] This does not mean that the authors or their arguments were unknown to Elizabethans; far from it, particularly for learned readers. Harrison cited Bodin's 1572 *Methodus* on the question of national origins, while Spenser's *View of the Present State of Ireland* cited *Six livres de la république* on the importance of shaping laws to the people for whom they were meant.[64] But neither in these nor in the engagements examined in Chapter 2 were these thinkers cited as authorities on the transformation of populations, despite the importance of this problem to everyone concerned. In his 1600 *State of England*, Thomas Wilson did cite Botero's *Relazioni universali* (translated in 1601) – but only to claim that Botero, "a stranger ... who never came within 1,000 mile of these countries," had wildly overestimated England's fighting strength.[65]

If Bodin and Botero were not major sources for Elizabethan engagements with multitudes, however, they would be widely read by Stuart authors. Further, they drew on some of the same intellectual sources and responded to some of the same problems as their English counterparts did. To the extent that they articulated as full-blown political theory what Tudor engagements with specific groups merely hinted at, each sheds light on the other's implications while exposing contextual differences. Juxtaposing them lets us see English engagements with troublesome groups of people not as part of an idiosyncratic process of state-formation but as posing conceptual challenges around degeneration and mobility that thinkers elsewhere confronted. By the same token, it draws out the significance of population, for reason-of-state theorists, not merely as a quantifiable resource but also as an object of qualitative transformation. This was a central implication of seeing policy as a perfective art – a view that Francis Bacon would theorize and that his followers would take up. These writers and projectors imbibed and adapted views of policy and of situation – a term that translated Botero's *sito* and included aspects of *utilità* – that owed much to reason of state.[66]

[63] Trace, "Only Early English Translation."

[64] Harrison, *Description of England*, p. 412; Spenser, *View*, p. 15.

[65] Thomas Wilson, *The State of England, 1600*, edited by F. J. Fisher [Camden Society, 3rd series, 70 (1936)], in Joan Thirsk and J. P. Cooper (eds.), *Seventeenth-Century Economic Documents* (Oxford: Oxford University Press, 1972), pp. 751–7, at 751.

[66] Botero, *Treatise*, p. 13, rendered *utilità* as "profit," comprising "commoditie of the scite," fertility, and ease of "conduct" (i.e., travel); compare Botero, *Delle cause*, p. 9. See also the chapter

Mobility, Mutability and Colonial Plantation

A second strand of thinking links policy, situation and the qualities of populations in the late Elizabethan and Jacobean eras: the literature and projecting of colonial plantation. This was the primary arena for discussions of overpopulation. Colonies were planned and promoted as outlets, dumping-grounds or safety-valves for excess numbers of unwanted people, extending the domestic mobility patterns of England's poor.[67] The primary material documenting English colonial expansion is copious, the secondary literature vast; there is no hope and no need to survey them here. Nevertheless, works advocating New World plantation between the 1580s and the 1630s show that the English Atlantic colonial enterprise, like Irish plantation, adopted and inflected ideas central to the conceptualization of population and its governance.[68] As with Tudor engagements with vagrants and the Irish, colonial projects constructed policy as an art that instrumentalized mobility against degeneration; still more than earlier efforts, colonial projects revealed the limits of corporeal metaphor as a framework for balancing qualitative multitudes. Instead, far-flung, discontinuous and expanding physical territory emerged as the space in which vast and growing numbers of bodies and souls were governed, while

"Of the Situation of Nations," in Giovanni Botero, *Relations of the Most Famous Kingdomes and Common-wealths thorowout the World*, translated by R. I. (London: Printed by Iohn Haviland, 1630), pp. 4–7.

[67] On this last point, see Bernard Bailyn, *The Peopling of British North America: An Introduction* (New York: Random House, 1988), pp. 20–5; Alison Games, *Migration and the Origins of the English Atlantic World* (Cambridge, MA: Harvard University Press, 1999), pp. 13–41. On colonies as outlets for excess population see Beer, *Origins*, pp. 32–52, which differentiates fear of overpopulation from anxiety about unemployment; Abbot Emerson Smith, *Colonists in Bondage: White Servitude and Convict Labor in America, 1607–1776* (New York: W. W. Norton, 1971), pp. 6–7, 44–5, 138; David Armitage, *The Ideological Origins of the British Empire* (Cambridge: Cambridge University Press, 2000), pp. 74–5; Alan Taylor, *American Colonies: The Settling of North America* (New York: Penguin, 2001), pp. 118–23; Timothy Sweet, *American Georgics: Economy and Environment in Early American Literature* (Philadelphia: University of Pennsylvania Press, 2002), pp. 16–17; Slack, *Invention of Improvement*, p. 126.

[68] See Nicholas Canny, *Kingdom and Colony: Ireland in the Atlantic World, 1560–1800* (Baltimore, MD: Johns Hopkins University Press, 1988); Jane H. Ohlmeyer, "'Civilizinge of Those Rude Partes': Colonization within Britain and Ireland, 1580s-1640s," and Nicholas Canny, "England's New World and the Old, 1480s-1630s," both in Nicholas Canny (ed.), *The Origins of Empire: British Overseas Enterprise to the Close of the Seventeenth Century* (Oxford: Oxford University Press, 1998), pp. 124–46 and 148–69; Andrew Hadfield, "Irish Colonies and the Americas," in Robert Applebaum and John Wood Sweet (eds.), *Envisioning an English Empire: Jamestown and the Making of the North Atlantic World* (Philadelphia: University of Pennsylvania Press, 2005), pp. 172–91. Horning, *Ireland in the Virginian Sea*, argues that Ireland was not a "testing ground" for New World colonialism. Yet distinctions between English knowledge of Ireland and of the New World, and between conditions of cross-cultural interaction in each, can be acknowledged without denying political, intellectual and other continuities.

natural and artificial aspects of situation shaped how human mutability could or should be managed over time.

Among the first authors to carry Elizabethan ideas of demographic governance into an Atlantic colonial context was Richard Hakluyt the younger, Church of England cleric, chronicler of travel and trade, and aspiring royal advisor.[69] His *Discourse of Western Planting* (as it came to be known) began as a policy paper written for Elizabeth at the request of Sir Francis Walsingham in 1584. It followed close on the heels of Hakluyt's synopsis of Aristotle's *Politics*, which played up the importance of "colonies" (*coloni*, villages) of families to the inculcation of virtue and hence to the health of the *polis*.[70] Hakluyt's purpose in the *Discourse* was to argue for English expansion. He appealed to several grounds: spreading "the glorious gospell of Christe," countering Spanish disruptions of seaborne commerce, restoring decayed trades, employing the idle and bridling the ambitions of Philip II.[71] The geopolitical cast of his arguments notwithstanding, Hakluyt echoed his contemporaries' thoughts on the role of policy in reforming "multitudes of loyterers and idle vagabondes" and "draw[ing] the Irishe … to more civilitie," exploiting mobility and mutability to that end.[72] What set him apart was that his locus of regeneration was an ocean away, a strategic point in a world of competing empires and creeds.

A global setting implied global numbers. Intimations of these appeared at several points in the *Discourse*. The most obvious contexts for thinking about world population in the sixteenth century, as for centuries earlier, were scriptural exegesis and sacred history. Exploration and expansion problematized both. While New World populations had to be reconciled with Noachic genealogy, Old World historical records challenged biblical chronology, necessitating the rapid population of the earth after the Great Flood. Scholars had recourse to ingenious speculations about ancient longevity, fertility and the relative demographic effects of the ante- and post-diluvian environments.[73] Hakluyt's longtime contact Sir Walter Ralegh

[69] See Peter Mancall, *Hakluyt's Promise: An Elizabethan's Obsession for an English America* (New Haven, CT: Yale University Press, 2007).
[70] Armitage, *Ideological Origins*, pp. 72–4.
[71] Richard Hakluyt, *A Discourse Concerning Western Planting Written in the Year 1584*, edited by Charles Deane (Cambridge, MA: John Wilson and Son, 1877), pp. 8–49.
[72] Hakluyt, *Discourse*, pp. 36, 85.
[73] See Patrick Wyse Jackson, *The Chronologers' Quest: Episodes in the Search for the Age of the Earth* (Cambridge: Cambridge University Press, 2006), pp. 13–31; James Barr, "Pre-Scientific Chronology: The Bible and the Origin of the World," *Proceedings of the American Philosophical Society* 143:3 (1999), 379–87. On the legacy of these arguments, see Buchwald and Feingold, *Newton and the Origin of Civilization*, pp. 164–94; McCormick, "Political Arithmetic and Sacred History," 829–57.

absorbed these apologetic strategies into his discussion of population in his unfinished *History of the World* (1614), and puzzled over the source of the New World's inhabitants, even raising the specter of polygenism.[74] A scriptural lens colored Hakluyt's view of the present, too. He gestured to the "infinite multitudes of these simple people that are in error," dangling "the gayninge of the souls of millions of these wretched people" for Christ before his readers' eyes and decrying Spain's "boastinge of [its] conversion of such multitudes of infidells" as a distortion of the atrocities and false religion of the *conquistadores* and the Inquisition.[75] The world was filled with numbers of souls, to be parceled out among empires and churches fighting for their conversion.

But many kinds of numbers – spectral and solid, real and imagined, future and past – populated Hakluyt's vision of imperial competition, and different kinds had conflicting implications. If vague numbers of real heathen souls might motivate English empire, specific numbers of imaginary Spaniards sustained Philip's tyrannical regime:

> Phillippe rather governethe in the West Indies by opinion, then by mighte; ffor the small manred of Spaine, of itself beinge always at the best slenderly peopled, was never able to rule so many regions, or to kepe in subjection such worldes of people as be there, were it not for the error of the Indian people … that doe ymagine that Phillippe hath a thousande Spaniardes for every single naturall subjecte that he hath there.[76]

This is not to say that opinion alone mattered. Calculators with knowledge of the relevant territories could explode implausible claims. For example, "any reasonable man that knoweth the barenes, desolation, and wante of men in Spaine" after two decades of war could reckon how "denuded" and "dispeopled" its empire must be.[77] Reports of the "more then Turkish cruelties" of Spanish rule in the Americas, too, included empirical information from which to work.[78] Here Hakluyt married shockingly large

---

[74] See Bonar, *Theories of Population*, pp. 11–39; Ernest A. Strathmann, "Ralegh on the Problems of Chronology," *Huntington Library Quarterly* 11:2 (1948), 129–48; Popkin, *Isaac La Peyrère*, pp. 35–6. On the *History*, see Nicholas Popper, *Walter Ralegh's History of the World and the Historical Culture of the Late Renaissance* (Chicago: University of Chicago Press, 2012). On the implications of biblical criticism for ideas about human origins and diversity, see Colin Kidd, *The Forging of Races: Race and Scripture in the Protestant Atlantic World, 1600–2000* (Cambridge: Cambridge University Press, 2006), pp. 54–78; Livingstone, *Adam's Ancestors*.

[75] Hakluyt, *Discourse*, pp. 8, 10, 12.

[76] Hakluyt, *Discourse*, pp. 56. See Mancall, *Hakluyt's Promise*, p. 147.

[77] Hakluyt, *Discourse*, p. 62.

[78] Hakluyt, *Discourse*, p. 71. Hakluyt cited Bartholomé de Las Casas, whose *Brevísima relación de la destrucción de las Indias* (1552) had been translated into English (via French) and printed the year before: Las Casas, *The Spanish Colonie, or Briefe Chronicle of the Acts and Gestes of the*

numbers to compelling territorial specificity: "of above three millions of soules" once living in Hispaniola, "there are not nowe twoo hundreth natives of the contrie."[79] The story was similar in Cuba, Jamaica and dozens of other islands: "in some of these isles more then five hundred thousand soules, and at this day there is not one only creature"; "All those iles conteyne above twoo thousande leagues and lande, and all are dispeopled and laid waste."[80] The story was similar on the mainland, an area that would reach from Seville to Jerusalem. Hakluyt closed with a grim global estimate: in all "there are deade more then fiftene millions of soules."[81]

The same fusion of scale and precision marked Hakluyt's predictions of an English empire's benefits. Here numbers were not ghosts of past extermination but premonitions of industry and growth. Hakluyt estimated that English trade had employed 14,000 people in Antwerp before its disruption; once new, colonial trades made good the loss of old, "it followeth, that the like number of people ... shal be sett on worke in England of our poore subjectes more than hath beene."[82] This inference fed optimistic extrapolation. Though Hakluyt agreed that "wee are growen mor populous than ever heretofore," and beset by "many thousandes of idle persons," empire could draw the sting of overpopulation:

> [W]here fooles for the swarminge of beggers alleage that the realme is too populous, Salomon saieth, that the honour and strengthe of a prince consisteth in the multitude of the people [Proverbs 14:28]. And if this come aboute, that worke may be had for the multitude, where the realme hath nowe one thousand for the defense hereof, the same may have five thousande.[83]

Economistic as it sounds, this prospectus resembled chronologists' apologetic projections of postdiluvian reproduction. Just as scriptural chronology dictated that what might have been must have been, the call to empire insisted that what could be would come to pass. Like humankind's beginning, England's future was one of boundless plenty:

> For when people knowe howe to live, and howe to mayneteyne and feede their wyves and children, they will not abstaine from mariage as nowe they

Spaniardes in the West Indies, Called the Newe World, for the Space of XL. Yeeres, translated by M. M. S. (London: Printed [by Thomas Dawson] for William Brome, 1583); see Mancall, *Hakluyt's Promise*, pp. 109–10.

[79] Hakluyt, *Discourse*, p. 73.
[80] Hakluyt, *Discourse*, pp. 73–4.
[81] Hakluyt, *Discourse*, p. 74. Las Casas had claimed 12 million; Mancall, *Hakluyt's Promise*, pp. 150–1.
[82] Hakluyt, *Discourse*, pp. 40, 42.
[83] Hakluyt, *Discourse*, pp. 37, 43.

doe. And the soile thus aboundinge with corne, fleshe, mylke, butter, cheese, herbes, rootes, and frutes, &c., and the seas that envyron the same so infynitely aboundinge in fishe, I dare truly affirme, that if the nomber in this realme were as greate as Spaine and Ffraunce have, the people being industrious, I say, there should be founde victualls ynoughe … to suffice them all.[84]

Hakluyt's emphasis on employment as the lynchpin of growth was not a matter of merely secular economy. It rested on God's Protestant sympathies and Nature's bounty.

It also depended on the transformative potential of planned mobility in specific situations. Hakluyt noted expansion's effects on particular groups. Seaborne empire would "breed" seamen.[85] Settlement among the heathen would reform clergymen "which by reason of idlenes here at home are nowe always coyninge of newe opinions."[86] "[T]he frye of the wandringe beggars of England that growe upp ydly" – wild rogues – could be saved from the gallows by being "unlade" and "better bredd upp" in colonies. Waste people and "waste countries" would improve each other.[87] Thieves would find redemption cutting wood in Newfoundland, working mines to the south or "plantinge … sugar canes, as the Portingales have done in Madera"; growing cotton, grain or fruit, "as the Portigales have done in the Azores"; dressing hides, gathering salt, hunting seals, packing feathers. Transformations would ramify along circuits of commercial exchange and knowledge production as well as civil government, recrossing the Atlantic and reaching up and down the social scale:

> In somme, the enterprice will mynister matter for all sortes and state of men to worke upon; namely, all several kindes of artificiers, husbandmen, seamen, marchauntes, soulders, capitaines, phisitions, lawyers, devines, cosmographers, hidrographers, astronomers, historiographers; yea, olde folkes, lame persons, women, and younge children, by many meanes … shalbe kepte from idlenes, and be made able by their owne honest and easie labour to finde themselves, without surchardginge others.[88]

Elizabethan statutes attacked idleness by lumping a motley of wastrels together as vagrants, a foreign presence in the body politic. Fusing discourses of depopulation and overpopulation with a nascent pro-natalism, Hakluyt assimilated every conceivable multitude into an industrious

[84] Hakluyt, *Discourse*, p. 43.
[85] Hakluyt, *Discourse*, pp. 3, 5, 89–94.
[86] Hakluyt, *Discourse*, p. 12.
[87] Hakluyt, *Discourse*, pp. 160–1. Timothy Sweet credits Hakluyt's namesake and cousin Richard Hakluyt (the elder) with coining the phrase "waste people"; Sweet, *American Georgics*, p. 20.
[88] Hakluyt, *Discourse*, pp. 37–8.

population distributed across continents, governed, civilized and set to work by imperial machinery.[89]

This machinery ran on colonial "commodities": the gold, silver, iron, salt, tar, timber, oil, fruit, fish and fowl to be caught, cut, gathered, packed, shipped and sold by half the groups Hakluyt named by, with or for goods and knowledge the other half supplied.[90] In turn, the key to commodities, their physical matrix, was "scituation." As in Botero, so in Hakluyt this was multifaceted, including location, salubrity, temperature, topography and even the nature of local inhabitants.[91] In relation to natural productions, however, it was first of all a matter of latitude, itself often synonymous with climate.[92] Thus, it was because England's putative American empire was "aunswerable in clymate to Barbary Egipte, Siria, Persia, Turky, Greece, all the islandes of the Levant sea, Italie, Spaine, Portingale, Fraunce, Flaunders, Highe Almayne, Denmark, Estland, Poland, and Muscovye" that Hakluyt believed it would "presently or within a shorte space afford us ... eyther all or a greate parte of the commodities" those countries produced.[93] But as this last phrase indicated, commodities "naturally" suited to the American climate might need to be transplanted from distant (though "answerable") locales by calculated, coordinated human effort.[94] With respect to botanical and human transplantations alike, situation was at once a condition and a product of the perfective power of art.

Hakluyt set the tone for subsequent colonialist arguments. In 1588, Thomas Hariot (or Harriot), a mathematician, atomist, teacher of Ralegh and visitor to Roanoke, promoted Virginian plantation in a work now best known for Theodore De Bry's engravings for the second edition, based on John White's paintings.[95] Commodities, fruits of situation, framed

[89] See Mancall, *Hakluyt's Promise*, pp. 143–5.
[90] On the meanings of "commodity" see Sweet, *American Georgics*, pp. 12–14.
[91] Hakluyt, *Discourse*, p. 21.
[92] See Karen Ordahl Kupperman, "The Puzzle of the American Climate in the Early Colonial Period," *American Historical Review* 87:5 (1982), 1262–89; Karen Ordahl Kupperman, *The Jamestown Project* (Cambridge, MA: Harvard University Press, 2009), pp. 158–62.
[93] Hakluyt, *Discourse*, p. 19.
[94] On later ideas of anthropogenic climate change, see Anya Zilberstein, *A Temperate Empire: Making Climate Change in Early America* (Oxford: Oxford University Press, 2016); Brant Vogel, "The Letter from Dublin: Climate Change, Colonialism, and the Royal Society in the Seventeenth Century," *Osiris* 26 (2011), 111–28.
[95] Thomas Hariot, *A Briefe and True Report of the New Found Land of Virginia of the Commodities and of the Nature and Manners of the Naturall Inhabitants* (Frankfurt: Typis Ioannis Wecheli, sumtibus vero Theodori de Bry, 1590). The first edition, lacking images, was printed at London in 1588. On Hariot's tract, see Raymond Phineas Stearns, *Science in the British Colonies of America* (Urbana: University of Illinois Press, 1970), pp. 68–71; Bauer, *Alchemy of Conquest*, pp. 401–8.

Hariot's tract: its three "parts" dealt with "Marchantable Commodities," "Commodities ... for victuall" (including a favorable description of maize) and miscellaneous information for planters, including "the nature and manners of the people" living there.[96] Like Hakluyt, Hariot grounded his optimism about the land's potential in latitude, "the nature of the climate being answerable to the Iland of Iapan, the land of China, Persia, Jury, the Ilands of Cyprus and Candy, the South parts of Greece, Italy, and Spaine."[97] Hariot brought more than a promoter's goggles to population questions, however. As "England's preeminent mathematician," he supplied Ralegh with historical demographic figures and tried to show in a manuscript of his own that "the issue from one man & one woman in 240 yeares may be more than can inhabit the whole earth" – at once a global vision of human numbers and a useful point for defenses of orthodox scriptural chronology.[98] Hariot was as engaged with demographic quantification as anyone could be.

In the *Brief and True Report*, the key demographic event was Indigenous mortality: not the dispeopling of continents by the millions, but local devastation by disease. Wherever the English found themselves challenged by any "subtile deuise," Hariot related, "within a few dayes ... the people began to die very fast ... in some townes about twentie, in some fourtie, in some sixtie, & in one six score, which in trueth was very many in respect of their numbers."[99] Far from indicating the insalubrity of the situation, this was – and was seen by English and Indigenous observers to be – exceptional, attributable either to the "invisible bullets" of English prayers or to the providential punishment of native transgressions.[100] (New England settlers would also interpret massive Indigenous mortality as a form of divine assistance.)[101] It underlined Hariot's claim that "in

---

On his mathematical and philosophical work, see Mordechai Feingold, *The Mathematicians' Apprenticeship: Science, Universities and Society in England, 1560–1640* (Cambridge: Cambridge University Press, 1984), pp. 104, 135–8; Christoph Meinel, "Early Seventeenth-Century Atomism: Theory, Epistemology, and the Insufficiency of Experiment," *Isis* 79:1 (March 1988), 68–103; Joyce E. Chaplin, *Subject Matter: Technology, the Body, and Science on the Anglo-American Frontier, 1500–1676* (Cambridge, MA: Harvard University Press, 2001), pp. 29–30, 125–7. On de Bry's illustrations, see Mancall, *Hakluyt's Promise*, pp. 195–6, 205–7; Bauer, *Alchemy of Conquest*, pp. 408–22.

[96] Hariot, *Briefe and True Report*, p. 15 (maize).
[97] Hariot, *Briefe and True Report*, p. 31.
[98] Feingold and Buchwald, *Newton*, p. 170.
[99] Hariot, *Briefe and True Report*, p. 28.
[100] Hariot, *Briefe and True Report*, p. 29; Greenblatt, *Shakespearean Negotiations*, pp. 21–30.
[101] See John Winthrop, "Reasons to Be Considered for Justifying the Undertakers of the Intended Plantation in New England and for Encouraging Such Whose Hearts Shall Move to Join with Them in It" (1629), in Samuel Eliot Moryson et al. (eds.), *Winthrop Papers*, vol. 2: *1623–1630*

respect of troubling our inhabiting and planting" the native inhabitants "were not to be feared." Their numbers were small, their largest town an affair "but of 30. houses."[102] Qualitative observations abetted quantitative claims: the people themselves were eminently malleable. Though "poor" and lacking "skill and iudgement" in European arts, they were "very ingenious" and apt "in short time" to be civilized and converted.[103] Virginian nature would succumb to European art.

Efforts to settle Roanoke repeatedly failed, but in 1606 James I chartered the Virginia Company, and from 1607 a colony took shape at Jamestown. Hope sprang anew. Robert Gray's 1609 promotional tract, *A Good Speed to Virginia*, said little about situation but expounded a familiar vision of policy as an art of transformative demographic and territorial governance. Gray placed overpopulation and plantation in a scriptural context. He quoted the Book of Joshua on Israel's growth and the consequent dispossession of the Canaanites and applied the moral to the Americas: "although the Lord hath giuen the earth to the children of men ... the greater part of it [is] possessed & wrongfully vsurped by wild beasts, and vnreasonable creatures, or by brutish savages."[104] England's demographic case matched Israel's. There once had been "roome enough in the land for euery man," "a surplussage of necessities" and "preferment in due correspondencie, for all degrees and sorts of men" – enough to maintain both numbers and distinctions of quality; now the country was blessed and "pestered with multitude," "ouercharged with swarmes of people," disordered and overcrowded in a land "too narrow for vs." The time had come to "imbrace euery occasion which hath any probabilitie" of alleviating the problem – including the "strange proiects" of transatlantic empire.[105] Like a second Joshua, the "faithfull and godly Prince" James I could provide for his children by supporting colonial adventures.[106]

Exegetical matters aside, Gray's thoughts on multiplication resembled Botero's (by then in print in English). He dismissed ancient and modern

(Boston, MA: Massachusetts Historical Society, 1931), pp. 138–45, at 141: "God hath consumed the Natiues with a great Plauge in those partes, so as there be few Inhabitantes lefte."
[102] Hariot, *Briefe and True Report*, p. 24.
[103] Hariot, *Briefe and True Report*, p. 25. De Bry's inclusion of several images "of the Pictes which in the olde tyme dyd habite" Britain likely underlined Hariot's stress on the transformative effects of civilization; but Hadfield, "Irish Colonies," pp. 181–6, argues that the images might instead have called Irish savagery to mind.
[104] Robert Gray, *A Good Speed to Virginia* (London: Printed by Felix Kyngston for William Welbie, 1609), sigs. B1r–B1v.
[105] Gray, *Good Speed to Virginia*, sigs. B2r–B2v.
[106] Gray, *Good Speed to Virginia*, sigs. B2v–B3r. Gray modified some implications of this typology, preferring the conversion of American "idolaters" to their destruction (sig. C1v).

attempts to restrain growth and quoted Proverbs 14:28 even as he qualified it territorially:

> There is nothing more daungerous for the estate of common-wealths, then when the people do increase to a greater multitude and number then may iustly parallel with the largeness of the place and countrey: for here-upon comes oppression, and diuerse kinde of wrongs, mutinies sedition, commotion, & rebellion, scarcitie, dearth, pouertie, and sundrie sorts of calamities[.][107]

Though Gray used corporeal metaphor to express the perils of overpopulation, he did so loosely, likening excessive numbers of people to "too much bloud in the body" at one moment and to nurslings draining the polity of its milk the next.[108] The body politic was a trove of evocative imagery rather than a framework for grasping ailments or cures. It could hardly be otherwise: Gray's remedy for the "degenerate and dunghill minds" overpopulation created lay not in restoring them to their places within the commonwealth but in "disburdening" it of their weight by moving them outside.[109]

At the same time, Gray echoed Botero's horticultural image of overpopulation – plants crammed in a nursery – invoking agriculture and apiculture to capture the territorial demands of growing population as well as the power of art over land and people:

> [M]any Nations perceyuing their people to increase aboue a due and proportionable number ... have sent their ouerflowing multitudes abroade into other countreyes and prouinces, to the ends they might preserue their owne in greater peace and prosperitie: so we see ye husbandman deale with his grounds when they are ouercharged with cattell, he remoues them from one ground to another, and so he prouideth [w?]ell both for his cattel and for his ground: and so doth the maister of the bee-garden, when his sees a hiue pestered with multitudes of bees, he driues the hiue, & so reapeth [?] greater gaine by his ware and honie.[110]

Rather than restricting the multitude to a "due and proportionable number," the king and the commercial and colonial agencies under his aegis were to cultivate growing, changing populations. This implied an elastic imperial geography to accommodate transplantations and an expansive temporal horizon for planning and evaluating colonial enterprise: "we are not borne like beasts for our selues, and the time present only ... posteritie

[107] Gray, *Good Speed to Virginia*, sig. B3v.
[108] Gray, *Good Speed to Virginia*, sig. B4r.
[109] Gray, *Good Speed to Virginia*, sigs. B4r–C1r.
[110] Gray, *Good Speed to Virginia*, sigs. B3v–B4r.

and the age yet ensuing haue not the least part in our life & labours."[111]
Future transformations, not present profits, underwrote the colonial project. "[I]f Art and industrie be vsed, as helpes to Nature," he argued – "Art
in cutting downe the trees and making the Countrie champion: Industrie
by taking paines to conquer and cast out those idolatrous Cananites, & to
plant themselves" – everything was possible. And "of all humane Artes,"
Gray wrote, "Politicall gouernment is the chiefest."[112]

Events in Virginia underscored the need for political government
to compel "so heady a multitude" to labor and manage the conflicting
interests of the groups involved.[113] William Strachey survived the wreck
of the *Sea Venture* in 1609 to find Jamestown on the verge of abandonment and reported the suppression of a series of mutinous plots in his
"True Reportory of the Wreck and Redemption of Sir Thomas Gates."
Remarking on the need for governors "to compel the adversant and irregular multitude," Strachey described the imposition of military discipline
in the colony by Gates, Thomas West (Baron De La Warr), and other
veterans of war in the Low Countries.[114] Yet he assured potential settlers
that Virginia "could produce as many fair births of plenty and increase"
as "any land under the heaven to which the sun is no nearer a neighbor";
given its "situation," industry and a suitable "form of government" were
all that was needed.[115] This form was not fixed. The coming of tobacco
in the 1620s brought new commercial prospects to territorial expansion,
deepening tensions between private profit, public order and security, and
helping to provoke the "Great Massacre" of 1622, the dissolution of the
Company and its replacement by royal authority in 1624.[116] Whatever the
flaws in planning or organization, however, the same conceptual links
between environment, art and policy continued to shape the mobilization
and improvement of populations in the nascent English empire.

---

[111] Gray, *Good Speed to Virginia*, sig. D1r.

[112] Gray, *Good Speed to Virginia*, sig. D2r.

[113] [William Strachey], "A True Reportory of the Wreck and Redemption of Sir Thomas Gates,
Knight, upon and from the Islands of the Bermudas: His Coming to Virginia and the Estate of
that Colony Then and After, under the Government of the Lord La Warr, July 15, 1610," in Louis
B. Wright (ed.), *A Voyage to Virginia in 1609: Two Narratives: Strachey's "True Reportory" and
Jourdain's Discovery of the Bermudas* (Charlottesville: University Press of Virginia, 1964), p. 65.

[114] [Strachey], "True Reportory," pp. 1–101. See Frederic W. Gleach, *Powhatan's World and Colonial
Virginia: A Conflict of Cultures* (Lincoln: University of Nebraska Press, 1997), pp. 74–5, 130–1.

[115] [Strachey], "True Reportory," pp. 51, 69, 77–8.

[116] See James Horn, "Tobacco Colonies: The Shaping of English Society in the Seventeenth-
Century Chesapeake," in Nicholas Canny (ed.), *Origins of Empire: British Overseas Enterprise to
the Close of the Seventeenth Century* (Oxford: Oxford University Press, 1998), pp. 170–92; Sweet,
American Georgics, p. 37; Gleach, *Powhatan's World*, pp. 3–4, 123–58.

Twelve years after Strachey's tour (and just weeks after the "Great Massacre" of 300 settlers), Patrick Copland reiterated Gray's optimism and his idea of demographic governance in a thanksgiving sermon to the Virginia Company in London.[117] Copland was a Scottish Presbyterian and former East India Company chaplain, and he sustained claims about Virginia's situation and commodities by appeal to his own "travailing to India and Iapan," confident that "if there be any odds, Virginia hath them."[118] His sermon celebrated the "happie ... landing of 800. People Men, Women, and children, all in health" and dwelt upon the colony's improving demographic record, expressed in number and proportion: "not one (but one, in whose roome there was another borne) of eight hundred" was lost in the recent voyage, "whereas in your former voyages scarce 80. of a 100. arrived safely in Virginia."[119] Such sparing use of "Gods rod of Mortality" was a sign of approval, as was the "voluntary" removal of "the Saluages" to make space for the colony, even "against the course of nature."[120] Providential prompts and favorable situation combined with the pressure of "number and multitude" at home set the stage for colonial settlement to do its demographic work. Copland repeated Gray's comparison of colonial expansion to husbandry almost verbatim. (He inserted passages lauding the London government's role as a "prudent and prouident husbandman" in "transporting of their overflowing multitude into Virginia," suggesting parallels between the colony and the hospital as objects of metropolitan munificence and as engines of human reclamation.)[121] Planned mobility defused domestic tensions and turned poor children into "men able to liue of themselues," "profitable to the Plantation, and to the Cittie" – a "conuersion" hardly less drastic that the saving of heathen souls.[122]

By the mid-1620s, Virginia was a locus of demographic transformation in fact, as well as in the promoters' projections. From the start, the majority of emigrants were poor servants, shipped initially for rental to settlers on Company land, and later as indentured labor for sale to private planters.[123] Other troublesome groups were also subject to transplantation.

---

[117] Patrick Copland, *Virginia's God Be Thanked, or a Sermon of Thanksgiving for the Happie Successe of the Affayres in Virginia this Last Yeare* (London: Printed by I. D. for William Sheffard and Iohn Bellamie, 1622), pp. 30–2.

[118] Copland, *Virginia's God Be Thanked*, p. 12.

[119] Copland, *Virginia's God Be Thanked*, pp. 2, 10.

[120] Copland, *Virginia's God Be Thanked*, pp. 24–6.

[121] Copland, *Virginia's God Be Thanked*, p. 31.

[122] Copland, *Virginia's God Be Thanked*, p. 32.

[123] Smith, *Colonists in Bondage*, pp. 8–16.

From 1617, the Lord Mayor of London had authorized the collection of funds to send poor children to the colony, and at least two shipments (the first of 100 transplantees) ensued.[124] Under Elizabethan statute, vagrants could be banished from the realm, though few were so sentenced; more commonly they were committed to Bridewell and made available to colonial merchants by the hospital itself.[125] By 1619, poor women were being sent as potential brides for colonists.[126] How well the results answered the projectors' promises is another question. The unruliness of the colonial multitude was a perpetual concern, exacerbated by demographic growth, the spread of tobacco and disruptive proselytism. If plantation did not reverse degeneration as hoped, however, it did turn poor English men, women and children into agents of territorial expansion, agricultural improvement and commercial profit.

From the point of view of demographic governance, the case of New England offers both parallels and contrasts with Virginia. Surveying arguments for plantation in 1629, the founder of the Massachusetts Bay Colony, John Winthrop, alluded to overpopulation as a matter of both excess number and moral degeneration: "This Land growes weary of her Inhabitantes," he wrote, "soe as man whoe is the most praetious of all creatures, is here more vile and base then the earth we treade vpon, and of lesse prise among vs then an horse or a sheepe."[127] Parishes struggled to maintain the poor families, their children and servants. "Intemperance" reigned among those with means; unnatural laws sought to restrain rather than sustain multiplication.[128] William Bradford, whose community had relocated to Leiden ten years before planting what became the Plymouth colony, similarly feared that his "posterity would be in danger to degenerate and be corrupted" if they stayed in place.[129] Though tinged with Puritan concerns, this was not out of line with earlier arguments for other projects. New England was imagined as an open space for settlement and multiplication – part "of those vast and unpeopled countries of America ... devoid of all civil inhabitants," as Bradford put it; "a whole Continent ... [lying] waste without any improuement," in Winthrop's words.[130]

---

[124] Smith, *Colonists in Bondage*, pp. 12, 148–9.
[125] Smith, *Colonists in Bondage*, pp. 137–41.
[126] Smith, *Colonists in Bondage*, p. 12.
[127] Winthrop, "Reasons," p. 139.
[128] Winthrop, "Reasons," p. 139.
[129] William Bradford, *Of Plymouth Plantation, 1620–1647* (New York: Random House, 1981), p. 26.
[130] Bradford, *Plymouth Plantation*, p. 26; Winthrop, "Reasons," p. 139.

The regeneration Bradford and Winthrop sought in New England, however, was of a more voluntary and austere sort than the empire touted by Hakluyt, a matter less of material profit or strategic advantage than of spiritual refuge. From our perspective, this distinction is one of degree, but the degree was significant enough to set Puritan descriptions of the colonial enterprise apart with respect to the context of demographic governance. For the Puritans described their goal as the formation of "an absolute church of themselves," independent and self-sufficient: a community in exile, not an instrumental extension of the metropole.[131] If corporeal analogy was loosening its hold on secular politics, organic "unity" remained central to most contemporary conceptions of religious community.[132] Bradford stressed the Plymouth settlers' conception of themselves as a fully fledged "body politic," an idea enshrined in the Mayflower Compact.[133] This was reinforced in practice by the fact that, in contrast to Virginia's largely single, male labor force, New England settlers commonly emigrated as intact families, natural units and building blocks of a polity.[134] Winthrop's "city upon a hill" was no hospital or workhouse writ large. Nor was it primarily a mechanism for the pacification or civilization of disaffected subjects on the margins of the realm, as sundry Irish plantations pretended. Nor was it to be a source of rich mines, exotic luxuries or cash crops as Virginia was becoming and as the Caribbean plantations were to be. (Nor, as Ralph Bauer observes, was it initially envisioned as a source of Indigenous converts to Christian civilization.)[135] New England thus fit imperial visions of demographic governance imperfectly – the more so once fear of overpopulation gave way, later in the century, to the belief that the colonies were draining metropolitan numbers.

On the other hand, situation played a major role in promoting New England, if not as a source of commodities then as a site of settlement. William Wood, about whom little is known other than that he spent time in Massachusetts, devoted the first part of *Nevv Englands Prospect*

---

[131] Bradford, *Plymouth Plantation*, p. 38.

[132] See Francis Bacon, "Of Unity in Religion," in Bacon, *The Essays or Counsels Civil and Moral* (1625), reprinted in Bacon, *Francis Bacon,* edited by Brian Vickers (Oxford: Oxford University Press, 1996), pp. 344–7.

[133] Bradford, *Plymouth Plantation*, pp. 57, 84.

[134] See Games, *Migration*, pp. 42–71. See also John Demos, *A Little Commonwealth: Family Life in Plymouth Colony*, 2nd ed. (New York: Oxford University Press, 2000); Ruth H. Bloch, *Gender and Morality in Anglo-American Culture, 1650–1800* (Berkeley: University of California Press, 2003), pp. 42–54; Joseph A. Conforti, *Saints and Strangers: New England in British North America* (Baltimore, MD: Johns Hopkins University Press, 2006), pp. 34, 44–5.

[135] Bauer, *Alchemy of Conquest*, p. 423.

(1634) to "the Situation," weather, climate, soil, flora and fauna of the region (the second part described different Indigenous groups and their relations with the English).[136] As in discussions of Virginia, situation took in latitude, location and topography – especially coastal features, with an eye to shipping.[137] But when Wood passed to climate and soil, he focused not on the potential for raising exotic plants but rather on the fitness of the region for "the temper of our English bodies" and its susceptibility to English improvements.[138] Indeed, as Timothy Sweet has noted, Wood argued that New England was better for English bodies than England itself.[139] Where English coastal "situations are counted most unwholesome," New England was "not often troubled with Mists, or unwholesome fogges, or cold weather from the Sea."[140] The harshness of its winters foretold "pleasant Spring-times, and fertile Summers, being iudged likewise to make much for the health of our English bodies," unlike Virginia, where "extreame hot Summers, hath dried up much English blood, and by pestiferous diseases swept away many lusty bodies, changing their complexion … into Palenesse."[141] Mobility to Virginia brought degeneration, a loss of English "complexion." The New England climate, by contrast, was preservative, even regenerative: "both men and women keepe their naturall complexions," and "If the Sunne doth tanne any, yet the Winters cold restores them … and as it is for the outward complexion, so it is for the inward constitution."[142]

Like Copland for Virginia, Wood grounded his claims for New England in demographic experience. In a manner that would mark colonial commentary throughout the period, personal observation and secondhand anecdote bled into the quantitative and classificatory language of bills and registers even as they echoed the environmental speculations of sacred history:

> I never knew any that had the Poxe, Measels, Greene-Sicknesse, Headaches, Stone, or Consumptions, &c. Many that have come infirm out of England, retaine their old grievances … and some that were long troubled

[136] William Wood, *Nevv Englands Prospect. A True, Lively and Experimentall Description of That Part of America, Commonly Called Nevv England: Discovering the State of That Countrie, Both As It Stands to Our New-Come English Planters; and to the Old Native Inhabitants* (London: Printed by Tho. Coates for Iohn Bellamie, 1634).
[137] Wood, *Nevv Englands Prospect*, pp. 1–3.
[138] Wood, *Nevv Englands Prospect*, p. 3.
[139] Sweet, *American Georgics*, p. 50.
[140] Wood, *Nevv Englands Prospect*, pp. 3–4.
[141] Wood, *Nevv Englands Prospect*, pp. 7–9.
[142] Wood, *Nevv Englands Prospect*, p. 9.

with lingering diseases, as Coughs of the lungs, Consumptions, &c. have beene restored by that medicineable Climate to their former strength and health. God hath beene pleased so to blesse men in the health of their bodies, that … out of that Towne from whence I came, in three yeares and a halfe, there dyed but three, one of which was crazed before he came into the Land; the other were two Children borne at one birth before their time…. To make good which losses, I have seene foure Children Baptized at a time, which wipes away that common aspersion, that women have no Children … there being as sweete lusty Children as in any other Nation, and reckoning so many for so many, more double births than in England[.][143]

A Londoner reading Wood's list of diseases might recall the headings of the weekly mortality bills. Wood could scarcely have been ignorant of these, so perhaps this was intended.[144] The learned reader, meanwhile, would see parallels between New England's fertility and chronologists' picture of the early postdiluvian Earth, where frequent births of twins had providentially accelerated the population of a new world.[145] Population was a matter of numbers: four births here compensated three deaths there. But numbers were neither merely secular nor independent of their environment. They were clues to situation, to the nexus between God's creation and humankind's art.

Looking to it as a new England rather than a surrogate Japan, Wood described colonial territory as a site of improvement. This led him, as Sweet notices, into a second paradox:

> For the naturall soyle, I preferre it before the countrey of Surry, or Middlesex, which if they were not inriched with continuall manurings, would be lesse fertile than the meanest ground in New England; wherefore it is neyther impossible, nor much improbable, that upon improvements the soile may be as good in time as England.[146]

New England was both naturally superior to improved English soil, and potentially, given improvements, just as good. Confused as this is, Wood was at pains to stress the goodness of the soil *and* its potential, were the "lazie" pattern of Indigenous subsistence to be replaced by English

---

[143] Wood, *Nevv Englands Prospect*, p. 9.
[144] See Robertson, "Reckoning with London"; Jenner, "Plague on a Page." Given the pattern of migration to New England, it is interesting that Wood addressed "women-readers"; see Wood, *Nevv Englands Prospect*, p. 94.
[145] In his *Chronologicarum demonstrationum libri tres* (1596), Johannes Temporarius advanced the idea that Noah's children had borne twins every year; see McCormick, "Political Arithmetic and Sacred History," p. 840. On demographic parallels between New England and the ante- or early postdiluvian world, see McCormick, "Statistics in the Hands of an Angry God."
[146] Wood, *Nevv Englands Prospect*, p. 12; Sweet, *American Georgics*, p. 51.

industry.[147] Over a decade after the "common course" of planting had been abandoned – derided by Bradford as a utopian attempt to circumvent human corruption by "taking away of property and bringing in community" – Wood remarked that "they were much deceived ... that ventured thither in hope to live in plenty and idlenesse" and advised "those men that are of weak constitutions to keepe at home"; "all New England," he wrote, "must be workers in some kinde."[148] Colonial improvement was not child's play: "he must have more than a boyes head, and no lesse than a mans strength, that intends to live comfortably," and he would need money for servants, cattle, buildings and enclosures to do much more than that.[149]

If Virginia's promoters enthused over what nature might provide, Wood emphasized what art could extract. Inasmuch as this shifted the burden of producing wealth from land to labor, it foreshadowed a deepening emphasis on populations as labor forces that is often tied to political arithmetic, explored in Chapter 4. Yet beneath this, a more basic idea persisted: that applying art to nature through planned mobility would improve territory and people alike. In this context, colonization would not only prevent the degeneration and improve the fortunes of settlers but also engender the civilization (figured by Wood as a *good* "degeneration") of the Indigenous inhabitants. Wood saw these as raw but pliable, possessed of strong, healthy bodies, "civility and good natures," "wisedome and pollicie" and, above all, the capacity to adopt the technology of improvement:

> The first plow-man was counted little better than a Iuggler: the Indians seeing the plow teare up more ground in a day, than their Clamme shels could scrape up in a month ... told the plow-man, hee was almost Abamocho, almost as cunning as the Devill; but fresh supplies of new and strange objects hath lessen'd their admiration, and quickned their inventions.... It is thought they would soon learne any mechanicall trades, having quicke wits, understanding apprehensions, strong memories, with nimble inventions, and a quick hand in using of the Axe or Hatchet ... much good might they receive from the English ... if they were not strongly fettered in the chains of idlenesse[.][150]

Just as colonization facilitated the quantitative growth and qualitative transformation of English people, it would break the chains that kept Americans idle. (Whether it would foster their numbers, Wood did not

[147] Wood, *Nevv Englands Prospect*, p. 12.
[148] Bradford, *Plymouth Plantation*, pp. 132–3; Wood, *Nevv Englands Prospect*, p. 48.
[149] Wood, *Nevv Englands Prospect*, pp. 48, 51.
[150] Wood, *Nevv Englands Prospect*, pp. 69, 72, 78.

say.) Wood noted that "already, as they have learned much subtiltie & cunning by bargaining with the English, so have they a little degenerated from some of their lazie customes, and shew themselves more industrious."[151] Interestingly, he also compared American customs and habits to those of the Irish – who, in the 1630s, seemed to have been pacified at last through multiple rounds of British plantation.[152] In New England, he argued, a similar transformation had begun.

The Bounds of Empire

Looking back on 1635 from the perspective of the distant future, the promises and projections surveyed in this chapter seem illusory. England was indeed on the verge of a new phase of state-building and imperial expansion, but neither in the way Hakluyt and his followers would have imagined nor as Bodin or Botero might have advised. New England colonies, in the midst of the Great Migration, were growing and multiplying and, in part for that reason, were coming to be viewed by their founders as a spiritual failure and by their metropolitan overlords as seedbeds of discontent and competition. In 1636, the Pequot War revealed the brutality of the colonial enterprise and the evanescence of any civilizing mission. In Virginia, for different reasons, the growth of plantation similarly threatened its own promise. There and in fledging Caribbean settlements, the glister of improvement faded on the individual level as the land yielded ever-greater wealth to large planters in the form of cash crops. Soon, too, the first indications of a developing slave-labor regime would appear. Back in Britain, meanwhile, idleness, poverty and periodic plague beset the still-growing population. Sweeping these concerns aside, a combination of religious and constitutional tensions would explode in revolt, rebellion and civil wars between 1637 and 1649. In Ireland, starting in 1641, an uprising against the ideas and practices of colonial plantation and English settlement rendered the island a de facto independent state – and, at times, a war zone – for much of the decade. The half-century or so that started with Hakluyt's *Discourse* and Botero's *Delle cause* ended with the Stuart realms in disarray.

Yet that same period witnessed significant and long-lasting changes in the way demographic knowledge and the governance of populations

[151] Wood, *Nevv Englands Prospect*, p. 78.
[152] Wood, *Nevv Englands Prospect*, pp. 65 (clothing), 68 (diet), 93 (mourning). For an overview of Irish developments, see David Edwards, "Political Change and Social Transformation, 1603–1641," in Jane H. Ohlmeyer (ed.), *The Cambridge History of Ireland, Volume II: 1550–1730* (Cambridge: Cambridge University Press, 2018), pp. 48–71.

were conceived and pursued. The idea of the body politic, with all its anatomical, physiological and medical trappings, survived in attenuated form, as a flexible source of powerful imagery rather than a coherent template for identifying and treating social ills. Policy moved further from ad hoc interventions to restore a social or political status quo toward routine activities of government requiring particular information and expertise. Its goal, moreover, was widely understood to be transformative. What Tudor engagements with vagrancy and Irish savagery implied, reason-of-state theorists and colonial promoters avowed: effective rule meant improving the quantity and the quality of people, and this meant measuring their numbers, moving and settling, mixing and unmixing their bodies, and imposing upon or instilling within them the qualities of desirable subjects: political allegiance, true religion and industry. It also meant knowing, improving and where necessary extending the territory they occupied. No single metaphor replaced the body politic, but governance – in its goals, methods and horizons – was incessantly compared with other modes and techniques of improvement and artisanship: agriculture, horticulture, animal husbandry and manual craft. "Politicall gouernment" was, as Gray had said, the chiefest of "humane Artes." Population was its material, territory its context, and situation – an amalgam of environmental features, geographical relations and human interventions – its guide.

This idea of policy as a perfective art, working with but ultimately transforming nature, has clear affinities with the operational idea of science that Francis Bacon advocated in his writings on natural philosophy and experimental method. Bacon's influence on the shape of political arithmetic was great, both through his own printed works and indirectly, via the projecting of the Hartlib Circle. Yet, as this chapter and Chapter 2 have shown, Bacon was but one of several sources for the idea of policy as art, and natural-philosophical discourse but one of several channels of influence – albeit a crucial one for the first political arithmeticians. Much as Deborah Harkness has suggested in another context, Bacon's importance lies in his philosophical appropriation of what others were thinking and doing.[153] As earlier chapters have also shown, the intellectual changes that let writers and projectors of Bacon's day see demographic governance in terms of the planned distribution of people across territories whose natural and artificial characteristics affected multiplication, health and industry were not the product of a sudden rupture. They emerged slowly, haltingly, piecemeal and from multiple directions.

[153] Harkness, *Jewel House*, pp. 211–53.

While Baconian ideas about nature shaped political arithmetic, the texture of demographic thought in Bacon's day is better judged by his popular *Essayes and Counsels, Morall and Civill*, the third edition of which appeared in 1625. His essay "Of Seditions and Troubles" denounced waste and luxury, and called for "the opening and well-balancing of trade; the cherishing of manufactures; the banishing of idleness" and "the improvement and husbanding of the soil." Beneath these jangling demands lay a quasi-Boterian view of governance as the management of population size and quality in relation to territory and resources:

> Generally, it is to be foreseen that the population of a kingdom ... do not exceed the stock of the kingdom which should maintain them. Neither is the population to be reckoned only by number; for a smaller number that spend more and earn less, do wear out an estate sooner than a greater number that live lower and gather more.[154]

The importance of quality as well as quantity reemerged in the essay "Of the True Greatness of Kingdoms and Estates," where Bacon repeated Botero's strictures on the importance of valor, without which numbers made for "great population and little strength."[155] Breeding a stout population meant restraining the multiplication of the nobility; maintaining order meant keeping nobility and commons divided.[156] Citing Roman example, Bacon also advocated liberal naturalization – the conversion of "strangers" into "natural subjects" – as a condition of imperial expansion.[157] In "Of Plantation," finally, he advocated "plantation in a pure soil," without displacement of preexisting inhabitants, without resort to "the scum of the people" to populate the colony, and without "sending too fast company after company" to choke it at birth.[158]

By the second quarter of the seventeenth century, it was possible even without large-scale, regular demographic data gathering to think and write of governance as a never-ending problem of managing the distribution of quantifiable populations across global territorial space so as to cultivate their growth and improvement through time toward an indefinitely distant future. This vision was anchored in the claims and assumptions of reason-of-state thinkers and colonial projectors whose writing appeared

---

[154] Bacon, *Francis Bacon*, p. 368.
[155] Bacon, *Francis Bacon*, pp. 398–9. Bacon compared (399) England and France, "whereof England, though far less in territory and population, hath been (nevertheless) an over-match; in regard the middle people of England make good soldiers, which the peasants of France do not."
[156] Bacon, *Francis Bacon*, pp. 369, 399.
[157] Bacon, *Francis Bacon*, p. 400.
[158] Bacon, *Francis Bacon*, pp. 407–9.

from the 1580s, and in the logistical challenges and material processes of mobilizing, transplanting and resettling large numbers of people across the Atlantic. One could think of this as a birth of population. Yet if, from one side, these theories and processes look pregnant with biopolitical significance, from another angle they can be seen as extensions of smaller-scale movements and mutations of local groups around the metropole and on its margins – adopting and adapting familiar goals even as they made nonsense of the framework of corporeal metaphor that had given qualitative multitudes their meaning. There was as yet no new framework to make sense of these physical populations as the body politic had made sense of functional multitudes. Over the next fifty years, this would change.

CHAPTER 4

Transmutation, Quantification and the Creation of Political Arithmetic

An Invention of Population

To this point, we have traced a shift in the focus of discourses and practices of demographic governance from relations between qualitative multitudes in a body politic to the multiplication and distribution of quantities
of people across expanding territory. These changes became manifest in
bits and pieces, episodically and in diverse ways – they were what Nicholas
Popper has called, in a related context, "improvisational responses to a
volatile social and political terrain."[1] There was no moment of rupture;
mobility and degeneration remained central even as mechanisms of mobilization and mutation were transformed from threats to instruments of
rule. Nor, despite new ideas about the uses of numerical information, can
we tie the shift that concerns us to the rise of quantification in any simple
way. Often, the quantitative language that characterized engagements
with populations in new economic, political and imperial settings was a
matter of verbal references to quantity rather than of actual numbers. This
is not to ignore the proliferation of censuses of the poor, lists of householders, colonial registers and bills of mortality in the decades around 1600.
But these entered into engagements with demographic governance as tools
rather than motors of change. The invention of population created new
contexts for quantification but was not a product of it.

"Invention" is a loaded term. It may seem inappropriate here, if only
because it suggests a creative instant or an epistemic rupture rather
than a complex and sinuous process of conceptual change. It can
also encourage confusion between analytical and historical categories, between "population" as a concept in the modern social sciences
and "population" as whatever human quantum our historical subjects
had in view. As was noted at the outset, in the eyes of many scholars,

---

[1] Nicholas Popper, "An Information State for Elizabethan England," *Journal of Modern History*,
90:3 (2018), 503–35, at 504.

the *invention* of population means the creation of a modern statistical object.[2] Population's modernity as a concept is stipulated before its origins are sought. No wonder, then, if its roots are found in eighteenth- or nineteenth-century anticipations of its typical modern representations, technological accouterments or institutional armatures – registration and surveillance, liberal political economy, scientific regimes of medicine and public health. And no wonder that historians have challenged this view less by questioning the connection between these representations, technologies or institutions and population than by arguing for the emergence of the complex earlier in time.[3] As long as population is defined as the object of modern scientific and governmental appropriations and interventions, it can hardly be otherwise.

Seeing population in terms of transformation as an aim of governance yields a different, nondefinitive, history. The ambition to manipulate the qualities of large groups worked itself out in different ways at different times, through a range of historically contingent discourses, projects and policies; the present account is one of many possible histories of the construction of population. At the same time, emphasizing the contingent relation of specific discourses or projects to a more enduring ambition does not exempt that ambition from historical contextualization. In the transition from the maintenance of a body politic of functional multitudes to the creation of governable subjects through mobilization and plantation, we have seen the emergence of a transformative idea of demographic agency – and of mobile, mutable and measurable populations as its object. Yet this was a response to emergent problems that had analogs, and provoked analogous responses, elsewhere. The evolution of transformative demographic governance in Tudor and Stuart Britain and its colonies helped produce a discourse, a political tradition and an empire of great reach and influence. But as a matter of grappling with the characteristics of large groups in space and time, the invention of population must have happened more than once.

Its English iteration is also significant, however, because it tied the new science of the seventeenth century to state formation and colonial expansion. Here, Francis Bacon was a key figure. Bacon's work has recently drawn new scrutiny. While Deborah Harkness has detailed his appropriation of the work of preexisting communities of scientific amateurs, Vera Keller has emphasized the common ground he shared with Botero, Jakob

---

[2] See Gregory, "Tabulation of England," 318; Charbit, *Classical Foundations of Population Thought*.
[3] See Pincus, "From Holy Cause to Economic Interest."

Bornitz and others.[4] As we have seen, Bacon's engagement with demographic governance in the context of civil government in the *Essays* was in some ways less innovative than Botero's earlier work, and his aspirations for Irish plantation echoed Botero's views on the role of colonies in drawing off excess numbers – and on the advantages of concentrating them in cities.[5] Even in England, neither Bacon's operational view of natural knowledge nor his claims for natural philosophy's political import were unique.[6] They surface in innumerable early seventeenth-century projects – for the improvement of land, the augmentation of timber, the drainage of the fens.[7] Yet Bacon synthesized these developments in a new methodology and an expansive vision of discovery.[8] These became key points of reference for much of the experimental work, projecting and polemic of the Hartlib Circle – the incubator for Petty's and his associates' ideas, and later for the Royal Society. Against an intellectual backdrop that included evolving ideas about reason of state, economy and empire, and the role of information and technology in each, Bacon's dicta and legacy framed the creation of political arithmetic as a way of knowing populations and a mode of projecting their transformation.

Inasmuch as political arithmetic was distinguished by treating populations as a matter of "number, weight and measure," however, Bacon's influence was indirect. In *The Advancement of Learning* (1605), he conventionally

---

[4] On the unity of Bacon's work, compare Julian Martin, *Francis Bacon, the State, and the Reform of Natural Philosophy* (Cambridge: Cambridge University Press, 1991); Markku Peltonen, "Politics and Science: Francis Bacon and the True Greatness of States," *Historical Journal*, 35:2 (1992), pp. 279–305; and Keller, *Knowledge and the Public Interest*, pp. 127–66. See also Carolyn Merchant, *The Death of Nature: Women, Ecology, and the Scientific Revolution* (San Francisco, CA: Harper and Row, 1990), pp. 164–91. On Bacon's appropriations and analogues, see Harkness, *Jewel House*, pp. 211–53; and Keller, *Knowledge and the Public Interest*, pp. 127–66.

[5] These connections are explored in Jamie Trace, "Giovanni Botero and English Political Thought," unpublished Ph.D. thesis, University of Cambridge (2018). See Francis Bacon, "Certain Considerations Touching the Plantation in Ireland, New Year 1609," in Basil Montagu (ed.), *The Works of Francis Bacon, Lord Chancellor of England: A New Edition*, 15 vols. (London: William Pickering, 1825–1834), vol. V, pp. 169–85; reproduced at CELT: Corpus of Electronic Texts (History Department, University College Cork, 2011) [https://celt.ucc.ie//published/E600001-015.html].

[6] On Bacon's idea of "operational" knowledge, see Peter Dear, *Discipline and Experience: The Mathematical Way in the Scientific Revolution* (Chicago: University of Chicago Press, 1995), pp. 155–9; Perez Zagorin, *Francis Bacon* (Princeton, NJ: Princeton University Press, 1998), pp. 93–5.

[7] See most recently Eric H. Ash, *The Draining of the Fens: Projectors, Popular Politics, and State-Building in Early Modern England* (Baltimore. MD: Johns Hopkins University Press, 2017). On Bacon's involvement with the drafting of patents under James I, see Cesare Pastorino, "The Philosopher and the Craftsman: Francis Bacon's Notion of Experiment and Its Debt to Early Stuart Inventors," *Isis* 108:4 (2017), 749–68.

[8] Bauer traces the origins of this conception of discovery to medieval alchemical and eschatological discourse but retains Bacon as its preeminent early modern exponent; Bauer, *Alchemy of Conquest*, pp. 430–70.

described mathematics as being "either Pure or Mixed." Pure mathematics included geometry and arithmetic, both treating of "Quantity determinate" and "severed from any axioms of natural philosophy." Mixed mathematics, on the other hand, dealt with "Quantity determined" in connection with "axioms or parts of natural philosophy"; applications included "Perspective, Music, Astronomy, Cosmography, Architecture, Enginery, and divers others."[9] In these contexts, mathematics acted as an auxiliary instrument in the determination of parts of nature – essential for the purposes of demonstration and thus for the creation of knowledge. But these parts of nature were not in themselves mathematical or quantitative entities. In *The New Organon* (1620), the first part of the projected *Instauratio magna*, Bacon reiterated – with an eye on neo-Platonist philosophers and mathematicians, including his contemporaries John Dee and Thomas Hariot – that mathematics "should only give limits to natural philosophy, not generate or beget it."[10] Political arithmetic, created well after Galilean and Cartesian fusions of mathematics with natural philosophy, and in the wake of Thomas Hobbes's application of geometrical reasoning to political and moral philosophy, made different assumptions.

In retrospect, Bacon's lack of interest in quantification is most striking where he examined human life most directly. The second section of the third part of his *Instauratio magna* was printed in 1623 as *Historia vitae et mortis* and published in a posthumous English translation as the *History Naturall and Experimentall, of Life and Death* (1638).[11] Here, as elsewhere, Bacon derived the value of practical knowledge from the idea of Christian charity.[12] In this context, long life was a blessing that discoveries might augment. Physicians thought the body's loss of "radical moisture" inexorable over time, but the ability of young bodies to heal and grow argued that "the Matter of Reparation might be Eternall, if the Manner of Reparation did not faile."[13] The question was how reparation failed, as less reparable parts of the body decayed, bringing others down with them, ending in the body's dissolution.[14] Bacon accordingly projected the *History* as an

---

[9] Bacon, *Francis Bacon*, p. 200.

[10] Bacon, *New Organon*, p. 79.

[11] Francis Bacon, *Francisci Baronis de Vervlamio, Vice-Comitis Sancti Albani, Historia vitae et mortis* (Londini: In officina Io. Haviland, impensis Matthaei Lownes, 1623); Francis Bacon, *History Naturall and Experimentall, of Life and Death. Or of the Prolongation of Life*, translated by W[illiam] R[awley] (London: Printed by Iohn Haviland for William Lee and Humphrey Mosley, 1638).

[12] Bacon, *Life and Death*, sig. A9v. On charity see *The Advancement of Learning*, in Bacon, *Francis Bacon*, p. 124.

[13] Bacon, *Life and Death*, sigs. A11v–A12r.

[14] Bacon, *Life and Death*, sigs. A12r–B1v.

investigation of longevity focusing on the *"Consumption, or Depradation"* of the body and its *"Reparation, and Renovation."*[15] But he began with a set of "Topick places" or questions connecting longevity to a range of conditions, from climate and location to "Hereditary" matters of *"Races, and Families"* to individual physiological and quasi-astrological factors such as "Complexion," stature and times of "Nativitie," to habits, character, diet and course of life.[16] These organized the "history" of human longevity as a natural phenomenon.

Bacon asked a series of questions about the observable, measurable effects of specifiable (and often quantifiable) conditions on length of life. These questions suggested the salience of environmental and inherited differences, as well as matters of custom or policy, in determining the lifespan of large numbers of people. Bacon's *History* likely influenced Petty's questions about the demographic implications of colonial settlement and his conception of a "Scale of Salubrity" that would tabulate the kinds of information Bacon sought as indices of the health of distinct geographical situations.[17] Yet Bacon gave no hint that the answers he sought were statistical. In discussing stages of life, he adhered to conventional ages for puberty (fourteen) and full stature (twenty), and rather than attempting to substantiate these with empirical data he set them against corresponding generic figures for other animals in order to suggest links between differentials in species' common ages and lifespans, as well as their physical qualities.[18] His figures for human longevity were based not on systematic observation but on Scriptural accounts of the patriarchs, pagan historiography and anecdotal reports of long-lived individuals.[19] A "rule of longevity" thus derived bore no relation to the "expectation of life" political arithmeticians later calculated from mortality data – data Bacon could have used, but did not.[20]

While Bacon's *History … of Life and Death* contributed nothing to quantitative demography, it did sketch physiological mechanisms – crude

---

[15] Bacon, *Life and Death*, sig. B2r.

[16] Bacon, *Life and Death*, pp. 5–7. Bacon sought to "omit, for the present, all *Astrologicall* Observations" beyond such "vulgar, and manifest Observations" as the approximate time, day and month of birth. On his view of astrology, see Zagorin, *Francis Bacon*, p. 108; H. Darrel Rutkin, "Astrology," in Katharine Park and Lorraine Daston (eds.), *The Cambridge History of Science, Volume 3: Early Modern Science* (Cambridge: Cambridge University Press, 2006), pp. 541–61, at 550–1.

[17] See Ted McCormick, "Governing Model Populations."

[18] Bacon, *Life and Death*, pp. 52–71.

[19] Bacon, *Life and Death*, pp. 88–136. Bacon's handling of longevity echoes his naturalizing treatment of other anomalous particulars; see Lorraine Daston and Katharine Park, *Wonders and the Order of Nature, 1150–1750* (New York: Zone Books, 2001), pp. 220–31.

[20] Bacon, *Life and Death*, p. 72.

and speculative, to be sure – that linked common experiences of health and longevity to climate and environment:

> In *Cold*, and *Northerne Countries*, Men live longer, commonly, than in Hot: which must needs be, in respect; The Skin is more Compact and close; And the Juyces of the body less dissipable; And the Spirits themselves less Eager to consume, and in better disposition to repair; And the Aire (as being little heated by the Sun-Beames,) lesse predatory.[21]

Tying character to climate was an ancient pursuit, and adding longevity to the congeries of qualities thus explained was no great leap. But Bacon indicated that, within broad climatic zones, more specific features of situation and topography were also relevant. Islands were more favorable than continents, for example, thanks to the moderating effects of sea air; "*High situations*," provided they were not mountain-tops, were preferable to low. Indigenes could, moreover, draw benefits from environs that were harmful to foreigners: such was the case in "*Marshes*, and *Fens*," which were "Propitious to the Natives, and Malignant to Strangers."[22] Though he did not speak in such terms, Bacon described a world in which a variety of environmental factors, grouped under the rubric of situation and acting on bodies through physically specifiable ways, shaped the demographic characteristics – the typical experiences of illness and lifespan, as well as the capacity to benefit or suffer from particular features of the landscape – of populations around the world.

Environmental factors were foremost in explaining common or collective experience, but other facts also mattered. On an individual level, the age, health and habits of parents, as well as matters of "complexion" (including hair and skin color and texture, and their changes over time) influenced longevity. So did height, weight and the proportion between parts of the body. These may or may not have been construed as individual characteristics; given Bacon's earlier discussion of animal lifespan in terms of size, he could have had common rather than personal traits in mind. Time of birth, an individual matter if ever there was one, might matter, but astrology was a doubtful business. More clearly consequential were the Hippocratic "non-naturals" of air, diet, exercise, sleep and the passions – the last linked, for Bacon's purposes, to particular religions and philosophical traditions.[23] Here, again, individual behaviors mingled with

---

[21] Bacon, *Life and Death*, pp. 139–40.
[22] Bacon, *Life and Death*, pp. 140–3.
[23] Bacon, *Life and Death*, pp. 145–63.

the effects of situation. Mental habits and philosophical orientations were personal, but diet perhaps less so, and air not at all. However these lines were drawn, it was apparent that longevity was subject both to some degree of individual determination and to broad environmental constraint. It was also evident that human collectivities acquired distinctive and sometimes complex vital characteristics in relationship to the situations they inhabited over time.

A crucial question that the *History* raised without answering was whether situation itself was receptive to intervention, and consequently whether collective longevity might be subject to technological manipulation. Bacon's utopian tract *The New Atlantis*, unfinished at his death, left little doubt on either point – if not with respect to present capacities, then at least in terms of experimental goals. The Father of Salomon's House, experimental center of the kingdom of Bensalem, described a series of instruments and stations devoted to "the knowledge of Causes, and secret motions of things; and the enlarging of the bounds of Human Empire, to the effecting of all things possible."[24] Among these were artificial caves in which experimenters sought medicines and hermits long life; medicinal wells; "Chambers of Health" for the medical improvement of air; baths for the treatment of disease and the preservation of strength; "orchards and gardens" where plants were made "by art" to grow more quickly or bear fruit out of season; "brewhouses, bake-houses, and kitchens," "shops of medicines," and so on.[25] Appended to the text was a wish-list of "*Magnalia Naturae, praecipue quoad usus humanos*" ("Miracles of nature, particularly as they apply to human use").[26] Longevity and its factors took pride of place:

> The prolongation of life.
> The restitution of youth in some degree.
> The retardation of age.
> The curing of diseases counted incurable.
> The mitigation of pain.
> More easy and less loathsome purgings.
> The increasing of strength and activity.
> The increasing of ability to suffer torture or pain.
> The altering of complexions, and fatness and leanness.
> The altering of statures.
> The altering of features.
> The increasing and exalting of the intellectual parts.

[24] Bacon, *Francis Bacon*, p. 480.
[25] Bacon, *Francis Bacon*, pp. 480–3.
[26] Bacon, *Francis Bacon*, pp. 488–9. See Keller, *Knowledge and the Public Interest*, pp. 154–7.

Some of these might pertain to individual lives. Others were necessarily wider in scope and impact: "Making of new species," "Transplanting of one species into another," as well as "Acceleration" of natural processes of growth and decay, "rich composts for the earth," and the invention of "new foods," among other things.[27]

Keller has distinguished Bacon's list of *optativa* – the category into which the *Magnalia Naturae* fall – from the broader set of philosophical or technological *desiderata*. The latter were heterogeneous goals of scientific and intellectual effort, while the former lay at the boundaries of the possible, in the realm of natural magic, marking the utmost limits of what human power might hope to achieve.[28] In this sense, the governance of longevity, health and other aspects of demography through the manipulation of its natural conditions was a distant dream. But in another sense, the shaping of situation, with a view to the instillation or improvement of qualities in numbers of people, was now a settled part of human art, policy and projects. We have seen it sketched in colonial contexts as early as Smith's plantation of the Ards, which yoked civilization to tillage. In Bacon's day, a more ambitious and sustained example was the draining of the fens. As Eric Ash has shown, this was a series of schemes, drawing on a combination of state and private support, intended to transform a landscape authorities saw as unprofitable and insalubrious into a healthy seat of productive agriculture – and, simultaneously, to improve an unhealthy and apparently idle local population.[29] In such projects, the possibility of improving not just the capacity of land but also the defining characteristics of a *situation*, with all their ramifications for the physical and moral qualities of its inhabitants, was to the fore. Basic to many contemporaneous projects, meanwhile, was the quantification of the material objects of improvement, and the quantitative projection of potential gains and timelines for their future achievement.[30] These developments converged

---

[27] Bacon, *Francis Bacon*, pp. 488–9.
[28] Keller, *Knowledge and the Public Interest*, p. 149.
[29] Ash, *Draining of the Fens*.
[30] See for example Arthur Standish, *The Commons Complaint* (London: Printed by William Stansby, 1611), which enjoined tree-planting to combat deforestation, included estimates of increased revenue per year per acre (2–5), and treated the territorial extent of forest land as a national problem, calling for "a suruay … of the woodes now growing in this Kingdome" (6); and Arthur Standish, *Nevv Directions of Experience* ([London]: s.n., 1613), which included "a neere estimation what millions of Acres the kingdome doth contain," as well as estimates of waste land, forest and area needed to produce sufficient wood for national consumption in perpetuity. See also Christopher Levett, *An Abstract of Timber-Measures* ([London]: Printed by William Iones, 1618), a tabular guide to calculating the board-foot content of timber. Thanks to Keith Pluymers for drawing my attention to these sources.

in the work of the Hartlib Circle – where, Keller argues, the lines between *desiderata* and *optativa*, between ordinary goals and extraordinary powers, broke down.[31]

Population, Projecting and Colonial Plantation in the Hartlib Circle

Nearly fifty years ago, Charles Webster's magisterial study of the circle around Samuel Hartlib emphasized its Puritan and Baconian commitments, painting a picture of a tight-knit set of philosophers, physicians, inventors and improvers collaborating in a programmatic reformation of knowledge, society, politics and religion.[32] No new conspectus has displaced this view, but recent scholars have questioned the tightness of the Hartlib Circle and the coherence of its program.[33] The "Hartlibians" were, it now appears, not so much a neo-Baconian cadre as a loose and shifting social and epistolary network. It centered on the German-born, London-based "intelligencer" Samuel Hartlib (1600–1662), but drew a wide range of figures into collaboration and mutual support through commitment to material improvement and spiritual transformation by means of the new science aided by the powers of the state. On one hand, this cautions us against seeking a definitively Hartlibian engagement with population. On the other, it helps explain why, in Hartlibian schemes touching the governance and transformation of groups of people (including the projects of early political arithmeticians), population's growth, qualities and susceptibility to improvement had a range of different, not always consistent, resonances.

The Hartlibians took up concerns familiar since before the turn of the century – feeding the poor, employing the idle, improving the land, defending the realm (and, in the midst of the Counter-Reformation, the Thirty Years' War and the Wars of the Three Kingdoms, the Protestant faith) against external threats and internal degeneration. So far as this goes, the transformations they sought to effect in groups of people were

---

[31] Keller, *Knowledge and the Public Interest*, p. 190.
[32] Charles Webster, *The Great Instauration: Science, Medicine and Reform 1626–1660* (London: Gerald Duckworth, 1975).
[33] See Thomas Leng, *Benjamin Worsley (1618–1677), Trade, Interest and the Spirit in Revolutionary England* (Woodbridge: Royal Historical Society/Boydell Press, 2008), pp. 3–7; Koji Yamamoto, "Reformation and the Distrust of the Projector in the Hartlib Circle," p. 376. An important collection of post-Webster Hartlibian studies is Mark Greengrass, Michael Leslie and Timothy Raylor (eds.), *Samuel Hartlib and the Universal Reformation: Studies in Intellectual Communication* (Cambridge: Cambridge University Press, 1994).

less remarkable than the scientific and political innovations by which they hoped to achieve these in the 1640s and 1650s. Framing these innovations were lattices of religious anxieties, moral visions and intellectual commitments that tied the problem of governing population to deeper questions of history, nature and Providence, as well as to pressing problems of imperial and confessional competition and political economy. From one perspective, these projectors built on emerging ideas about the growth, mobility and change of populations across vast territory as objects of political attention. From another, their interest in the methods and power of the new science applied to a malleable nature, and in the economic and strategic potential of colonies in a time of political tumult, led them to connect local improvements, colonial projects and global processes of human multiplication in new ways.

The first and most ambitious attempt to articulate the relationship between improvement and population was the work of Gabriel Plattes (1600–1644). Plattes was a mysterious figure, known personally to few of Hartlib's associates but much sought-after and read – and, after he died in penury, lamented.[34] In 1639, he published two brief treatises dealing with the technological exploitation of natural processes to produce material wealth. *A Discovery of Infinite Treasvre, Hidden since the Vvorlds Beginning* advocated a program of agricultural improvements; *A Discovery of Subterranneall Treasure* focused on mining and metallurgy.[35] In both, Plattes outlined an alchemical theory of wealth that implied the possibility of infinite growth. Not metals alone, but all the Earth's fruits – and, indirectly, all the products of human artifice – originated in the propagation and mixture of subterranean and celestial vapors.[36] In Plattes's view, which was shared by many of his Baconian contemporaries but rooted in older and broader artisanal attitudes toward nature, all art – from the weaving of cloth to the transmutation of metals – worked by channeling, exploiting or perfecting the operations of nature.[37] In doing so, it cooperated with

[34] See for instance Peter Smith to [John Beale?], 7 April 1656, in Hartlib Papers [hereafter HP] 67/23/1a–17b, at 17b.

[35] Gabriel Plattes, *A Discovery of Infinite Treasvre, Hidden since the Worlds Beginning* (London: Printed by I.L. and are to be sold by George Hutton, 1639); Gabriel Plattes, *A Discovery of Subterranneall Treasure* (London: Printed by J. Okes for Jasper Emery, 1639).

[36] Plattes, *Discovery of Subterranneall Treasure*, pp. 1–8; Plattes, *Discovery of Infinite Treasure*, sigs. C3v–C4r, pp. 23–4.

[37] On artisanal knowledge and the new science, see Long, *Artisan/Practitioners and the Rise of the New Sciences*, pp. 30–61; Glacken, *Traces on the Rhodian Shore*, pp. 461–97; Pamela H. Smith, *The Body of the Artisan: Art and Experience in the Scientific Revolution* (Chicago: University of Chicago Press, 2004); and, on alchemy, William R. Newman, *Promethean Ambitions: Alchemy and the Quest to Perfect Nature* (Chicago: University of Chicago Press, 2004).

God, who had ordained "the superficiall, and subterraneall Treasures of the Earth ... for the releese and sustenance of mens livings."[38] If the vital spirit that remained after these vapors had congealed into various forms of wealth could be returned to the earth, art could not only build on but also augment nature's fertility. Improvement was a continuous, cumulative, ramifying interaction between art and nature.[39]

The *Discovery of Infinite Treasvre* applied the possibility of "good improvements of the earth" to the problems of "an over-peopled Common-wealth."[40] Like Botero, Plattes linked the exploitation of resources and the expansion of territory to the growth of population. Like Bacon, he saw improvement in providential terms as both material progress and recovery of the prelapsarian world: "there is nothing wanting but willing mindes," he wrote, "to make this Countrey the Paradise of the World."[41] Unlike both, however, he saw long-term improvement as an alternative to rather than a justification or tool of colonial expansion. While he acknowledged that "the new world called America, doth for the present give aide and succour for the maintenance of the surplusage of people increased in those Countryes," he also observed that "the finding of new worlds, is not like to be a perpetuall trade." Rather than trying to manage multiplication by exporting excess numbers, then, "it seemeth to agree with providence, to begin to improve the Lands formerly peopled, in such manner that by their industry there may be raised maintenance for double the number."[42] The bulk of the *Discovery* described the array of improvements – enclo-sures and tree-planting, soil preparations and fertilizers, irrigation and drainage, Persian wheels and seed drills – that would bring this about.[43]

Here and in his later works *Macaria* (1641) and *The Profitable Intelligencer* (1644), Plattes not only argued that such improvements could double England's demographic capacity in the near term, he also implied that

[38] Plattes, *Discovery of Subterraneall Treasure*, sig. B1v.
[39] On the Hartlib Circle's engagement with alchemy and economic thought, see Carl Wennerlind, "Credit-Money as the Philosopher's Stone: Alchemy and the Coinage Problem in Seventeenth-Century England," *History of Political Economy* 35: Supplement (2003), 234–61; Wennerlind, *Casualties of Credit*, pp. 44–80. On Plattes, see Ted McCormick, "Alchemy into Economy: Material Transmutation and the Conceptualization of Utility in Gabriel Plattes (*c.* 1600–1644) and William Petty (1623–1687)," in Guillaume Garner and Sandra Richter (eds.), *"Eigennutz" und "gute Ordnung": Ökonomisierungen im 17. Jahrhundert* (Wiesbaden: Harassowitz Verlag, 2016), pp. 339–52. On Hartlibian projects touching population, see Ted McCormick, "Food, Population, and Empire in the Hartlib Circle, 1639–1660," in Emma Spary and Anya Zilberstein (eds.), *Critical Histories of Food and the Sciences: Osiris* 35 (2020), 60–83.
[40] Plattes, *Discovery of Infinite Treasvre*, sig. A3v.
[41] Plattes, *Discovery of Infinite Treasvre*, sigs. A3v–A4r.
[42] Plattes, *Discovery of Infinite Treasvre*, sig. C3v.
[43] Plattes, *Discovery of Infinite Treasvre*, pp. 23–58.

they obviated territorial limits to growth.[44] On one hand, this reflected his reading of Providence. God had made humans "infinite by propagation," yet confined them to limited space; though Plattes was alert to the expansion of trade and colonial plantations, "the fruits of the Earth for their food, and cloathing" could be made "infinite" only by the development of art.[45] On the other, it allowed Plattes to describe the population as subject to the same natural-cum-artificial levers of governance, whether considered in national or in global terms. In this sense, Plattes joined the sacred-historical vision of biblical chronologists and the political ambitions of reason-of-state under the banner of the new science. *The Discovery of Infinite Treasvre* presented multiplication as ever pressing toward historically and technologically conditioned limits of subsistence. Only timely breakthroughs in production prevented disaster:

> [F]or three severall times the people growing too numerous for their maintenance, God hath given understanding to men to improve the earth is such a wonderful manner, that it was able to maintaine double the number ... for when there were but few, they were maintained by Fish, Fowle, Venison, and Fruits; freely provided by Nature: but when they grew too numerous for that food, they found out the Spade and used industry to augment their food ... then they growing too numerous againe, were compelled to use the plough, the chiefest of all engines ... whereby all Commonwealths have ever since been maintained[.][46]

Plattes's improvements were the next stage in this history of adjustment between art and numbers, linking Providence to policy. The utopian tract *Macaria* spelled this out: under the ideal regime Plattes sketched, landowners were enjoined to adopt improvements on pain of fines and even the loss of their estates.[47] In the real world, too, improvement was an increasingly vital instrument in the management of human multiplication; as the population grew, "Art" and policy displaced "Nature, and accident" at every level.[48] While individuals must contribute to improvement, the most important earthly agent of this governance was the state.

---

[44] [Gabriel Plattes], *A Description of the Famous Kingdome of Macaria; Shewing Its Excellent Government: Wherein the Inhabitants Live in Great Prosperity, Health, and Happinesse; the King Obeyed, the Nobles Honoured; and All Good Men Respected, Vice Punished, and Vertue Rewarded* (London: Printed for Francis Constable, 1641), p. 11; Gabriel Plattes, *The Profitable Intelligencer, Communicating His Knowledge for the Generall Good of the Common-Wealth and All Posterity* (London: Printed for T. U., 1644), sig. A2r. On the authorship of *Macaria*, once attributed to Hartlib, see Charles Webster, "The Authorship and Significance of Macaria," *Past and Present*, 56 (1972), 34–48.

[45] Plattes, *Profitable Intelligencer*, sig. A2r.

[46] Plattes, *Discovery of Infinite Treasvre*, sig. C3r.

[47] [Plattes], *Macaria*, pp. 3–4.

[48] Plattes, *Profitable Intelligencer*, sig. A3v.

Plattes was imaginative in connecting specific, small-scale improvements – having servants gather waste materials to sell for fertilizer, for instance, enabling them to marry – to an overarching vision of terrestrial fertility and human multiplication.[49] Surviving correspondence suggests that this vision influenced his Hartlibian readers less than did the particular improvements he touted. Yet their later projects, too, used improvements as levers of demographic governance at different levels. Where Plattes dwelt on England's capacity for numbers, however, later projectors took up the distribution and composition of populations. Two contexts make sense of this shift. First, as real demographic growth slowed and then stagnated by mid-century, early Stuart anxiety about overpopulation, assumed in Plattes's writing, gave way to concern about maintaining numbers in the face of war and epidemic in the Three Kingdoms and economic and military competition with France and the Dutch Republic. Second, and related, the period saw an expansion of colonial schemes, culminating in the Cromwellian conquest of Ireland from 1649 and the misfired Western Design against the Spanish West Indies from 1655, which resulted in the conquest of Jamaica. Where Plattes had counterpoised improvement and expansion, later Hartlibians put each in the other's service. Rather than seeing colonies as outlets for excess numbers, they treated the movement, qualities and relations of populations around the Atlantic as dynamic factors of an imperial political economy.[50]

Between 1645 and 1649, the Huguenot exiles Hugh L'Amy and Peter Le Pruvost sought parliamentary support for a series of linked improvements to agriculture, fisheries and trade that exemplify this imperial demographic governance.[51] Like Plattes, the two called for the adoption of fertilizers for "dunging and fattning" soil, new crop rotations and seed preparations to prevent disease.[52] Unlike him, they emphasized that these improvements should be contracted voluntarily.[53] They also linked domestic improvement

---

[49] Plattes, *Profitable Intelligencer*, sig. A1r.

[50] I have learned much from Abigail L. Swingen, *Competing Visions of Empire: Labor, Slavery, and the Origins of the British Atlantic Empire* (New Haven, CT: Yale University Press, 2015). See also Abigail L. Swingen, "Labor: Employment, Colonial Servitude, and Slavery in the Seventeenth-Century Atlantic," in Philip J. Stern and Carl Wennerlind (eds.), *Mercantilism Reimagined*, pp. 46–73; Keith Pluymers, "Taming the Wilderness in Sixteenth- and Seventeenth-Century Ireland and Virginia," *Environmental History* 16:4 (2011), 610–32.

[51] The scheme is discussed in Koji Yamamoto, *Taming Capitalism before Its Triumph: Public Service, Distrust, and 'Projecting' in Early Modern England* (Oxford: Oxford University Press, 2018), pp. 109–12.

[52] Hugh L'Amy and Peter Le Pruvost, "Copy Proposals in Hand B," undated, HP 12/61a–63b; Hugh L'Amy and Peter Le Pruvost, "Proposals of Hugh L'Amy & Peter Le Pruvost," undated, HP 12/93a–98b; Peter Le Pruvost, "Draft Petition in [John] Dury's Hand, Peter Le Pruvost to House of Lords," undated, HP 12/150a–b.

[53] Hugh L'Amy and Peter Le Pruvost, "Copy, Propositions of High L'Amy & Peter Le Pruvost to House of Commons," HP 12/142a–143b.

directly to the state-backed colonial plantation. Those who "shall follow the way of improoving husbandrie" in England, they wrote, should be "obliged allwaies in time to come ... to furnish one man of their kindred of friends for the service of the Plantation" at a rate of one man per seventy acres improved – on pain of confiscation and a £1,000 fine.[54] As for earlier colonial promoters, improved husbandry in the colonies would absorb and employ the idle, vagrant and poor, as well as otherwise unemployed soldiers from the New Model Army.[55] But in doing so, it would "furnish ... men" to promote other innovations, for instance in the catching and preservation of fish from the Atlantic and the North Sea.[56] These improvements would have further ramifications. More and better victuals would lower shipping costs; expanded shipping would produce more seamen for service in trade and war. Rather than merely being drained from the mother country, the men thus supplied would "enlarge the borders of Great Brittaine" by carrying improvement to New World colonies and securing a British, Protestant empire against the forces of the Counter-Reformation.

In L'Amy and Le Pruvost's vision, this empire of improvements stood in stark contrast to rival Atlantic empires, preeminently the Spanish, which had been built on "mines of Gold or Silver or the Trade of spices and sugar" rather than honest agricultural labor or fishing, and which moreover were "burden[ed] ... with Negros."[57] Interlinked projects of plantation for improvement, cultivation and trade, by contrast, would produce British colonial populations distinguished not only by their Protestantism and their industry but also by their color.[58] L'Amy and Le Pruvost's allusions to Spain echoed the "Black Legend" of Iberian greed and brutality – culminating in massive depopulation across the New World – as it had taken shape under Elizabeth, in works like Hakluyt's *Discourse of Western Planting*. Looking forward in time, it also anticipated the ideology of Protestant, commercial,

---

[54] L'Amy and Le Pruvost, "Copy Proposals in Hand B," HP 12/142a.
[55] L'Amy and Le Pruvost, "Copy Proposals," HP 12/62a; Hugh L'Amy, "Copy Proposals for Husbandry," HP 12.65s.
[56] L'Amy and Le Pruvost, "Copy Proposals," HP 12/61a–b.
[57] Hugh L'Amy and Peter Le Pruvost, "Copy Memo in Hand ?, Hugh L'Amy and Peter Le Pruvost to House of Commons," HP 12/7a–8b. Both in this sense and in their alchemical aspects, Hartlibian projects arguably continue the "White Legend" that Bauer argues English proponents of expansion counterpoised to the "Black Legend" of Spanish empire in the New World; Bauer, *Alchemy of Conquest*, p. 370.
[58] On John Dury's connection to L'Amy and Le Pruvost and their project for a Huguenot colony in the West Indies, see Jeremy Fradkin, "Protestant Unity and Anti-Catholicism: The Irenicism and Philo-Semitism of John Dury in Context," *Journal of British Studies* 56: 2 (2017), 273–94, at 273; on their influence on the Hartlibian projector and economic writer Benjamin Worsley, see Leng, *Benjamin Worsley*, pp. 35–6.

maritime and free empire described by David Armitage.[59] From another perspective, the pointed distinction between industrious, improving, white colonists and the "burden" of enslaved Africans might reflect the emergence of a proto-liberal idea of free (that is, mobile and waged) labor counterpoised to archaic forms of servitude – ironically so, in an era when colonial dependence on indentured labor was giving way to dependence on chattel slavery. Such ironies were not hard to come by in the period; Mary Nyquist has juxtaposed the rhetoric of "slavery" in early modern political thought with the reality of chattel slavery, and William Pettigrew has shown that later arguments about English liberty underpinned the deregulation of the slave trade.[60] But bringing enslaved and free populations into relation as objects of demographic governance, at a moment when racial distinctions were being constructed as natural, is another matter. What role would racism play in the transformative manipulation of populations?

It is worth asking, to begin with, what "Negros" meant in the context of mid-century projecting. Enslaved African people had an ambiguous place in Hartlibian colonial schemes, and in English demographic thinking. There was an obvious tension between a line of the population thought that valorized both mobility and mutability, on one hand, and the emergence of racialized slavery as a basis of plantation and of racial difference as a purportedly immutable natural fact, on the other.[61] This tension would, indeed, shape the experience of the enslaved, both synchronically and diachronically.

[59] On the "Black Legend," see Margaret R. Greer, Walter D. Mignolo and Maureen Quilligan, "Introduction," in Margaret R. Greer, Walter D. Mignolo and Maureen Quilligan (eds.), *Rereading the Black Legend: The Discourses of Religious and Racial Difference in the Renaissance Empires* (Chicago: University of Chicago Press, 2007), pp. 1–24; on the ideology of empire, see Armitage, *The Ideological Origins of the British Empire*.

[60] Mary Nyquist, *Arbitrary Rule: Slavery, Tyranny, and the Power of Life and Death* (Chicago: University of Chicago Press, 2013); William A. Pettigrew, *Freedom's Debt: The Royal African Company and the Politics of the Atlantic Slave Trade, 1672–1752* (Chapel Hill: University of North Carolina Press, 2013).

[61] "Race" is a vexed term. Colin Kidd denies the presence of "clearly articulated theories of racial difference" – products rather than antecedents of Atlantic slavery, in his view – before the eighteenth century, but admits "racist attitudes" much earlier; Kidd, *The Forging of Races*, p. 54; see also Livingstone, *Adam's Ancestors*, p. 65; Philip D. Morgan, "British Encounters with Africans and African-Americans, Circa 1600–1780," in Bernard Bailyn and Philip D. Morgan (eds.), *Strangers within the Realm: Cultural Margins of the First British Empire* (Chapel Hill: University of North Carolina Press, 1991), pp. 157–219. A compelling account of racism as a proslavery ideology in North America is Barbara Jeanne Fields, "Slavery, Race, and Ideology in the United States of America," *New Left Review* 1:181 (1990), 95–118. Hannaford, *Race*, pp. 147–84, suggests a seventeenth-century European intellectual origin for later ideas of race; Jennifer Morgan presents evidence that ideas of fundamental and morally significant physical differences shaped English views of enslaved African people in the Caribbean by the mid-seventeenth century; Jennifer L. Morgan, *Laboring Women: Reproduction and Gender in New World Slavery* (Philadelphia: University of Pennsylvania Press, 2004), pp. 12–49.

As Christina Sharpe has written, the "forced movements" which underlay so many projects of transformation and improvement entailed in the case of slavery not only more systematic violence but also the "containment, regulation, punishment, capture and captivity" that made "blackness ... the symbol, par excellence, for the less-than-human being condemned to death."[62] Yet as Sharpe and others note, "dehumanization" fails to capture either the ambiguities central to plantation slavery – in which purported deficiencies in intellect or sensitivity justified subjection, even as presumptions of rationality and responsibility justified punishment – or the pattern of analogous yet distinct attempts to reshape Black people as well as white before and after the abolition of the slave trade and of slavery itself.[63] If the long eighteenth century witnessed a hardening of racial categorizations, this was less a complete exclusion than what Zakiyyah Iman Jackson calls "the violent imposition and appropriation – inclusion and recognition – of black(ened) humanity in the interest of plasticizing that very humanity."[64] At the end of the period, even abolitionist arguments emphasizing the mutability of the enslaved (and hence their capacity for civilization) reinscribed hierarchical distinctions that justified distinct forms of governance. Some of these echoed early modern responses to vagrancy and idleness – but criminality now attached to the unrestrained mobility of elaborately racialized current or former captives, and pathology to their bodies, childrearing and cultural practices.[65]

These latter developments lay in the future, but the tensions that produced them color mid-seventeenth century projects. Among the Hartlibians and their immediate successors, the construction of Africans as distinct from (and, as Petty and others speculated, naturally inferior to) Europeans at the same moment that enslaved African people were becoming essential to English plantation made for contradictory conclusions.[66]

---

[62] Christina Sharpe, *In the Wake: On Blackness and Being* (Durham, NC: Duke University Press, 2016), p. 21.

[63] Zakiyyah Iman Jackson, *Becoming Human: Matter and Meaning in an Antiblack World* (New York: New York University Press, 2020), p. 39 (thanks to Chanda Prescod-Weinstein for drawing my attention to this work); Sasha Turner, *Contested Bodies: Pregnancy, Childrearing, and Slavery in Jamaica* (Philadelphia: University of Pennsylvania Press, 2017), pp. 27, 35, 212–13.

[64] Jackson, *Becoming Human*, p. 12.

[65] Turner, *Contested Bodies*, pp. 40, 45, 49–50, 188; Saidiya V. Hartman, *Scenes of Subjection: Terror, Slavery, and Self-Making in Nineteenth-Century America* (Oxford: Oxford University Press, 1997), pp. 6, 62, 98, 132–3, 145; Rana Hogarth, *Medicalizing Blackness: Making Racial Difference in the Atlantic World, 1780–1840* (Chapel Hill: University of North Carolina, 2017).

[66] On Petty's ambiguous ideas of African difference, see Rhodri Lewis, *William Petty on the Order of Nature: An Unpublished Manuscript Treatise* (Tempe: Arizona Center for Medieval and Renaissance Texts and Studies, 2012), pp. 58–9. For contemporaneous investigations of color difference by Petty's Royal Society colleagues, see Cristina Malcolmson, *Studies of Skin Color in the Early Royal Society: Boyle, Cavendish, Swift* (London: Routledge, 2016).

L'Amy and Le Pruvost's solution, as we have seen, was to exclude such people as a "burden" on the Spanish empire that the English could simply shed. Another and more influential response, however, was to include them as both human and something less than persons. Defined at once by immutable difference and by radical mobility, enslaved Africans and their descendants were marginalized in the later seventeenth and early eighteenth centuries by a mode of demographic governance that exploited mixture and mutability in the cause of moral as well as material improvement. They were, indeed, barely visible to political arithmeticians like Petty as governable populations at all.[67] Yet at this same moment, their putatively natural capacities for both productive and reproductive labor in colonial climes and conditions were, as Jennifer Morgan has shown, becoming central to the economic calculation and projection on which visions of empire as a site of improvement rested.[68]

Another projector in Hartlib's network, Cressy Dymock, illuminates this seeming paradox. Dymock was descended from a landed Lincolnshire family and entered Gray's Inn in 1629, following in his father's footsteps. He surfaces in Hartlib's correspondence from the late 1640s as an inventor and promoter of agricultural improvements from orchard-keeping and rabbit-breeding to new crop rotations and to instruments, including a seed drill designed to reduce wastage. Among his projects was a model for the more efficient organization of farmland, which Hartlib published in 1653 as *A Discovery for Division or Setting out of Land, as to the Best Form*.[69] In this as in other projects, Dymock – like other Hartlibians, and further informed by the experience of fen drainage in Lincolnshire – advocated for enclosure and the creation of "single" (as opposed to "mixt") interests in land.[70] This, he argued, would help new techniques tried by "reall experience" triumph over an irrational popular attachment to "custom."[71]

---

[67] McCormick, *William Petty*, pp. 231–2.

[68] Morgan, *Laboring Women*, pp. 69–106. The boundaries of mutability were themselves shifting; for security reasons, colonial authorities in eighteenth-century Jamaica allowed the legal "whitening" of some descendants of enslaved African women and English men: see Brooke N. Newman, *A Dark Inheritance: Blood, Race, and Sex in Colonial Jamaica* (New Haven, CT: Yale University Press, 2018), esp. pp. 67–142; Daniel Livesay, *Children of Uncertain Fortune: Mixed-Race Jamaicans in Britain and the Atlantic Family, 1733–1833* (Chapel Hill: University of North Carolina Press, 2018).

[69] Samuel Hartlib, *A Discoverie for Division or Setting out of Land, as to the Best Form* (London: Printed for Richard Wodenothe, 1653). The original scheme is set out in Cressy Dymock to [Samuel Hartlib?], undated, HP 62/29/1a-4b.

[70] Cressy Dymock, "Memorandum on the Advantages of Enclosure," 1649, HP 64/18/1a–2b, at 1b. See Richard Grove, "Cressey Dymock and the Draining of the Fens: An Early Agricultural Model," *The Geographical Journal* 147:1 (1981), 27–37; Ash, *Draining of the Fens*, pp. 285–9.

[71] Dymock to Hartlib, letter, undated, HP 62/9/2a–b, at 2a.

Beyond facilitating technological change, however, a single interest would transform both the land and the people dwelling upon it:

> Each man shall bee blest according to his good endeavour[.] Many comod-
> ityes [will be] found to be vendible, not formerly knowne ... And those
> that are aboundantly increased both in quantitye & quallitye ... Thus this
> kingdome might within one age iustly merritt the title of the garden of the
> world ... Nor could there bee any other pore but Indigents, & they would
> easily & plentifully bee supplyed[.][72]

Multiplying the fruits of the earth would employ and feed greater numbers. Any number of Hartlibian and earlier projects showed similar concern with population, but Dymock's package of projects for the English
countryside had a more radical qualitative thrust. By individualizing
interest, enclosure incentivized industry and improvement more systematically than any workhouse ever could. In so doing, it altered the relationship of people to the land and the commonwealth. Enclosure itself
was the most important improvement of all, making "men's minds ...
soe much more settled & fitt to serue god" and "their affaires ... contracted into order & more Moderate & inobled labour."[73] Improvement
would transform the population into something it was not yet: An
aggregate of self-interested, laboring, predictable particulars. And "The
wealth of each perticuler thus encreased would ... vastly advance the
publique revenue."[74]

In one sense, Dymock's project for a perpetual motion machine,
which he first described to Hartlib in 1648 as a means of "turning of
grind stones[,] winnowing of Corne, churning of butter, or the like," fits
this picture neatly.[75] Like the alchemical transmutation that influenced
Petty's demographic vision in the 1670s, the perpetual motion was a scientific desideratum that later became an emblem of delusion.[76] In both
cases, eighteenth-century mockery obscures seventeenth-century meaning. Though grander than a new crop or seed drill, the perpetual motion

---

[72] Dymock, "Memorandum on the Advantages of Enclosure," HP 64/18/2a.

[73] Dymock, "Memorandum on the Advantages of Enclosure," HP 64/18/2b.

[74] Dymock, "Memorandum on the Advantages of Enclosure," HP 64/18/2b. See Katherine Bootle
Attié, "Enclosure Polemics and the Garden in the 1650s," *Studies in English Literature, 1500–1900*
51:1 (2011), 135–57. See also Ted McCormick, "Improvement, Projecting, and Self-Interest in the
Hartlib Circle, c. 1640–1660," in Christine Zabel (ed.), *Historicizing Self-Interest in the Modern
Atlantic World: A Plea for Ego?* (Abingdon: Routledge, 2021), pp. 25–43.

[75] Cressy Dymock to Hartlib, 25 December 1648, HP 62/50/2a–b, at 2a.

[76] See Simon Schaffer, "The Show That Never Ends: Perpetual Motion in the Early Eighteenth
Century," *British Journal for the History of Science* 28:2 (1995), 157–89; Keller, *Knowledge and the
Public Interest*, 326–31.

was of a piece with other Hartlibian innovations in its providential significance (Dymock described himself as "impregnate with an issue which by … devine blessing is now brought forth" and the engine as "a living male childe cal'd the Marriage of Strength and tyme") and in its capacity to expand the power of art to transform nature.[77] In particular, perpetual motion promised to enable various kinds of work to be done "without the helpe of wind or water, man, or beast (except the helpe of a man to sett itt first goeing, & looke to itt while itt doth goe)."[78] Its uses were myriad: Dymock's 1651 pamphlet, *An Invention of Engines of Motion Lately Brought to Perfection*, listed thirty-two applications for the machine, from ploughing and draining land, to grinding paint and plaster, to driving cranes and boring pipes.[79]

Yet the machine's agricultural functions shaped Dymock's sense of its potential. In March 1649, retrenching his initial claims, Dymock suggested that the engine might "doe the Worke of 3. Or 4. Horses with one" rather than none at all.[80] In May, he described the engine's capacity "to draw the Plough (or rather Spade-plough … and the grand or second roulers, and the New harrowes. Etc.[)]."[81] When he began soliciting purchasers for shares in the invention, he specified the cost of modifying it to grind wheat or malt.[82] Meanwhile, he also came to identify this not-quite-perpetual-motion engine more precisely as a "Marriage of Strength and tyme," as he put it in October.[83] An undated "Memo Concerning a Utility Engine" elaborated: The machine would "Marrye strength and tyme togather, or bring them closer each to other then vsuall enginges doe" by reducing the animal and human labor needed to plough a given area or grind a given volume in a day:

> As to ploughing/Vsually men haue in their teemes to plough 4 -5- or -6 horses or 8 oxen, & to guide these and the plough two men or a man & a boy att least, with which they plough about one acre a day[.] I hope without any horse with 6 men onely or lesse to plough with two ploughs att once of the same strength or bignes … two acres a day of the same or the lyke ground[.]

[77] Cressy Dymock to [Hartlib?], 25 October 1649, HP 62/50/9a–10b, at 9a.

[78] Dymock to Hartlib, HP 62/50/2a.

[79] Cressy Dymock, *An Invention of Engines of Motion Lately Brought to Perfection* (London: Printed by Richard Woodnoth, 1651).

[80] Cressy Dymock, "Copy Extract in Hartlib's Hand, Cressy Dymock on Perpetual Motion," 16 March 1649, HP 62/50/11a–b, at 11a.

[81] Cressy Dymock to [?], 25 May 1649, HP 62/50/3a–4b, at 3a-b.

[82] Cressy Dymock, "Memo on Perpetual Motion," HP 67/17/1a–2b, at 1a.

[83] Dymock to [Hartlib?], HP 62/50/9a.

> As to the grinding of Corne Malt &c.... Horse mills to moue them effectually require 3- or -4 horses to worke att a tyme & some must bee kept to releiue them/But I hope to grind -30- or -40- quarters of malt ... or towards 20 quarters of hard corne in a day without any of the foresaid vsuall helpes perticulerly without horses & with onely two men in their turnes[.][84]

Dymock's engine would shift the balance between human and animal labor, making the rural population more productive while eliminating horses and oxen – and thus the need for fodder. Combined with his other projects, it would make the English countryside a garden, land disposed and labor exploited as efficiently as possible for the production of food. The effect, as an anonymous paper likely by Dymock put it, was that "by this Invention the Land will maintain on[e] 3d part of men at the least more then now it doth."[85]

So far, perpetual motion was of a piece with other domestic improvement schemes and with the providential framework of technologically assisted multiplication in which Plattes, for example, set them. But, like L'Amy and Le Pruvost, Dymock also projected his invention into colonial spaces:

> If my engine bee made vse of in the Barbadoes for the grinding of sugar there will nessesarily follow (besides all private benefitts) this publique advantage that whereas they are now forced to lett many acres ly for fother [i.e., fodder] for those draught cattle winter & somer the proffitt thence arrising beeing far short of what the same land would yeild if planted with sugar canes, cotton, Indico, or the lyke, by this meanes all that land may bee converted to those more beneficiall vses, to the great increase & trade of those more staple comodityes.[86]

Perpetual motion's function – the elimination of animal labor and thus fodder – was the same everywhere, but its fruits depended on location: food and employment in England, cash crops in the Caribbean. While the former would support population growth, employment for free labor and improvement based on a mixture of large and small freeholdings, the latter would have more complex demographic and social effects. In keeping with the logic of the 1651 Navigation Act (partly the work of another Hartlibian, Benjamin Worsley), an increase of colonial staples would mean

---

[84] Cressy Dymock, "Memo Concerning a Utility Engine" (undated), HP 67/13/1a–2b, at 1a-b.
[85] "Notes on Perpetual Motion," HP 58/21a–22b. The document lists thirty-three uses of perpetual motion resembling the thirty-two in Dymock's *An Invention of Engines of Motion*, and it echoes other papers of his on the subject.
[86] Cressy Dymock, "Memorandum about Engines," undated, HP 62/8a–b, at 8a.

an increase in shipping; regulated trade might prove a nursery of seamen.[87] But eliminating fodder would transform demography on Barbados, too, where the impulse to plant every possible acre with sugar already made food scarce in the later 1640s.[88] A paper probably by Dymock explained "that in the plantations horses etc are dearer, & shorter lived then Negroes, & more troublesome and charegeable to keep then Negroes."[89] There was thus an obvious use for an "Invention ... wher by the hands of 4 or 6 Negroes at a spell the same work could bee dispatched, both as to strength and time, which is now done by 4 horses or 8 cattle."[90]

Thus the same technological intervention that promised to make England the world's garden, populated by industrious, adaptable and rational improvers, cast enslaved Africans in the Caribbean as a cheaper and easier substitute for livestock. However, poorly such assumptions matched the reality of plantation, they bear out, in an economic register, Jackson's observation that "repudiation of 'the animal' has historically been essential to producing classes of abject humans."[91] At the same time, they instantiate the kind of violent, "plasticizing" inclusion she substitutes for the frame of dehumanization. The projection of perpetual motion into sugar plantations implicitly denied "Negroes" the rationality (to say nothing of the self-interest) Dymock appealed to and sought to cultivate in the English population; but it also defined them against animals as a less "chargeable," less "troublesome" and longer-lasting supply of work. In essence, enslaved Africans would be whatever plantation required them to be. Yet if "Negroes" and white Englishmen were both subject to a mode of governance that instrumentalized mobility and aimed at qualitative as well as quantitative transformation, the place of the former was quietly yet brutally bounded by the interests of the latter. In England, the perpetual motion would transform land, trades and people together, imposing a second and better nature and transforming the country into another Eden. In Barbados, it would turn every possible inch of land to the production of

---

[87] On Worsley and the Navigation Act, see Leng, *Benjamin Worsley*, pp. 53–79. See also Steven C. A. Pincus, *Protestantism and Patriotism: Ideologies and the Making of English Foreign Policy, 1650–1668* (Cambridge: Cambridge University Press, 1996), pp. 40–75; Maurice Ashley, *Financial and Commercial Policy under the Cromwellian Protectorate* (London: Frank Cass, 1962), pp. 20–5, 157–73.

[88] See Richard S. Dunn, *Sugar and Slaves: The Rise of the Planter Class in the English West Indies, 1624–1713* (New York: W. W. Norton, 1973), p. 59.

[89] "Memo on Types of Mills," undated, HP 67/8/1a–2b, at 1b. The anonymous paper uses Dymock's signature formulation of "strength and time" to describe the invention, and its estimates of animal labor inputs and the comparative efficiency of different kinds of mills are similar to those in Dymock's "Memo Concerning a Utility Engine."

[90] "Memo on Types of Mills," undated, HP 67/8/1b.

[91] Jackson, *Becoming Human*, p. 11.

staples for export. The private profits of the improved colonial plantation would accrue to planters, the public benefits to the metropole.

The differential demographic implications of Dymock's perpetual motion reflected the differentiation of colony and metropole as well as of enslaved and free within an emerging imperial political economy. Colonies derived their value in the first instance from their capacity – once settled, planted and improved – to produce commodities whose transportation, refinement and sale supplied the metropolitan state and population with revenue and employment. The 1650s witnessed several important events in the elaboration of this empire. Two stand out: the 1651 Navigation Act restricted trade with English colonies to English ships, setting the stage for the naval triumphs of the First Anglo-Dutch War; Cromwell's 1654 "Western Design" against Spanish power in the Atlantic eventuated in embarrassing defeat at Hispaniola and the desultory conquest of Jamaica in 1655.[92] The third set of developments, underway before 1650, framed Dymock's calculations and accelerated during the decade: the rise of sugar cultivation across most of the English West Indies, the concomitant resort to enslaved African labor and the lagging codification of race (on a muddle of theoretical bases) as a principle of domination.[93] By the Restoration, the territorial extent, economic function, racist character and legal armature of the English empire in the Caribbean as it would exist through the eighteenth century were already taking shape.[94]

Writers on "mercantilism" have focused on the fiscal and economic aspects of this complex.[95] Though the "pro-populationism" of Restoration economic writing, its links to new forms of demographic and economic quantification – synonymous with political arithmetic – and its legacy in pronatalist social legislation (the 1695 Marriage Duty Act, for example) are well known, they are often considered as quantitative and as concerned simply with labor, revenues, or military strength rather than as essays in more ambitious forms of social engineering.[96] Historians of slavery and

---

[92] On the Western Design, see Swingen, *Competing Visions of Empire*, pp. 32–55; Carla Gardina Pestana, *The English Conquest of Jamaica: Oliver Cromwell's Bid for Empire* (Cambridge, MA: Harvard University Press, 2017).

[93] Dunn, *Sugar and Slaves*.

[94] See Susan Dwyer Amussen, *Caribbean Exchanges: Slavery and the Transformation of English Society, 1640–1700* (Chapel Hill: University of North Carolina Press, 2007), pp. 106–44.

[95] On mercantilism as a language, see Magnusson, *Mercantilism*; on the concept, see Philip J. Stern and Carl Wennerlind, "Introduction," in Wennerlind and Stern (eds.), *Mercantilism Reimagined*, pp. 3–22.

[96] See for example Overbeek, *History of Population Theories*, p. 2. For these connections and their social ramifications in England and France, however, see Rusnock, *Vital Accounts*; Tuttle, *Conceiving the Old Regime*. On the Marriage Duty Act, see Brooks, "Projecting, Political Arithmetic and the Act of 1695," 31–53.

colonialism, while far from ignoring either numbers or economies, have probed the qualitative and transformative impact of empire-formation on populations and ideas about population.[97] This work shows that for advocates of colonial and commercial expansion, and for the human and non-human targets of their attention, transoceanic flows of goods, bodies and coin were intertwined with qualitative as well as quantitative changes in demography and its governance. Agricultural improvements, new trades and new policies fueled and fed on the creation of industrious and self-interested individuals at home, the transplantation and transmutation of others in colonial settlements and the reduction of still others to the position of self-reproducing engines, immobilized and isolated (at least in theory) from the body of subjects. By the later seventeenth century, policing the qualities, boundaries and relations of subject populations – by technological and juridical means, and at local and imperial levels – were tasks as central to empire as numbering the people.

Survey, Transplantation and Settlement in Cromwellian Ireland

One of the largest, most contentious and most consequential projects of the Cromwellian era was William Petty's "Down Survey" of Ireland.[98] More than most Hartlibian projects, the Survey was an effective practical instrument of colonization. Petty pitched it from his position as physician to the New Model Army in Ireland, a post that Hartlibian connections had probably helped him secure.[99] Though it is often described as the first scientific mapping of Ireland (indeed, of any European state), the Survey's object was more specific. In 1641, an uprising against Protestant encroachments broke out in Ulster. Spreading quickly across Ireland, the revolt was almost immediately construed as an attempt to exterminate the Protestant settler population; the figure of 154,000 murdered

[97] See for example Turner, *Contested Bodies*; Morgan, *Labouring Women*; Newman, *Dark Inheritance*; Chaplin, *Subject Matter*.

[98] Petty compiled a documentary of the survey to answer critics: William Petty, *History of the Cromwellian Survey of Ireland, A.D. 1655–6, Commonly Called "the Down Survey,"* edited by T.A. Larcom (Dublin: Irish Archaeological Society, 1851). See Smyth, *Map-Making*, pp. 166–97; McCormick, *William Petty*, pp. 84–118; Henry, "William Petty," 1–20; and Hugh Goodacre, *The Economic Thought of William Petty: Exploring the Colonialist Roots of Economics* (Abingdon: Routledge, 2018), pp. 26–45.

[99] On the Hartlibians' interest in Ireland, see Toby Barnard, "The Hartlib Circle and the Cult and Culture of Improvement in Ireland," in Mark Greengrass et al. (eds.), *Samuel Hartlib and Universal Reformation: Studies in Intellectual Communication* (Cambridge: Cambridge University Press, 1994), pp. 281–97; Fradkin, "Protestant Unity and Anti-Catholicism," 273–94.

Protestants, though implausible to informed observers, became canonical.[100] From 1642, a Catholic Confederacy, bringing together Gaelic Irish and Old English, governed most of the country, in effect autonomously.[101] Civil war in England forestalled an adequate military response for most of the decade, but the 1642 Adventurers' Act established the idea behind the settlement Cromwell would impose after his conquest of the island in 1649–1652: those who paid for Ireland's subjugation would be repaid in rebels' lands. Undertaken during thirteen months from early 1655 on territory earmarked for Cromwellian soldiers (in lieu of arrears), and later extended to "adventurers'" lands, the Down Survey measured the extent and assessed the quality of these lands, facilitating their transfer from Catholic to Protestant control. The upshot was a transformation of Irish landownership that survived the Restoration and the Revolution of 1688–1691 to furnish the material basis of Protestant dominion for much of the eighteenth century.[102]

The Down Survey and the settlements it served were epochal events in Irish and British history. Petty's work was also a major technical achievement. This was less because of its accuracy as a surveying and cartographic exercise – it overestimated the area of land covered – than because of its organization and execution as a state-backed yet effectively autonomous project.[103] Taking his own payment in land debentures (and buying more at a discount as the army despaired of seeing theirs redeemed), Petty cut costs by using soldiers instead of professional surveyors, equipping them with cheap instruments made of mass-produced, interchangeable parts and giving them just enough training to produce rough maps and assign land to basic categories that more expert eyes could vet and compile. The initial Down Survey took just thirteen months to complete – a fraction of the time Petty's Hartlibian rival Benjamin Worsley, then

---

[100] On 1641 see Jane Ohlmeyer, "Introduction: A Failed Revolution?" in Jane Ohlmeyer (ed.), *Ireland from Independence to Occupation, 1641–1660* (Cambridge: Cambridge University Press, 1995), pp. 1–23, and Eamon Darcy, *The Irish Rebellion of 1641 and the Wars of the Three Kingdoms* (Woodbridge: Royal Historical Society/Boydell Press, 2013); on Protestant views and their legacy, John Gibney, *The Shadow of a Year: The 1641 Rebellion in Irish History and Memory* (Madison: University of Wisconsin Press, 2013).

[101] See Jane H. Ohlmeyer, "Ireland Independent: Confederate Foreign Policy and International Relations During the Mid-Seventeenth Century," in Jane H. Ohlmeyer (ed.), *Ireland from Independence to Occupation, 1641–1660* (Cambridge: Cambridge University Press, 1995), pp. 89–111; Micheál Ó Siochrú, *Confederate Ireland, 1642–1649: A Constitutional and Political Analysis* (Dublin: Four Courts Press, 1999).

[102] See John Cunningham, *Conquest and Land in Ireland: The Transplantation to Connacht, 1649–1680* (Woodbridge: Boydell Press, 2011); Ohlmeyer, *Making Ireland English*, pp. 301–35.

[103] See John Harwood Andrews, *Shapes of Ireland: Maps and Their Makers 1564–1839* (Dublin: Geography Publications, 1997), pp. 121–48.

Surveyor-General of Ireland, had suggested.[104] As noted, it furnished an imperfect yet invaluable body of measurements and valuations that underpinned a fundamental reorganization of landholding in Ireland – and, by extension, of the political geography of that kingdom as well as its relationship to the other two. However flawed, it was a major contribution to English knowledge of and Protestant control over Ireland.[105] By the same token, it forged Petty's path not only to personal wealth but also to political survival and continued influence in Irish affairs long after 1660 when Hartlib and his reforming circle were hastily forgotten.

The case for Ireland's importance in the formation of Petty's Restoration political arithmetic has been made.[106] What matters here is the multiplicity of ways in which the Down Survey, as a Hartlibian project and an instrument of state policy and colonial plantation, touched on the governance of populations. The Survey itself was an impressive exercise in the construction and management of a certain kind of collective body. Petty framed his use of roughly 1,000 soldiers less as a simple economy than in terms of their characteristic qualities and experiences, as well as their capacity to receive new skills. Surveying a conquered yet not fully subdued country required

> [S]uch as were able to endure travaile, ill lodginge and dyett, as alsoe heates and colds, beinge alsoe men of activitie, that could leape hedge and ditch, and could alsoe ruffle with the severall rude persons in the country, from whome they might expect to be often crossed and opposed.

These "qualifications" Petty "found among severall of the ordinary shouldiers, many of whom, havinge bin bread to trades, could write and read sufficiently for the purposes intended." What they lacked, moreover, could quickly be supplied them, "if they were but headfull and steddy minded, though not of the nimblest witts": "how to make use of their instruments," "How to judge observation points, the value of lands, etc."[107] Before the work of surveying even began, the project required the molding of a labor force from suitable material into a new form, able to endure

[104] See Irma Corcoran, *Thomas Holme, 1624–1695: Surveyor General of Pennsylvania* (Philadelphia: American Philosophical Society, 1992), pp. 35–46; T. C. Barnard, "Miles Symner and the New Learning in Seventeenth-Century Ireland," *Journal of the Royal Society of Antiquaries of Ireland* 102:2 (1972), 129–42.

[105] See Smyth, *Map-Making*, pp. 166–97, and Henry, "William Petty"; see also Cronin, "Writing the 'New Geography,'" 58–71.

[106] McCormick, *William Petty*; Reungoat, *William Petty*; Goodacre, *Economic Thought of William Petty*.

[107] Petty, *History*, pp. xv–xvi.

a trying physical environment and to produce, by means of instruments, calculation and observation, a particular kind of information.

This was nothing in comparison with the effects envisioned for the Irish population. Historians of the Irish land settlement have understandably focused upon two features: first, the real transformation it wrought in landownership (from roughly 59 percent Catholic in 1641 to about 22 percent in 1688, declining further thereafter); and second, the never-completed Cromwellian plan to "transplant" Irish Catholics (more accurately, Irish Catholic landowners, though views differed at the time) from Ulster, Leinster and Munster across the River Shannon into Connacht, with the further idea of settling English soldiers along a kind of *cordon sanitaire* traversing the island from northeast to southwest.[108] At a minimum, the Cromwellian settlement projected the subjugation of the Irish Catholic populace to such a degree – its political leadership gone, its territorial power shrunken and restricted, and its bulk either laboring on English plantations or (as some English Protestants hoped) confined to a remote province – that rebellion would be impossible.[109] Beyond this goal, however, a host of more elaborate and conflicting ideas about the future state of Ireland and the future character and place of its national and confessional subpopulations proliferated among representatives of different factions and interests in the English army, the Protestant elite, the Dublin administration and the government in Westminster.

Beneath massive quantitative shifts lurked the question of the populations and their malleability. In part, this reflected the circumstances of the conquest; a key legacy of 1641 was a refreshed image (substantiated by specious numbers) of Irish Catholics bent on the slaughter of Protestants. But, as we have seen, English authority and plantation in Ireland had been important loci for thinking about degeneration and mutability since at least the 1570s, while the forcible expulsion, relocation or dispersion of troublesome religious and ethnic minorities – Muslims and Jews in the Iberian case, Catholics and Protestants elsewhere – was a familiar feature

---

[108] T. C. Barnard, "Conclusion: Settling and Unsettling Ireland: The Cromwellian and Williamite Revolutions," in Jane H. Ohlmeyer (ed.), *Ireland from Independence to Occupation 1641–1660*, (Cambridge: Cambridge University Press, 1995), pp. 265–91, at 269; Cunningham, *Conquest and Land*; Smyth, *Map-Making*, pp. 168–9.

[109] A key proponent of collective guilt as a justification for removal was Colonel Richard Lawrence, who debated the matter with Petty's associate Vincent Gookin: see Lawrence, *The Interest of England in the Irish Transplantation, Stated* (Dublin: William Bladen, 1655), written in response to Vincent Gookin, *The Great Case of Transplantation in Ireland Discussed* (London: I.C., 1655), and answered in Vincent Gookin, *The Author and Case of Transplanting the Irish into Connaught Vindicated, from the Unjust Aspersions of Col. Richard Laurence* (London: Printed by A.M. for Simon Miller, 1655).

of early modern political experience.[110] The most significant debate on this head in the Ireland of the 1650s, entwining a sense of long-term failure with the immediate experience of crisis, concerned the transplantation into Connacht.[111] Petty criticized the scheme from an instrumental point of view: his surveyors depended on Catholic informants, "mearsmen," with vital knowledge of local boundaries, whom transplantation put to flight before the work was done.[112] A deeper argument with which Petty sympathized, however, and whose implications he would take up in his Restoration political arithmetic, was Vincent Gookin's *The Great Case of Transplantation in Ireland Discussed* (1655).[113]

Gookin was the son of a Protestant planter in County Cork. An MP in the nominated Barebone's Parliament, he aligned himself with the Munster-based, Old Protestant Boyles – whose children included the political giant Roger (Lord Broghill) and the budding chymist and natural philosopher Robert (linked via Hartlib to Petty and Worsley). Like Petty, Gookin grew close to Henry Cromwell, who supplanted Charles Fleetwood as Lord Deputy between 1655 and 1657.[114] Though dedicated to Fleetwood, *The Great Case of Transplantation* attacked a central policy of his administration favored by radical sectarians in the army. Gookin himself spoke for established Protestant planters, whose anti-Catholicism was countervailed by the need for agricultural labor. Besides being unjust, the wholesale removal of the Catholic Irish on the basis of "national blood-guilt" would harm "the Publick-Good." For

---

[110] For a recent overview, see Nicholas Terpstra, *Religious Refugees in the Early Modern World: An Alternative History of the Reformation* (Cambridge: Cambridge University Press, 2015).

[111] Besides Cunningham, *Conquest and Land*, see Patricia Coughlan, "Counter-Currents in Colonial Discourse: The Political Thought of Vincent and Daniel Gookin," in Jane H. Ohlmeyer (ed.), *Political Thought in Seventeenth-Century Ireland: Kingdom or Colony*, (Cambridge: Cambridge University Press, 2000), pp. 56–82; and Sarah Barber's insightful "Settlement, Transplantation and Expulsion: A Comparative Study of the Placement of Peoples," in Ciaran Brady and Jane H. Ohlmeyer (eds.), *British Interventions in Early Modern Ireland* (Cambridge: Cambridge University Press, 2005), pp. 280–98.

[112] Petty, *History*, pp. 29, 35, 118, 123.

[113] Petty's descendant and first modern biographer credits him with co-authorship of the pamphlet, and Petty listed "A Discourse against the Transplantation into Connaught," in "A Collection of W. Petty's Severall Works and Writings since the Yeare 1636" (compiled 1671). See Edmond Fitzmaurice, *The Life of Sir William Petty, 1623–1687* (London: John Murray, 1895), p. 31; William Petty, *The Petty Papers: Some Unpublished Writings of Sir William Petty*, edited by Marquis of Lansdowne, 2 vols. (London: Constable, 1927), vol. II, pp. 260–1. I am unaware of further evidence for this claim.

[114] See P. Little, "Gookin, Vincent (c. 1616–1659), politician and author," *Oxford Dictionary of National Biography*, retrieved May 15, 2019 [https://o-www-oxforddnb-com.mercury.concordia .ca/view/10.1093/ref:odnb/9780198614128.001.0001/odnb-9780198614128-e-11008]. On the political context, see Patrick Little, *Lord Broghill and the Cromwellian Union with Ireland and Scotland* (Woodbridge: Boydell Press, 2004), pp. 59–90.

one thing, "The Revenue of Contribution of Ireland is generally raised out of Corn, and the Husbandmen of that Corn are generally Irish, the removal therefore of these necessarily infers the failure of that."[115] For another, soldiers receiving land "have neither Stock, nor Money ... nor (for the most part) skill in Husbandry: But by the labours of the Irish on their Lands, together with their own industry, they may maintain themselves, improve their Lands ... and by degrees inure themselves sutably to that course of life."[116] Removing the Irish "leaves these poor mens proportions of Land totally wast."[117] The Irish were vital to improvement.

Gookin did not, however, argue for a return to the early Stuart status quo. Instead, he envisioned the final conversion of the Irish to Protestantism. This was no new wish. But in contrast to earlier, halfhearted projects for training clergymen or translating texts, Gookin saw a mixture between English and Irish as the *sine qua non* of Irish transformation. Isolation could only deepen divisions, either by preventing positive change or by inviting degeneration:

> If ... these Papists be suffered to continue in the English plantations, they may enjoy the labours of Godly able Ministers, the encouragements of Protestant professors, and the Catechizings of private Christians, all which are powerfull morall instruments to conversion; but if they be transplanted, as their consocation may probably settle them on their old lees, so their separation certainly deprives them of these advantages; And by a persistence in their former Principles, continue them Papists still, or by a forgetting them (if possible) and no better distil'd into them, make them turn Atheists.[118]

Rather than blaming the fecklessness and criminality of the Irish on inherent or inherited barbarism, Gookin explained their behavior in terms of their concrete circumstances, exacerbated by irrational legislation. The leaders of the rebellion were dead or gone:

> [As] for the poor Commons, the Sun never shined (or rather not shined) upon a Nation so completely miserable; There are not one hundred of them in 10000. who are not by ... the act of settlement under the penalty of losing life and estate; The Tax sweeps away their whole Subsistence; Necessitie makes them turn Theeves and Tories, and then they are prosecuted with fire and sword for being so.[119]

---

[115] Gookin, *Great Case*, pp. 7, 15.
[116] Gookin, *Great Case*, p. 15.
[117] Gookin, *Great Case*, p. 16.
[118] Gookin, *Great Case*, p. 6.
[119] Gookin, *Great Case*, p. 13.

If the goal of converting the Irish was antiquated, and if Gookin's optimism on the subject looks naïve – as when he suggested that the example of 1641 would act as a moral argument against Catholicism – his analysis of and solution for the obstacles to conversion were novel in their expression and still more their implications.[120] Irish difference was not a natural fact but a political artifact. Changing it was a matter of demographic mobility and mixture.

Conversion itself figured less as a spiritual than a political transformation. It was, in effect, Anglicization. Gookin considered the age-old and apparently well-founded objection "that the English may degenerate, and turn Irish" if the mixture were allowed. His response anticipated Petty's promise to transmute the Irish into English:

> Of future contingents no man can pass a determinate judgement; but if we speak morally, and as probably may be, it may much rather be expected that the Irish will turn English. Those Topicks before instanced concerning Religion do infer it as very probable, that with the Religion professed by the English, it is likely they may receive their Manners also. And this is confirmed by experience of all of that Nation who embraced the Protestant Religion.[121]

Religious change was sought not for its own sake but because it would mean a change in manners tantamount to turning the Irish English. Gookin's framing of this expectation is also important. Like any Elizabethan or Stuart commentator, he invoked history. But instead of citing the degeneration of the Old English as an argument against mixture, as others did, he appealed to experience and moral probability in support of it. What made the difference was the situation in which mixture would henceforth take place: "as to former experience, even that likewise seems to add weight to this expectation, because whatever inducements perswaded the English formerly to turn Irish, the same more strongly invite the Irish now to turn English."[122] The Irish were defeated; Protestants controlled the state, land, wealth, law and the language in which these operated.

> The Irish numbers (now so abated by Famin, Pestilence, the Sword, and Forein Transportations) are not like to overgrow the English as formerly, and so no fear of their being obnoxious to them hereafter: but being mixed with, they are likelyer to be swallowed up by the English, and incorporated into them; so that a few Centuries will know no difference present, fear none to come, and scarce believe what were pass'd.[123]

---

[120] Gookin, *Great Case*, pp. 2–3.
[121] Gookin, *Great Case*, p. 18.
[122] Gookin, *Great Case*, pp. 18–19.
[123] Gookin, *Great Case*, pp. 21–2.

Only isolation could preserve Irish Catholics as a distinct group. Mixture would create a unified, governable, Protestant and English population. Isolation and mixture, mobility and confinement, transplantation and transformation: these were the tools of effective policy. Numbers of people – but more than that, the qualities and relations of the populations concerned – were its objects.

Though Gookin's opposition to transplantation has put him in a favorable light, from a present-day perspective, it is not difficult to see his program of digestion, predicated on the planned eradication of meaningful cultural difference, as a kind of genocide – albeit less violent than that sometimes attributed to Cromwell or portended by the transplantation scheme itself. In this regard, Gookin's project of assimilation was almost identical to Petty's Restoration project of transmutation. Whether or not Petty contributed to Gookin's pamphlet, its arguments no doubt influenced Petty's thinking. Both sought to preserve Irish numbers while destroying Irish distinctiveness, insofar as this was politically troublesome. The difference was that Petty, penning his proposals in the midst of royal pushes for toleration in the early 1670s and mid-1680s, ceased to frame Protestantism as essential to political inclusion and laid greater stress on the English language and manners. This shift of emphasis had implications for Petty's understanding of how demographic mixture might affect qualitative change. What matters for present purposes is that the idea of the subject population as not just an object but also a *product* of large-scale, transformative political interventions – the defining characteristic of Restoration political arithmetic, and the culmination of decades of thinking about the mobility and mutation of problematic groups – animated criticism of policy and visions of improvement by the mid-1650s.

This is not to say that this way of thinking was hegemonic or widely accepted. Gookin's stance was oppositional and Petty's (his stewardship of the survey notwithstanding) that of the projector. On the other side was Richard Lawrence, an English army colonel and, like his master Fleetwood, a supporter of transplantation.[124] Yet even as Lawrence echoed older views of the Irish in dismissing Gookin, he departed from Spenserian vitriol in related ways. The very title of *The Interest of England in the Irish Transplantation* answered Gookin's appeal to the public good not by decrying Irish barbarism but by insisting that Ireland's "National Interest" must be destroyed for the sake of England's.[125] The problem

---

[124] On Lawrence, see Toby Barnard, "Interests in Ireland: The 'Fanatic Zeal and Irregular Ambition' of Richard Lawrence," in Brady and Ohlmeyer (eds.), *British Interventions in Early Modern Ireland*, pp. 299–314.

[125] Lawrence, *Interest of England*, p. 22.

was not incivility or Catholicism but the integrity of the Irish nation. Lawrence denied that the transplantation was a collective punishment; yet he blamed "the most horrid, causeless Rebellion and bloudy Massacre that hath been heard of, in these latter ages of the World" not on "particular persons or parties of the Irish Nation," but on "the whole Irish Nation it self, consisting of Nobility, Gentry, Clergie, and Commonalty." These were "all engaged as one Nation in this quarrel, to root out and whoolly extirpate all English Protestants from amongst them."[126] In such circumstances, "promiscuous and scattered inhabiting amongst the Irish" would leave the English "as sheep prepared for the slaughter." Given irreconcilable national divisions, numbers carried the case: The Irish "were in all places far the greater number, and in most a hundred to one."[127] Only by excluding the Irish nation and admitting "no more Irish Papists ... to live within them, than what they might have ... visibly at their mercy" could English plantations be safe.[128]

Where Gookin treated national distinctions as congeries of religion and manners, incidental obstacles to the absorption of individuals into a single subject population, Lawrence took the Irish nation far more seriously as a social and political reality. Thus, while Gookin could only regard Irish Catholic isolation as an obstacle to assimilation, Lawrence saw transplantation both as a vital safety measure for English settlement and as a positive attack on the Irish nation as such. Relocating the Irish would dislocate the relations – landlord–tenant ties as well as sept organization – that sustained them as a collective entity with a distinct interest.[129] To put it another way: while Gookin saw planned mixture as the key to converting the Irish into English, Lawrence less optimistically (or more realistically) looked to planned, coerced mobility and segregation as the first step toward eradicating Irish identity by disrupting its social matrix. Both saw the problem as a political one, and both understood the proximate task of policy as controlling the mobility, mixture and mutability of populations on a national scale. These similarities, which set Gookin *and* Lawrence apart from most Tudor writers on degeneration, are as important as any differences between their specific prognoses or their points of view.

As Gookin's reply to Lawrence indicated, new approaches made use of older strictures. Gookin cited Sir John Davies and even the Jesuit Campion as authorities on the Irish and Old English, while he picked holes in the

---

[126] Lawrence, *Interest of England*, p. 13.
[127] Lawrence, *Interest of England*, p. 17.
[128] Lawrence, *Interest of England*, p. 18.
[129] Lawrence, *Interest of England*, pp. 25–6.

logic of Lawrence's claims about the precautionary and limited nature of the transplantation.[130] But his reassertion of the importance of mixture underscored the extent to which the two differed over tactics more than over long-term goals:

> Cohabiting with the English was a means probably to have quasht the Rebellion, if other wholsome concurrents (apointed by Law) had been duly executed; as, 1. Care taken for spreading the Protestant Religion, the neglect of which left them to their own, the strongest incentive to Rebellion, and tie to unanimity in it.... 2. Educating their Gentry in Civility and Religion, for which the Court of Wards was erected, and doubtlesse was then convenient there for that Nation. 3. Suppressing their Language, Manners, Laws, Septs &c.... These and such like things neglected, next ... were the causes of that horrid bloudy Rebellion, and not their dwelling among English, which if helpt with the assistance of such provisions as the Law did make, might probably have produced the contrary[.][131]

The question was not what needed to be done to the Irish but whether transplantation or mixture was the best way to do it in the circumstances. Gookin now argued not that transplanting the Irish was excessive but that it "prevents not Rebellion, and so is too narrow a plaister to cover the sore of Ireland." It would "lay the seeds of an everlasting feud ... perpetuating the distinctions of English and Irish, Protestant and Papist," "joyning Irish forces" and "sequestring them, to give them the advantage of privacy in all their conspiracies."[132] Lawrence wrote as if the Irish were on the verge of another rebellion; for Gookin "the Tables are just turned":

> [T]hey are few, the English many; we may overspread them, and incorporate them into our selves, and so by an onenesse take away the foundation of difference and fear together; we may breed up their youth, habituate them to our customs, cause a disuse of their Language: we have opportunities of communicating better things unto them, and probabilities they may be received[.][133]

Events overtook this debate, and the shape of the settlement matched neither of these competing visions. On the ground, Gookin and the Old Protestant perspective he represented were the more obvious winners, as most soldiers sold their debentures and the transplantation stalled. Yet the English failed to convert or digest the Catholic Irish, whose interest – complicated by revisions to the settlement under Charles II – survived

130 Gookin, *Author and Case*, pp. 18–38.
131 Gookin, *Author and Case*, p. 38.
132 Gookin, *Author and Case*, p. 39.
133 Gookin, *Author and Case*, p. 41.

in sufficiently coherent form to keep Irish landownership and Protestant hegemony live issues through the next several decades.[134] It was just these issues that gave rise to political arithmetic.

"Number, Weight, and Measure": Political Arithmetic in the Restoration

"Political arithmetic" was coined sometime around 1670.[135] It has appeared ever since as the invention of a new, scientific and, above all, quantitative age. Its inventor, Petty, has often seemed precocious in his focus on "number, weight and measure," his imaginative exploitation of demographic and economic figures running well ahead of the empirical data at his disposal over a century before the census.[136] While John Graunt's "shop arithmetique" revealed a world of relationships hidden in the rows and columns of London's weekly bills of mortality and in the patchy parish registers of baptisms, marriages and burials, Petty promised nothing less than a new "Instrument of Government" for the Stuart kingdoms and the growing transatlantic colonial empire, predicated on the collection and analysis of vast amounts of information.[137] Most of this was numerical. Throughout his printed works – from the 1662 *Treatise of Taxes and Contributions*, through the 1674 *Discourse … Concerning the Uses of Duplicate Proportion*, to the posthumously printed *Political Arithmetick* (1690) and *The Political Anatomy of Ireland* (1691) – and in dozens of manuscript tracts, Petty announced the need for enumeration and calculation in the making of

---

[134] On the Restoration settlement, see Karl Bottigheimer, "The Restoration Land Settlement in Ireland: A Structural View," *Irish Historical Studies* 18:69 (1972), 1–21; Kevin McKenny, "The Restoration Land Settlement in Ireland: A Statistical Interpretation," in Coleman A. Dennehy (ed.), *Restoration Ireland: Always Settling and Never Settled* (Aldershot: Ashgate, 2008), pp. 35–52. On the Catholic "new interest," whose landownership rested on the land settlement, see Eoin Kinsella, "'Dividing the Bear's Skin before She Is Taken': Irish Catholics and Land in the Late Stuart Monarchy, 1683–91," in Dennehy (ed.), *Restoration Ireland*, pp. 161–78.

[135] The manuscript of *Political Arithmetick* was in circulation by 1672. For examples see BL Additional MS 21128, ff.2–37, Royal Society Library MS 366 and Trinity College Dublin MS 544, each of which is dated 1671/2.

[136] For "Number, Weight, and Measure," see Petty, *Political Arithmetick*, sigs. A4r, A4v, 21. The phrase originated in the apocryphal Wisdom of Solomon (11:20), but a more proximate source for Petty may have been Gabriel Plattes, who used it in *The Discovery of Infinite Treasvre* to describe the creation of the world (pp. 1–2). The iatrochemist Arthur Dee, whom Petty may have read, applied it to the elementary composition of animals, vegetables and minerals: Arthur Dee, *Fasciculus Chemicus: Or Chymical Collections. Expressing the Ingress, Progress, and Egress, of the Secret Hermetick Science, out of the Choicest and Most Famous Authors* (London: Printed by J. Flesher for Richard Mynne, 1650), pp. 48–9.

[137] Graunt, *Natural and Political Observations*, sig. A4r; William Petty, "The New Instrument of Government" (1682), BL Additional MS 72880, ff.60–71v.

policy. People should be numbered, land measured, hearths and windows counted, births, deaths and marriages tracked. Numbers, too, expressed the goals of policy: The largest population, the best ratio of "hands" to "lands," the highest rate of marriages.[138] Such were the aims of a political arithmetic that came of age in an era of commercial expansion, fiscal innovation, colonial settlement and Continental war.

In this light, it is not surprising that Petty's creation should appear at the beginning of accounts of statistics, quantification and calculation during the long eighteenth century. The label "political arithmetic" came into wider use from the 1690s, and as Peter Buck, Joanna Innes, and most recently William Deringer have shown, associated forms of demographic data-gathering and quantitative argumentation colored political and social, as well as religious and natural philosophical debate up through the 1750s.[139] By this time, a substantial subgenre of "medical arithmetic" had formed around questions of epidemic disease, environmental salubrity and inoculation, as Andrea Rusnock and others have explored; subsequent decades saw actuarial calculations transformed by new discussions of life expectancy, based on the amateur collection and circulation of data from far-flung locales.[140] By the 1780s, political arithmetic embraced statistical approaches to everything from agriculture to natural theology. Beyond these varied realms of technical application – and despite criticism from the likes of David Hume and Adam Smith – the cultural power of numbers, and in particular of demographic quantification, appeared in literary genres from satires, to novels, to pastoral verse. To all these interlinked developments, Malthus's *Essay* (1798) and the national census (1801) were a kind of coda.

Yet the line from Petty to Malthus was a broken one. Petty's mode of quantitative argument – as distinct from his conceptualization of economic relationships and his Baconian rhetoric – was largely irrelevant to later political economy, and his assumptions about the power and legitimacy of state intervention were opposed to those of Smith and his followers. Petty's reputation for mathematical prowess has not survived careful juxtaposition with Graunt's work, let alone that of eighteenth-century calculators such as Richard Price.[141] Perhaps most important, as

---

[138] See for instance William Petty, "Of Lands & Hands" (1686), BL Additional MS 72866, ff.27–52v; *Political Arithmetick*, p. 65.

[139] Peter Buck, "Seventeenth-Century Political Arithmetic: Civil Strife and Vital Statistics," *Isis* 68:1 (1977), 67–84; Buck, "People Who Counted"; Innes, *Inferior Politics*, pp. 109–75; Deringer, *Calculated Values*, pp. 1–46.

[140] Rusnock, *Vital Accounts*; Glass, *Numbering the People*.

[141] On Petty's mathematical abilities, see Goodacre, *Economic Thought of William Petty*, p. 75; Reungoat, *William Petty*, pp. 33–41.

William Deringer argues, was that despite Petty's enduring association with political arithmetic, the specific calculative practices that developed during the eighteenth century under that title originated not with Petty's court-oriented projects in the 1660s and 1670s but only later, with Charles Davenant's "Country" critiques of the administration in the 1690s. As Deringer implies, Restoration political arithmetic was a different sort of enterprise. Its essence was not (as Davenant put it in his 1698 *Discourses on the Public Revenues*) "Reasoning, by Figures, upon Things relating to Government," but "social engineering"; not quantification but transformation.[142]

Ironically, then, recent work on political arithmetic as a quantitative practice underlines the main theme of this book: The creation of population as an object of qualitative transformation. If Petty contributed less to quantification than has been thought, he was more preoccupied with qualitative change. But what was the significance of his engagement with the latter, and were the two connected? In an earlier book, I argued that Petty's peculiar background – his Parisian encounters with the materialist and corpuscularian natural philosophies of Descartes, Mersenne and Hobbes; his Dutch training in iatrochemistry and alchemy; and his projecting as a member of the Hartlib Circle, culminating in the Down Survey – enabled him to tackle the problems of Irish settlement and the politics of religion in the Restoration through a program of "transmutation" by which subpopulations could be moved, mixed and converted to suit the needs of the Stuart monarchy.[143] Acting on an analogy between populations and material substances, Petty construed policy as demographic chemistry: Its task was the imposition of desirable natures on populations. The paradigm case was the transmutation of the Irish into English. Here, a systematic exchange ("counter-transplantation") of English and Irish women would compel intermarriage in Ireland, inserting English women – bearers of language, manners and children – into Irish households. Within a generation, the Irish would be English.

Petty's transmutative project was novel in important respects. But in a broad sense, his ambitions – the transformative core of his political arithmetic – were neither new nor idiosyncratic. Shorn of its circumstantial targets and trappings, Petty's work looks less like the precocious anticipation of eighteenth-century calculation or nineteenth-century political economy,

---

[142] Deringer, *Calculated Values*, p. 18; Charles Davenant, *Discourses on the Public Revenues, and on the Trade of England* (London: Printed for James Knapton, 1698), p. 2.
[143] McCormick, *William Petty*.

and more like an attempt at furnishing a systematic, naturalistic formula for tendencies that had come to color engagements with troublesome populations over the course of a century. Many if not most of the qualitative questions we have encountered in earlier chapters – the loyalty and civility of the Irish, the industry or idleness of the English, the relationships between different groups, and the effects of confinement, settlement and mobility on the character of successive generations and across the metropolitan and colonial territory – recur in Petty. Whereas earlier writers tackled these as unique problems, however (whether through ad hoc projects or by making them central issues of government), the quantitative rhetoric, mechanical logic and serial application of political arithmetic implied that the solution to all these challenges and more lay in the adoption of a single set of methods for the permanent management of population as such.

The corpuscularian understanding of alchemical transmutation Petty likely learned as a student of medicine and philosophy in Leiden, Utrecht and Amsterdam – reinforced by prior familiarity with dyeing, encounters with Hartlibian alchemical projectors and acquaintance with mechanical philosophers such as Robert Boyle – supplied the intellectual matrix for this new articulation of demographic governance.[144] Other metaphors were available. Gookin's use of digestion to describe the assimilation of the Irish is one example, while Petty's description of "political anatomy" (applied most elaborately to Ireland) has sometimes been taken as an alternative or rival to political arithmetic.[145] But inasmuch as alchemy included multiple kinds of intentional manipulation, while incorporating quantification into its procedures, it was applied to problems that neither the unidirectional, organic process of digestion nor the analytical and diagnostic procedures of anatomical dissection could easily capture.[146] Petty's Hartlibian background is especially pertinent here, for as we have seen, Gabriel Plattes (who likewise invoked "number, weight and measure" as ordering principles of creation) had already extended transmutation to explain productive material transformations of *all* kinds.[147] An art,

---

[144] McCormick, *William Petty*, pp. 14–83.

[145] William Petty, *The Political Anatomy of Ireland* (London: Printed by D. Brown and W. Rogers, 1691), sig. A5r-v; Tony Aspromourgos, "Political Economy, Political Arithmetic and Political Medicine in the Thought of William Petty," in Peter D. Groenewegen (ed.), *Physicians and Political Economy: Six Studies of the Work of Doctor-Economists* (London: Routledge, 2001), pp. 10–25.

[146] As Bauer has shown, alchemy had a long history of metaphorical use in Spanish imperial thought, though how much of this was known to Petty is unclear from his writings; Bauer, *Alchemy of Conquest*.

[147] See note 36 in this chapter.

devoted at its deepest level to the controlled imposition of desirable qualities on matter, was a fitting analog to a mode of governance that centered
on the imposition of desirable natures on people. This parallel implied
not only in the language of Petty's projects but also in their method, ties
his Restoration work to mid-century intellectual contexts and early Stuart
legacies; it frames both his uptake of longstanding challenges to governance and his distinctive clarity and ruthlessness in proposing solutions.

Seen diachronically, Petty's work was a series of projects framed under
an increasingly clear rubric – almost, as "essays in political arithmetick"
proliferated in his last years, a methodological brand.[148] His limited printed
corpus, his reliance on manuscript publication and the ad hoc nature of his
proposals (often directed to contacts at court in Dublin and Westminster)
have been studied.[149] An underexamined implication of understanding
Petty as a projector rather than an economic thinker, however, is that it
makes political arithmetic a continuation of his Cromwellian-era work
rather than a Restoration novelty. This is clearest with respect to Ireland.
The project of settlement Petty helped directly in the 1650s and defend
in the 1660s continued, in his repeated proposals for "transmuting the
Irish into English" by means of a "counter-transplantation" or "Exchange
of Women," first in the early 1670s and again under James II.[150] Here,
the systematic, coercive insertion of marginalized English women into
Irish households would transform "the Manners, Language & perhaps
the Religion" – the politically salient qualities – of the host population.[151]
The same concerns animated Petty's final substantial work, "A Treatise of
Ireland" (1687). This text, lately examined by Hugh Goodacre, envisioned

---

[148] See William Petty, *Another Essay in Political Arithmetick, Concerning the Growth of the City of London: With the Measures, Periods, Causes, and Consequences Thereof. 1682* (London: Printed by H.H. for Mark Pardoe, 1683); William Petty, *Two Essays in Political Arithmetick, Concerning the People, Housing, Hospitals, &c. Of London and Paris.* (London: Printed for J. Lloyd, 1687); Petty, *Five Essays in Political Arithmetick.*

[149] Frances Harris, "Ireland as a Laboratory: The Archive of Sir William Petty," in Michael Hunter (ed.), *Archives of the Scientific Revolution: The Formation and Exchange of Ideas in Seventeenth-Century Europe* (Woodbridge: Boydell Press, 1998), pp. 73–90; McCormick, *William Petty*, pp. 259–84.

[150] For various iterations of this idea, see Petty, "An Opinion of what is possible to bee done" (1670), BL Additional MS 72865, ff.140–142; Petty, *Political Anatomy*, pp. 29–31; Petty, "About Exchanging of Women" (1674), BL Additional MS 72897, ff.71–72v; Petty, "A Proposal for Ireland" (1675), BL Additional MS 72879, ff.98–103v; Petty, "A Dialogue about the Reconciling of the English and Irish, and also the Papists and Non-papists" (1686), BL Additional MS 72882, ff.15–18v; Petty, "Advantages in particular to Ireland by the Transplantation and other prac-tises…" (1686), BL Additional MS 72882, ff.65–66v; Petty, "For the Union of English & Irish" (1686), BL Additional MS 72881, ff.88–89v; Petty, "The grand settlement of Ireland" (1687), BL Additional MS 72885, ff.114–117v.

[151] Petty, "About Exchanging of Women," BL Additional MS 72897, f.71r.

"Transplanting a Million of People ... out of Ireland into England," both as an economic strategy and to make the religious composition of the British population safer for a Catholic monarchy.[152]

The content of proposals changed with political circumstance, and the state patronage Petty enjoyed under Cromwell never returned. He joined other beneficiaries of the Cromwellian land settlement in resisting the retrenchments imposed in the Acts of Settlement (1662) and Explanation (1665), and other planters in arguing against export restrictions on cattle in 1663 and 1665. But the idea of transmuting the Irish first appeared in 1670, at a moment when Charles II's Cabal ministry, French alliance, and push for religious toleration heightened fears of popish power at court, while Irish Catholics lobbied hard against the land settlement.[153] By the latter half of the decade, with the Test Act (excluding Catholics from the office) law, the Second Anglo-Dutch War past, the Cabal dissolved and the Old Protestant Duke of Ormond reinstalled as Lord Lieutenant of Ireland, evidence of the project fades from the archive. It returned to Petty's agenda only in 1686, by which point James II was not only pushing for toleration but had begun appointing Catholic officers to civil and military posts in England and Ireland.[154] Petty thus pressed the transmutation of the Irish on his contacts and patrons at just those moments when Irish Catholic interests appeared closest to overturning the statutory basis of Protestant supremacy in Ireland, and when royally decreed religious toleration (which Petty favored) seemed closest to realization in England.

The scale and scope of the transmutation, or at least of the transplantation of people that underpinned it, varied. *The Political Anatomy of Ireland* (printed in 1691, but circulating in 1672) envisioned an annual exchange of

---

[152] William Petty, "A Treatise of Ireland" (1687), printed in Charles Henry Hull (ed.), *The Economic Writings of Sir William Petty*, 2 vols. (Cambridge: Cambridge University Press, 1899), vol. II, pp. 545–621, at 551. The manuscript "Treatise" is in BL Additional MS 21128, ff.52–91v. See Goodacre, *Economic Thought of William Petty*, pp. 26–45; McCormick, *William Petty*, pp. 209–258.

[153] On Charles II's policies and aims, see John Miller, *Charles II* (London: Weidenfeld and Nicholson, 1991), pp. 175–219. On Irish politics see Anne Creighton, "'Grace and Favour': The Cabal Ministry and Irish Catholic Politics, 1667–1673," in Dennehy (ed.), *Restoration Ireland*, pp. 141–60. See also Tim Harris, *Restoration: Charles II and His Kingdoms, 166–1685* (New York: Penguin, 2006), pp. 43–84.

[154] On James's goals see John Miller, *James II* (New Haven, CT: Yale University Press, 2000); Scott Sowerby, *Making Toleration: The Repealers and the Glorious Revolution* (Cambridge, MA: Harvard University Press, 2013), pp. 23–56. D. W. Hayton emphasizes the role of the Irish Catholic community and the Earl of Tyrconnell in shaping developments: D. W. Hayton, *Ruling Ireland, 1685–1742: Politics, Politicians and Parties* (Woodbridge: Boydell Press, 2004), pp. 8–34. See also Tim Harris, *Revolution: The Great Crisis of the British Monarchy, 1685–1720* (New York: Penguin, 2006), pp. 39–65, 101–43.

several thousand women between England and Ireland, based on an estimate of the number of "unmarried marriageable women" in the smaller
kingdom:

> There are among the 600 M. ... poor Irish, not above 20 M. of unmarried
> marriageable Women; nor would above two thousand per Ann. grow and
> become such. Wherefore if ½ the said Women were in one year, and ½ the
> next transported into England, and disposed of one to each Parish, and as
> many English brought back and married to the Irish ... the whole Work of
> natural Transmutation and Union would in 4 or 5 years be accomplished.[155]

In a March 1674 paper "About Exchanging of Women," Petty revised
his estimates – both of numbers and of the time needed for a complete
transmutation – upward. Now there were "700,000 Irish or 140,000 familys," among whom "There are yeerly but 7000 marriages." Thus "If 7000
English poore Women were yearly brought out of England" and married to "the like Number of poorer Irish Men Then in 20 Yeares The
Mother or Mistress of every of the said familys would bee an English
protestant woman, And Consequently The Manners, Language & perhaps the Religion of all the sayd familys would bee English."[156] Though
predicated on quantitative claims, the logic of the project in these and
contemporaneous iterations rested on Petty's conventional understanding
of women as charged with maintaining households and rearing children,
modified by more idiosyncratic confidence that households produced the
qualities of populations just as mechanically as corpuscles did those of
physical substances.[157]

Petty's proposals in James's reign maintain confidence in the means and
the goal of transmuting the Irish. Yet they also suggest changes in scale,
speed and proximate purpose of transmutation as the Irish Catholic lobby
triumphed and the politics of toleration threatened relations between the
Catholic king and his Protestant subjects. A 1687 paper on "The grand settlement of Ireland," for example, began not with numbers of Irish women
or marriages but with trends in the proportional change in Catholic populations in England and Ireland since the Reformation: "Whereas the number of Roman Catholiques, have decreased in England, within the last
150 years from 280 to one ... t'is now thought, they May (within the next
7 yeares) contrariwise Encrease from one to 36; without the Clergy; The

[155] Petty, *Political Anatomy*, p. 30.
[156] Petty, "About Exchanging of Women," BL Additional MS 72879, f.71r.
[157] Ted McCormick, "Alchemy in the Political Arithmetic of Sir William Petty (1623–1687)," *Studies in History and Philosophy of Science* 37:2 (2006), 290–307.

proportions in Ireland Continuing as they now are."[158] The previous year, Petty had suggested that an exchange of poor populations between the two kingdoms might be "a great step towards the returne of England to that [i.e., the Roman] faith, without persecution or violence," presumably because it would increase the Catholic proportion of the English population.[159] The same exchange that furthered the transmutation of the Irish into English in Ireland was now also billed, for the benefit of an embattled Catholic monarch, as a means of transmuting Protestants into Catholics in England. The 1687 "Treatise of Ireland," written as the possibility of a Dutch invasion loomed, called for the wholesale removal of a million Irish into England with similar ends in view.

Besides displaying the projector's free hand in disposing of the poor and colonized, these changes reveal the increasing centrality of the politics of religion to political arithmetic and its adaptability to political reversals. As striking as the shift from Anglicizing the Irish to Catholicizing the English may seem, however, they were compatible uses of Petty's instrument. The common thread was the governability of the population. For Ireland, this meant redistributing Irish women thinly across England's ten thousand parishes to learn the "Oeconomy & manners of England," while pressing Englishwomen to institute the same "Oeconomy of the Family" – including language, manners, "Diet, Apparel, &c." – in Irish households.[160] Like earlier writers, Petty described his project as a way "to Civilise the Irish."[161] Civilizing people also meant changing the landscape:

> I would have above all, The Irish Cabbins, which are worse then hogstyes, to bee changed into English Cottages with Gardens, and good ones to bee built in Tythings & Townships whereby Milk, Butter and Cheese, as also Linnen and Woollen may bee better wrought, and wherein English women might bee contented to Live, when they shall bee maried to Irish Men[.][162]

Petty's reliance on the bodies and minds of young women as the agents of positive rather than negative change signals a departure from earlier denunciations of Irish barbarism and Old English degeneracy, however. (It also contrasts with ideas emerging at the same time about the governance of enslaved African women in the Caribbean, whose reproductive

[158] Petty, "The grand settlement of Ireland," BL Additional MS 72885, f.116r.
[159] Petty, "For the Union of English & Irish," BL Additional MS f.89r.
[160] Petty, "A Proposal for Ireland," BL Additional MS 72879, f.100v; Petty, *Political Anatomy*, pp. 30–1.
[161] William Petty, "A Briefe & Generall Proposal for Religion in England & Ireland" (1686), BL Additional MS 72888, ff.125–126v, at f.125v; see also Petty, "Advantages in Particular to Ireland," BL Additional MS 72882, f.66r.
[162] Petty, "A Dialogue about Reconciling," BL Additional MS, f.17v.

labor was instrumentalized even as their bodies and childrearing practices were denigrated.)[163] Civility was spread not threatened by mixture; it was produced in the home and in the womb. It was a demographic fact. Rather than residing in blood or milk, however, it was a matter of national traits. A population that spoke, ate, dressed and worked in English ways – ways instilled by women and sustained by material improvements – was civilized for English purposes.

More than Spenser's, steeped as his was in humanist ethnography, Petty's equation between civility and Englishness was overtly political, and therefore circumstantial. Irish civilization was whatever set of transformations made the union between the Irish and English easier, Irish land more productive and the English crown safer. This was why, given the religious leanings of the monarchs Petty served, transmutation need not involve Protestantization.[164] It is also why, unlike earlier plantation schemes, political arithmetic was applied with equal force – though with wildly unequal practical implications, given relations between the Three Kingdoms – to metropolitan and colonial (but, notably, not African) populations alike. In the first instance, English women were essential to the scheme. From Petty's first framing of the scheme, they were presumed to be just as subject to "impressment" into reproductive service abroad as Irish women were to mass removal.[165] As much as the direction of transmutation – from Irish to English – implied a familiar elevation of metropolitan civilization over colonial barbarism, the logic and the logistics of "counter-transplantation" erased the distinction between colonial and metropolitan populations; indeed, as he noted in 1670, "I understand that the qualitys of Exchangd women to bee alike."[166] As an instrument of government, political arithmetic erased distinctions between English and Irish populations not only with respect to each other (they would merge indissolubly) but also in relation to the state that manipulated them.

Beyond the thousands of English women required for the transmutation of the Irish, Jacobite iterations of Petty's counter-transplantation

---

[163] See Jennifer Morgan, *Laboring Women*, pp. 12–49, 69–106; Jackson, *Becoming Human*, p. 13.

[164] In *The Political Anatomy of Ireland*, Petty spoke of transforming "The Manners, Language & *perhaps* the Religion" of the Irish (emphasis added). As he wrote elsewhere, "I suppose no force upon Conscience in Religion." William Petty, "Of Counter-Transplanting the Irish & English" [1670s], BL Additional MS 72879, ff.117–118v, at f.117r.

[165] Petty noted: "the King has power to Imprest men to serve in War. Methinks hee may doe the same to prevent war." William Petty, "Of Counter-Transplanting the Irish & English" [1670s], BL Additional MS 72879, BL Additional MS 72879, f.117v.

[166] William Petty, "Of Counter-Transplanting the Irish & English" [1670s], BL Additional MS 72879, BL Additional MS 72879, f.117r.

scheme compassed the possibility of exchanging as many as 100,000 poor English and Irish families, in the interests of revenue as much as civilization.[167] Nor were the poor or the marginalized the only groups subject to social engineering. Contemporaneous manuscripts took up the manipulation of England's confessional composition – both the relative proportions of Catholic and Protestant numbers in the population and the drift of future religious change. The relocation of a million Catholic Irish into Britain that Petty's "Treatise of Ireland" envisioned would not only contribute to English revenues and Irish economic subjugation, as has been studied; it would also "So ... order the People of both Nations and Religions, that there may be in England about 8 Non-Catholicks to one Roman Catholick," furthering for the sake of "Profit, Pleasure, and Security" both the "Union of the two Nations" and what Petty elsewhere called the "Catholication of ye 3 Kingdomes."[168] In all of this, what was consistent was not the distinction between colonial and metropolitan populations but rather the idea that profit and security both depended on active, systematic and potentially massive interventions in the mobility, mixture and mutations of populations across the Three Kingdoms.

National and confessional differences shaped the political crises that sparked Petty's most ambitious proposals and framed his creation of political arithmetic. It is thus a mistake to isolate Petty's economic thought from his engagements with the politics of religion and Irish plantation. By the same token, the transplantation and transmutation schemes with which he met crises in these latter contexts, though extreme, were of a piece with political arithmetic's less jarring, more routine uses in England and abroad.

---

[167] William Petty, "For Raising 3 Stocks of 3 Millions of One Million in Each in the Kingdom of Ireland" (1686), BL Additional MS 72882, ff.33–34v, at f.33v.

[168] Petty, "Treatise of Ireland," in Hull (ed.), *Economic Writings*, vol. II, pp. 557, 561, 577; William Petty, "Of Catholication of the 3 Kingdomes of England Scotland & Ireland" (1686), BL Additional MS 72888, ff.37–38v; see also William Petty, "Questions and Assertions Ariseing from & Depending Upon the Maine Question of Transporting a Million of People out of Ireland into England" [1686?], BL Additional MS 72882, ff.59–62v. Sabine Reungoat reads this as an insincere attempt to flatter James; Reungoat, *William Petty*, p. 191. The Protestant Duke of Ormond, longtime Lord-Lieutenant of Ireland and a frequent recipient of Petty's proposals, was less sanguine about Petty's commitment to the Protestant interest, writing in late 1686: "Sir William Pet[t]y is not so very confident of the assurance given him but that hee thinks it prudence to secure himself by applications to men in power & if hee can not save all will try to save one"; James Butler, Duke of Ormond, to Sir Robert Southwell, 27 October 1686, BL Additional MS 21484, ff.64–65v, at f.64v. Goodacre sees the "Treatise" as Petty's most ambitious articulation of population management, but – emphasizing a "sharp distinction between the metropolitan and colonial worlds" – says little about the confessional implications of the transplantation for Britain; Goodacre, *Economic Thought of William Petty*, p. 40. See also David Armitage, "The Political Economy of Britain and Ireland after the Glorious Revolution," in Ohlmeyer (ed.), *Political Thought in Seventeenth-Century Ireland*, pp. 221–43.

If the Irish required transmuting into English, and the population of the Three Kingdoms needed confessional recalibration, Petty's economic writing – in particular, *A Treatise of Taxes and Contributions* (1662) and *Political Arithmetick* (circulated 1672, printed 1690) – suggested more prosaic but no less pervasive interventions in the qualities of the general population. Like his transmutation proposals and his ideas for populating American colonies, Petty's vision of governance was predicated on the malleability of metropolitan as well as colonial populations and posited the state's control of their politically salient qualities as well as their numbers.[169]

A Treatise of Taxes gave an economic turn to the truism that numbers were the glory of the prince. "Fewness of people," Petty wrote, "is real poverty"; underpopulation led to idleness and the degeneration of skill. "If the people be so few, as that they can live, *Ex sponte Creatis*, or with little labour," he wrote, "they become wholly without Art."[170] Because the need for labor and hence the spur to art originated in a struggle for subsistence, numbers of people gained meaning in relation to territory.[171] As Petty put it, "the *Ratio formalis* of Riches" lay "rather in proportion than quantity": "a Nation wherein are Eight Millions of people, are more then twice as rich as the same scope of Land wherein are but Four."[172] This put a premium on population density as a measure of economic potential, as Hugh Goodacre has shown.[173] It also implied policies such as the encouragement of multiplication and immigration (especially of skilled artisans), and what Petty called "an universal Reformation of what length of time hath warped awry" in the professions.[174] Here, he advocated "lessen[ing] the number of Students in Divinity, Law, and Medicine, by lessening the use of those Professions." Analysis of economic and demographic data – including the mortality bills John Graunt was exploring – would set the "requisite" numbers of lawyers, doctors and divines, leaving the rest of the population available for agriculture and manufactures.[175] At the same

---

[169] On Petty's extension of political arithmetic to trans-Atlantic colonies, see McCormick, "Governing Model Populations."

[170] William Petty, *A Treatise of Taxes and Contributions* (London: Printed for N. Brooke, 1662), pp. 16–17.

[171] Conversely, Petty criticized the "mistake, that the greatness and glory of a Prince lyeth rather in the extent of his Territory, then in the number, art, and industry of his people, well united and governed"; Petty, *Treatise of Taxes*, p. 5.

[172] Petty, *Treatise of Taxes*, pp. 9, 16.

[173] Goodacre, *Economic Thought of William Petty*, pp. 95–177. Petty thought it a "false opinion, that our Countrey [England] is full peopled," and judged that Ireland had "not above the 1/5th part so many as the Territory would maintain," Petty, *Treatise of Taxes*, pp. 4–5, 28.

[174] Petty, *Treatise of Taxes*, p. 9.

[175] Petty, *Treatise of Taxes*, pp. 9–11.

time, "certain constant Employments for … indigent people" would "keep their mindes to discipline and obedience, and their bodies to a patience of more profitable labours when need shall require it."[176]

Even before "political arithmetic" was coined, Petty treated population – its changing size, national, religious and occupational makeup, geographical and social distribution, and bodily and mental discipline – as the definitive object of policy. *Political Arithmetick* fleshed this out, notably in its praise of the Dutch. Admired for its commercial prowess, the Dutch Republic stood in Petty's work for the power of "situation, trade, and policy" working together.[177] A narrow, flat, coastal territory had compelled Dutch industry and art, favoring the growth of shipping.[178] The result was a uniquely well-adapted and adaptable population:

> Husbandmen, Seamen, Soldiers, Artizans and Merchants, are the very Pillars of any Common-Wealth; all the other great Professions, do rise out of the infirmities … of these; now the Seaman is three of these four. For every Seaman of industry and ingenuity, is not only a Navigator, but a Merchant, and also a Soldier … wherefore to have the occasion of abounding in Seamen, is a vast conveniency.[179]

Seamen emblematized and embodied productive mutability. Petty also lauded Dutch toleration as an accommodation to human nature, "it being natural for Men to differ in Opinion in matters above Sense and Reason."[180] By fitting policy to the environment and human nature, the Dutch had created a population that reflected their situation yet overcame its limitations, expanding political horizons. It was this adaptive interaction between policy and circumstance, mediated by the qualities of population, which Britain and Ireland must emulate.[181] Petty's invocation of nature was pregnant with implications. But from a seventeenth-century perspective, what stood out was his expansion of transformative demographic governance from ad hoc problem-solving to a mainspring of effective rule in economic, politico-religious and colonial matters alike.

[176] Petty, *Treatise of Taxes*, pp. 12–13.
[177] Petty, *Political Arithmetick*, pp. 1–34.
[178] Petty, *Political Arithmetick*, pp. 20–1.
[179] Petty, *Political Arithmetick*, p. 17.
[180] Petty, *Political Arithmetick*, p. 25.
[181] Petty's counterpoint to Johan de Witt's Dutch Republic was Louis XIV's France, pursuing naval expansion on a scale Petty thought disproportionate both to its natural harbors and to its existing population of seamen ("natural, and perpetual Impediments" to a doomed policy); see Petty, *Political Arithmetick*, pp. 51–63 (quotation at p. 51).

The Meaning of Numbers

It is this expansive view of demographic transformation that makes sense of Petty's vaunted interest in quantification. Striking rhetorical, visual and discursive features of his printed corpus – the label "political arithmetic," the triad of "number, weight and measure," the tables and calculations that pepper his books – have encouraged historians of social science to view Petty as many of his contemporaries did: the "best computer" of his era, to quote both the Duke of Ormond and Gregory King.[182] While positive assessments treat him as a prophet of calculation, critical views focus on his computational mistakes, the faultiness of his numbers or on his role in constructing numbers themselves as disinterested and unassailable facts.[183] This focus is understandable. Petty often lamented his compatriots' ignorance of measurable trends and the paucity of numbers with which he had to work.[184] As he noted in *A Treatise of Taxes*, "it will be objected, that these computations are very hard if not impossible to make; to which I answer onely this, that they are so, especially if none will trouble their hands or heads to make them, or give authority for so doing" – yet only on such a basis could decisions about "Trade" and other matters be saved from the vagaries of chance and "false judgments."[185]

Indeed, taken together, Petty's proposals entailed an unprecedented expansion of data-gathering, involving church and state in the regular collection and analysis of demographic statistics (as well as maps, surveys, meteorological and epidemiological records, and even astrological observations) in the Three Kingdoms and across England's colonial territories. Perhaps the most thorough single statement was Petty's "New Instrument of Government" (1682), a description of a projected work that would detail

---

[182] James Butler, Duke of Ormond, to Sir Robert Southwell, 8 November 1679, in Historical Manuscripts Commission, *Fourteenth Report, Appendix, Part VII. The Manuscripts of the Marquis of Ormonde, Preserved at the Castle, Kilkenny*, 2 vols. (London: Historical Manuscripts Commission, 1895), vol. II, pp. 294–6, at 294; Gregory King, "'The LCC Burns Journal': A manuscript notebook containing workings for several projected works" (*c.* 1695–1700), facsimile reproduction in Peter Laslett (ed.), *The Earliest Classics: John Graunt and Gregory King* (Farnborough: Gregg International Publishers, 1973), p. 49. King himself accused Petty of exaggerating his demographic estimates.

[183] A. M. Endres, "The Functions of Numerical Data in the Writings of Graunt, Petty, and Davenant," *History of Political Economy* 17:1 (1985), 245–64; Richard Olson, *The Emergence of the Social Sciences, 1642–1792* (New York: Twayne Publishers, 1993), pp. 57–70; Stephan Gregory, "The Tabulation of England: How the Social World Was Brought in Rows and Columns," *Distinktion: Scandinavian Journal of Social Theory* 14:3 (2013), 305–25; Poovey, *History of the Modern Fact*, pp. 92–143.

[184] See for example Petty, *Treatise of Taxes*, p. 4; Petty, *Political Arithmetick*, sigs. A1v–A2r.

[185] Petty, *Treatise of Taxes*, p. 34.

Ireland's administrative divisions, place-names, acreages, soil quality, land use, natural and transplanted flora, houses, mills, markets, fairs, rents, cattle, shipping, internal trade, arms and horses, as well as "the Age, Sex, State, Trade, Office, Religion and Country of Each Inhabitant," the "Births, Burialls and mariages, as also the Removeals of the Inhabitants from place to place," and "Every 6th yeare … the Age, Sex, Stature, Haire, Eye & other marks of each person of above 16 years old."[186] This "instrument," elements of which recur in Petty's papers on England and its overseas colonies, was no mere census.[187] It combined fiscal and demographic questions with surveying, cartography, natural history and the surveillance of individuals, networks and migrations. In this sense, it is tempting to see Petty as envisioning a kind of information state that would only become practicable in the later nineteenth century and functional in the twentieth.[188]

Paradoxically, however, Petty was more skeptical of calculation and more open about the limitations of numbers than his historiographical profile indicates. In a manuscript dialogue from the 1660s entitled "How All Persons & Things May Contribute Proporti[onally] to Their Government & Defence," he tied the practical limits of computation to those of sense and reason. "When Wee have proceeded as far as wee can by Number weight & measure, and have apply'd them to the smallest parts our senses can discerne," Petty's mouthpiece explained, then what remained was "leaving things to the Opinions of men, or to lott."[189] This was less a matter of chance than of trusting experts. When Petty's interlocutor criticized "estimate & opinion," his spokesman responded:

> [I]n drawing … a circle of an Inch diameter, the most Mathematicall Limner useth no scale nor Compasses but measures properties both of lines and angles by the estimat of his Eye. Upon the Violin there are no frets or divisions upon the Neck but by estimate & yet the music intended to bee exact. Those that play best at Tenis & billiards use no instruments for the angles of Incidence & Reflection, At bowles there is no computation of the lines and radius which the bowles describe.... If a man would divide an

[186] Petty, "New Instrument of Government," BL Additional MS 72880, ff.61v–62r.

[187] Compare for example William Petty, "Quaeries Concerning the Nature of the Natives of Pensilvania" (1686), BL Additional MS 72867, ff.74–77v, printed in Lansdowne (ed.), *Petty Papers*, vol. II, pp. 115–19.

[188] Higgs, *Information State in England*, pp. 62–3, 131–2, sees the formative period as extending from 1880 to 1914; but compare Popper, "Information State for Elizabethan England"; Slack, "Government and Information"; Groebner, *Who Are You?*; Soll, *Information Master*.

[189] William Petty, "How All Persons & Things May Contribute Proporti[onally] to Their Government & Defence" (1660s), BL Additional MS 72865, ff.6–13, at f.7r.

Inch into 100 visible parts hee needs make scarse halfe so many lineary distinctions, & so of 1000 more particulars. Wherefore there is more exactnes in the conjectures of some Mens hand & Eyes then in Measures or weights. And this judgment of reason to Men of grosse sensation bears the same proportion as Lott doth to the finest of all human computations.[190]

Exactness need not mean calculation or measurement. It was sometimes a matter of expert conjecture. This was so not only where objects were beyond the reach of the senses, but also where an issue was "effect of so many & so Minute causes [as] the sense of Man cannot compute."[191] Though "wee must stick to Number Weight & Measure, till our senses & Instruments ... fayle us," at some point the hand or eye of a skilled practitioner – "the Estimate bona fide made by those of greatest practise & Experience" – beat the false precision of a faulty computer.[192]

This caveat suggests that even Petty's best-known articulation of his quantitative approach is not quite what it seems. The Preface to *Political Arithmetick* closed with a description of the method that has sustained many accounts of Petty as a quantifier:

> The Method I take to do this, is not yet very usual; for instead of using only comparative and superlative Words, and intellectual Arguments, I have taken the course (as a Specimen of the Political Arithmetick I have long aimed at) to express my self in Terms of *Number*, *Weight*, or *Measure*; to use only Arguments of Sense, and to consider only such Causes, as have visible Foundations in Nature; leaving those that depend upon the mutable Minds, Opinions, Appetites, and Passions of Particular Men, to the Consideration of others: Really professing my self as unable to speak satisfactorily upon those Grounds ... as to foretel the cast of a Dye; to play well at Tennis, Billiards, or Bowles, (without long practice) by virtue of the most elaborate Conceptions that ever have been written *De Projectilibus & Missilibus*, or of the Angles of Incidence and Reflection.[193]

Superficially, this reads as a vindication of empirical, numerical fact against subjective and spectral opinion. Yet the passage gives the very same examples of matters beyond calculation – tennis, billiards, bowls – as the manuscript dialogue quoted, and it links them, again, not simply

[190] Petty, "How All Persons & Things May Contribute Proporti[onally] to Their Government & Defence," BL Additional MS 72865, ff.7v-8r.
[191] Petty, "How All Persons & Things May Contribute Proporti[onally] to Their Government & Defence," BL Additional MS 72865, f.8r.
[192] Petty, "How All Persons & Things May Contribute Proporti[onally] to Their Government & Defence," BL Additional MS 72865, f.8v.
[193] Petty, *Political Arithmetick*, sig. A4r.

to chance or ignorance but to practice and judgment. By distinguish-ing number, weight and measure from such "considerations," Petty was not asserting the superior exactitude of quantitative method but, to the contrary, demarcating its limits. Numbers captured and made calcu-lable the visible, sensible aspects of the objects of government, including population. At the same time, reliance on empirical numbers reflected the *imprecision* of political arithmetic.

This explains Petty's otherwise puzzling description of the numbers he used. These "Observations or Positions expressed by *Number, Weight*, and *Measure*," he continued, "are either true, or not apparently false" – hardly an endorsement of their accuracy. Further, he added,

> [I]f they are not already true, certain, and evident, yet [they] may be made so by the Sovereign Power, *Nam id certum est quod reddi potest* ["for that is certain which may be made so," a legal maxim], and if they are false, not so false as to destroy the Argument they are brought for; but at worst are sufficient as Suppositions to shew the way to that Knowledge I aim at.[194]

Numbers were *not* exact representations of empirical reality. Despite his reputation as a peddler of quantitative facts, Petty conspicuously failed – in this, his baldest declaration of his method – to vouch for the exactitude of his figures or even for their broad truth. He offered them instead as expressions of the visible aspects of population and as indicators of politi-cal possibility. They were "true, certain, and evident" only to the extent that they might be "made so by the Sovereign Power." Their value hinged on the power, and their accuracy depended on the action, of the state. The point of political arithmetic was not that numerical facts should deter-mine policy; policy governing population would determine the numerical facts. Transformation, not calculation, was the key.

Transformations of the kind Petty envisioned fostered ambitious demands for information. Graunt's work on the mortality bills, the legacy of the Down Survey and the mathematization of natural-philosophical argument led Petty to frame his arguments in quantitative language and to draw on empirical figures in distinctive ways. Yet in practice, he relied on rough estimates derived or extrapolated from patchy, pre-existing sources and he was open and unapologetic about doing so. He described the goals of his demographic governance – which were funda-mentally qualitative – more often in terms of simple proportions (the ratio of Catholics to Protestants) or unities (the union of the English and the

---

Irish) than as complex calculations with precise outcomes. Transmutation involved ratios and aggregates, but on the ground level, it depended on the operation of passions and the mutability of minds. What made political arithmetic a new instrument of government was its generalization of demographic transformation as a mode of policy. This created uses for old numbers and suggested roles for new ones as raw material for arguments and as expressions of political goals. But what Petty tried to create, the sovereign power that governed the population, was as much an alchemical monarchy as it was an information state.

CHAPTER 5

Improving Populations in the Eighteenth Century

Demographic Subjectivity in the Age of Political Arithmetic

Petty's projecting reveals much about the creation of population as an object of knowledge and power, but his rhetoric is a fallible guide. "Number, weight and measure" framed his discussion of his method. Yet even as he affirmed numbers as his chosen idiom, he undercut their empirical veracity, referring their value to the power of the state and locating their truth in a possible future – a future predicated on the adoption of measures that his numbers ostensibly underpinned. The quantification of human and other material invites expansive visions of data-gathering and computation as techniques of rule; yet Petty's proposals rested on rough, reasoned estimates or extrapolations from old sources. He defined his political goals in terms of the imposition of desirable natures on human masses of uncertain size but known qualities. He projected future population growth in figures but aimed at achieving broad ratios and proportions between populations defined by mutable political, cultural and economic characteristics. Numbers furnished a medium for describing and at times dissembling the objects of qualitative transformation along these multiple axes. It was the goal of transformation, however, not quantification, which drove change. Quantification took hold once planned mobility and directed mutation had become central tasks of governance. It did not create these tasks.

Petty's transmutative projects came to nothing, however. His quantitative rhetoric endured. Political arithmetic was revived after the Revolution of 1688 as a series of computational practices suited to Parliamentary government rather than a social engineering program befitting an absolute monarch. Posthumously known by his printed works, Petty (alongside or in place of Graunt) anchored a steadily growing canon of calculators. This roster eventually included heroes of quantification from Edmund Halley (who based a "Life Table" on Breslau mortality data in 1693),

Gregory King (who tabulated the population of England by ranks and degrees in 1695) and Charles Davenant (who defined political arithmetic as an "Art of Reasoning, by Figures" in 1698), through William Maitland (who debated the size and growth of London with Continental statisticians in the 1730s and 1740s) to Arthur Young (who published series of agricultural statistics as "political arithmetic" in the 1770s). It also included a sizeable subset of "medical arithmeticians," from champion of inoculation and Secretary of the Royal Society James Jurin, in the early 1720s, through physician and statistician William Black, in the late 1780s.[1] By the time Adam Smith published *The Wealth of Nations* in 1776, political arithmetic was so strongly identified with "computations" based on numerical data that to doubt one was, for Smith, to "have no great faith" in the other.[2]

The historiography of quantification in the long eighteenth century is deep, and less inclined than it once was to take Petty's rhetoric at face value.[3] One consequence has been a demotion of Petty-as-computer in favor of Graunt on the one hand and Davenant on the other. Yet severing the links between Restoration and Augustan political arithmetic risks obscuring significant legacies. If Davenant radically repurposed Petty's invention, this does not mean that Petty's ambitions had no sequel. After all, these transformative ambitions were not Petty's alone, but products of a century and more of engagement with the challenges and possibilities of moving large numbers of people around, mixing or separating them, and manipulating their qualities. His vision of population was never merely quantitative, and nor was it ever merely his. Just as the construction of population as an object of qualitative manipulation had a history prior to its alchemical climax in Petty's proposals, so it manifested itself in a host of less colorful but more effectual ways afterward. If we are to see these continuities, it is the perspicuity of quantification as a category of analysis – and of the quantifying spirit as a historical cause – that needs to be rethought.

---

[1] A version of this canon appears in Thomas Short, *New Observations, Natural, Moral, Civil, Political, and Medical, on City, Town, and Country Bills of Mortality. To Which Are Added, Large and Clear Abstracts of the Best Authors Who Have Wrote on That Subject. With an Appendix on the Weather and Meteors* (London: Printed for T. Longman and A. Millar, 1750), pp. xi–xii. On medical arithmetic see Rusnock, *Vital Accounts*, esp. pp. 65–6.

[2] Comparing calculations relating to the grain trade in Book IV, Smith wrote: "I have no great faith in political arithmetic, and I mean not to warrant the exactness of either of these computations." Adam Smith (ed. Edwin Cannan), *An Inquiry into the Nature and Causes of the Wealth of Nations*, 2 vols. (London: Methuen and Co., 1904), vol. II, p. 36.

[3] See especially Deringer, *Calculated Values*.

One approach is to consider the eighteenth century as less an age of numbers than one of projects.[4] It was also, taking up the legacy of seventeenth-century projectors, an era of improvements; of celebratory reflections on progress in the arts and sciences; of confrontation between ancient and modern wisdom and policy; and, at mid-century, of ruminations on the nature and causes of long-term social, economic and intellectual development. Population figured in these myriad, interlinked discourses as a set of ideas and as a series of quantities. As historians of politics and social policy have shown, engagements with demographic figures or trends played instrumental and discursive roles in the justification and criticism of policies and of governments.[5] Numbers of people figured, too, in the numerous bits of local legislation, administrative measures, church initiatives and charitable efforts – "inferior politics," as Joanna Innes calls them – that supplied the legal and social infrastructure of improvement in Augustan and Hanoverian Britain.[6] Historians of probability have explored the development of annuities and the creation of an insurance industry, which put a premium on more sophisticated mathematics and more precise empirical knowledge of life expectancy.[7] These political, fiscal and economic applications fueled calls for systematic enumeration that, as D. V. Glass and others have traced, led eventually to the national census.[8]

Yet the census came at the end of the century. It was the prior history of projects and policies geared toward improvement, and predicated on qualitative ideas about population, that created a world wherein the regular, systematic, empirical gathering of demographic numbers made sense. Conversely, it was the regularity, systematicity and empiricism of the census, not the quantification of population per se, which made it new. In quantitative terms, projections of human multiplication backward to Adam and forward to the full peopling of the planet (or the apocalypse)

---

[4] See Maximilian Novak (ed.), *The Age of Projects* (Toronto: University of Toronto Press, 2008). The title is a reference to Defoe's description of his time as "The Projecting Age": Daniel Defoe, *An Essay upon Projects* (London: Printed by R.R. for Tho. Cockerill, 1697), p. 1.

[5] See Buck, "People Who Counted"; Hoppit, "Political Arithmetic."

[6] Innes, *Inferior Politics*, pp. 109–75; see also Julian Hoppit, *Britain's Political Economies: Parliament and Economic Life, 1660–1800* (Cambridge: Cambridge University Press, 2017), pp. 3–37, 66–101.

[7] D. O. Thomas, *The Honest Mind: The Thought and Work of Richard Price* (Oxford: Oxford University Press, 1977), pp. 127–50; Lorraine J. Daston, "The Domestication of Risk: Mathematical Probability and Insurance, 1650–1830," in Lorenz Krüger, Lorraine J. Daston and Michael Heidelberger (eds.), *The Probabilistic Revolution, Volume 1: Ideas in History* (Cambridge, MA: MIT Press, 1987), pp. 237–60; Hacking, *Emergence of Probability*, pp. 92–121.

[8] Glass, *Numbering the People*; Levitan, *Cultural History of the Census*.

had long fueled arguments about scriptural history, the date of the Flood, the division of the Earth among the sons of Noah and the formation of historical empires. Graunt offered one account of human "doubling" since Creation in his *Observations*, while Petty furnished clergymen with mathematical arguments showing the plausibility of biblical history and even of bodily resurrection. Political-arithmetical calculations diverged from sacred-historical precedent less in their chronological or doctrinal implications (which were typically orthodox) than in their use of empirical sources and, in histories of the earth like Thomas Burnet's and William Whiston's, in their adaptation of new ideas about human fertility, salubrity and longevity to the changing states of the pre- and postdiluvian world.[9]

By the second decade of the eighteenth century, such influential writers as William Derham – whose Boyle Lectures, printed as *Physico-Theology* in 1714, became standard reading throughout the Anglo-American world – had domesticated the idea of multiplication as both a natural process accessible to measurement and an object of providential care, an index of divine judgment and human freedom.[10] Long tasked with gathering vital data, and more recently concerned with surveying the numerical strength of dissent, as in the Compton Census of 1676, the church now publicized and propagated demographic ideas for apologetic and pastoral purposes.[11] In a 1701 sermon to the London Society for the Reformation of Manners, Anglican archdeacon (later Bishop of Peterborough) White Kennett enthused that "By a moderate Calculation, no less than Thirty Thousand Persons have been convicted for prophane Cursing and Swearing," and "Near the same number of Lewd and Disorderly Persons … brought to a merciful Punishment."[12] Such quantitative summaries of the struggle against vice generated annual "Accounts."[13] Across the Atlantic, the Puritan Cotton Mather copied Kennett's numbers into his

---

[9] See McCormick, "Political Arithmetic and Sacred History."

[10] On Derham and the Boyle Lectures, see Margaret C. Jacob, *The Newtonians and the English Revolution, 1689–1720* (Ithaca, NY: Cornell University Press, 1976), pp. 143–61. On the Atlantic career of physico-theology, see Susan Scott Parrish, *American Curiosity: Cultures of Natural History in the Colonial British Atlantic World* (Chapel Hill: University of North Carolina Press, 2006), pp. 44–54.

[11] On the Compton Census see Anne Whiteman, "The Compton Census of 1676," in Kevin Schurer and Tom Arkell (eds.), *Surveying the People: The Interpretation and Use of Document Sources for the Study of Population in the Later Seventeenth Century* (Oxford: Leopard's Head Press, 1992), pp. 78–96; Anne Whiteman (ed.), *The Compton Census of 1676: A Critical Edition* (London: Oxford University Press, 1986).

[12] White Kennett, *A Sermon Preach'd at Bow-Church, London, before the Societies for Reformation, on Monday the 29th of December, 1701* (London: Printed for A. and J. Churchil, 1702), p. 48.

[13] See Shelley Burtt, "The Societies for the Reformation of Manners: Between John Locke and the Devil in Augustan England," in Roger D. Lund (ed.), *The Margins of Orthodoxy: Heterodox Writing and Cultural Response, 1660–1750* (Cambridge: Cambridge University Press, 1995), pp. 149–69, at 153.

commonplace book, while quoting Graunt's findings on life expectancy in minatory sermons to his Massachusetts flock.[14] While politicians bent demographic calculation to new polemical uses, parishioners heard God's will revealed in patterns of mortality.

The language of political arithmetic, the history of human multiplication and the idea of demographic governance entered public consciousness by several paths. Sermons – especially but not only prominent series such as the Boyle Lectures – were read even more widely than they were heard. New kinds of publication further broadcast demographic numbers and processes. While popular print reproduced snatches of political-arithmetical or physico-theological argumentation verbatim, once recondite numbers, ratios and ideas also coalesced in new literary forms.[15] The materials and mentalities of political arithmetic became public property, ripe for serious or satirical use. In 1692, the Tory mathematician John Arbuthnot introduced "the Force of Numbers" not only through familiar games of cards and dice but also through a series of demographic wagers:

> There is … a Calculation of the Quantity of Probability founded on Experience, to be made use of in Wagers about any thing; for example, it is odds, if a Woman is *with Child*, but it shall be a *Boy*; and if you would know the just odds, you must consider the Proportion in the Bills that the Males bear to the Females: The Yearly Bills of Mortality are observ'd to bear such Proportion to the live People as 1 to 30, or 26; therefore it is an even Wager, that one out of thirteen, dyes within a Year…. It is but 1 to 18 if you meet a *Parson* in the Street, that he proves to be a *Non-Juror*, because there is but 1 of 26 that are such. It is hardly 1 to 10, that a *Woman* of Twenty Years old has her *Maidenhead*, and almost in some Wager, that a *Town-Spark* of that Age has not been *clap'd*.[16]

Where Graunt had drawn natural and political lessons for philosophers and statesmen, Arbuthnot invited ordinary readers to see their neighbors (and, implicitly, themselves) as so many demographic units, products of probability. Arbuthnot amplified his praise of private and public computation thirty years later in *An Essay on the Usefulness of Mathematical*

[14] "Cotton Mather's Quotations," in the *Microfilm Edition of the Cotton Mather Papers*, 19 reels (a joint publication of the Massachusetts Historical Society and the American Antiquarian Society), reel 7 [vol. 6: *Sermons, essays, and other works, 1680–1724*], fr.84–156, at fr.101–102. See McCormick, "Statistics in the Hands of an Angry God?"

[15] Cohen, *Calculating People*, p. 83.

[16] John Arbuthnot, *Of the Laws of Chance, or, a Method of Calculation of the Hazards of Game, Plainly Demonstrated, and Applied to Games at Present Most in Use, Which May Be Easily Extended to the Most Intricate Cases of Chance Imaginable* (London: Printed by Benj. Motte, 1692), sigs. A8r, A9v–A10v.

Learning, defending Petty as the author of a pleasant and useful "art."[17] Adopting a quantitative view of the social and political world was part of embracing empirical, experimental, scientific knowledge, for rulers and householders alike.[18]

It may seem paradoxical that Arbuthnot's friend and fellow "Scriblerian" satirist Jonathan Swift – who knew Petty's writings and daughter, Anne – should have penned the most biting critique of political arithmetic ever written.[19] Even Swift's harsh appraisal, however, recognized the power of demographic thinking. *A Modest Proposal* (1729) lampooned Petty's projecting in its blithe attitude to human life and in its deft, amoral calculation:

> The Number of Souls in *Ireland* being usually reckoned one Million and a half; of these I calculate there may be about Two hundred Thousand Couple whose Wives are Breeders; from which Number I subtract thirty thousand Couples, who are able to maintain their own Children ... this being granted, there will remain an Hundred and Seventy thousand Breeders. I again subtract Fifty Thousand, for those Women who miscarry, or whose Children die by Accident, or Disease, within the Year. There only remain an Hundred and Twenty Thousand Children of poor Parents, annually born: The Question therefore is, How this Number shall be reared, and provided for?[20]

Swift's disdain for political arithmetic predated *A Modest Proposal* and reflected more than concern for the Irish. In *Gulliver's Travels* (1726), the King of Brobdingnag laughed at Gulliver's "odd Kind of Arithmetick (as he was pleased to call it) in reckoning the Numbers of our People by a Computation drawn from the several Sects among us in Religion and Politicks" – harking back to the Compton Census.[21] Swift had earlier adverted to the corrosive, even atheistic tendencies of calculation in *An Argument against Abolishing Christianity* (written 1708–11):

> It is likewise urged, that there are, by Computation, in this Kingdom, above ten Thousand Parsons, whose Revenues added to those of my Lords the

---

[17] John Arbuthnot, *An Essay on the Usefulness of Mathematical Learning, in a Letter From a Gentleman in the City to His Friend in Oxford*, 2nd ed. (Oxford: Printed by L. Lichfield for S. Wilmot, 1721), p. 19.

[18] On Arbuthnot as a "Tory Newtonian," see Deringer, *Calculated Values*, pp. 94–5.

[19] See Peter M. Briggs, "John Graunt, Sir William Petty, and Swift's Modest Proposal," *Eighteenth-Century Life* 29:2 (2005), 3–24.

[20] Jonathan Swift, *A Modest Proposal for Preventing the Children of Poor People in Ireland, from Being a Burden to their Parents or Country; and for Making them Beneficial to the Publick* [1729], in Robert A. Greenberg and William B. Piper (eds.), *The Writings of Jonathan Swift* (New York: W. W. Norton, 1973), pp. 502–9, at 503. See Sussman, "Colonial Afterlife of Political Arithmetic."

[21] Jonathan Swift, *Travels into Several Remote Nations of the World* [1726], in Greenberg and Piper (eds.), *Writings of Jonathan Swift*, pp. 1–260, at 107. See note 11.

> Bishops, would suffice to maintain, at least, two Hundred young Gentlemen
> of Wit and Pleasure, and Free-thinking ... who might be an Ornament to
> the Court and Town: And then again, so great a Number of able (bodied)
> Divines might be a Recruit to our Fleet and Armies.[22]

For Swift, the same computational rationality that Arbuthnot enjoined
gave birth to monstrous absurdities. For all the distance between their
personal assessments, however, the two authors agreed on the analytical
and practical import of calculation, on the increasing centrality of population as an object of this calculation and on the prominence of a new,
metrical, demographic mindset.

Thus a kind of demographic subjectivity fed upon new awareness of
demographic thinking and measurement as political and cognitive tools.
In part, this sense of belonging to population reflected the impact of political-arithmetical concepts and practices on much older ideas of biblical
genealogy: all people were descended from Adam, but Adam's progeny
now appeared more and more often as a continuously growing quantum
of which each individual was a unit. Rather than reducing the individual
to a "mere" statistic, this made statistics matters of divine concern. Such
was the gist of Mather's use of Graunt in a 1708 funeral sermon:

> Children, Go unto the Burying-place; There you will see many a Grave
> shorter than your selves. 'Tis now upon Computation found, That more
> than half the Children of men Dy before they come to be Seventeen Years
> of Age. And what needs any more be said, for your Awakening, to Learn
> the Holy Scriptures![23]

Similar ideas appeared in more elegiac and less monitory modes, and in
literary rather than religious venues. In 1711, Joseph Addison and Richard
Steele's *The Spectator* encouraged readers to visualize their place within
natural demographic regularities, in a text later known as "The Vision
of Mirzah." Supposedly a manuscript discovered by a visitor to Cairo,
describing an encounter with a sage, it set mortality tables in a sacred-historical and providential context, figuring life as the crossing of an ancient
and dilapidated bridge:

[22] Jonathan Swift, *An Argument to Prove, that the Abolishing of Christianity in England, May, as
Things Now Stand, Be Attended with Some Inconveniences, and Perhaps, Not Produce Those Many
Good Effects Proposed thereby* [1708–1711], in Greenberg and Piper (eds.), *Writings of Jonathan
Swift*, pp. 460–71, at 464.
[23] Cotton Mather, *Corderius Americanus: An Essay on the Good Education of Children* (Boston, MA:
Printed by John Allen, 1708), p. 18. This was in fact a funeral sermon for Massachusetts schoolmas-
ter Ezekiel Chambers; compare Cotton Mather, *Seasonable Thoughts Upon Mortality. A Sermon
Occasioned by the Raging of a Mortal Sickness in the Colony of Connecticut, and the Many Deaths*

The Bridge thou seest, said he, is humane Life; consider it attentively.... I found that it consisted of threescore and ten entire Arches, with several broken arches, which added to those that were entire made up the Number about an hundred. [T]he Genius told me, that this Bridge consisted at first of a thousand Arches; but that a great Flood swept away the rest.... But tell me further, said he, what thou discoverest on it. I see Multitudes of People passing over it, said I, and a black Cloud hanging on each End of it. As I looked more attentively, I saw several of the Passengers dropping thro' the Bridge, into the great Tide that flowed underneath it; and upon further Examination, perceived there were innumerable Trap-doors that lay concealed in the Bridge, which the Passengers no sooner trod upon, but they fell through.... These hidden Pit-falls were set very thick at the Entrance of the Bridge, so that Throngs of People no sooner broke through the Cloud, but many of them fell into them. They grew thinner towards the Middle, but multiplied and lay closer together towards the End of the Arches that were entire.[24]

Daniel Defoe's *A Journal of the Plague Year* – printed in 1722 as the work of "a Citizen who continued all the while in London" during the 1665 epidemic – put demographic observation before the public in another way, again inviting readers to imagine themselves as candidates for grim enumeration.[25] Besides commenting on medical and administrative responses to plague, Defoe quoted the bills of mortality and criticized them for failing to give "a full Account," blaming inattentive or skittish parish officers.[26] The Restoration naval administrator and Fellow of the Royal Society Samuel Pepys, who had tracked the plague's progress via the bills during the outbreak, had voiced similar concerns in his diary.[27] Sixty years on, anxiety about these numbers was fodder for novels.

These examples suggest that a demographic subjectivity – in which ordinary readers and listeners might understand themselves as demographic observers and calculators *and* as objects of demographic observation and

of Our Brethren There (Boston, MA: Printed by T. Green, 1712), pp. 14–15, and Cotton Mather, *Life Swiftly Passing and Quickly Ending. A Very Short Sermon, on the Shortness of Humane Life* (Boston, MA: Printed by T. Fleet and T. Crump, 1716), pp. 7–10. See McCormick, "Statistics in the Hands of an Angry God?"; Daniel Scott Smith and J. David Hacker, "Cultural Demography: New England Deaths and the Puritan Perception of Risk," *Journal of Interdisciplinary History* 26:3 (1996), 367–92.
[24] *The Spectator* 160, September 1, 1711. See Bonar, *Theories of Population*, pp. 123–4, 131–2.
[25] [Daniel Defoe], *A Journal of the Plague Year: Being Observations or Memorials, of the Most Remarkable Occurrences, as Well Public as Private, which Happened in London during the Last Great Visitation in 1665* (London: Printed for E. Nutt, J. Roberts, A. Dodd and J. Graves, 1722).
[26] Defoe, *Journal of the Plague Year*, pp. 3–8, 115–17.
[27] See entries from late May to mid-September 1665, in Robert Latham and William Matthews (eds.), *The Diary of Samuel Pepys*, 10 vols. (London: G. Bell and Sons, 1970–83), vol. VI, pp. 108–225.

calculation – was possible because demographic figures and tables themselves were ever more present in media and public discourse.[28] Numbers were news. The London mortality bills had been printed for over a century; as Mark Jenner has shown, they featured alongside prayers and medical remedies in "Lord Have Mercy Upon Us" broadsides issued during plague outbreaks since the early Stuart period.[29] In the seventeenth century, however, this practice was limited to London. In the early eighteenth century, it ceased to be so. As newspapers multiplied in London, spread to provincial cities (facilitated by the lapse of the Licensing Act in 1695) and sprang up in such distant and diverse colonial outposts as Boston, New York, Philadelphia and Charleston, mortality data became a routine part of the news by the early 1730s.[30] Just as the growth of news and of reliable communications networks fostered new senses of synchronicity and national and imperial belonging, so the familiarization of measurable population processes and of a standard if crude sense of demographic history encouraged a sense of individual and generational demographic location as well as of communal size and power.[31]

Indications of demographic subjectivity raise the question of agency. What did it mean to be one of a fluctuating number? Here histories of medicine and the family have been most suggestive. Examining debates over smallpox inoculation in Boston and London in the early 1720s, Andrea Rusnock has shown how demographic numbers drove bitter public polemics, as doctors and divines argued the ethics and efficacy of new medicine. Even more bluntly than the political wrangles of Court and Country computers, inoculation debates revealed fundamental issues at stake in the public engagement with population. Mortality statistics were assumed on all sides to reveal God's judgment. But what was the verdict? Were numbers of the dead an indication that plague must be suffered

---

[28] For a Foucauldian account of the significance of tabulation, see Gregory, "The Tabulation of England," 305–25. Gregory argues (p. 316) that "it is quantification itself that transforms society. And it is the table which can be regarded as its most efficient medium." Tabulation reduced "a multi-dimensional reality to the two-dimensionality of a paper sheet" (p. 319), imposing categorical distinctions that use made indisputable and initiating bio-power by constituting populations as objects of strategic calculation (pp. 318–19). I argue that quantification followed rather than drove the constitution of populations as objects of manipulation. Notwithstanding the instrumental use of tabular representation, examples such as "The Vision of Mirzah" suggest it was just one of several ways of making population visible.

[29] Jenner, "Plague on a Page."

[30] See Sommerville, *The News Revolution in England*, p. 66; Glaisyer, *The Culture of Commerce in England, 1660–1720*, pp. 172, 176; Cassedy, *Demography in America*, pp. 120–6; Klepp, "The Swift Progress of Population," pp. 3–15.

[31] On the impact of news and correspondence see Sommerville, *New Revolution in England*; Rachel Scarborough King, *Writing to the World: Letters and the Origins of Modern Print Genres*

as a condign punishment, or did the measurable effects of inoculation show the legitimacy of human intervention? Might individual assertions of agency – or failures to assert it, where science allowed – tempt God? How might personal decisions imperil the wider community? Empirical population data, marshaled for the purpose, printed in pamphlets and sent in letters across the Atlantic, limned the moral as well as mortal consequences of an individual decision to undertake inoculation, or not.[32] With respect to inoculation, at least, political arithmetic came to mediate personal agency in matters touching health, faith and family.

Questions about demographic agency were and are complicated by boundaries of geography, status, gender and race. On the most basic level, numbers were inescapably mediated by various forms of literary, religious and scientific communication, as we have seen, and access to the pertinent genres of print and speech (and literacy and numeracy skills) was both unevenly distributed and changing over the course of the century. Even for those with access, the same set of numbers – the London mortality figures published by Graunt and recycled by Cotton Mather, for example – could have different implications for individuals depending on geographical, cultural and generic context.[33] More than this, however, conceptions of demographic agency both reflected and produced as well as challenged existing and emerging inequalities. As Swift's use of "breeders" caustically implied, the pronatalist thrust of political arithmetic – which appealed, as earlier Hartlibian projects had, to the self-interest of male householders, planters and administrators – left little space for reasoned calculation or indeed for choice on the part of what Graunt and Petty called "teeming women," and still less in Ireland than in Britain.[34] As Jennifer Morgan, Sasha Turner and Rana Hogarth have shown for different periods, moreover, the simultaneous instrumentalization and pathologization of the bodies of African- and colonial-born Black people, especially women, denied outright or stigmatized and punished

---

(Baltimore, MD: Johns Hopkins University Press, 2018), pp. 23–85. This literature is indebted to Benedict Anderson, *Imagined Communities: Reflections on the Origin and Spread of Nationalism*, rev. ed. (London: Verso, 2006). A counterpoint to arguments for the production of modern temporal sensibility through early newspapers is Tony Claydon, "Daily News and the Construction of Time in Late Stuart England, 1695–1714," *Journal of British Studies* 52:1 (2013), pp. 55–78.

[32] Rusnock, *Vital Accounts*, pp. 41–106.

[33] McCormick, "Statistics in the Hands of an Angry God?"

[34] See for example Petty, *Another Essay in Political Arithmetick*, pp. 13–14. On the cultural and scientific politics of pronatalism in eighteenth-century Britain, see Lisa Forman Cody, *Birthing the Nation: Sex, Science, and the Conception of Eighteenth-Century Britons* (Oxford: Oxford University Press, 2005).

reproductive, childrearing and medical choices inconsistent with the demands of plantation, production or – as in Hogarth's account of the Philadelphia yellow fever epidemic of 1793 – the convenience of white populations.[35] By the same token, resistance to various aspects of colonial and patriarchal demographic governance, from pronatalism to racialized medicine, meant assertions of agency – around childbirth, childrearing, and individual and collective health – from below.

These were themselves sometimes articulated in demographic terms. The demographic subjectivity in play during the inoculation debates and implied in contemporaneous physico-theological tracts, essays and sermons, for example, anticipated the reformulation of women's reproductive agency that Susan Klepp traces in British North America after the Seven Years' War. Klepp describes a conscious "switch from 'natural' (and presumptively unmediated) childbearing to goal-oriented and limited family size" by about 1800.[36] What was new here was not women's power over reproduction altogether, but rather the context in which, tools by which and purposes for which urban, middle-class, literate women exercised this power. Instead of using contraception on an ad hoc basis, these women came to envision a target family size and to organize their reproductive careers accordingly: clustering births, spacing pregnancies and ceasing to bear children once their goals were reached.[37] They thus brought not just their bodies but their reproductive lives out of the realm of unimproved nature and into that of conscious calculation.[38] In this, Klepp argues, they pioneered a control over fertility that became normal elsewhere only in the late nineteenth and twentieth centuries – a transition seen in retrospect as a key feature of industrial civilization and a gauge of social and economic modernity.[39]

Quantification played instrumental and symbolic roles in this transition, just as in political arithmetic.[40] Numbers of children and measures of wealth and time displaced continuity of lineage as the aim of procreation, against a backdrop of spreading numeracy and public awareness of population

---

[35] Morgan, *Laboring Women*; Turner, *Contested Bodies*; Hogarth, *Medicalizing Blackness*, especially pp. 17–47.

[36] Klepp, *Revolutionary Conceptions*, p. 4.

[37] Klepp, *Revolutionary Conceptions*, pp. 49, 70, 122–3. For a complementary account of the career of the "bachelor," see John Gilbert McCurdy, *Citizen Bachelors: Manhood and the Creation of the United States* (Ithaca, NY: Cornell University Press, 2009).

[38] Klepp, *Revolutionary Conceptions*, p. 70.

[39] Klepp, *Revolutionary Conceptions*, pp. 5–6, 262. On "fertility transition" see Etienne van de Walle, "Fertility Transition, Conscious Choice, and Numeracy," *Demography* 29:4 (1992), 487–502.

[40] On demographic enumeration in colonial American contexts, see Molly Farrell, *Counting Bodies: Population in Colonial American Writing* (Oxford: Oxford University Press, 2016).

as a factor of national strength.[41] Yet more than numbers lay behind the assumption of individual control over reproductive planning, just as more than numbers had underlain projections of state control over the multiplication and mutation of mankind. In both cases, the imperative to improve natural material, to impose a second nature upon it, supplied the matrix within which quantification and calculation made sense. In both cases, a sense of human power over physical nature and of technology – whether agricultural or contraceptive – as the instrument of this power was essential. Indeed, Klepp notes a "slippage between the productivity of women and the productivity of agriculture."[42] The same slippage had linked the improvement of land with the regeneration of human groups since the late sixteenth century. The difference between the two cases was not the role of numbers but the locus of agency, which no longer emanated from the metropolitan seats of imperial strategy but was now scattered across the middling households of women and their husbands, calculating for themselves on the periphery.

As this dispersal of agency suggests, one of the major questions raised by the emergence of population as an object of public knowledge and calculation and a locus of subjectivity was that of who held, or should hold, power over its collective qualities. Keeping to the problem of transformation, we might ask more precisely: Where did the power to transform populations reside? In one way or another, this question dogged practical engagements with population over the whole of the long eighteenth century, from Petty to Malthus. Closely bound up with it was a second question: What were the limits of demographic governance? What forces or conditions limited the quantitative and, especially, the qualitative manipulation of human populations? There was no consensus on either of these questions between 1660 and 1800. At the end of the period, however, Malthus gave firm and influential answers that broke with those the prior history of demographic governance through Petty-style projecting had often implied – and that were at odds, too, with a growing sense of public and individual demographic agency.

Nature, Place and the Power of Improvement

Petty had suggested ways of thinking about the limits of policy. These centered on two elastic ideas: "Nature," a heavily burdened concept with a complex career ahead of it; and "situation," a synonym for place that Petty and

---

[41] Klepp, *Revolutionary Conceptions*, pp. 115–17, 213–14; van de Walle, "Fertility Transition," argues for numeracy as a necessary condition for control over fertility (though not for the use of techniques such as birth spacing on other grounds).
[42] Klepp, *Revolutionary Conceptions*, p. 56.

his contemporaries complicated and enriched.[43] Because he used these terms in aphoristic dicta rather than explaining them at length, their meaning is hard to abstract from their purposes in specific arguments. Nevertheless, their implications for policy can help us to mark where Petty departed from his predecessors and to compare his sense of the limits of policy to those of his successors. Broadly speaking, his arguments pointed in two directions. One was toward a complicated series of negotiations between demography and various senses of nature, construed as more or less local and malleable or universal and immutable. The second was toward an understanding of the size, growth and quality of populations not just as a goal of policy but also as a criterion of political judgment in Britain and across the Atlantic. The following two sections will deal with the first, while the final section will turn to the second.

In *Political Arithmetick*, Petty invoked the triad of "Situation, Trade, and Policy" to explain the success of Dutch commerce, to predict the failure of French naval policy and to indicate the unexploited potential of English and Irish land and labor.[44] "Situation" was a common word. In sixteenth-century works, it denoted geographical location, topographical position or physical orientation. The 1532 translation of Xenophon's *Oeconomicus* recommended that "the situation" of a house "be very moche southward" so as to maximize light in winter and shade in summer.[45] William Cunningham's 1559 *Cosmographicall Glasse* eschewed speculation on "the situation of Paradice," proposing instead "to consider the temperature of Regions, Cities, and Townes, in what Zone, & vnder what Clymate and Parallele they are situated."[46] Astrologers noted the "situation of the starres."[47] On an anatomical level, situation described the disposition of limbs or organs, as when Christopher Langton explored in 1545 the "figure, situation, and action" of the human "guttes and entrayles."[48] In

---

[43] On the history of the concept of nature, see Glacken, *Traces on the Rhodian Shore*; Lorraine Daston, "Description by Omission: Nature Enlightened and Obscured," in John Bender and Michael Marrinan (eds.), *Regimes of Description: In the Archive of the Eighteenth Century* (Stanford, CA: Stanford University Press, 2005), pp. 11–24; Pierre Hadot, *The Veil of Isis: An Essay on the History of the Idea of Nature*, translated by Michael Chase (Cambridge, MA: Harvard University Press, 2006). On Petty's idea of "situation," see McCormick, *William Petty*, pp. 170–3.

[44] Petty, *Political Arithmetick*, pp. 1–2, 10.

[45] Xenophon, *Xenophons Treatise of Housholde*, translated by Gentian Hervet (London: Printed by Thomas Berthelet, 1532), p. 31.

[46] William Cuningham, *The Cosmographical Glasse Conteinyng the Pleasant Principles of Cosmographie, Geographie, Hydrographie, or Nauigation* (London: Printed by John Day, 1559), sigs. Aiiij^v–Av^r.

[47] Joachim Camerarius, *The History of Strange Wonders*, (London: Printed by Roulande Hall, 1561), sig. Cviii^r.

[48] Christopher Langton, *An Introduction into Phisycke wyth an Vniuersal Dyet* (London: Printed by Edwarde Whytchurche, [1545?]), p. xxxv.

Galenic terms, it might distinguish salubrious or insalubrious locations.[49] In each case, however, situation was preeminently spatial. It was also "natural," in the sense of given: it supplied the context for policy, the starting point for intervention.

So understood, situation was a component of what Barbara Shapiro calls the "grid" of early modern empirical political knowledge: a genre that fused travel and diplomatic reportage with natural history to convey the "present state" of various nations.[50] It was in this vein that Thomas Smith's *Discourse of the Common Weal* celebrated learning for revealing "the scituation, temperature, and qualities of everie countrie in the world."[51] Instantiating this, Thomas Washington's 1585 translation of Nicolas de Nicolay's account of the Ottoman realms discussed the "foundation, force, and situation of the city of Algiers," noting that "she is situated vpon the Mediterane Sea, vpon the hanging of a mountaine enuironed with strong walles."[52] Situation was to the fore in the promotion and evaluation of colonies. For Hakluyt, "Scituation" and "commodities" were the two key descriptive categories; the *Discourse of Western Planting* delineated the former in terms of latitude, climate, salubrity and soil, all of which shaped the products of a place and the nature of its inhabitants.[53] Thirty years later, in the context of Irish plantation under James I, Matteo de Renzi warned Lord Deputy Chichester of the "Eminent daungers England is like to be subiect vnto. by reason of [Ireland's] goodly harbours, braue & able men, & the well situation of the land."[54] Situation as spatial context was a basic type of political information.

Seventeenth-century writing on trade and economy gave situation a further set of historical and artificial connotations. Though situation continued to be spatial and natural (both in the sense of embracing the natural features of a place and in the sense of being given), its boundaries broke down; it came to include demographic, cultural and technological legacies as well as recent political histories, blurring the distinction between

---

49 On environment in early modern medical thought, see Andrew Wear, *Knowledge and Practice in English Medicine, 1550–1680* (Cambridge: Cambridge University Press, 2000), pp. 184–99.

50 Shapiro, "Empiricism and English Political Thought, 1550–1720."

51 [Smith], *Discourse of the Common Weal*, p. 26.

52 Nicolas de Nicolay, *The nauigations, peregrinations and voyages, made into Turkie by Nicholas Nicholay Daulphinois, Lord of Arfeuile, chamberlaine and geographer ordinarie to the King of Fraunce*, translated by T. Washington and ed. John Stell (London: Printed by Thomas Dawson, 1585), pp. 7–8.

53 Hakluyt, *Discourse*, pp. 21–2.

54 Matteo de Renzi to Lord Deputy Chichester, July 18, 1615, National Archives, De Renzi Papers, SP 46/90, f.24.

setting and action. The effect of this extension was to turn an idea of environment as a backdrop to human activity into a partial and provisional product of that activity. We have already seen a dramatic instance of this: Gabriel Plattes's account of the succession of improvements that had expanded the carrying capacity of the Earth since the invention of agriculture to his own time.[55] As a concept, situation went from distinguishing natural and artificial realms at any given scale to suggesting that environments and populations were historically produced through mutual interaction. In other words, situation came to denote a space where nature and art as well as past and present met and interacted, a boundary zone where the power and limits of policy to shape a future from what was given were tested.

Perhaps because trade policy was their focus, economic writers envisioned these interactions on a national scale. In 1650, John Keymor contrasted the poor character of English and Irish fishermen with the possibilities their situation offered:

> The merchandizes of France, Portugal, Spain, Italy, Turkey, East, and West-Indies are transported most by the Hollanders ... into the ... Kingdoms of Pomerland, Spruceland, Poland, Denmark, Swethen, Leifland, and Germany; and the merchandise brought from the last mentioned Kingdoms ... are likewise by the Hollanders ... transported into the Southern and Western Dominions; and yet the scituation of England lieth far better for a store-house to serve the Southern, East, and North-east Regions then they, and hath far better means to do it[.][56]

John Smith made the same point a decade later: "The scituation of our Country" he wrote, "is such, that for the convenience of all kind of Marts the world hath not the like ... it is fix'd, as it were, by Art and Nature, the fittest Staple for both Northern and Southern Commodities." England need only be "a little industrious."[57] Thomas Mun's *England's Treasure by Forraign Trade*, printed in 1621 and reprinted in 1664, elaborated. Mun blamed the constraints of "situation" for Genoese decline and – remarking "How much Art doth add to Nature" – enthused about "*Englands* Largeness, Beauty, Fertility, Strength ... in multitude of warlike People, Horses, Ships, Ammunition, advantageous situation for Defence and

---

[55] See Chapter 4.
[56] John Keymor, *A Cleare and Evident Way for Enriching the Nations of England and Ireland, and for Setting Very Great Numbers of Poore on Work* (London: Printed by T.M. & A.C., 1650), p. 4.
[57] John Smith, *The Trade & Fishing of Great-Britain Displayed: With a Description of the Islands of Orkney and Shotland* (London: Printed by William Godbid, 1661), pp. 11–13.

Trade."[58] Yet situation was only as good as policy made it. Left to itself, "great plenty" had made the English *"vicious* and *excessive*, wastful of the means we have" and "improvident and careless" of the gains to be had from industry properly applied. Compare the Dutch, whom a barren perch had made "wise and industrious."[59] Situation was an incitement "to add *Art* to *Nature*" for the purpose of producing industrious people.[60]

These ideas drove Petty's arguments in *Political Arithmetick*. "I take the Foundation of [Dutch] atchievements," he wrote, "to lie originally in the Situation of the Country, whereby they do things inimitable by others, and have advantages whereof others are incapable."[61] From access to waterways, all blessings flowed. "Situation hath given them Shipping," Petty wrote, and "Shipping hath given them in effect all other Trade"; now "Forreign Traffick must give them as much Manufacture as they can manage themselves, and ... make the rest of the World but as workmen to their Shops."[62] On this rendering, situation determined what policy could achieve: Far from "the fruit of their contrivance," Dutch successes "could not almost have been otherwise."[63] Likewise, but in a contrary direction, French coastal geography furnished "natural, and perpetual Impediments" to the rapid expansion of Louis XIV's navy.[64] However absolute the French monarchy, attempts to overawe the givens of situation would fail. On the other hand, any gap between the state of a nation and the potential of its situation marked a failure of effort – a matter of policy.

As far as this goes, situation may seem impervious to interference after all. Yet when Petty talked about "nature" as a constraint on action, its relationship to situation was ambiguous. In the preface to the *Treatise of Taxes*, he described the task of reforming Ireland as a matter of "pass[ing] into Positive Laws whatsoever is right reason and the Law of Nature," and explained that *"res nolunt male administrari*, and that (say I what I will or can) things will have their course, nor will nature be couzened."[65] Yet the same passage portrayed Ireland not as a complex and intractable situation but, to the contrary, "as a white paper" – a blank slate.[66] Perhaps, in a preface

[58] Thomas Mun, *England's Treasure by Forraign Trade. Or, the Ballance of Our Forraign Trade Is the Rule of Our Treasure* (London: Printed by J.G. for Thomas Clark, 1664), pp. 150, 175–6.

[59] Mun, *England's Treasure by Forraign Trade*, pp. 182–3.

[60] Mun, *England's Treasure by Forraign Trade*, p. 181.

[61] Petty, *Political Arithmetick*, p. 10.

[62] Petty, *Political Arithmetick*, pp. 20–1.

[63] Petty, *Political Arithmetick*, p. 21.

[64] Petty, *Political Arithmetick*, p. 51.

[65] Petty, *Treatise of Taxes*, sigs. A4r–A4v.

[66] Petty, *Treatise of Taxes*, sig. A4r.

written in 1662, the point was to flatter the Duke of Ormond's power and seek his patronage rather than to theorize the relationship between art and nature. Nevertheless, the same tag, *res nolunt malè administrari* ("things will not be ill managed") recurred in Petty's 1674 *Discourse ... Concerning Duplicate Proportion* and in later writing.[67] The *Discourse* described natural, proportional relationships – such as those between the strength of a light and the distance from which it could be seen, or between age and probability of death – that art might exploit but could not alter.

The nature of "things" (*res*), in this sense, was fixed. Petty and others made use of this idea, often with its Latin tag, to argue against policies that contradicted the essence of their objects. The paradigm case of such a policy was religious uniformity, which sought not merely to change opinions or interests but to deny an inherent and universal human tendency, demonstrated around the world and throughout history, to differ in matters of belief.[68] This was unnatural in a different way than French naval expansion would be. It was neither the essence of ships nor that of men that doomed Louis XIV's plans; it was France's alleged paucity of natural harbors and trained seamen. If these were "natural" obstacles, they were also local ones. Readers may also have wondered whether they were as "perpetual" as Petty claimed. Numbers of seamen could grow over time. Even harbors could be created, or at least improved; the Duke of Tuscany's construction of the port of Livorno was famous.[69] When we set Petty's description of Dutch transformation next to his predictions of

---

[67] See Petty, *Discourse ... Concerning Duplicate Proportion*, sig. A12r; Petty, "Speculum Hiberniae," (1686), BL Additional MS 72884, ff.25–37v, at f.25r. The more familiar form of the quotation, "*res nolunt diu male administrari*," is often translated as "things refuse to be mismanaged long." I can find no source for Petty's abridgment of it, which later became common. It appeared on the title page of the second edition of Henry Neville, *Plato Redivivus: or, a Dialogue Concerning Government* (London: Printed for S.I., 1681); in William Penn, *A Perswasive to Moderation to Dissenting Christians...* (London: Printed by Andrew Sowle, 1685), p. 42, which likened government to sailing while dependent on changing winds; and in Peter Pett, *The Happy Future State of England* (London: s.n., 1688), in English at pp. 42 and 66 (as "things will not be ill administered") and in Latin at p. 250 – where it was attributed, following Bede, to Aristotle via Cicero (in the form "*nolunt entia malè gubernari*"). In the latter passage, Pett echoes Petty's distinction (in *Political Arithmetick*, sig. A4r) between causes with "Foundations in Nature" and "the mutable Minds, Opinions, Appetites, and Passions of particular men"; Pett contrasts human minds, which may be maladministered, with being, which will not be. Petty knew Penn and Pett well and may have known Neville through their shared connection to James Harrington. Robert Wood told Petty of the contents and authorship of *Plato Redivivus* shortly after its publication; see Wood to Petty, March 1, 1681, BL Additional MS 72850, f.271–272v.

[68] Petty, *Political Arithmetick*, pp. 23–7.

[69] Botero, *On the Causes of the Greatness and Magnificence of Cities*, p. 32. See Tazzara, *The Free Port of Livorno*, pp. 20–47.

French stasis, it is hard not to suspect him, as Davenant and others did, of inconsistency.[70]

Nature thus entered into discussions of policy in several distinct, conflicting ways. With respect to inherent human qualities or the mathematical laws of natural philosophy, it represented an inflexible barrier. But in the guise of situation, nature was subject to and sometimes demanded extensive manipulation in the form of improvements that, over time, became part of the landscape confronting new generations of projectors and statesmen. This process of adaptive interaction between policy and situation, and between land and population, was complex. Physical transformations played a large role, as in fen drainage or forest clearance. Recent work shows that projectors and colonial promoters saw such measures not only as making land more productive – thereby altering social relations and facilitating government – but also as inducing climate change and improving the habitability of the places affected.[71] Thus, in 1670, the *Philosophical Transactions* printed a summary of Italian antiquarian Giovanni Battista Donius's *De restituenda salubritati agri romani*, projecting the regeneration of the Roman region: "that Country not being unwholesome of its own Nature, but from adventitious causes," the editor noted, "it is probable, that those may be remov'd" by new plantation:

> [A]s the insalubrity of that Campagne began only after it was wasted and dispeopled, by the incursions of those Barbarous Nations, that invaded Italy, and destroyed the habitations that were there; so the Air would recover its former good temperature, if that Country were again Inhabited, and tilled as before.[72]

Irish bogs stirred similar hopes in Petty's compatriots and successors.[73] His own interest in a "scale of salubrity" hinted at the potential of manipulations of situation to improve the demographic conditions of colonial

---

[70] See Davenant, *Discourses on the Public Revenues*, pp. 5–6. Compare McCormick, *William Petty*, pp. 297–8, which is too dismissive of Davenant's criticism.

[71] See Ash, *Draining of the Fens*; Zilberstein, *Temperate Empire*; Vogel, "The Letter from Dublin."

[72] Jo. Battista Donius, "An Accompt Given by a Florentin Patrician, Call'd Jo. Battista Donius, Concerning a Way of Restoring the Salubrity of the Country About Rome: Extracted out of the Ninth Italian *Giornale De Letterati*; and English't as Follows," *Philosophical Transactions of the Royal Society* [hereafter *PTRS*] 5 (1670), 1017–19.

[73] See for example Gerard Boate, *Irelands Naturall History* [1652], reprinted in *A Collection of Tracts and Treatises Illustrative of the Natural History, Antiquities, and the Political and Social State of Ireland, at Various Periods Prior to the Present Century* (Dublin: Alexander Thom & Sons, 1860), pp. 1–148, at pp. 134–5; William Temple, *An Essay Upon the Advancement of Trade in Ireland* (Dublin: s.n., 1673), p. 18; William King, "Of the Bogs and Loughs of Ireland" (1684), in BL Additional MS 4811, ff.57v–61, printed in K. Theodore Hoppen (ed.), *Papers of the Dublin Philosophical Society, 1683–1709*, 2 vols. (Dublin: Irish Manuscripts Commission, 2008), pp. 217–26.

settlement.[74] But the Dutch case indicated subtler connections, too. The link between shipping and trade depended as much on information as on ships or ports: "Those who predominate in Shipping … have more occasions than others to frequent all parts of the World, and to observe what is wanting or redundant every where."[75] Situation produced particular kinds of people, who then exploited it in characteristic ways.

Petty's triad of "Situation, Trade, and Policy" was *sui generis*. But in an age of revived interest in Hippocratic medicine and multiplying natural histories, environments' effects on their inhabitants and the power that molding these environments or managing exposure to them might afford over population, were main threads of both natural investigation and projecting from the late seventeenth century through the mid-eighteenth.[76] Queries or instructions for travelers – which proliferated in this period, fueled by natural-historical and colonial as well as antiquarian concerns – regularly asked about climate, seasons and local diseases.[77] The data collected fueled medical speculation. In 1685, Robert Boyle, whose own "General Heads" shaped the genre of queries, published two essays touching the subject.[78] In *An Essay of the Great Effects of Even Languid and Unheeded Motion*, Boyle envisioned a "natural History of the Air" and noted "that among the six principal Causes" of its "healthfulness or insalubrity" were "the Climate, the Soil, the Situation of the Place, the Seasons of the Year, the raigning winds and Contingencies (whether more or less frequent) and especially Subterraneal Steams."[79] The accompanying essay, *An Experimental Discourse of Some Little Observed Causes of the Insalubrity and Salubrity of the Air and Its Effects*, accounted for the healthfulness of particular places by reference their general characteristics

---

[74] McCormick, "Governing Model Populations," 179–98.

[75] Petty, *Political Arithmetick*, p. 15.

[76] On Hippocratic ideas and their legacies, see Glacken, *Traces on the Rhodian Shore*, pp. 80–115; Rusnock, *Vital Accounts*, pp. 109–36; Jan Golinski, *British Weather and the Climate of Enlightenment* (Chicago: University of Chicago Press, 2007), pp. 143, 150, 182; Suman Seth, *Difference and Disease: Medicine, Race, and the Eighteenth-Century British Empire* (Cambridge: Cambridge University Press, 2018), pp. 25–87; see also Slack, *Invention of Improvement*, p. 21.

[77] See Adam Fox, "Printed Questionnaires, Research Networks, and the Discovery of the British Isles, 1650–1800," *The Historical Journal* 53:3 (2010), 593–621.

[78] Robert Boyle, "General Heads for the Natural History of a Country, Great or Small," *Philosophical Transactions* 1 (1665–1666), 186–9. See Michael Hunter, "Robert Boyle and the Early Royal Society: A Reciprocal Exchange in the Making of Early Modern Science," *British Journal for the History of Science* 40:1 (2007), 1–23.

[79] Robert Boyle, *An Essay of the Great Effects of Even Languid and Unheeded Motion. Whereunto Is Annexed an Experimental Discourse of Some Little Observed Causes of the Insalubrity and Salubrity of the Air and Its Effects* (London: Printed by M. Flesher for Richard Davis, 1685), sig. A2v.

(marshy land was typically insalubrious, for example), inferring the local presence of disease-bearing or -blocking "effluvia" or "vapours, and exhalations" from the earth both as causal mechanism of "endemical diseases" and to explain any empirical deviations from the norm (mining countries with unusually healthy populations, for instance).[80] While Boyle did not spell out the implications of these links for improvement, later medical arithmeticians would.

Taking up similar connections on a global-historical scale, meanwhile, were the new sacred histories and theories of the Earth that rose to meet challenges to Scripture following the Isaac la Peyrère's publication of his pre-Adamite theory in 1655–6.[81] In different ways, late Stuart thinkers such as the Cartesian Thomas Burnet and the Newtonian William Whiston posited links between the nature of the early Earth and the demographic characteristics of its inhabitants.[82] Scholars and exegetes then and for decades afterward speculated about the natural mechanisms and physiological implications of the transition from ante- to postdiluvian longevity and fecundity. From the start, this work was motivated by the need to defend one or another scriptural chronology.[83] But this apologetic work used political arithmetic to think about the history of population not merely as a changing number but also as an environmentally conditioned, and therefore historically conditioned, set of natural processes. Of course, the environmental manipulations at issue – the Earth's

---

[80] Robert Boyle, *An Experimental Discourse of Some Little Observed Causes of the Insalubrity and Salubrity of the Air and Its Effects* (printed with in *An Essay of the Great Effects of … Motion* but paginated separately), pp. 3–5, 19, 23.

[81] Isaac la Peyrère, *A Theological Systeme Upon That Presvpposition, That Men Were before Adam. The First Part* (London: s.n., 1655); Isaac la Peyrère, *Men before Adam. Or a Discourse Upon the Twelfth, Thirteenth, and Fourteenth Verses of the Fifth Chapter of the Epistle of the Apostle Paul to the Romans. By Which Are Prov'd, That the First Men Were Created before Adam* (London: s.n., 1656).

[82] See Thomas Burnet, *The Theory of the Earth: Containing an Account of the Original of the Earth, and of All the General Changes Which It Hath Already Undergone, or Is to Undergo, Till the Consummation of All Things. The Two First Books Concerning the Deluge, and Concerning Paradise.* (London: Printed by R. Norton, for Walter Kettilby, 1684), pp. 22–3, 39–42, 180–92; William Whiston, *A New Theory of the Earth, from Its Original to the Consummation of All Things. Wherein the Creation of the World in Six Days, the Universal Deluge, and the General Conflagration, as Laid Down in the Holy Scriptures, Are Shewn to Be Perfectly Agreeable to Reason and Philosophy* (London: Printed by R. Roberts for Benj. Tooke, 1696), pp. 174–87.

[83] See Matthew Hale, *The Primitive Origination of Mankind, Considered and Examined According to the Light of Nature* (London: Printed by William Godbid, for William Shrowsbery, 1677), pp. 203–7; Richard Bentley, *The Folly and Unreasonableness of Atheism Demonstrated from the Advantage and Pleasure of a Religious Life, the Faculties of Human Souls, the Structure of Animate Bodies, & the Origin and Frame of the World* (London: Printed by J.H. for H. Mortlock, 1693), pp. 20–2; William Nicholls, *A Conference with a Theist* (London: Printed by T.W. for Francis Saunders and by Tho. Bennet, 1696), pp. 66–80.

creation and its transformation by the Great Flood – were the work not of human politicians but of a providential God. Still, the idea that environmental change explained qualitative and quantitative changes in population informed natural-philosophical defenses of Scripture through the mid-eighteenth century.[84]

Meanwhile, the circulation of mortality bills and vital data in periodicals such as the *Philosophical Transactions* and in the correspondence of interested amateurs provided fodder for ideas about the qualitative effects of local or specific environments on population.[85] From Graunt's time onward, one major distinction was between the city – that is, London – and the countryside. Comparing the London bills with parish registers from elsewhere, Graunt had established that London increased its size only by recruiting rural emigrants. Successive waves of bills and commentary refined and elaborated this picture of the city as a sink of disease, vice and death. Gregory King took extensive notes on Graunt (and Petty) and looked for further testimony to the "disposition of the London Climate and Air as to health" in the bills of his own day, finding that a decrease in the bills in 1700 "must be occasioned by Decrease of the People or from a greater Salubrity."[86] On the one hand, the disparity between life in the capital and in rural areas cautioned against generalizing from urban data. On the other hand, as Edmund Halley argued, London itself was no typical city. Halley thought the city of Breslau – less subject to in- and out-migration, situated in a similar latitude and with air "but indifferently salubrious" – might better be "proposed for a Standard" upon which to base a life table.[87] Through the 1720s and 1730s, extracts of bills from

---

[84] See Francis Walsh, *The Antediluvian World; or, a New Theory of the Earth* (Dublin: Printed by S. Powell, 1743), pp. 31–52; Benjamin Parker, *A Review of the State of the Antediluvian World* (London: Printed for W. Reeve, 1748), pp. 20–7; Patrick Cockburn, *An Enquiry into the Truth and Certainty of the Mosaic Deluge* (London: Printed for C. Hitch and M. Bryson, 1750), pp. 45–116. Such concerns are marginal but present in Short, *New Observations*, pp. 249–64.

[85] Several abstracts of bills and registers with commentary are in Cl. P/17, Classified Papers, Royal Society Library, including Richard Corbet's "A Method of Computing the People" (Document 19, undated), annual totals of christenings and burials in London Bills from 1664 to 1728 (Document 43) extracts of registers from the parish of Addle by Thomas Kirke (Document 25, dated 1693–4) and the villages of the Middle and Lower Mark (Document 29, dated 1698), and European bills of mortality communicated by Conrad Sprengell (Document 42, dated 1726) and Johann (or Jean; or John) Scheuchzer (Document 44, dated 1728–9); see note 88.

[86] "Considerations on the general Bill of Mortality ao. 1700" and "Positions in Grants Epistle Ded. To my Ld Roberts of Truro Ld Pr. Seal," (undated), Papers of Gregory King, National Archives, T 64/302.

[87] Edmund Halley, "An Estimate of the Degrees of the Mortality of Mankind, Drawn from Curious Tables of the Births and Funerals at the City of Breslaw; with an Attempt to Ascertain the Price of Annuities Upon Lives," *PTRS* 17 (1693), 596–610, at 597 and 610.

London, Dublin, Breslau, Dresden, Augsburg and other cities illustrated not only "the great Vicissitudes of sublunary Affairs, in the vast Disparity between the aforesaid Cities" (as historian William Maitland put it) but also the challenges of constructing a model from what Charles Brand called "imperfect and chimerical Returns."[88]

Under the influence of Hippocratic ideas, medical arithmeticians from the 1720s to the 1760s traced the effects of location to a combination of factors. Taking advantage of the practice of weather recording promoted by the Royal Society, and following the line of enquiry indicated earlier by Boyle, many focused on the air.[89] The Coventry- and later Sheffield-based physician Thomas Short assembled a massive collection of mortality bills and weather observations, eventually publishing *A General Chronological History of the Air* that chronicled "its different Effects at sundry Times, in various Places, on human Bodies" from the Great Flood to the present day.[90] Given contemporaneous thinking about the warming effects of forest clearance and cultivation and the drying effects of fen-drainage, Hippocratic thinking underscored the link between changes in the landscape and improvements in salubrity and thus in population. But similar views were also current beyond the world of medicine. William Brakenridge, a clergyman and F.R.S. who contributed several contentious demographic letters

[88] William Maitland, "Remarks Upon the Aforesaid Bills of Mortality for the Cities of Dresden and Augsburgh," *PTRS* 38 (1733), 98; John Smart and Charles Brand, *Tables of Interest, Discount, Annuities, &c. First Published in the Year 1724, by John Smart, and Now Revised, Enlarged, and Improved, by Charles Brand. To Which Is Added an Appendix, Containing Some Observations on the General Probability of Life* (London: Printed for T. Longman, T. Cadel and N. Conant, 1730), pp. 190–7. For examples of Continental bills in the *Philosophical Transactions*, see Conrad Joachim Sprengell's communication of extracts from the *Acta Bratislaviensia* in *PTRS* 32 (1722), 454–69; 33 (1724), 25–35; and 35 (1727), 365–74, as well as Conrad Joachim Sprengell, "The Bills of Mortality for the Town of Dresden, for a Whole Century, Viz. from the Year 1617 to 1717, Containing the Numbers of Marriages, Births, Burials, and Communicants," *PTRS* 38 (1733), 89–93; Conrad Joachim Sprengell, "The Bills of Mortality for the Imperial City of Augsburg, from the Year 1501 to 1720 Inclusive, Containing the Number of Births, Marriages, and Burials," *PTRS* 38 (1733), 94–7; and Jean Gaspard Scheuchzer, "The Bills of Mortality in Several Parts of Europe, for the Years 1724 and 1725. Extracted from the *Acta Bratislaviensia*, by the Same," *PTRS* 36 (1729), 110–23. Sprengell (or Sprengwell) was a knight, a Fellow of the Royal Society and the royal College of Physicians, and author of *The Aphorisms of Hippocrates and the Sentences of Celsus* (London: Printed for R. Bonwick, W. Freeman, Tim. Goodwin et al., 1708). Scheuchzer, a Swiss-born physician, naturalist, and antiquary, was foreign secretary to the Royal Society and later librarian to Hans Sloane; see Andrea Rusnock, "Scheuchzer [Scheutzer], John Gaspar (1702–1729), physician and naturalist," *Oxford Dictionary of National Biography*.
[89] See Golinski, *British Weather*.
[90] "A Collection of Several Bills of Mortality and Registers of the Weather, Collected in the Year 1732/3, etc., by Thomas Short, M.D., of Sheffield," BL Additional MS 10591; Thomas Short, *A General Chronological History of the Air, Weather, Seasons, Meteors, &c. in Sundry Places and Different Times; More Particularly for the Space of 250 Years* (London: Printed for T. Longman and A. Millar, 1749), p. v.

to the *Philosophical Transactions* in the 1750s – he argued that the national population was in decline by critiquing extrapolations from unusually healthy parishes – suggested that the improvement of wastelands alone might permit a 50 percent increase in carrying capacity.[91] Taking trade into account, he wrote, "if the land in both the British Isles was duly cultivated, they might sustain about six million more people than they do now; that is as many people as England now contains." Indeed, he thought "the whole Globe of the Earth" capable of supporting "above twenty-six times the present number of mankind."[92] Of course, this was a claim about numbers. But it was an argument that rested on the power of improvement, driven by policy, to create environments that fostered better health and longer life.

Neither as a determinant of population nor as an object of policy was place just a matter of airs and waters. Financial calculators such as Smart, public-spirited clergymen like Brakenridge, and physicians such as Short all emphasized the local cooperation of moral and economic in conjunction with natural causes. London was a graveyard for migrants in part because it was a sinkhole of vice. Among Smart's arguments against generalizing from Halley's life table was the observation that Breslau was "inhabited chiefly by Sober, Industrious People, Strangers to Luxury … whereas London is a City, abounding with Luxury amongst the Rich, and Debauchery amongst too many both of the Rich and the Poor."[93] Brakenridge explained what he saw as London's decreasing population by reference to "three causes … that may all operate jointly": first, "the vicious custom … of drinking

[91] William Brakenridge, "A Letter to George Lewis Scot, Esq; F. R. S. Concerning the Number of People in England," *PTRS* 49 (1755), 268–85, at 275–7. For Brakenridge's arguments concerning depopulation, see also William Brakenridge, "A Letter from the Reverend William Brakenridge, D.D. and F.R.S. to George Lewis Scot, Esq; F.R.S. Concerning the Number of Inhabitants within the London Bills of Mortality," *PTRS* 48 (1753), 788–800; William Brakenridge, "A Letter to the Right Honourable the Earl of Macclesfield, President of the Royal Society, Concerning the Method of Constructing a Table for the Probabilities of Life at London," *PTRS* 49 (1755), 167–82; and William Brakenridge, "A Letter to the Right Honourable the Earl of Macclesfield, President of the Royal Society, from the Rev. William Brakenridge, D.D. F.R.S. Containing an Answer to the Account of the Numbers and Increase of the People of England, by the Rev. Mr. Forster," *PTRS* 50 (1757), 465–79. Replies to Brakenridge include George Burrington, *An Answer to Dr. William Brakenridge's Letter Concerning the Number of Inhabitants within the London Bills of Mortality* (London: Printed for J. Scott, 1757), and several letters to the Royal Society from the Berkshire cleric Richard Forster, two of which appeared as "An Extract of the Register of the Parish of Great Shefford, near Lamborne, in Berkshire, for Ten Years: With Observations on the Same" and "A Letter to the Rev. Thomas Birch, D. D. Secr. R. S. Concerning the Number of the People of England," in *PTRS* 50 (1757), 356–63 and 457–65, respectively. Further letters – which, to Forster's chagrin, were not printed – are in British Library Additional MS 4440, ff.176–185v and 189.
[92] Brakenridge, "Letter … Concerning the Number of People in England," 277.
[93] John Smart to George Heathcote, February 25, 1737/8, BL Additional MS 4434, ff.237–41, at f.237v.

spirituous liquors"; second, "the fashionable humour of living single, that daily increases"; and third, "the great increase of trade in the northern parts of Britain, that keeps the people there employed at home."[94] More systematically than these authors, Corbyn Morris, an influential mid-century economic writer, customs official and promoter of public improvements, blamed London's surplus of burials over baptisms on a combination of "the large number of Servants" who died without issue, "The Unhealthiness of the Air," "The Discouragement to Matrimony" by reason of expense and "the enormous Use of spirituous Liquors" among the poor.[95]

All four causes were amenable to local improvement, driven chiefly, in Morris's view, by government. Unwittingly echoing Plattes, Morris advised "that the Cleansing of this City … be put under one uniform publick Management," which would oversee the removal of urban refuse into the country, "where it would be of great benefit to the Lands." Likewise, he suggested "That several Foundling-Hospitals be established in different Parts of this Town," under public administration, and charged with "receiving all without exception." He called for the cutting of new, parallel streets leading out of the city, "By which Measures the Air of London would be free from many of the poisonous Particles loading it at present; and a new Circulation of pure Air introduced" – as well as a new circulation of London's inhabitants, who would enjoy new and regular access to the country air.[96] While the church supported physicians' findings (and manufacturers' interests) by inveighing against liquor consumption, taxes might curb "The Luxury of great Families" and end their servants' artificial celibacy.[97] At the same time, barring bachelors "from setting up anew, in any Retail Business" would encourage them to marry. Morris also envisioned, finally, the total suppression of "Hawkers and Pedlars … A Set of unmeriting People, who carry Luxury into all Corners; and sollicit and enflame the Pride of every Farmer's Wife and Daughter in the Kingdom."[98] Here was a complex program of political reforms and administrative projects, directed to a variety of different areas of life, with the common purpose of transforming London's physical, economic and moral landscape in order to improve the health and industry of its population.

---

[94] Brakenridge, "Letter … Concerning the Number of Inhabitants within the London Bills of Mortality," 798–9.
[95] Corbyn Morris, *Observations on the Past Growth and Present State of the City of London* (London: s.n., 1751), pp. 1–3.
[96] Morris, *Observations*, p. 24.
[97] Morris, *Observations*, pp. 23–5.
[98] Morris, *Observations*, p. 25.

Improving Population as a Public Project

Morris's vision was far from unique; it reflected a historical vision and a "projecting" turn that many of his contemporaries shared. Meanwhile, many of the policies he suggested – especially concerning incentives for marriage and childbearing – were familiar less from the suggestions of a Petty than from the pronatalist endeavors of Louis XIV and his successors in France, or from the history of ancient states and populations.[99] Montesquieu's comments in the *Lettres Persanes* (originally printed in 1721 and translated into English the following year) connected the two and set the tone for comparisons of ancient and modern policy; while his Persian observers found Paris "thickly populated" and lauded the multiplying power of "benign government," they also found the planet "less populous than it once was," and castigated religious customs, colonial emigration and the abrogation of ancient "penalties against those who refused to marry" for the change.[100] In Britain, the 1753 debate between the Church of Scotland minister Robert Wallace and the philosopher and essayist David Hume over the relative populousness of the ancient and modern worlds followed a similar logic. Wallace followed Montesquieu in arguing against Hume that ancient slavery had promoted multiplication and in approving the practice of subjecting bachelors to social and political exclusion.[101] Hume, for his part, echoed Montesquieu's emphasis on the role of government in promoting population, as well as that of improvement in altering climate.[102] Similar issues arose in arguments over the putatively depopulating effects of "commerce and the arts" – a subset of the wider debate over the dangers of luxury – later in the same decade.[103]

---

[99] On Louis XIV's policies, see Tuttle, *Conceiving the Old Regime*. On French responses to perceived depopulation, see Blum, *Strength in Numbers*.

[100] Charles de Secondat, baron de Montesquieu, *The Persian Letters*, translated by George R. Healy (Indianapolis: Hackett, 1999), pp. 190–8, 202–5. The first of several eighteenth-century English editions was *Persian Letters*, translated by John Ozell, 2 vols. (London: Printed for J. Tonson, 1722). See Tomaselli, "Moral Philosophy and Population Questions in Eighteenth Century Europe" and Blum, *Strength in Numbers*, pp. 11–20.

[101] Robert Wallace, *A Dissertation on the Numbers of Mankind in Antient and Modern Times: In Which the Superior Populousness of Antiquity Is Maintained* (Edinburgh: Printed for G. Hamilton and J. Balfour, 1753), pp. 89–91, 93–5. Compare Hume, "Populousness of Ancient Nations," pp. 386–96.

[102] Hume, "Populousness of Ancient Nations," pp. 381–2, 448–9.

[103] See especially William Bell, *A Dissertation on the Following Subject: What Causes Principally Contribute to Render a Nation Populous? And What Effect Has the Populousness of a Nation on Its Trade?* (Cambridge: Printed by J. Bentham, 1756), and William Temple, *A Vindication of Commerce and the Arts; Proving That They Are the Source of the Greatness, Power, Riches and Populousness of a State* (London: Printed for J. Nourse, 1758). On the wider luxury debate, see

Whether or not they read Montesquieu, Wallace and Hume, however –
and whatever their view of quantitative demographic trends in the distant
or recent past – Morris and others like him drew on the transformative
logic of projects taking physical and institutional shape in the cities and
country around them. As historians including Donna Andrew, Joanna
Innes and Sarah Lloyd have shown, the early eighteenth century saw a
shift in the locus of charitable activity from the parish – the locus of poor
relief before and after Elizabethan legislation – in two directions.[104] On
the one hand was the central state, with Parliament a key resource for
the pursuit of specific, local improvements, whether this meant enclosure
acts or hospital subventions. On the other hand was an emerging civil
society: a matrix of public-spirited, privately backed and highly visible
philanthropic and reform-oriented activities and associations. Working
in concert as often as in competition, and legitimating their efforts in
terms of national interest, these engines powered projects that made the
augmentation, discipline and care of the population an object of public as
well as state intervention.

Examples of such interventions are innumerable and suggestively heterogeneous. An early instance noted earlier was the Society for the Reformation
of Manners. Beginning in London and emulated with varying success
in more than a dozen other cities and towns between the 1690s and the
1740s, this was a "private, voluntary association" that drew support from
the Church of England and enlisted the civil courts in an attempt not to
enforce theological orthodoxy but rather to ally Anglicans and Dissenters
in the production of a "moral populace" through the surveillance, reporting and prosecution of vice.[105] As we have seen, a distinguishing feature
of Societies was a regular "Account" of numbers of prosecutions and con-
victions secured.[106] Series of enumerations furnished preachers like White
Kennett with publishable metrics of successful reform:

David Spadafora, *The Idea of Progress in Eighteenth-Century Britain* (New Haven, CT: Yale
University Press, 1990), pp. 213–16; Christopher J. Berry, *The Idea of Luxury: A Conceptual and
Historical Investigation* (Cambridge: Cambridge University Press, 1994), pp. 126–76. On discus-
sions in France, see John Shovlin, *The Political Economy of Virtue: Luxury, Patriotism, and the
Origins of the French Revolution* (Ithaca, NY: Cornell University Press, 2006).

[104] Donna T. Andrew, *Philanthropy and Police: London Charity in the Eighteenth Century* (Princeton,
NJ: Princeton University Press, 1989); Innes, *Inferior Politics*; Lloyd, *Charity and Poverty in
England*.

[105] See Burtt, "Societies for the Reformation of Manners," (quotations at pp. 152 and 155);
Hindle, *On the Parish*, p. 186. See also Shelley Burtt, *Virtue Transformed: Political Argument in
England, 1688–1740* (Cambridge: Cambridge University Press, 1992), pp. 15–38.

[106] See Slack, *Invention of Improvement*, p. 213.

> There have been several Lists printed of the Names … of many Thousands of Lewd and Scandalous Persons, who by the endeavours of the Societies for promoting a Reformation of Manners, have been legally Prosecuted and Convicted.… And for this one year that is now expiring, I am credibly inform'd, that above a thousand have been convicted, and duly punish'd for Lewd and Disorderly Persons.[107]

Yet what the numbers indicated were the transformations wrought: the maintenance of public order, the improvement in the moral landscape, the mobilization of problematic segments of the population and their transmutation from idle criminals into useful members of society.

> Several thousands more have been convicted for exercising Trade on the Lord's Day, for Cursing, Swearing, Revelling, Tipling, and other Riot and Excess.… [A]bove six hundred Lewd and Licentious Houses have been actually supprest … great numbers of prostituted Women, to avoid Infamy and Pain, have Transported themselves to foreign Parts … a greater number have taken up to an Honest Industrious course of Life, who often acknowledge that their Punishment was their Conversion.[108]

The upshot of this disciplinary alchemy, "the working of this Publick Spirit" (as Kennett put it in his sermon of 1701) or of these "Combinations and publick Confederacies" (as the recurring preface to the numerical appendices of other sermons to the Societies had it), was not an augmentation of numbers but a qualitative change visible in "the Publick Houses … the Markets … the Streets of this City."[109] The project of reform was "a necessary war" on vice that paralleled wars on foreign foes in enlisting the entire nation as "Intelligencers, Informers, Witnesses, and … Officers" as well as in conducing to the power of the state.[110] Victory would be borne in the physical bodies and social interactions as well as in the souls of its inhabitants.[111]

---

[107] Kennett, *Sermon Preach'd at Bow-Church*, pp. 47–8.

[108] Kennett, *Sermon Preach'd at Bow-Church*, p. 48.

[109] Kennett, *Sermon Preach'd at Bow-Church*, p. 50. For examples of the appendix containing numerical reports (the "Account of the Progress Made"), see St. George Ashe, *A Sermon Preached to the Societies for Reformation of Manners, at St. Mary-le-Bow, on Monday, December the 31st, MDCCXVI* (London: Printed by J. Downing, 1717); William Butler, *A Sermon Preached to the Societies for Reformation of Manners, at St. Mary-le-Bow, on Monday, January the 1st, MDCCXXI* (London: Printed by J. Downing, 1722); Arthur Bedford, *A Sermon Preached to the Societies for Reformation of Manners, at St. Mary-le-Bow, on Thursday, January 10, 1733* (London: Printed for Jos. Downing, 1734).

[110] Thomas Bray, *For God, or for Satan: Being a Sermon Preached at St. Mary le Bow, before the Societies for the Reformation of Manners, December 27. 1708* (London: Printed by J. Downing, 1708), p. 30; Edward Chandler, *A Sermon Preached to the Societies for Reformation of Manners, at St. Mary-le-Bow, on Monday January the 4th, 1724* (London: Printed for James Knapton, 1724), p. 8; Joseph Burroughs, *A Sermon Preached to the Societies for Reformation of Manners; at Salters-Hall, on Monday, the 28th of June, 1731* (London: Printed for E. Matthews, 1731), p. 10.

[111] See Withington, *Society in Early Modern England*, p. 199.

The Societies for the Reformation of Manners (SRMs) foundered on a combination of Church ambivalence about collaboration with Dissent and public ambivalence about the power of the courts to eliminate vice. It may be indicative that after *The Fable of the Bees* appeared in 1714, SRM sermons often attacked its author, Dutch-English physician and economic writer Bernard Mandeville, for his claim that "private vices" were, economically speaking, "public benefits."[112] Yet even Mandeville's mockery of projecting – like Swift's – attested to the power and to the pervasive acceptance of demographic management as a public concern. In his satirical *A Modest Defence of Publick Stews* (1724), Mandeville decried "the Tendency [whoring] has to dispeople a Nation; and that both by the destruction of the Bastard Infants, and by ruining young Males Constitutions so much, that, when they marry, they either beget no Children, or such as are sickly and short-liv'd."[113] His concerns about barrenness and disease echoed those of Graunt and many afterward. Mandeville's solution, however, was not to contravene human nature, as the SRMs sought, but to contain and direct its dangerous tendencies by institutional means. "But alas!" he wrote, "violent Love for Women is born and bred with us; nay, it is absolutely necessary to our being born at all."[114] The "Torrent of Lewdness" nature unleashed being "too strong to be opposed by open Force," he went on, "let us see if we can find out an Expedient to divert it by Policy, and prevent the Mischief tho' we can't prevent the Crime."[115]

Mandeville framed his proposal as a problem in political arithmetic: "As there is constantly in the Nation, a certain Number of young Men, whose Passions are too strong to brook any Opposition: Our Business is to contrive a Method how they may be gratify'd, with as little Expence of Female Virtue as possible."[116] The answer (not a new one, in an early modern context) was to make the supply and regulation of sex work the business of civil government:

> Let a hundred or more Houses be provided in some convenient Quarter of the City, and proportionably in every Country Town, sufficient to contain

[112] See Bernard Mandeville, *The Fable of the Bees: Or, Private Vices Publick Benefits* (London: Printed for J. Roberts, 1714); E. J. Hundert, *The Enlightenment's Fable: Bernard Mandeville and the Discovery of Society* (Cambridge: Cambridge University Press, 1994).
[113] Bernard Mandeville, *A Modest Defense of Publick Stews* (London: Printed by A. Moore, 1724). I have used the scholarly edition in Bernard Mandeville (ed. Irwin Primer), *Bernard Mandeville's "A Modest Defence of Publick Stews": Prostitution and Its Discontents in Early Georgian England* (Basingstoke: Palgrave Macmillan, 2006); quotation at p. 68.
[114] Mandeville, *Modest Defense* p. 57.
[115] Mandeville, *Modest Defense,* p. 84.
[116] Mandeville, *Modest Defense,* pp. 86–7.

two Thousand Women ... let a hundred Matrons be appointed, one to each House, of Abilities and Experience enough to take upon them the Management of twenty Courtezans each.... [T]here must be ... an Infirmary, and Provision made for two able Physicians, and four Surgeons at least. Lastly, there must be three Commissioners appointed to superintend the whole, to hear and redress Complaints, and to see that each House punctually observes such Rules and Orders as shall be thought Necessary for the good Government of this Community.[117]

Mandeville's stated goal was not, it bears noting, the suppression of vice. It was, rather, the moral and physical improvement of the population as a whole. Public brothels calibrated to the sexual needs of the male population and the physical capacities of women would result in the most efficient management of ineradicable appetites: "we shall not have one Woman employ'd in the Publick Service more than is absolutely necessary, nor one less than is fully sufficient."[118] While the population was made healthier and more fertile, "the Nation would receive a general Benefit by having such a considerable Number of its most disorderly Inhabitants brought to live after a regular civiliz'd Manner." That is, "a certain Number of young Women" would "arrive gradually, Step by Step, at the highest Degree of Impudence and Lewdness."[119]

Though he offered it sarcastically, Mandeville's demographic and governmental rationale for public brothels was rhetorically effective because it mirrored contemporary thinking about the means and ends of social legislation and philanthropic projects. His apology for "public stews" was not far removed from earnest arguments in favor of institutions such as foundling hospitals – nor, indeed, from moralizing criticisms of such institutions as accessories to vicious living. When Morris proposed a series of foundling hospitals and a policy of general admission in 1751, Thomas Coram's London Foundling Hospital had been receiving abandoned infants, on a selective basis, for a decade; between 1756 and 1760 Parliamentary support would allow unrestricted admissions.[120] Much as Mandeville's satire anticipated, opinions of the hospital ranged from blame for subsidizing fornication and harming marriage to praise for preserving lives otherwise lost to the nation.[121] Like Mandeville's brothels, too, Coram's hospital

---

[117] Mandeville, *Modest Defense,* pp. 60–1. On the regulation of sex work, see Strasser, *State of Virginity,* especially pp. 56–85.
[118] Mandeville, *Modest Defence,* pp. 87–8.
[119] Mandeville, *Modest Defence,* pp. 62–3.
[120] See Alyssa Levene, *Childcare, Health and Mortality at the London Foundling Hospital, 1741–1800: 'Left to the Mercy of the World'* (Manchester: Manchester University Press, 2007), pp. 1–15.
[121] Andrew, *Philanthropy and Police,* pp. 58–60.

proposed not only to save lives but also to make them useful to the nation through medical, administrative and educational interventions. Unlike these brothels, however, the hospital was real.

Studies of Coram's hospital paint a bleak picture. In an age of high but decreasing infant mortality, children admitted to the hospital fared better than inmates of workhouses, but not as well as "even the most poorly off infants in the country" – and still worse during the period of general admission.[122] Allowing for the circumstances of their reception, however, this is not surprising, and after infancy the foundlings' statistical divergence from the rest of the London population abated.[123] In any case, abandoned infants were by definition a marginalized population subject to a range of disadvantages: disproportionately born to poor parents, often out-of-wedlock, they were increasingly placed in the hospital at the behest not of mothers but of parish officials (who may have been some distance away, aggravating the hazards of the first days).[124] More remarkable was what awaited the infants after admission. Within a matter of days, each healthy child was assigned a place within a network of paid wet-nurses and removed from London – some as nearby as Surrey, others as far away as Yorkshire. There they remained until the age of five or six, watched over by a network of volunteer inspectors, before returning to London and the hospital for school and apprenticeships.[125] Clothed, fed, moved and molded by the hospital and its agents, they reentered the general population and traversed the empire as servants, laborers, seamen and craftsmen: useful people.[126]

In "preserving lives, which might otherwise be lost," as its governor Jonas Hanway put it, Coram's hospital was a model of eighteenth-century projecting.[127] Yet it also embodied ideas of demographic governance in formation since the later sixteenth century, inflected by the uptake of political and medical arithmetic after 1660 and articulated in a post-Revolutionary language of public welfare.[128] The foundlings' very marginality

---

[122] Levene, *Childcare, Health and Mortality*, p. 55.
[123] Levene, *Childcare, Health and Mortality*, p. 64.
[124] Levene, *Childcare, Health and Mortality*, pp. 68–89.
[125] Levene, *Childcare, Health and Mortality*, pp. 8–9.
[126] Levene, *Childcare, Health and Mortality*, p. 204. See most recently Helen Berry, *Orphans of Empire: The Fate of London's Foundlings* (Oxford: Oxford University Press, 2019).
[127] Jonas Hanway, *A Proposal for Saving from 70,000 l. to 150,000 l. (a) to the Public; at the same time rendering 5000 young persons of both sexes more happy in themselves and more useful to their country, than if so much money were expended on their account (25 February 1764)* (London: s.n., 1764), p. 1.
[128] The hospital was responsible for over 600 children at the outset of the general admission period, and over 6,000 at its height; Berry, *Orphans of Empire*, p. 91.

and mobility opened them to new kinds of intervention; starting in 1766, for example, they were the first population in Britain to receive systematic smallpox inoculation.[129] Not unlike the children of Elizabethan vagrants, their removal from their natal environment was instrumental to their reformation. Some wondered whether they had been removed far enough. Sharing his thoughts with hospital treasurer George Whatley in 1756, Henry Etough, rector of Lowick and Islip in Northamptonshire, inveighed against wet-nurses not only because "Their milk is frequently prejudiced by numerous irregularities" but also because "To ye government of ye passions, people of ye lowest rank are utterly unaccustomed."[130] The "State of ye country" itself inhibited health and multiplication:

> All iniquities are supported by ye Great Number of public houses, who in order to procure business, contrive all sorts of diversions within & without doors, to ye later of which there is an unfailing confluence of both sexes of all ages. Fairs, Church Feasts, & horse races are productive of innumerable mischiefs.

Some of these were ancient ills, others of recent vintage. Worst was tea, which involved a "prodigious ... waste of time ... preparing sipping & chattering" and produced a "faintness & dejection" for which "spirituous liquors are ye sure relief." The result was neglect of "Proper food cloathing & proper business" among the lower sort and the addiction of their "Children ... to this parent of nervous disorders & propagator of ... dismal sensations." Etough traced "ye decrease of ye people" itself "to this vile fashionable drug." Removing foundlings from such influences might turn the tide, but "ye want of a strict Police, & ... incorrigible depravities in ye customs & manners of ye Populace" threatened.[131]

Etough did not speak for everyone. A set of notes on "The intent of the Publick in suporting an Hospitall for Exposed Children," dated *c.* 1752 and attributed to circuit judge and then-Hospital treasurer Taylor White, contrasted the hospital favorably with other institutions for the marginalized.[132] As the first line indicated, the author considered the hospital not as a private project but first and foremost as a manifestation of the public

---

[129] Levene, *Children, Health and Mortality*, p. 201. See Daniel Sutton to Jonas Hanway, July 13, 1766, in London Metropolitan Archives (hereafter LMA) A/FH/M/01/005/7–8. Inoculation involved moving the children in batches, 100 per fortnight, to Sutton's infirmary in Ingatestone, Essex.

[130] Henry Etough to George Whatley, September 15, 1756, LMA A/FH/M/01/002/023–024, at 023. Etough thought "nursing by hand" with "Sea biskets" and water more "simple & innocent."

[131] Etough to Whatley, September 25, 1756, LMA A/FH/M/01/002/031–034, at 031–032.

[132] [Taylor White?], "The intent of the Publick in suporting [*sic*] an Hospitall for Exposed Children," *c.* 1752, LMA A/FH/M/01/004, item 012. On White see Berry, *Orphans of Empire*, pp. 81, 91.

will. It was the public that desired "to give a relief equally to every Child, whom its Parents can not or will not suport," and "Till this End is accomplished the Publick remains disatisfied." The governors' task was thus "to give a right turn to the publick zeal" in aiding the hospital's operations. "The Publick," he went on,

> Are ... acquainted with the powers Given to the Governors by the King & the Legislature, they have seen the Rule by which as well the Corporation as the Domestick Oeconomy is managed, they know how the children are taken in nursed & employed, & they may have heard that upwards of a Thousand Children have been taken & maintained.... They see the Buildings you have made & the uses to which they are aplied. & in general they have aproved[.]

Not just the fact that the orphans were saved but also the specific administrative, fiscal and even physiological mechanisms by which their transformation into laborers was effected were public concerns – as was the scope of the transformation. For "what [the public] also see is that every taking in of Children many are rejected. & that many remain in Workhouses & under Parrish nurses ready to Perish." The public saw the limits of the hospital's "Capital" in proportion to its "Expenses" and the constraints on this capital's growth. The public would deliberate and act on what it saw. It must therefore be informed, lest it "[consider] that the End proposed by this great undertaking is impossible to be effected, or is too remote ... to be worth their imediate attention"; "the more the publick sees done the great benefactions will be given."[133]

White, if he was the author, suggested half-a-dozen ways out of debt and toward universal admission. These included the pursuit of private donations as well as the purchase of reversions on other charitable endowments, but the first was "a carefull management of the Childrens Industry, whose labour are a part of the Estate of the Corporation" and the most "material" was empowering the corporation to compel parishes to hand over (and pay for) foundlings and orphans. The hospital would cease to be a local and limited charity and become instead the steward and improver of an otherwise wasted national subpopulation, its work justified by its contribution to the public interest and its superiority over existing institutions. "[W]ith regard to the Publick," White argued, "it aparently tends to the preservation of many Lives ... now lost under the care of Parish Officers[,] some by neglect others by the closeness & bad air of Workhouses." Beyond mere preservation,

---

[133] [White?], "Intent of the Publick," LMA A/FH/M/01/004, item 012.

[I]t will bring up many good servants to the commonwealth. & in the stations they are most wanted, as to the sea husbandry & laborious employments & their education will be taken such care of, that they will go into the world instructed in the principles of Virtue industry & the xian Religion.

From the dregs of idleness and sin, the hospital – given sufficient support and political leeway – would generate industry and virtue. This transformation, centered on systematically manipulating the qualities of a population, was of the essence of projecting. Like many projectors before him, too, White allowed the possibility of "Reasonable" doubt about "the trusting so important a concern to any corporation, who may in time be corrupt." His answer was likewise glib: "when that evil arises the Legislature can easily correct the abuse."[134]

There was room for disagreement about the proper source of support for and power over demographic governance, and about the goals, instruments and oversight of the institutions tasked with it. What was widely accepted by the middle decades of the eighteenth century was that such questions – centered on the means of instilling desirable characteristics in a measurable population – were public ones. For White and Etough alike, foundlings were an isolated and fragile but also a nationwide and recurring phenomenon, to be governed by a dedicated institution and formed in body and mind by passing through its wards and along its circuits before being dispatched to fitting stations in the wider imperial polity. They were thus an emblem and a part of a wider phenomenon of demographic governance that linked private and public projects to a congeries of natural, historical, moral, medical and political-economic ideas and debates about how populations worked and what could be done with them – in field and household, at sea and on the march, in Britain and across the world. From his provincial rectory, Etough invoked French and Italian policies and Indigenous American and African practices to argue that nursing could reverse national decline, just as sacred historians traced the postdiluvian population of the earth to the neonatal habits of the ancient Israelites. In his Essex infirmary, Daniel Sutton undertook to inoculate the hospital foundlings with smallpox, forty years after Cotton Mather and James Jurin had argued for the providential and statistical legitimacy of the technique. In the midst of the Seven Years' War, the General Committee of the Foundling Hospital considered its role in

---

[134] [White?], "Intent of the Publick," LMA A/FH/M/01/004, item 012.

"obviat[ing] those Calamitous mischiefs" that military life visited upon the women and children of a global British empire.[135]

Multiplication, Race and the Demographic Governance of Empire

One enduring distinction in demographic thought was that between city and country; another was between metropolitan and colonial environments. Jacobean colonial promoters had leaned heavily on latitude as a guide to climate. But the reports of New England and Virginia settlers complicated this, as did the invasion and plantation of more southerly locales, especially in the Caribbean.[136] In the latter context, ideas about climate, character and physiology fed arguments about the hazards of settlement for Englishmen and about the suitability of Africans for labor in colonial locales. Notwithstanding constructions of blackness as a marker of permanent and deep difference, not least through medicine, questions of transformation were central to the projected fates of both groups.[137] As Joyce Chaplin, Suman Seth and others have explored, a discourse of "seasoning" developed from the early seventeenth century, according to which English bodies gradually adjusted to their new environments.[138] During the Restoration, both colonists and the enslaved were seen to require seasoning. The extent of this varied between bodies and according to destination. Thus, in 1662, the Cromwellian veteran and first English governor of Jamaica, Edward D'Oyley, contrasted the island – "wonderfull healthfull for Negroes … very few or none dyeing" – with Virginia, where "the Blacks require a seasoning in the Winter as the English in the Summer."[139] From the later seventeenth century, Seth argues, thinking about this process crystallized around the idea of a "seasoning sickness" that effected a once-for-all transformation in the bodies of the transplanted.[140] By the early eighteenth century, metropolitan commentators saw colonial populations, free and enslaved, as qualitatively distinct from their European and

---

[135] Letter, "31 July 1759/From Dr. Brocklesby/Read in the General Committee the 1st August 1759," in LMA A/FH/M/1/005/168–169.

[136] See Chapter 3.

[137] See Chapter 4.

[138] See Chaplin, *Subject Matter*, pp. 175–6; Seth, *Difference and Disease*. But compare Hogarth, *Medicalizing Blackness*, pp. 53–4 and 76, which emphasizes that discourses of seasoning and blackness worked together.

[139] "The relation of Collonell Doyley upon his returne from Jamaica directed to the Lord Chancellor" (*c.* 1662), BL Additional MS 11410, ff.10v–15r, at f.12r.

[140] Seth, *Difference and Disease*, pp. 5, 91–164.

African cousins.[141] Creoles were products of a process linking geographical mobility to bodily change, a process vital to the political economy of the British Empire.

In contrast to shifting environmental ideas, the emergence of scientific constructions and justifications of racism in Britain and other imperial metropoles is well documented.[142] At first glance, frameworks of distinction based on climate and on race might appear incompatible. Just as gender, status and location constrained demographic agency, so racialized hierarchies implied limits on mixture and mutation tools of demographic governance from above, regardless of environment. An ideological commitment to fixed divisions between races might seem to mark the boundaries of population as an object of improvement. It is hard to see, for example, how members of the "white" and "negro" races David Hume posited in his 1748 essay "Of National Characters" could ever have been governed as components of a single population – since, for Hume, only the whites were capable of meaningful education or achievement.[143] Hume drew criticism, but such views were already common in the plantation colonies and became so in Britain after 1760. The idea that natural boundaries were not to be crossed was one even Petty, for all his ambitions, endorsed. Between the mid-seventeenth century and the later eighteenth century, creeping naturalization of the social and legal inequalities slavery brought to the plantation colonies of the Caribbean and North America further constrained the mobility and mutability envisioned between different groups. Yet, as we have also seen, this constraint coexisted with assumptions of radical malleability, with the violent "plasticizing" of a racialized other as at once animal and human, property and person.

Much as metropolitan and colonial policies and projects proposed to instill a second nature in marginalized or laboring populations by calculated uses of mobility and mixture, so in the context of a plantation

[141] On the early development and persistence of a metropolitan "discourse of alterity" directed at settlers, see Jack P. Greene, *Evaluating Empire and Confronting Colonialism in Eighteenth-Century Britain* (Baltimore, MD: Johns Hopkins University Press, 2013), pp. xii–xiii, 50–83.

[142] See for example Kidd, *The Forging of Races*, pp. 79–120; Hogarth, *Medicalizing Blackness*; Andrew Curran, *The Anatomy of Blackness: Science and Slavery in the Age of Enlightenment* (Baltimore, MD: Johns Hopkins University Press, 2011); Hannaford, *Race*, pp. 187–233.

[143] Hume specifically asserted that "negroes" were "naturally inferior to the whites," that there was "scarcely ever ... a civilized nation of that complexion," that they had "No ingenious manufactures, no arts, no sciences" and that even as individuals they had attained no eminence "either in action or speculation." This all stood in contrast, Hume claimed, to the achievements and capacities of even "the most rude and barbarous of the whites." David Hume, "Of National Characters," reprinted in Eugene F. Miller (ed.), *Essays, Moral, Political and Literary*, revised ed. (Indianapolis, IN: Liberty Fund, 1985), pp. 197–215, at 208 n.10.

system predicated on coerced mobility (the slave trade) and qualitative transformation (seasoning), purportedly natural divisions were entrenched and policed – but also, on occasion, renegotiated – by means of legal, social and eventually medical classifications and restrictions on mobility and mixture. Colonial schemes in Elizabethan and Jacobean England and Ireland proposed to civilize Gaels and tame rogues by disrupting and reorienting their geographic, social and legal relationships; Caribbean planters sought to maintain clear distinctions between free and unfree labor both by fusing this distinction to incipient notions of race and by restricting the physical and social mobility and the legal capacities of the enslaved and the non-white. Marriages between English women and Irish men (and English men and Indigenous women) had been a vital instrument of Petty's transmutative schemes. Conversely, "miscegenation" between English and African or African-descended people became a key target of colonial legislators fearful of degeneration. It was outlawed in Antigua in 1644, in Barbados, Maryland, Virginia and Bermuda in the 1650s and 1660s, and in Massachusetts, the Carolinas and Pennsylvania in the first quarter of the eighteenth century.[144] Conceptual frameworks and practical means of demographic governance that had taken shape through metropolitan attempts to assimilate marginal groups into a single loyal and productive population now served to naturalize a distinction between free and enslaved – even as each was subject to various kinds of manipulative intervention, often (in the context of imperial economy) for complementary ends.

And yet colonial circumstances often produced, and imperatives of economy and security sometimes enjoined, violations of these putatively natural boundaries.[145] Miscegenation bans notwithstanding, sexual relationships crossed racial lines and generated "mixed-race" people whose status was ambiguous and unstable. In the Caribbean, where enslaved people vastly outnumbered free, three generations' removal from mixture sufficed to restore physiological "whiteness."[146] Quantitative imbalances set the stage for qualitative transformations: in Jamaica, Brooke Newman and Daniel Livesay have shown that a policy of selective legal "whitening" developed as a positive strategy of governance.[147] Against the backdrop

---

[144] See Winthrop D. Jordan, *White over Black: American Attitudes toward the Negro, 1550–1812* (Baltimore, MD: Penguin, 1968), pp. 136–78; Richard S. Dunn, *Sugar and Slaves: The Rise of the Planter Class in the English West Indies, 1624–1713*. (New York: W. W. Norton, 1973), p. 228.

[145] For examples see Chaplin, *Subject Matter*, pp. 157–98.

[146] This stood in stark contrast to the mainland North American colonies, where "black blood … stained a man and his heirs forever." Dunn, *Sugar and Slaves*, pp. 254–5.

[147] Newman, *Dark Inheritance*; Livesay, *Children of Uncertain Fortune*.

of the Maroon War of 1728–39, thin European emigration and growing numbers of enslaved people stoked fears of rebellion. From 1733, distant descendants of mixed-race unions were thus permitted to seek the legal status of whites – in effect, regenerating a white elite from the degenerate products of mixture. The colonial legislature repeatedly revised the conditions of whitening between the 1730s and the 1760s to suit the planter elite. Thus, in practice, whiteness was a congeries of bloodline, skin color, wealth and British education that made nonsense of the essentialist theories of difference articulated at the same time and, indeed, by Jamaican planters like Edward Long themselves.[148] If climate justified the enslavement of Africans, and medicine proclaimed their racial otherness, security and interest dictated that some of their descendants must become English nevertheless. Before Tacky's Revolt (1760–1) scared planters and the Treaty of Paris (1763) fueled new debate on colonial government, much intellectual, political and familial effort went into effecting this transmutation.[149]

Political arithmetic came late to these discussions and engaged more explicitly with situation than with race. Petty had been interested in imperial schemes, but setting his Irish projects aside, he produced only rough notes on New England's population, queries about the health and other characteristics of "the Natives of Pennsylvania," and a sketchy proposal for a "scale of salubrity" that may have been designed to facilitate colonial settlement.[150] More sustained application of political arithmetic to colonial settlement in the Atlantic developed gradually after 1688. Cotton Mather's use of Graunt's mortality table in early eighteenth-century funeral sermons has been noted. Mather also sent the Royal Society his own observations of long-lived and fecund individuals, which duly appeared in the *Philosophical Transactions*.[151] In contrast to his pastoral use of Graunt's table, which stressed the proximity of death at all stages of life, when working as a natural historian Mather emphasized the distinctive fertility and longevity of his neighbors in comparison with their London compatriots. Whereas long life and plentiful progeny were

---

[148] On Long, see Vincent Brown, *Tacky's Revolt: The Story of an Atlantic Slave War* (Cambridge, MA: Harvard University Press, 2020), p. 227.

[149] Newman, *Dark Inheritance*, p. 106; Livesay, *Children of Uncertain Fortune*, p. 58; Greene, *Evaluating Empire*, pp. 156–99. On the aftermath of Tacky's Revolt, see Brown, *Tacky's Revolt*, pp. 208–36.

[150] McCormick, "Governing Model Populations."

[151] Cotton Mather, "An Extract of Several Letters from Cotton Mather, D. D. to John Woodward, M. D. And Richard Waller, Esq; S. R. Secr.," *PTRS* 29 (1714), 62–71. See McCormick, "Statistics in the Hands of an Angry God?"

"no rare thing" in Massachusetts, he told Richard Waller (Secretary of the Royal Society), "you inform us, That but 64 out of an hundred of the children that are born, are alive at 6 years old." For Mather, this divergence implied not only New England's superior healthfulness but also its greater proximity – in terms of demographic norms – to the "First Ages" of the Earth.[152] Mather said little about the cause of the difference, but his account ruled out diet, exercise or constitution.[153] Environment remained.

American fecundity became a major theme of transatlantic discourse a generation later, in the context not of multiplication in New England but of Anglo-French competition across North America. Here, too, situation was central. But it was sometimes treated in a more systematic and abstract way, more amenable to political economy than to sacred historiography, less interested in remarkable individuals and families than in connecting broad trends to the geography of settlement, the availability of land and the competence of government. Its foremost analyst was the philosopher, projector and political arithmetician Benjamin Franklin.[154] As early as 1747, his satirical "Speech of Miss Polly Baker" argued that to constrain multiplication "in a new Country that really wants People" by prohibiting "Fornication" was to "turn natural and useful Actions into Crimes" – in contravention of "the Publick Good" and "the first and great Command of Nature, and of Nature's God, Encrease and Multiply."[155] Better that nature should take its course, Franklin implied, and policy follow. He moved beyond pronatalist satire and the defense of natural policy to describe the mechanism of increase and the role of situation in his *Observations Concerning the Increase of Mankind* (written in 1751, printed in 1755).[156] Here, Alan Houston argues, Franklin combined "the straitlaced methods of political arithmetic" with the vision of Enlightenment stage theory to produce "an important precursor to modern population doctrines."[157]

[152] Cotton Mather to Richard Waller, November 12, 1712, in Royal Society Library, Early Letters, EL/M2/33.

[153] Mather, "Extract of Several Letters," 71.

[154] See Joyce E. Chaplin, *Benjamin Franklin's Political Arithmetic: A Materialist View of Humanity* [Dibner Library Lecture] (Washington DC: Smithsonian Institution Libraries, 2006).

[155] Benjamin Franklin, "The Speech of Miss Polly Baker," *The General Advertiser*, London, April 15, 1747, reprinted in Alan Houston (ed.), *The Autobiography and Other Writings on Politics, Economics, and Virtue* (Cambridge: Cambridge University Press, 2004), pp. 177–9, at 178–9.

[156] Benjamin Franklin, *Observations Concerning the Increase of Mankind, Peopling of Countries, &c.*, in [William Clarke], *Observations on the Late and Present Conduct of the French, with Regard to Their Encroachments upon the British Colonies in North America …* (Boston, MA: 1755), reprinted Alan Houston (ed.) *Autobiography and Other Writings*, pp. 215–21.

[157] Houston, *Benjamin Franklin*, pp. 109, 124–5.

From this perspective, Franklin's appreciation of the American situation, combined with his uptake of quantitative methods and his engagement with Enlightenment ideas of progress, underpinned projections of demographic expansion and colonial growth. Seen in another light, however, Franklin extended the transmutative ambitions of demographic governance to the "improvement" of humanity's racial complexion.[158] These two sides of Franklin's political arithmetic – Franklin as apostle of growth and as racial alchemist – illuminate the complex legacies of transformative demographic governance in the later eighteenth century. By the same token, they show what is at stake in shifting our focus from the rise of quantification to the ambition to transform. With them, then, we will conclude.

Franklin began by arguing, like Mather, that "Bills of mortality, Christenings, &c. of populous Cities, will not suit Countries; nor will Tables form'd on Observations made in full settled old Countries, as Europe, suit new Countries, as America."[159] But rather than simply pointing to the prolific qualities of the American climate or colonies, Franklin sketched distinct demographic trajectories for old and new, settled and frontier territories. The different futures open to each depended on causal links between the facts of human nature, the logic of multiplication and the context of material constraints. Here, as Houston suggests, Franklin – like Hume, and at the same moment – pushed demographic thinking away from Scripture and toward political economy. "People increase," he wrote, "in Proportion to the Number of Marriages, and that is greater in Proportion to the Ease and Convenience of supporting a Family. When Families can be easily supported, more Persons marry, and earlier in Life." In cities, competition for a livelihood, the cost of maintaining a family and the pressures of luxury conspired against early marriage and stifled growth; in countries long settled, like Europe, competition for land long since settled, divided and "improved to the Heighth" did the same.[160] In America, by contrast, cities were scarce and land "plenty." "Hence Marriages ... are more general, and more generally early, than in Europe." Hence, Franklin computed, "our People must at least be doubled every 20

---

[158] Houston notes that "The relationship between skin color and specific racial or ethnic characteristics remained unsystematic" when Franklin wrote, and that he "often invoked national identities ... to call attention to their plasticity"; Houston, *Benjamin Franklin*, p. 135. I would suggest that plasticity – the mutability central to demographic governance and, as Jackson argues, to the construction of blackness – does not contradict but underlies Franklin's application of political arithmetic to race. See Jackson, *Becoming Human*, pp. 1–44.
[159] Franklin, *Observations Concerning the Increase of Mankind*, p. 215.
[160] Franklin, *Observations Concerning the Increase of Mankind*, p. 215.

Years."[161] Despite this growth, "so vast is the Territory of North-America, that it will require many Ages to settle it fully."[162]

Insofar as Franklin tied the prospect of multiplication to the availability of land and the consequent economic incentive to early marriage, he left little obvious scope for social engineering. This allows Houston to see him primarily as a precursor to Malthus (indeed, as the latter's superior).[163] But Franklin's projections depended on assumptions about the civilizational qualities of different kinds of people, and his application of them reflected hopes and fears about the possibility of transmutation or degeneration through interracial contact and mixture. For America was not in fact unsettled. Not only was it, Franklin acknowledged, "chiefly occupied by Indians" at present; it had also been "as fully settled as it well could be by Hunters" when Europeans first arrived.[164] Paradoxically, America was fully occupied in 1492 yet still unsettled in 1750. The source of the paradox was a silent shift of perspective from settlement as occupation by (Indigenous) people to settlement as occupation by (white) farmers. Only by equating settlement with agriculture, and agriculture with white colonization, could Franklin discount the Indigenous settlement of America almost as soon as he mentioned it and expound on the natural demographic advantages of a vast and vacant New World over a populous and dying Old. The laws of growth that ensured a happy future for Franklin's America made the historical conditions and economic behavior of Europeans and their colonial descendants the measure of nature.

Franklin was not alone among Enlightenment writers in naturalizing the social relations and economic motivations of commercial agriculture. Important here, however, is not only the analytical point that qualities associated with historically and geographically specific social formations shaped the delineation and function of supposedly universal demographic mechanisms but also Franklin's further claim that the qualities of populations – in particular, their cultural and racial character – might and must be controlled and cultivated with an eye to moral, material and aesthetic improvement. This adds nothing to Franklin's proto-Malthusian credentials but does much to locate him in the intellectual history this book has traced. To make it clear, he contrasted white multiplication in mainland

---

[161] Franklin, *Observations Concerning the Increase of Mankind*, p. 216. Franklin estimated that American colonists married twice as often (two rather than one per 100 people per year) and had twice as many births per marriage (eight rather than four) as Europeans.

[162] Franklin, *Observations Concerning the Increase of Mankind*, p. 216

[163] Houston, *Benjamin Franklin*, pp. 142–3.

[164] Franklin, *Observations Concerning the Increase of Mankind*, pp. 215–16.

British North America with the situation in the plantation colonies of the Caribbean. Listing causes that "must diminish a Nation," he noted loss of territory and trade, "insecure Property" and high taxation. Then came slavery:

> The Negroes brought into the English Sugar Islands, have greatly diminish'd the Whites here; the Poor are by this Means deprived of Employment, while a few Families acquire vast Estates, which they spend on Foreign Luxuries, and educating their Children in the Habit of those Luxuries; the same Income is needed for the Support of one that might have maintain'd 100.[165]

The use of enslaved "Negroes" distorted the behavior of free "Whites," curtailing the opportunities poorer whites should expect in colonial circumstances while engendering costly tastes in the planter class, artificially reproducing the effects of Old World urbanization and settlement. But the cost of slavery ran deeper – for white people.

> [T]he Whites who have Slaves, not labouring, are enfeebled, and therefore not so generally prolific.... Slaves also pejorate the Families that use them; the white Children become proud, disgusted with Labour, and being educated in Idleness, are rendered unfit to get a Living by Industry.[166]

The problem with slavery, viewed as an obstacle to white multiplication, was not just economic. Surrounded by enslaved people of African birth or descent, whites became physically and morally incapable of reproduction or industry. In a word, they degenerated.

Promoting white population therefore meant opposing luxury, tyranny and slavery. It also meant securing and protecting opportunities for families to form; transplantation or naturalization schemes like those promoted in the last century, designed to fill perceived "vacancies" by "The Importation of Foreigners," were at worst harmful and at best otiose. In fully peopled countries immigrants could only, Franklin noted without apparent irony, "eat the Natives out."[167] Where space existed, "natural Generation" would fill it:

> Who can now find the Vacancy made in Sweden, France or other Warlike Nations, by the Plague of Heroism 40 Years ago; in France by the Expulsion of the Protestants; in England, by the Settlement of her Colonies; or in Guinea, by 100 Years Exportation of Slaves, that has blacken'd half America? – The thinness of Inhabitants in Spain is owing to National

---

[165] Franklin, *Observations Concerning the Increase of Mankind*, pp. 217–18.
[166] Franklin, *Observations Concerning the Increase of Mankind*, p. 218.
[167] Franklin, *Observations Concerning the Increase of Mankind*, pp. 219–20.

Pride and Idleness ... rather than to the Expulsion of the Moors, or to the making of new Settlements.[168]

Such examples of natural increase grounded Franklin's fundamental claim that the only "Bound to the prolific Nature of Plants or Animals" was "their crowding and interfering with each others Means of Subsistence." Malthus would emphasize the constraints this implied, but from a New World perspective the future looked bright. "A Nation well regulated," Franklin enthused, "is like a Polypus; take away a Limb, its Place is soon supply'd; cut it in two, and each deficient Part shall speedily grow out of the part remaining." Given "Room and Subsistence enough," therefore, "you may ... increase a Nation ten fold in Numbers and Strength."[169] As Houston notes, this argument by analogy answered the recurring accusation that colonial emigration depopulated the metropole.[170] Closer to a polyp than to a human body, the British imperial population would expand as long as territorial acquisitions created the necessary space.[171]

Franklin's vision of multiplication and his estimate of a twenty-five-year doubling period for the white colonial population underpinned his argument for the annexation of Canada after the British capture of Québec in 1759.[172] They also informed Rhode Island minister and political arithmetician Ezra Stiles's *Discourse on the Christian Union* (1761), an annexationist sermon that approved Franklin's doubling figure based on its closeness to scriptural example and modern testimony.[173] Franklin spoke of the "extended population" of Great Britain; Stiles projected the propagation of churches by "natural increase" across North America.[174] For both, the key implication of colonial growth was territorial: only by annexing the vast expanse of Canada (and not the tiny French Caribbean island of Guadeloupe) could

---

[168] Franklin, *Observations Concerning the Increase of Mankind*, p. 220.

[169] Franklin, *Observations Concerning the Increase of Mankind*, pp. 220–1.

[170] Houston, *Benjamin Franklin*, p. 128.

[171] See Benjamin Franklin, *The Interest of Great Britain Considered, with Regard to Her Colonies, and the Acquisitions of Canada and Guadeloupe* (London: Printed by T. Becket, 1760), pp. 24–5. On Franklin's use of the polyp, see Chaplin, *Benjamin Franklin's Political Arithmetic*, p. 26.

[172] Franklin, *Interest of Great Britain Considered*, pp. 17–23.

[173] The modern testimony included Henry Neville's fictional story of interracial polygamy in the *Isle of Pines*, which Stiles took for a real account. Ezra Stiles, *A Discourse on the Christian Union: The Substance of Which Was Delivered before the Reverend Convention of the Congregational Clergy in the Colony of Rhode-Island; Assembled at Bristol, April 23, 1760* (Boston, MA: Printed by Edes and Gill, 1761), pp. 102–5, 108–10, 113–14. For Stiles's interest in the strength of different confessional groups in the colonies, see Ezra Stiles, *Extracts from the Itineraries and Other Miscellanies of Ezra Stiles, D.D., Ll.D., 1755–1794, with a Selection from His Correspondence*, ed. Franklin Bowditch Dexter (New Haven, CT: Yale University Press, 1916).

[174] Franklin, *Interest of Great Britain Considered*, p. 18; Stiles, *Discourse on the Christian Union*, p. 51.

Britain accommodate coming generations of English Protestants. Both this territorial vision and the doubling period proved influential. The medical arithmetician Thomas Short quoted the latter, citing Franklin and Stiles; others, including Malthus, would cite it through Short.[175] By the 1770s, radicals on both sides of the Atlantic used colonial increase to criticize the failings of British administration. As radical Dissenter and supporter of American independence Richard Price noted in 1779, "In the English colonies in North America there has for many years been an increase scarcely ever before known among mankind."[176] This stood in contrast to "the progress of depopulation in this kingdom" since 1688.[177] For Price, these trends condemned English luxury, war, taxation and debt.[178] For his correspondent Stiles, they showed what was at stake in the establishment of "Romish Idolatry over two Thirds of the Territoryes of the British" – a reference to the Quebec Act – and a "System of Domination" over the colonies.[179]

Franklin's articulation of colonial increase in the *Observations* was, and was seen to be, a defense of the colonies in quantitative terms.[180] Yet as his words and their legacy before and during the American Revolution indicate, it was also an argument against the admixture of "Foreigners" and, at least implicitly, an excuse for the expulsion of religious and ethnic minorities. "Why should Pennsylvania, founded by the English," he had asked regarding German immigration, "become a Colony of Aliens, who ... will never adopt our Language or Customs, any more than they can acquire our Complexion?" The complexion of populations was more than a local concern, as he revealed in a closing "Remark":

> That the Number of purely white People in the World is proportionably very small. All Africa is black or tawny. Asia chiefly tawny. America (exclusive of the new Comers) wholly so. And in Europe, the Spaniards, Italians, French,

[175] Thomas Short, *A Comparative History of the Increase and Decrease of Mankind in England, and Several Countries Abroad, According to the Different Soils, Situations, Business of Life, Use of the Non-Naturals, &c.* (London: Printed for W. Nicoll, 1767), pp. ii–iv; Thomas Robert Malthus, *An Essay on the Principle of Population, as It Affects the Future Improvement of Society*, pp. 20–1. See Chaplin, *Benjamin Franklin's Political Arithmetic*, pp. 37–8.

[176] Richard Price, *An Essay on the Population of England, from the Revolution to the Present Time* (London: Printed for T. Cadell, 1780), p. 31. On Price's radicalism see Thomas, *Honest Mind*, especially pp. 151–73.

[177] Price, *Essay on the Population of England*, p. 17.

[178] Price, *Essay on the Population of England*, pp. 17–18, 29–33.

[179] Ezra Stiles to Richard Price, April 4, 1775, American Philosophical Society, Richard Price Papers, B P93, 1–2. On contention over the Quebec Act see most recently Hannah Weiss Muller, *Subjects and Sovereign: Bonds of Belonging in the Eighteenth-Century British Empire* (Oxford: Oxford University Press, 2017), pp. 121–65.

[180] See Chaplin, *Benjamin Franklin's Political Arithmetic*, pp. 24–5.

Russians and Swedes, are generally of what we call a swarthy Complexion; as are the Germans also, the Saxons only excepted, who with the English, make the principal Body of White People on the Face of the Earth, I could wish their Numbers were increased.[181]

Like Hume, but more fastidiously, Franklin described a world population divided by color. Where Hume had asserted the intellectual superiority of "the whites" in an essay on national character, however, Franklin voiced a positive wish to change the demographic proportions between the races – and this in a tract on population and policy. This was not simply a matter of shaping Pennsylvania's character by favoring immigrants with stereo-typically desirable cultural habits. To the contrary, Franklin described the process of colonization as a work of global racial cleansing. In this context, he argued unambiguously for the prevention of African multiplication; black (and, generally, dark) life was a polyp that must stay contained in the Old World. Whitening the world's population was as much a part of progress as clearing the land:

And while we are, as I may call it, Scouring our Planet, by clearing America of Woods, and so making this Side of our Globe reflect a brighter Light to the Eyes of Inhabitants in Mars or Venus, why should we in the Sight of Superior Beings, darken its People? why increase the Sons of Africa, by Planting them in America, where we have so fair an Opportunity, by excluding all Blacks and Tawneys, of increasing the lovely White and Red?[182]

Printed in 1755, this final passage was omitted from later printings of the *Observations*, which ended instead with the polyp analogy. Struggling with its racism, Houston suggests that, because its antislavery implications were politically impracticable in the 1750s, it is best read as satire.[183] Yet the polyp analogy also rested on the presumption of unlimited territory for white families, and Franklin's comments on the "Sugar Islands" – where slavery was inhibiting white multiplication – were evidently sincere. Franklin's vision was perhaps wittingly grandiose. But in an age of colonial massacre and encroachment on occupied yet "vacant" land; of mass enslavement and forced migration; and of projects to codify and adjust the boundaries of color-coded race to improve the security and complexion of real populations, it was no joke.

---

[181] Franklin, *Observations Concerning the Increase of Mankind*, p. 221.

[182] Franklin, *Observations Concerning the Increase of Mankind*, p. 221. On Franklin's opposition to German immigration, see also Benjamin Franklin, "Benjamin Franklin to James Parker, 20 March 1751," in Alan Houston (ed.), *Autobiography and Other Writings*, pp. 222–5.

[183] Houston, *Benjamin Franklin*, p. 136. Compare Chaplin, *Benjamin Franklin's Political Arithmetic*, pp. 22–5.

Demographic Subjectivity and Demographic Governance in the Revolutionary Era

By the fourth quarter of the eighteenth century, even as Adam Smith and his followers disavowed political arithmetic, ideas about demographic governance were so widely diffused in politics and public discourse as to seem ubiquitous. In Britain, medical arithmetic flourished as never before, represented not only by the works of Thomas Short but also by the ambitious data-gathering, clinical reform and smallpox inoculation projects of Thomas Percival in Manchester, John Haygarth in Chester and John Heysham in Carlisle, among others.[184] Older philanthropic projects of social reclamation and public utility targeting specific groups, such as Coram's Foundling Hospital or Jonas Hanway's Marine Society, persisted or revived.[185] So too, for a time, did older reformative approaches to poverty and vagrancy: Paul Slack estimates that by 1782, when Gilbert's Act restricted their use to "impotents," workhouses were available to one in three English parishes.[186] In the Caribbean colonies, fear of Maroon war and slave rebellion on the one hand, and anxiety about the possibility of abolition on the other, fueled new efforts to police racial difference, redress demographic imbalances or, in the case of the abolitionists Sasha Turner examines, remold the enslaved for a regime of "free" labor through familiar but now racialized projects of surveillance, enforced industry and pronatalist interventions in households, childrearing and medicine.[187] These manipulations provoked resistance. On the British North American mainland, too, colonial women began to articulate their control over their reproductive careers in ways that would come to define modern demographic behavior.[188] Throughout the British world, not merely the augmentation but the qualitative control of populations – their moral characteristics, physical condition, cultural compatibility and racial classification – mediated engagements with political and social questions of all kinds.

---

[184] Rusnock, *Vital Accounts*, pp. 92–106, 137–75; Lisbeth Haakonssen, *Medicine and Morals in the Enlightenment: John Gregory, Thomas Percival and Benjamin Rush* (Amsterdam: Rodopi, 1997), pp. 94–186; Francis M. Lobo, "John Haygarth, Smallpox and Religious Dissent in Eighteenth-Century England," in Andrew Cunningham and Roger French (eds.), *The Medical Enlightenment of the Eighteenth Century* (Cambridge: Cambridge University Press, 1990), pp. 217–53.

[185] Lloyd, *Charity and Poverty in England*, pp. 56–7.

[186] Slack, *English Poor Law*, pp. 35–6.

[187] Livesay, *Children of Uncertain Fortune*, pp. 90–142; Newman, *Dark Inheritance*, pp. 229–68; Turner, *Contested Bodies*.

[188] Susan E. Klepp, "Revolutionary Bodies: Women and the Fertility Transition in the Mid-Atlantic Region, 1760–1820," *Journal of American History* 85:3 (1998), 910–45; Klepp, *Revolutionary Conceptions*.

Examples could easily be multiplied. As these few indicate, however, there was no consensus on the ultimate possibility or impossibility, desirability or direction of the quantitative transformations such multifarious policies and projects sought to effect. Every initiative had its backers and its critics, the former promising transformations that the latter decried as impossible or dangerous. But this is the most significant thing about the phenomenon: ideas about demographic governance – about the capacity of public or state intervention to maintain or improve the qualities of the population – could be, and were, taken up on either side of a plethora of questions of government or social welfare. A way of thinking that had first taken shape around discrete confrontations with particular Tudor multitudes (vagrants; the Irish), and whose seventeenth-century rearticulation in the language of Baconian science and empirical quantification had been bound up with a particular discourse (political arithmetic), was by the eighteenth century so much a part of thinking about the problem and possibilities of civil society and imperial government that it becomes as difficult to isolate from its expression in particular contexts as any other common idiom.

One question raised by many debates around matters of demographic governance, however, was the proper locus of authority: clerical or medical (at issue in projects for smallpox inoculation), public or private (central to the changing scope of the Foundling Hospital's activities), metropolitan or colonial (of concern to Franklin and Stiles, as well as to the Jamaican Assembly and the Board of Trade), collective or individual. This last distinction, in particular, energized criticism of projects for the improvement of populations – much as it continues to anchor liberal and libertarian arguments against "social engineering" – founded on ideas of self-interest and spontaneous order.[189] Perhaps most famously, Adam Smith's metaphorical figure of the "Invisible Hand," together with his and others' portrait of the calculating, self-seeking individual as the fundamental social unit, inherently undermined not only anthropomorphic ideas of the body politic but also models of demographic governance that treated populations as objects for mechanistic or alchemistic manipulation in the conscious pursuit of some collective good.[190] In practice, liberal political economy

---

[189] For examples of this tension in twentieth-century engagements with world population, see Connelly, *Fatal Misconception*.

[190] On the Invisible Hand as a self-regulating mechanism, see Otto Mayr, *Authority, Liberty, and Automatic Machinery in Early Modern Europe* (Baltimore, MD: Johns Hopkins University Press, 1986), pp. 164–80.

proved compatible with violent essays in qualitative transformation. The freedom and opportunity Franklin sought to secure for his lovely white polyps, after all, were the flip side of the exclusion or assimilation he proposed for those of darker hue or rougher manners.[191] But locating rights and agency in individual subjects or citizens, while making order a natural and inevitable product of their aggregate behavior, put the legitimacy as well as the logic of projects of collective improvement in question. No one voiced his doubts more strongly or more influentially than the celebrated founder of the science of demography, Thomas Robert Malthus.

[191] On Franklin's economic vision, see Drew R. McCoy, *The Elusive Republic: Political Economy in Jeffersonian America* (Chapel Hill: University of North Carolina Press, 1980). On the tensions and historical links between liberal individualism and racism after the end of slavery, see Hartman, *Scenes of Subjection*, especially pp. 115–24.

Conclusion: Malthus, Demographic Governance and the Limits of Politics

The Malthusian Division

From the perspective of the Henrician humanists, Elizabethan pamphleteers, Jacobean colonial promoters, Interregnum projectors, Restoration political arithmeticians and Enlightenment-era physicians, philanthropists and philosophers who have populated this book, T. R. Malthus's 1798 *Essay on the Principle of Population* appears, scarcely less than the French Revolution, to mark the end of an age.[1] The demographic governance that emerged during the three centuries before Malthus wrote was defined by the assumption that groups of people could be transformed by means of purposive interventions: policies and projects exploiting the mobility and the malleability of subject populations with the aim of improving their political and economic nature. The interventions at issue ran the gamut from forced transoceanic transplantation to domestic moral surveillance. Their proximate goals also varied, from the redress of rural depopulation to the inculcation of productive habits and skills, to the assuagement of political-cum-confessional hatreds, to the prevention of epidemics and to the civilization of the colonized. But at their heart – from before the rise of quantification or the birth of statistics, to both of which they gave meaning – was the construction of intentional control over the collective qualities of subjects as a central problem of political rule, social order and, eventually, human flourishing. Into this baroque edifice slammed the wrecking ball of Malthusian principle.

In beginning with a *principle* of population – an unchanging and universal law of nature immanent in all species – Malthus's essay departed sharply from the rhetoric and method of early modern demographic governance.[2] His subject in the 1798 *Essay* was not this or that population,

---

[1] Malthus, *Essay* (1798).
[2] Important recent works on Malthus include Robert J. Mayhew, *Malthus: The Life and Legacies of an Untimely Prophet* (Cambridge, MA: Harvard University Press, 2014); Alison Bashford and Joyce E. Chaplin, *The New Worlds of Thomas Robert Malthus: Rereading the Principle of Population*

but population as such. The contrast with the episodic, ad hoc and local projects we have encountered here could scarcely be greater; and, as is well known, Malthus's assertion of this fatal principle undercut the optimistic premises on which many of these projects rested. Though radical preachers of boundless improvement and revolutionary proponents of equality (the Marquis de Condorcet, William Godwin and Richard Price) were his proximate targets, the weak points on which Malthus focused his attacks – belief in the transformative power of institutions and policies and, beyond that, in the radical mutability of humankind – were shared by almost every thinker and schemer touched on in this book. Building on the economic and moral thought of Adam Smith, Malthus too sought to explain human society in terms of the constant and beneficial (for the clergyman, Providential) operation of a few natural laws, in the face of which even the most well-meant interventions were at best counterproductive. He, thus, replaced the baroque alchemy of political arithmetic with the liberal logic of political economy.

Yet reading the *Essay* in light of generations of engagement with demographic governance reveals continuities that too narrow a contextualization of Malthus obscures. As much as Malthus undermined the basis of particular projects, he employed some of the same conceptual tools their authors had developed – invoking "situation" as a key factor in multiplication, assessing policies in terms of their conformity to nature and worrying about the degenerative or morally improving effects of different institutional arrangements designed to manipulate the qualities of groups. His distinctive approach and views notwithstanding, then, Malthus's arguments touched on the ambitions and assumptions of early modern projectors more ambivalently and at many more points than initially appears.[3] For this reason, reading the *Essay* with this longer history in mind also allows us to reassess what it was that made Malthus different. What emerges is not an outright rejection of transformative demographic governance. Rather, it is a more specific denial of demographic agency to the early modern motley of publics, institutions and governments that

---

(Princeton, NJ: Princeton University Press, 2016); and essays in Robert J. Mayhew (ed.), *New Perspectives on Malthus* (Cambridge: Cambridge University Press, 2016). My interpretation of Malthus's *Essay* here builds on an essay in the latter volume.

[3] Sylvana Tomaselli points out that Malthus's work was "part of a general and very important controversy about the extent to which and the manner in which population growth or decline were subject to human control." Sylvana Tomaselli, "Political Economy: The Desire and Needs of Present and Future Generations," in Christopher Fox, Roy Porter and Robert Wokler (eds.), *Inventing Human Science: Eighteenth-Century Domains* (Berkeley: University of California Press, 1995), pp. 292–322, at 313.

claimed it, and the reassignment of this power to the weak reasoning of passionate individuals and the hard benevolence of "nature's God."[4]

The *Essay* opened with "an obvious truth ... taken notice of by many writers": namely, "that population must always be kept down to the level of the means of subsistence." Botero had said nearly as much. Malthus's concern, however, was "the means by which this level is effected," and his point that "a view of these means ... forms ... the strongest obstacle in the way to any very great future improvement of society."[5] The *Essay*'s first chapter traced hope for improvement to "great and unlooked for discoveries" in science, an "unshackled spirit of inquiry" fueled by print and "new light on political subjects" culminating in the French Revolution. All fostered a sense "that we were touching on a period big with the most important changes, changes that would in some measure be decisive of the future of mankind."[6] All misled. Two postulates exposed the deceit: "First, That food is necessary to the existence of man," and "Secondly, That the passion between the sexes is necessary, and will remain nearly in its present state."[7] The need for food tied life to land whose productivity – *pace* Plattes – allowed only finite additions; constant sexual passion entailed rapid multiplication. "Population, when unchecked, increases in a geometrical ratio. Subsistence increases only in an arithmetical ratio."[8] These were not contingent observations but axiomatic truths. The "natural inequality of the two powers of population, and of production in the earth" was unrelenting. Checks – "waste of seed, sickness, and premature death" in plants and animals, "misery and vice" in human beings – leveled it. The inevitability of checks made the "perfectibility of society" an idle dream.[9]

As others have recognized, Malthus's attack on improvement was a thought-experiment grounded in general claims about human nature, the power of population and the limits of production.[10] By comparison with optimistic visions based in stage theories of past social development – the boldest of which was Condorcet's *Esquisse d'un tableau historique des progrès d'esprit humain* (1795) – this was a kind of conjectural

---

4 Malthus, *Essay* (1798), p. 350.
5 Malthus, *Essay* (1798), p. iii.
6 Malthus, *Essay* (1798), pp. 1–2.
7 Malthus, *Essay* (1798), p. 11.
8 Malthus, *Essay* (1798), p. 14.
9 Malthus, *Essay* (1798), pp. 15–16.
10 Keith Tribe describes "The numerical element of Malthus's reasoning" as "purely speculative"; Keith Tribe, *Land, Labour and Economic Discourse* (London: Routledge & Kegan Paul, 1978), p. 128.

anticonjectural history. Like the conjectural historians of the French and Scottish Enlightenments (including not only Condorcet but also Smith), Malthus was more concerned with inferring the nature and limits of change from models of social organization than with offering an empirical account of any particular set of events.[11] The very conflict between the powers he identified implied that "in no state that we have yet known, has the power of population been left to exert itself with perfect freedom."[12] Checks, preventing or punishing excess, operated always and everywhere, at every stage of civilizational development.[13] The *Essay*'s second chapter, thus, moved from universal claims to contrasting models of human multiplication under notionally minimal and maximal degrees of constraint.

As the nearest approximation of untrammeled multiplication, Malthus took America.[14] Here, "where the means of subsistence have been more ample, the manners of the people more pure, and consequently the checks to marriages fewer, the population has been found to double itself in twenty-five years."[15] Malthus drew explicitly on the numbers (and echoed the contradictory assumptions) of Benjamin Franklin, painting a picture of vacant New World land spurring early marriage and fostering the closest thing possible to unchecked population growth. In the "modern states of Europe," by contrast, limited opportunities were "calculated to prevent, and certainly do prevent, a very great number in all civilized nations from pursuing the dictate of nature in an early attachment to one woman."[16] Natural sexual appetites, lacking the outlet of marriage, produced vice; the alternative was misery. Rather than a progress, the history of settled nations was and must be a perpetual oscillation. Overpopulation meant food scarcity, raising the cost of subsistence while lowering wages. Bringing misery

---

[11] Dugald Stewart's 1793 biography of Smith described "*Theoretical* or *Conjectural History*" as a "species of philosophical investigation" akin to "natural history" in Hume's usage, the goal of which was, "when we cannot trace the process by which an event *has been* produced ... to show how it *may have been* produced by natural causes." He noted that "In most cases, it is of more importance to ascertain the progress that is most simple, than the progress that is most agreeable to fact; for, paradoxical as the proposition may appear, it is certainly true, that the real progress is not always the most natural." Dugald Stewart, *Account of the Life and Writings of Adam Smith, LL.D.*, in Adam Smith (ed. W. P. D. Wightman, J. C. Bryce and I. S. Ross), *Essays on Philosophical Subjects* (Oxford: Oxford University Press, 1980), pp. 269–351, at 293, 296.

[12] Malthus, *Essay* (1798), p. 19.

[13] On Malthus's use of stage theory, see Ronald L. Meek, *Social Science and the Ignoble Savage* (Cambridge: Cambridge University Press, 1976), p. 223.

[14] See Bashford and Chaplin, *New Worlds of Thomas Robert Malthus*.

[15] Malthus, *Essay* (1798), p. 20.

[16] Malthus, *Essay* (1798), pp. 20, 28. On Malthus's privileging of colonists' (and Franklin's) views in his discussion of America, see Alison Bashford and Joyce E. Chaplin, "Malthus and the New World," in Mayhew (ed.), *New Perspectives on Malthus*, pp. 105–27, at 106, 110.

in the near term, however, this eventually led to increasing application of labor to land, raising production and ameliorating the lives of the masses long enough to set the cycle going once more.[17] "The restraints to population are in some degree loosened; and the same retrograde and progressive movements with respect to happiness are repeated."[18] Change, in the sense of escape from the trap finite abundance set for boundless passion, was illusory.

Chapters 3 and 4 applied this argument, respectively, to the situation of "the savage or hunter state" – "the rudest state of mankind," represented here by an undifferentiated Indigenous society in America – and "the state of mixed pasture and tillage, in which ... the most civilized nations must always remain."[19] Here and later, Malthus reproduced Franklin's strange bifurcation of "America": on one hand, it was a vacant space for unconstrained settler multiplication, and hence an approximation of the power of population unbound; on the other, it was a savage society already fully peopled in relation to the resources suited to its mode of subsistence and therefore suffering the inevitable checks. At the same time, and in common with conjectural historians, Malthus also connected the misery and want he ascribed to "savage" America with the desperate migration of Europe's past barbarians, whose "congregated bodies at length obscured the sun of Italy, and sunk the whole world in universal night."[20] Here was a picture of inevitable want driving migration – with disastrous consequences not only for its immediate victims but also for the more civilized world next door. Yet, despite appearances, "the superior power of population" over "the means of subsistence" obtained in civilized no less than in barbarian societies.[21] If "the greater part of Europe is more populous now than it was in former times" – Malthus here touched on the debate between Wallace and Hume – this was only because "the industry of the inhabitants has made these countries produce a greater quantity of human subsistence."[22] So far as this went, Plattes might have agreed.

The principle of population wrought different effects in civilized than in barbarian nations, however. In fact, Malthus argued, growth slowed as European societies passed from pastoralism to mixed agriculture, as political arithmeticians' accounts of "doubling periods" – Franklin's figure for

[17] Malthus, *Essay* (1798), pp. 29–30.
[18] Malthus, *Essay* (1798), p. 31.
[19] Malthus, *Essay* (1798), pp. 39, 53.
[20] Malthus, *Essay* (1798), p. 45.
[21] Malthus, *Essay* (1798), p. 45.
[22] Malthus, *Essay* (1798), p. 55.

colonial settlers here became a proxy for primitive European society –
allegedly showed:

> In examining the principal states of modern Europe, we shall find, that
> though they have increased very considerably in population since they
> were nations of shepherds, yet that, at present, their progress is but slow;
> and instead of doubling their numbers every twenty-five years, they require
> three or four hundred years, or more, for that purpose. Some, indeed, may
> be absolutely stationary, and others even retrograde.[23]

This stagnation was due, moreover, to a new combination of factors.
Certainly, civilization brought no abatement of the passion between the
sexes, and "positive" checks to growth operated in all states of society;
the civilized poor could starve as well as the barbarous.[24] But a second,
"negative" check to multiplication now emerged, in the form of rational
foresight – indeed, fear – of the economic and social consequences of marriage. This negative check could only operate in civilized societies, for two
reasons. First, and central to Malthus's attack on Enlightened or radical
egalitarianism, the fear behind the negative check centered on a loss of
relative status that was only possible in conditions of inequality – that is,
where "Two or three steps of descent in society" constituted "a real and
essential evil."[25] Fear of downward mobility drove rational restraint. But
what made such demotion an object of fear was not primarily the threat of
exposure to the positive checks that menaced society's poorest members,
but rather the obstacle that relative poverty presented to "free, equal, and
reciprocal" participation in society.[26] Loss of status was an affront not to
survival, that is, but to independence.

A few things about this are important. One is that "The love of independence" was effectively specific to people of some economic standing
in modern nations. These alone had some kind of independence to lose
through marriage and the burdens of family. The universal nature of the
principle of population notwithstanding, a historically and culturally specific quality thus played an important role in shaping demographic agency
and thereby changing the nature of the checks that met multiplication –
confining the positive check "chiefly, though not perhaps solely, to the lowest orders of society," as Malthus argued in Chapter 5.[27] Second, this love
of independence worked its effects on demographic behavior through the

---

[23] Malthus, *Essay* (1798), pp. 61–2.
[24] Malthus, *Essay* (1798), pp. 62–3.
[25] Malthus, *Essay* (1798), p. 65.
[26] Malthus, *Essay* (1798), p. 65.
[27] Malthus, *Essay* (1798), p. 71.

rational foresight of individuals. No more than Smith's rational self-interest could it be imposed from above. Intentional demographic agency, to the extent that anyone exercised it on earth, was, thus, the prerogative of rational and propertied individuals. Third, however, it was by the same token a historical and social achievement, subject like other aspects of society to the benign or malign influence of policy and projects. As with Smith, Malthus's focus on the harmful consequences of intervention – especially the Poor Laws – has loomed largest for his readers: "the parish law of England ... is a system of all others the most calculated gradually to weaken this sentiment, and in the end, may eradicate it completely."[28] But the sentiment at issue was itself a product of situation and of education. The love of independence was a demographically consequential quality as much engendered and preserved by one sort of governance as weakened or extinguished by another. To this extent, at least, Malthus tasked government with shaping population as urgently as any of his predecessors.

When Malthus turned to the Poor Laws in Chapter 5, therefore, he presented them as an artificial mechanism – an unnatural policy, as Petty would have understood it – with unintended but real and disastrous consequences for the love of independence that alone reduced the role of positive checks in favor of negative in civilized nations. By making payments to the poor while ignoring the iron link between produce and land, "Their first obvious tendency is to increase population without increasing the food for its support."[29] Like religious uniformity in Petty's rendering, which produced rebels and hypocrites rather than converts, these laws ignored the natural and permanent grounds of the problem they purported to solve, thereby worsening it. Second,

> [T]he quantity of provisions consumed in workhouses upon a part of society, that cannot in general be considered as the most valuable part, diminishes the shares that would otherwise belong to more industrious, and more worthy members; and thus in the same manner forces more to become dependent.[30]

Not only did the parish relief system promote dependency (a form of moral degeneration as well as economic degradation) by shifting resources from the more to the less worthy, however. The settlement laws also prevented the mobility required for labor markets to function on a national scale to facilitate the natural oscillation between the demand for labor and

[28] Malthus, *Essay* (1798), pp. 67–8.
[29] Malthus, *Essay* (1798), p. 83.
[30] Malthus, *Essay* (1798), p. 84.

the reduction of excess population Malthus had sketched at the start.[31] Population was not only a natural force but also (still) a political problem whose management involved the instrumentalization of mobility as well as of self-interest. It was essential to grant "liberty and freedom of action to the peasantry of England … to settle without interruption, wherever there was a greater plenty of work and a higher price for labour," Malthus argued. "The market of labour would then be free": free, that is, to shape the demographic calculations of individuals.[32] This was not an argument against attempts to shape the qualities of populations but rather an argument about what those qualities should be and what kind of governance could instill and maintain them.

"To prevent the recurrence of misery, is, alas! beyond the power of man," Malthus averred.[33] Yet misery did not strike equally everywhere. Foresight limited its empire among the civilized to the ignorant, shiftless and poor; colonial expansion – if one assumed the disappearance of Indigenous people, as Malthus, like Franklin, did in Chapter 6 – opened vistas of vacant land: "new colonies settled in healthy countries, where there was plenty of room and food, have constantly increased with astonishing rapidity in their population."[34] The former colonies of British North America had excelled all others in the regard was testament to the influence of political institutions – in particular, a "liberty and equality" favoring early marriage – even where land was putatively free.[35] Given "want of room and food," however, institutions mattered less.[36] This was the case in Britain itself, and by extension in other modern nations:

> In the natural progress of the population of any country, more good land will, *cæteris paribus*, be taken into cultivation in the earlier stages of it than in the later. And a greater proportional yearly increase of produce will almost invariably be followed by a greater proportional increase of population.[37]

As better land was exhausted and worse pressed into use, increases in produce declined before population; crowding, poor diets and epidemics followed, and with them "discouragements to marriage … vicious habits, war, luxury, the silent though certain depopulation of large towns, and the

[31] Malthus, *Essay* (1798), p. 92.
[32] Malthus, *Essay* (1798), p. 95.
[33] Malthus, *Essay* (1798), p. 98.
[34] Malthus, *Essay* (1798), p. 101.
[35] Malthus, *Essay* (1798), p. 104.
[36] Malthus, *Essay* (1798), p. 109.
[37] Malthus, *Essay* (1798), p. 123.

close habitations, and insufficient food of many of the poor."[38] While "the fact" of checks to population was inescapable, however, "the modes which nature takes to prevent or repress a redundant population" varied.[39] Banishing misery was an idle dream, but its nature and scope might change.

This was cold comfort for revolutionaries and utopians. Much of the rest of the *Essay* attacked the bold and sunny speculations of Wallace, Price, Condorcet and especially Godwin in greater detail. These critiques, all of them grounded in the inevitable clash between the power of population and that of the earth's production, have been studied thoroughly and need no elaboration here. Yet even in this most polemical portion of the *Essay*, the keynote of Malthus's commentary on the power of policy – or, more generally, human art – to ameliorate the effects of nature was ambivalence rather than flat denial. Perfectibility was a sham.[40] Lifespan was fixed.[41] Equality was impossible.[42] The passion between the sexes was constant.[43] Art could no more alter the results of this than (contra Godwin) policy could be blamed for it:

> [T]he truth is, that though human institutions appear to be the obvious and obtrusive causes of much mischief to mankind; yet, in reality, they are light and superficial, they are mere feathers that float on the surface, in comparison with those deeper seated causes of impurity that corrupt the springs, and render turbid the whole stream of human life.[44]

This gave the lie to projects: far from changing the river's course, as projectors and legislators imagined, their schemes and engines were so many feathers drifting on its surface. And yet, the misery Godwin decried as the fruit of bad laws Malthus upheld as "the result of the laws of nature, which human institutions, so far from aggravating, have tended considerably to mitigate, though they can never remove."[45] Policy was not without power; art was not without effect.

The question was where this power was located and how far through society and into nature's empire these effects might reach. Where did demographic agency reside and what might it accomplish? One locus for effective

[38] Malthus, *Essay* (1798), p. 126.
[39] Malthus, *Essay* (1798), p. 128.
[40] Malthus, *Essay* (1798), ch. 8.
[41] Malthus, *Essay* (1798), ch. 9.
[42] Malthus, *Essay* (1798), ch. 10.
[43] Malthus, *Essay* (1798), ch. 11.
[44] Malthus, *Essay* (1798), p. 177.
[45] Malthus, *Essay* (1798), p. 179.

demographic calculation, we have seen, was the rational individual. Here was the basis for a shift, among elites in civilized nations, from positive to negative checks. Yet, as the chapters directed against Godwin underlined, there were severe limits to this – physical limitations that no power of mind could touch.[46] There were physical limitations, too, on the cultivation of mind. The struggle for subsistence made it improbable "that the lower classes of people in any country, should ever be sufficiently free from want and labour, to attain any high degree of intellectual improvement."[47] Not only the lower orders of society but also women as a sex were excluded – by "their different education," paradoxically – from acquiring the habit of "vigorous mental exertion" needed for reason to master passion.[48] To the degree that these limitations *were* matters of education – the impossibility of attaining it, in the case of the lower orders; its failure to cultivate rational exertion, in the case of women – they might seem accidental rather than essential obstacles, and susceptible to change. But the material circumstances of life and the inequalities scarcity dictated in modern, settled societies made them effectively insurmountable. The demographic agency of the rational individual was available only to the few.

Beneath the radicals' failure to grasp the necessary effects of circumstance lay a more basic mistake: the exaltation of mind over body. "Mr. Godwin," Malthus wrote, "considers man too much in the light of a being merely intellectual."[49] Attributing human formation originally to sense impressions, in a Lockean vein, Godwin and others proposed to transform character by means of institutions.[50] Yet "a great number of those impressions which form character," Malthus insisted, "remain absolutely independent of the will of man" and, thus, beyond the grasp of any such remolding.[51] Moreover, human beings – even rational, civilized men and a fortiori members of inferior sexes, orders and societies – were compounds of mind and body, and "the decision of the compound being is different from the conviction of the rational being."[52] Mind could no more overrule body than men could become angels. Any idea of transforming the relationship between spirit and flesh was illusory – not because of the limits of the earth or modes of subsistence but because of the very nature

---

[46] Malthus, *Essay* (1798), p. 223.
[47] Malthus, *Essay* (1798), p. 218.
[48] Malthus, *Essay* (1798), pp. 238–9.
[49] Malthus, *Essay* (1798), p. 252.
[50] Malthus, Essay (1798), pp. 266–8.
[51] Malthus, *Essay* (1798), p. 270.
[52] Malthus, *Essay* (1798), p. 255.

of the human frame. Malthus here attacked the philosophical and psychological assumptions of late eighteenth-century radicalism. But in so doing, he implicitly called in question any scheme purporting to impose a better second nature on degenerate human material – any policy predicated on the malleability of human nature or the mutability of people's qualities.

In almost the same breath, however, Malthus voiced another very different objection. Here, his starting point was not the impossibility of improvement but rather its potentially hazardous consequences. With an eye on the history of agriculture and botany, he admitted that purposive changes were possible; art had manifestly manipulated nature in these realms.[53] The danger was that, carried beyond a certain indefinable point, such manipulation ultimately damaged and deformed its object. The stakes of such experimental error might seem small,

> But an experiment with the human race is not like an experiment upon inanimate objects. The bursting of a flower may be a trifle. Another will soon succeed it. But the bursting of the bonds of society is such a separation of parts as cannot take place without giving the most acute pain to thousands: and a long time may elapse, and much misery may be endured, before the wound grows up again.[54]

Far from a hopeless daydream, improvement was a potentially devastating nightmare – only too efficacious, but liable to slip out of control, causing the degeneration of its human objects and dissolving the ties that bound them to society. In this fleeting moment, Malthus embraced fears of mutability and social breakdown that in many respects resemble those with which this book started. But he voiced these not in the context of seeking to restrain mobility or restore a static body politic – like any stage theorist he knew history would not hold still, as his comments on America made clear.[55] He spoke, rather, in horror at what attempts to harness human mutability and alter the nature of society had done. He did not merely look forward with derision to vain attempts at social engineering; he looked back with apprehension at its real effects.

For demographic governance was the prerogative of Nature and, thus, of Nature's God, whose designs demanded the unceasing oscillation between growth and want Malthus everywhere discerned. This providential plan was the subject of Chapters 18 and 19, which closed the *Essay*.

---

[53] On Malthus and agriculture, see Fredrik Albritton Jonsson, "Island, Nation, Planet: Malthus in the Enlightenment," in Mayhew (ed.), *New Perspectives on Malthus*, pp. 128–52.

[54] Malthus, *Essay* (1798), p. 275.

[55] Malthus, *Essay* (1798), p. 343.

Here, Malthus described how the "book of nature, where alone we can read God as he is," revealed

> [A] constant succession of sentient beings, rising apparently from so many specks of matter, going through a long and sometimes painful process in this world; but many of them attaining, ere the termination of it, such high qualities and powers, as seem to indicate their fitness for some superior state.[56]

This, then, was the secret of the world's design and population's place within it: not a quick transformation of waste into wealth but a slower, truer transmutation of matter into spirit. The principle of population kept "the inhabitants of the earth always fully up to the level of the means of subsistence; and is constantly acting upon man as a powerful stimulus ... to the further cultivation of the earth," feeding further growth, new needs and more activity.[57] The misery and want built into earthly life was but "the mighty process of God, not for the trial, but for the creation and formation of mind," needed "to awaken inert, chaotic matter into spirit, to sublimate the dust of the earth into soul, to elicit an ethereal spark from the clod of clay."[58] Or, as Malthus put it later, "Evil exists in the world, not to create despair, but activity."[59] "The sorrows and distresses of life" were not punishments, but "excitements" meant "to soften and humanize the heart, to awaken social sympathy, to generate all the Christian virtues, and to afford scope for the ample exertion of benevolence."[60] No craft could counterfeit this process; art, efficacious in small things, was a poor mimic of grand designs. "The constancy of the laws of nature" was "the foundation of the industry and foresight of the husbandman; the indefatigable ingenuity of the artificer; the skilful researches of the physician, and anatomist; and the watchful observation, and patient investigation, of the natural philosopher."[61] Intellect – human worth – emerged not only from policies or projects but also from the condition of a species destined by a beneficent but distant deity for moral and material struggle. Between these individuals, with their strong passions and weak reason, and the Almighty, with His perfect and painful machine of nature, no legitimate agent of real transformation existed.

---

[56] Malthus, *Essay* (1798), pp. 351–2.
[57] Malthus, *Essay* (1798), p. 365.
[58] Malthus, *Essay* (1798), p. 353.
[59] Malthus, *Essay* (1798), p. 395. On the *Essay* as a theodicy, see Brian Young, "Malthus among the Theologians," in Brian Dolan (ed.), *Malthus, Medicine, and Morality: 'Malthusianism' after 1798* (Amsterdam: Rodopi, 2000), pp. 93–113.
[60] Malthus, *Essay* (1798), p. 372.
[61] Malthus, *Essay* (1798), p. 363.

Agency and the Limits of Transformation

Scholars have explored Malthus's changes to the *Essay* between the first edition and the second, printed in 1803. In particular, the disappearance of the final two chapters on Providence, the augmentation of statistical data for Britain and other countries (buoyed by the appearance of the national census in 1801) and – most significant – a new emphasis on "moral restraint" as a third check to population have all been held to signify a retrenchment of some of the first *Essay*'s direr implications.[62] To the extent that moral restraint was an individual prerogative that might prevent misery and avoid vice, it mitigated the human weakness that so marked the first *Essay*. Yet inasmuch as this mode of demographic agency brought rational calculation to bear on inborn passions, moral restraint only underlined the spiritual nature of the transformation of humankind that Malthus avowed – the slow and painful transmutation, effected at massive cost by the entire system of Nature, of a speck of matter into a spark of divinity. It also confirmed the assignment of responsibility for navigating the process to the individual rather than the state or the public. As A. M. C. Waterman has described it, this was a Christian political economy.[63] In light of the previous three centuries of engagement with the role of situation and policy in the qualities of human groups, however, it was also a particular answer to the question of the nature, seat and purposes of demographic governance. The subsequent history of philanthropy, policing and population policy in the metropole – to say nothing of the pursuit of civilization and discipline in the colonies – argues that, over the long term, it remained a minority position.

Though Malthus's *Essay* sits at one end – from our perspective, the liberal end – of a spectrum of views on demographic governance, it belongs to a tradition of qualitative engagements with population spanning the early modern period. Against a dominant historiographical trend, this book has argued that what these engagements had in common was not a quantifying spirit, much less a concrete reliance on empirical, numerical data. Many of them predated quantitative demographic sources and many others simply failed to use such numbers as existed. More to the point, numbers figured (so to speak) in a far wider and more complex set of ways than as proto-statistics. In the context of the sixteenth-century body

---

[62] See Samuel M. Levin, "Malthus and the Idea of Progress," *Journal of the History of Ideas* 27:1 (January 1966), 92–108, at 93; Young, "Malthus among the Theologians," pp. 102–5.

[63] A. M. C. Waterman, *Revolution, Economics and Religion: Christian Political Economy 1798–1833* (Cambridge: Cambridge University Press, 1991).

politic, they drew their force from the symbolic weight of proportions or the biblical resonance of multitudes; in the guise of seventeenth-century political arithmetic, they pointed to the power of the new science and the capacity of state-sponsored projects to create new futures; for eighteenth-century publics, they indexed the triumphs of improvement and public spirit over waste, idleness and vice. No more than a single mode of quantification was a single view of the economy or polity shared across these engagements; the modern British state and the Empire developed and were contested in the midst of them – and through them. The common denominator was the ambition to transform people, to impose or instill a second nature on or in them, by means of constraining, facilitating or compelling their mobility and mixture and by manipulating their environments.

This ambition emerged historically in attempts to define and address specific problems associated with particular groups of people. These locally, historically and/or functionally defined multitudes – husbandmen, vagrants, the mere Irish, the Old English – drew attention to the role of unconstrained mobility and mixture in degeneration. But they also raised the possibility of instrumentalizing the same or analogous processes – planned or coerced mobility, resettlement or confinement, transplantation and colonial expansion, even mixture – for the sake of regenerating lost virtues or producing new ones. Locating the origins of population in these contexts has significant methodological and historiographical implications. For one thing, decentering quantification forces us to look beyond the history of statistics, of the census and indeed of the information state. Ideas of population were not dictated by numbers nor, exclusively, by state actors. Rather, anxieties about mobility and degeneration and hopes for their reversal created the context for new kinds of information and intervention, by no means all centrally directed or state-driven. These anxieties and hopes emerged in specific geographical and social contexts. The scope and consequent limitations of the present work aside, exploring these contexts more fully requires attention to historiographies – of agriculture and rural life, poverty and vagrancy, colonialism and race, labor and technology – that lie off the beaten path of the intellectual history of social science.

By the same token, the transformative ambition at the heart of population's emergence from engagements with multitudes left traces in a wide variety of sources and genres of print, only a fraction of them examined here. It is not enough to trawl the canon of political theory or economic writing and extract changing ideologies of or attitudes to population from the haul. Rogue pamphlets and literary works, sermons and sacred histories, colonial propaganda and technological projects, newspapers, novels and essays in natural philosophy all bore witness to ideas about the mobility, mixture and mutability of populations. Much as interpreting uses of number in these sources requires more than mathematical ability, reading them requires not only the tools and the vision of different sub-fields within history but also those of different disciplines. This book has leaned heavily in places on the work of historians of science and literary scholars, in particular; but other kinds of source will dictate other analytical borrowings. A narrow approach to intellectual history will not do when the material in question is of such a scattered and varied nature, nor when the subject itself – the history of demographic governance, agency and subjectivity; the making of population as a way of seeing, doing and being – involves (to oversimplify) both changing ideas about society and society's changing engagement with those ideas.

One of the most pressing questions this history raises is how such contingent, diverse and diversely mediated engagements with the qualities of groups shaped the meaning of population after Malthus. To put it another way: what might the early modern history of demographic governance tell us about the persistence or reemergence of concerns about the mobility, mixture and mutability of populations in the nineteenth, twentieth and twenty-first centuries? Instances of such concern are not only numerous but also fundamental to received interpretations of modern history. So central are they, in fact, that under the rubric of "population politics," they have sometimes been taken as definitively and uniquely modern phenomena.[64] It would be pointless to argue that there was nothing new in the creation of an industrial proletariat; in the definition, documentation and policing of ethnic and national masses; in the concoction of eugenics programs purporting to combat criminal traits and protect a putative white race from degeneration; or in the technological rationalization and central planning of genocide in the name of hygiene. And yet their scale, impact and specific technological and ideological contexts notwithstanding, neither the qualitative focus, the violent means nor the radical goals of such processes and projects were always so new as is imagined. At their core was the assumption that population – whether manifested

---

[64] See for example Eric D. Weitz, "Racial Politics without the Concept of Race: Reevaluating Soviet Ethnic and National Purges," *Slavic Review* 61:1 (2002), 1–29; Eric D. Weitz, "From Vienna to the Paris System: International Politics and the Entangled Histories of Human Rights, Forced Deportations, and Civilizing Missions," *American Historical Review* 113:5 (2008), 1313–43; Connelly, *Fatal Misconception*.

in ideological terms as a confessional group, a labor force, a nation or a race – concretized qualities whose control, preservation or alteration was a central task of governance. This assumption was not a modern creation but an early modern inheritance.

This in turn suggests that thinking in terms of demographic governance gives us one way of connecting a variety of distinct historical developments over the long term, and of seeing modern population politics as fundamentally continuous with developments that began in the sixteenth century. Here, however, the English and Anglophone focus of the present study reveals its limitations. If the discourse of degeneration links modern eugenics with premodern colonialism or vagrancy legislation, for example, surely we should also ask (as some scholars have) about the legacy of forced conversion, the valuation of *limpieza di sangre* and the transplantation and expulsion of Jews and Moriscos from Spain – or the regulation of Jewish populations in Italian and German territories – or the management of Romani mobility across Europe – or any number of other examples, from the late medieval period onward, where key elements of what I have described as demographic governance are, or at least appear to be, at issue.[65] This book has offered one of many possible histories of demographic governance, in the hope of reinforcing and opening up other lines of enquiry rather than of imposing strict definitions and rigid chronologies. At the same time, the prominence of Malthus's name and work, the influence of "Baconian" thinking about art and nature, the spread of political arithmetic in policy debates and in multiple print genres, and the endurance of Britain's colonial empire help account for the special resonance that some of the ideas, arguments and projects that form part of this particular history have.

A focus on demographic governance might also connect the histories of class, race and gender, complementing suggestions in recent work on the history of the body.[66] In particular, anxieties about the possibility and more especially the danger of mutability appear to mark the crystallization of each of these ideas from the long eighteenth century onward.

---

[65] For suggestive accounts of such instances, see Mary Elizabeth Perry, *The Handless Maiden: Moriscos and the Politics of Religion in Early Modern Spain* (Princeton, NJ: Princeton University Press, 2005); Geoffrey Symcox, "Toleration and *Ragion Di Stato*: Jews and Protestants in the Savoyard State, Ca. 1650–1750," in Hans Erich Bödeker, Clorinda Donato and Peter Hanns Reill (eds.), *Discourses of Tolerance and Intolerance in the European Enlightenment* (Toronto: University of Toronto Press, 2009), pp. 27–52; David Cressy, *Gypsies: An English History* (New Haven, CT: Yale University Press, 2018).

[66] See, for example, Kevin Siena, *Rotten Bodies: Class and Contagion in Eighteenth-Century Britain* (New Haven, CT: Yale University Press, 2019), pp. 228–52.

Differences between male and female, Black and white, and rich and poor came to be naturalized, in part by means of anatomical investigation and medical commentary, in part by means of philosophical and religious speculation. Broadly speaking, the boundaries of the full-blooded, rational, responsible, political and economic subject came to be drawn more sharply over the course of the nineteenth and into the twentieth centuries. The exclusion of those on the wrong side of each line, meanwhile, was justified as natural even as the lines themselves were defended as bulwarks of social order and indeed of civilization. And yet a belief in the possibility and desirability of transformation has also lingered and spread – most obviously in opposition to the repressive nature of rigid class, gender and racial hierarchies, but also as an instrument for the maintenance of hierarchy itself. In the present, promises of biotech-driven "human upgrades" compete for attention with calls for cultural assimilation and "social cohesion."[67] The endless adjustments demanded of precarious workers by a faltering "gig" economy, of migrants by changing border regimes and of marginalized citizens by projects of disenfranchisement are a constant reminder that political inclusion, social acceptance and economic worth remain tied to the promises and perils of transformation.

---

[67] For speculation about human upgrades, see Yuval Noah Harari, *Sapiens: A Brief History of Humankind* (New York: Harper, 2015), ch. 20. On social cohesion, see for example "Assimilation is counter-terrorism," Raymond Odierno and Michael O'Hanlon, Opinion, *USA Today*, April 18, 2016.

Afterword

I wrote the last lines of this book in the midst of a global pandemic; I write this just days after having received the first dose of a vaccine, while medical authorities warn of a fourth wave of infection. Over the past year, COVID-19 has made the effects of global mobility and the perils of mixture, the safety of confinement and the rapid transformation of social behavior the stuff of everyday conversation and media commentary – as well as of municipal decree, national politics and international negotiation. Far from introducing new ideas, it seems, this worldwide catastrophe has breathed new life into centuries-old fears of contamination, degeneration and social breakdown, and given new force to technologically mediated variations on old answers: regulating mobility, controlling mixture, changing behavior. Though the language has changed, we are all at work imposing second natures or having them imposed on ourselves, our families and our communities. Numbers – the daily, weekly, monthly numbers of the infected, the hospitalized, the recovering and the dead; the changing rates of transmission and hospitalization; the percentages of hospital beds and intensive care units filled to or beyond capacity; the 2 meters or 6 feet of distance we are to maintain around ourselves for the sake of safety; the average efficacy of the several competing vaccines among different age groups – govern our lives and delimit our horizons more fully than the Bills of Mortality did those of Pepys and his fellow Londoners during the Great Plague. But for us as for them, behind the numbers lurk deeper anxieties: are we sick even now? Are we spreading disease and death? Are we making the changes necessary to have a future we want? Do we even have the power to do so? Transformations are upon us whether we will or no.

I wrote, too, during a summer of unprecedented popular protest, led by the Black Lives Matter movement, against racist police brutality and white violence – especially but not only in the United States – against Black people, as well as Indigenous people and people of color. Here is another demand for transformation, voiced by the targets of an ideology of white supremacy rooted partly in processes traced in this book. If early modern demographic governance hinged on the mutability of populations, nascent constructions of racial difference in the seventeenth and eighteenth century set limits to this, excluding those supposedly incapable of civilization from political personhood as well as from the kind of economic subjectivity and demographic agency increasingly demanded in the later eighteenth century by writers like Smith and Malthus of rational and moral individuals. It is no dismissal of the peculiar and grotesque history of "race" in the United States since Independence to say that we are still, also, reckoning with these prior denials of personhood and of rationality. Indeed, under cover of mythmaking about the trans-historical unity and singularity of Western Civilization, in the revival of pseudo-scientific racism in the form of speculative linkages between IQ and "races" (often euphemized as "populations") and in the denunciation of institutional and governmental policies of inclusivity and equity as "social engineering," these denials are daily reaffirmed.

On one hand, we can still see everywhere the poisonous legacies, contested histories and continuing echoes of early modern engagements with the qualities of populations – up to and including colonization, genocide, mass enslavement, forcible transplantation, economic, sexual and environmental exploitation, and political and social exclusion over the course of centuries. On the other, we see, too, the persistent promise of the ambition to transform people – once the prerogative of states and projectors concerned with loyalty and industry but now, it may be, appropriated by antiracist, environmentalist and other broadly based movements for overdue and emancipatory change. These different but historically connected legacies of engagement with populations may be reflected in the current contrast between reactionary dismissals of inclusivity and mixture as unnatural social engineering, and the more progressive recognition that our capacity for radical and lasting transformation – muted and individualized in liberal conceptions of economic rationality and travestied in neoliberal celebrations of "disruption" – is, on a collective basis, essential to our prospects for survival. We will either change or perish.

Bibliography

Archives and Libraries

American Philosophical Society, Philadelphia.
British Library, London.
London Metropolitan Archives, London.
National Archives, Kew.
Royal Society Library, London.

Online Archives, Digital Projects and Non-Print Media

CELT: Corpus of Electronic Texts. Cork: University College Cork, 1997–2020. Available at https://celt.ucc.ie

Early English Books Online (EEBO). ProQuest LLC, 2003–2020. Available at https://eebo.chadwyck.com

Eighteenth Century Collections Online (ECCO). Gale/Cengage Learning. Available at https://gale.com/c/eghteenth-century-collections-online-part-i

Greengrass, M., M. Leslie, and M. Hannon, eds. *The Hartlib Papers*. Sheffield: Digital Humanities Institute, University of Sheffield, 2013. Available at https://dhi.ac.uk/hartlib

The Holinshed Project. Oxford: Digital Humanities Institute, University of Oxford, 2008–2013. Available at https://cems.ox.ac.uk/holinshed

Microfilm Edition of the Cotton Mather Papers, 19 reels. Worcester and Boston: Massachusetts Historical Society and the American Antiquarian Society.

Printed Periodicals

Journal des Sçavans
Philosophical Transactions of the Royal Society
The Spectator

Printed Books and Scholarly Editions

A Letter sent by I.B. Gentleman vnto his very frende Mayster R.C. Esquire, vvherein is contained a large discourse of the peopling & inhabiting the Cuntrie called the Ardes, and other adiacent in the North of Ireland. London: Printed by Henry Bonneman for Anthony Kitson, 1572.

An Ease for Overseers of the Poore Abstracted from the Statutes, Allowed by Practise, and Now Reduced into Forme, as a Necessarie Directorie for Imploying, Releeuing, and Ordering of the Poore. London: Printed by Iohn Legat, 1601.

Arbuthnot, John. *An Essay on the Usefulness of Mathematical Learning, in a Letter from a Gentleman in the City to His Friend in Oxford,* second edition. Oxford: Printed by L. Lichfield for S. Wilmot, 1721.

Arbuthnot, John. *Of the Laws of Chance, or, a Method of Calculation of the Hazards of Game, Plainly Demonstrated, and Applied to Games at Present Most in Use, Which May Be Easily Extended to the Most Intricate Cases of Chance Imaginable.* London: Printed by Benj. Motte, 1692.

Ashe, St. George. *A Sermon Preached to the Societies for Reformation of Manners, at St. Mary-le-Bow, on Monday, December the 31st, MDCCXVI.* London: Printed by J. Downing, 1717.

Bacon, Francis. *Francis Bacon: The Major Works.* Ed. Brian Vickers. Oxford: Oxford University Press, 2008.

Bacon, Francis. *The History of the Reign of King Henry VII.* London: Hesperus Press, 2007.

Bacon, Francis. *The New Organon.* Trans. and ed. Lisa Jardine and Michael Silverthorne. Cambridge: Cambridge University Press, 2000.

Bacon, Francis. *The Works of Francis Bacon, Lord Chancellor of England: A New Edition.* Ed. Basil Montagu, 15 vols. London: William Pickering, 1825–1834.

Bacon, Francis. *History Naturall and Experimentall, of Life and Death. Or of the Prolongation of Life.* Trans. [W]illiam [R]awley. London: Printed by Iohn Haviland for William Lee and Humphrey Mosley, 1638.

Bacon, Francis. *Francisci Baronis de Vervlamio, Vice-Comitis Sancti Albani, Historia vitae et mortis.* Londini: In officina Io. Haviland, impensis Matthaei Lownes, 1623.

Barnes, Jonathan, ed. *The Complete Works of Aristotle: The Revised Oxford Translation,* 2 vols. Oxford: Oxford University Press, 1985.

Bedford, Arthur. *A Sermon Preached to the Societies for Reformation of Manners, at St. Mary-le-Bow, on Thursday, January 10, 1733.* London: Printed for Jos. Downing, 1734.

Bell, William. *A Dissertation on the Following Subject: What Causes Principally Contribute to Render a Nation Populous? And What Effect Has the Populousness of a Nation on Its Trade?* Cambridge: Printed by J. Bentham, 1756.

Bentley, Richard. *The Folly and Unreasonableness of Atheism Demonstrated from the Advantage and Pleasure of a Religious Life, the Faculties of Human Souls, the Structure of Animate Bodies, & the Origin and Frame of the World.* London: Printed by J.H. for H. Mortlock, 1693.

Bland, Alfred Edward, Philip Anthony Brown, and Richard H. Tawney, eds. *English Economic History: Select Documents*. London: G. Bell and Sons, 1914.

Boate, Gerard. *Irelands Naturall History* [1652], reprinted in *A Collection of Tracts and Treatises Illustrative of the Natural History, Antiquities, and the Political and Social State of Ireland, at Various Periods Prior to the Present Century*. Dublin: Alexander Thom & Sons, 1860, pp. 1–148.

Bodin, Jean. *The Six Bookes of a Commonweale*. Ed. Kenneth Douglas McRae. Trans. Richard Knolles. Cambridge: Harvard University Press, 1962.

Bodin, Jean. *The Six Bookes of a Common-weale*. Trans. Richard Knolles. London: [Printed by Adam Islip] and G. Bishop, 1606.

Bodin, Jean. *Six livres de la république*. Paris, 1576.

Botero, Giovanni. *On the Causes of the Greatness and Magnificence of Cities*. Trans. Geoffrey Symcox. Toronto: University of Toronto Press, 2012.

Botero, Giovanni. *The Reason of State*. Trans. P. J. Waley and D. P. Waley. London: Routledge and Kegan Paul, 1956.

Botero, Giovanni. *Relations of the Most Famovs Kingdomes and Common-wealths thorowout the World*. Trans. R. I. London: Printed by Iohn Haviland, 1630.

Botero, Giovanni. *A Treatise, concerning the Causes of the Magnificencie and Greatnes of Cities, Deuided into Three Bookes*. Trans. Robert Peterson. London: Printed by T. P[urfoot] for Richard Ockould and Henry Tomes, 1606.

Botero, Giovanni. *The Trauellers Breuiat, or, an Historicall Description of the Most Famous Kingdomes in the World Relating Their Situations, Manners, Customes, Ciuill Gvernment, and Other Memorable Matters*. Trans. Robert Johnson. London: Printed by dm. Bollifant for Iohn Iaggard, 1601.

Botero, Giovanni. *Le relationi universali*. Venice: Appresso Giorgio Angelieri, 1596.

Botero, Giovanni. *Della ragion di stato libri dieci*. Venice: Appresso I. Gioliti, 1589.

Botero, Giovanni. *Delle cause della gradezza delle città libri III*. Rome: Appresso Giovanni Martinelli, 1588.

Boyle, Robert. *An Essay of the Great Effects of Even Languid and Unheeded Motion. Whereunto Is Annexed an Experimental Discourse of Some Little Observed Causes of the Insalubrity and Salubrity of the Air and Its Effects*. London: Printed by M. Flesher for Richard Davis, 1685.

Bradford, William. *Of Plymouth Plantation, 1620–1647*. New York: Random House, 1981.

Bray, Thomas. *For God, or for Satan: Being a Sermon Preached at St. Mary le Bow, Before the Societies for the Reformation of Manners, December 27. 1708*. London: Printed by J. Downing, 1708.

Burnet, Thomas. *The Theory of the Earth: Containing an Account of the Original of the Earth, and of All the General Changes Which It Hath Already Undergone, or Is to Undergo, Till the Consummation of All Things. The Two First Books Concerning the Deluge, and Concerning Paradise*. London: Printed by R. Norton, for Walter Kettilby, 1684.

Burrington, George. *An Answer to Dr. William Brakenridge's Letter Concerning the Number of Inhabitants within the London Bills of Mortality*. London: Printed for J. Scott, 1757.

Burroughs, Joseph. *A Sermon Preached to the Societies for Reformation of Manners; at Salters-Hall, on Monday, the 28th of June, 1731.* London: Printed for E. Matthews, 1731.

Butler, William. *A Sermon Preached to the Societies for Reformation of Manners, at St. Mary-le-Bow, on Monday, January the 1st, MDCCXXI.* London: Printed by J. Downing, 1722.

Camerarius, Joachim. *The History of Strange Wonders.* London: Printed by Roulande Hall, 1561.

Campion, Edmund. *A Historie of Ireland* [MS 1571]. London, 1633; New York: Scholars Facsimiles and Reprints, 1940.

Certayne Causes Gathered Together, Wherin Is Shewed the Decaye of England, Only by the Great Multitude of Shepe, to the Utter Decay of Houshold Keping, Mayntenance of Men, Dearth of Corne, and Other Notable Dyscommodityes Approued by Syxe Olde Prouerbes. London: Printed by Heugh Syngelton, 1552.

Chandler, Edward. *A Sermon Preached to the Societies for Reformation of Manners, at St. Mary-le-Bow, on Monday January the 4th, 1724.* London: Printed for James Knapton, 1724.

Cockburn, Patrick. *An Enquiry into the Truth and Certainty of the Mosaic Deluge.* London: Printed for C. Hitch and M. Bryson, 1750.

Copland, Patrick. *Virginia's God Be Thanked, Or a Sermon of Thanksgiving for the Happie Successe of the Affayres in Virginia this Last Yeare.* London: Printed by I. D. for William Sheffard and Iohn Bellamie, 1622.

Cuningham, William. *The Cosmographical Glasse Conteinyng the Pleasant Principles of Cosmographie, Geographie, Hydrographie, or Nauigation.* London: Printed by John Day, 1559.

Davenant, Charles. *Discourses on the Public Revenues, and on the Trade of England.* London: Printed for James Knapton, 1698.

Davies, John. *A Discoverie of the Trve Cavses why Ireland Was Neuer Entirely Subdued, nor Brought vnder Obedience of the Crowne of England, vntill the Beginning of His Maiesties Happie Raigne* [1612], reprint. Shannon: Irish University Press, 1969.

Dee, Arthur. *Fasciculus Chemicus: Or Chymical Collections. Expressing the Ingress, Progress, and Egress, of the Secret Hermetick Science, out of the Choicest and Most Famous Authors.* London: Printed by J. Flesher for Richard Mynne, 1650.

Defoe, Daniel. *A Journal of the Plague Year: Being Observations or Memorials, of the Most Remarkable Occurrences, as Well Public as Private, Which Happened in London during the Last Great Visitation in 1665.* London: Printed for E. Nutt, J. Roberts, A. Dodd, and J. Graves, 1722.

Defoe, Daniel. *An Essay upon Projects.* London: Printed by R.R. for Tho. Cockerill, 1697.

Erasmus, Desiderius. *The Education of a Christian Prince.* Ed. Lisa Jardine. Trans. Neil M. Cheshire and Michael J. Heath. Cambridge: Cambridge University Press, 1997.

Erasmus, Desiderius. *Ten Colloquies.* Trans. Craig R. Thompson. Indianapolis: Bobbs-Merrill, 1957.

Franklin, Benjamin. *Autobiography and Other Writings.* Ed. Alan Houston. Cambridge: Cambridge University Press, 2004.

Franklin, Benjamin. *The Interest of Great Britain Considered, with Regard to Her Colonies, and the Acquisitions of Canada and Guadeloupe.* London: Printed by T. Becket, 1760.

Gerrard, William. "Lord Chancellor Gerrard's Notes of His Report on Ireland," *Analecta Hibernica* 2 (1931): 93–291.

Graunt, John. *Natural and Political Observations, Mentioned in a Following Index, and Made upon the Bills of Mortality.* London: Printed by Thomas Roycroft for John Martin, James Allestry, and Thomas Dicas, 1662.

Gray, Robert. *A Good Speed to Virginia.* London: Printed by Felix Kyngston for William Welbie, 1609.

Gookin, Vincent. *The Author and Case of Transplanting the Irish into Connaught Vindicated, from the Unjust Aspersions of Col. Richard Laurence.* London: Printed by A. M. for Simon Miller, 1655.

Gookin, Vincent. *The Great Case of Transplantation in Ireland Discussed.* London: I.C., 1655.

Hakluyt, Richard. *A Discourse concerning Western Planting Written in the Year 1584.* Ed. Charles Deane. Cambridge: John Wilson and Son, 1877.

Hale, Matthew. *The Primitive Origination of Mankind, Considered and Examined According to the Light of Nature.* London: Printed by William Godbid, for William Shrowsbery, 1677.

Hanway, Jonas. *A Proposal for Saving from 70,000 l. to 150,000 l. (a) to the Public; at the Same Time Rendering 5000 Young Persons of Both Sexes More Happy in Themselves and More Useful to Their Country, than If So Much Money Were Expended on Their Account (25 February 1764).* London: s.n., 1764.

Hariot, Thomas. *A Briefe and True Report of the New Found Land of Virginia of the Commodities and of the Nature and Manners of the Naturall Inhabitants.* Frankfurt: Typis Ioannis Wecheli, sumtibus vero Theodori de Bry, 1590.

Harrison, William. *The Description of England: The Classic Contemporary Account of Tudor Social Life.* Ed. George Edelen. New York: Dover, 1968.

Hartlib, Samuel. *A Discoverie for Division or Setting out of Land, as to the Best Form.* London: Printed for Richard Wodenothe, 1653.

Historical Manuscripts Commission. *Fourteenth Report, Appendix, Part VII. The Manuscripts of the Marquis of Ormonde, Preserved at the Castle, Kilkenny,* 2 vols. London: Historical Manuscripts Commission, 1895, vol. II, pp. 294–6.

Holinshed, Raphael. *Chronicles of England, Scotland, and Ireland,* 6 vols. London, 1587.

Hume, David. "On the Populousness of Ancient Nations," in *Essays Moral, Political, and Literary,* revised edition. Ed. Eugene F. Miller. Indianapolis: Liberty Fund, 1987, pp. 377–464.

Hume, David. "Of National Characters," in *Essays, Moral, Political and Literary,* revised edition. Ed. Eugene F. Miller. Indianapolis: Liberty Fund, 1985, pp. 197–215.

Kennett, White. *A Sermon Preach'd at Bow-Church, London, before the Societies for Reformation, on Monday the 29th of December, 1701.* London: Printed for A. and J. Churchil, 1702.

Keymor, John. *A Cleare and Evident Way for Enriching the Nations of England and Ireland, and for Setting Very Great Numbers of Poore on Work.* London: Printed by T. M. & A. C., 1650.

King, Gregory. "'The LCC Burns Journal': A Manuscript Notebook Containing Workings for Several Projected Works" (c.1695–1700). Facsimile Reproduction in *The Earliest Classics: John Graunt and Gregory King.* Ed. Peter Laslett. Farnborough: Gregg International Publishers, 1973.

Kinney, Arthur F., ed. *Rogues, Vagabonds, and Sturdy Beggars: A New Gallery.* Amherst: University of Massachusetts Press, 1990.

Langton, Christopher. *An Introduction into Phisycke wyth an Vniuersal Dyet.* London: Printed by Edwarde Whytchurche, [1545?].

Las Casas, Bartholomé de. *The Spanish Colonie, or Briefe Chronicle of the Acts and Gestes of the Spaniardes in the West Indies, Called the Newe World, for the Space of XL. Yeeres.* Trans. M. M. S. London: Printed [by Thomas Dawson] for William Brome, 1583.

Latham, Robert and William Matthews, eds. *The Diary of Samuel Pepys,* 10 vols. London: G. Bell and Sons, 1970–1983.

Lawrence, Richard. *The Interest of England in the Irish Transplantation, Stated.* Dublin: William Bladen, 1655.

Leadam, Isaac Saunders, ed. *The Domesday of Enclosures, 1517–1518.* London: Longmans, Green and Co., 1897.

Levett, Christopher. *An Abstract of Timber-Measures.* [London]: Printed by William Iones, 1618.

Lewis, Rhodri. *William Petty on the Order of Nature: An Unpublished Manuscript Treatise.* Tempe: Arizona Center for Medieval and Renaissance Texts and Studies, 2012.

Luther, Martin. *The Book of Vagabonds and Beggars with a Vocabulary of Their Language and a Preface by Martin Luther.* Ed. David Biron Thomas. Trans. J. C. Hotten. London: Penguin, 1932.

Malthus, Thomas Robert. *An Essay on the Principle of Population, or, A View of Its Past and Present Effects on Human Happiness, with an Inquiry into Our Prospects Respecting the Future Removal or Mitigation of the Evils Which It Occasions.* London: John Murray, 1826.

Malthus, Thomas Robert. *An Essay on the Principle of Population, as It Affects the Future Improvement of Society. With Remarks on the Speculations of Mr. Godwin, M. Condorcet, and Others.* London: Printed for J. Johnson, 1798.

Mandeville, Bernard. *Bernard Mandeville's "A Modest Defence of Publick Stews": Prostitution and Its Discontents in Early Georgian England.* Ed. Irwin Primer. Basingstoke: Palgrave Macmillan, 2006.

Mandeville, Bernard. *A Modest Defense of Publick Stews.* London: Printed by A. Moore, 1724.

Mandeville, Bernard. *The Fable of the Bees: Or, Private Vices Publick Benefits.* London: Printed for J. Roberts, 1714.

Mather, Cotton. *Life Swiftly Passing and Quickly Ending. A Very Short Sermon, on the Shortness of Humane Life.* Boston: Printed by T. Fleet and T. Crump, 1716.

Mather, Cotton. *Seasonable Thoughts Upon Mortality. A Sermon Occasioned by the Raging of a Mortal Sickness in the Colony of Connecticut, and the Many Deaths of Our Brethren There.* Boston: Printed by T. Green, 1712.

Mather, Cotton. *Corderius Americanus: An Essay on the Good Education of Children.* Boston: Printed by John Allen, 1708.

More, Thomas. *Utopia.* Eds. George M. Logan and Robert M. Adams. Cambridge: Cambridge University Press, 1989.

Morison, Samuel Eliot, et al., eds. *Winthrop Papers,* 5 vols. Boston: Massachusetts Historical Society, 1929–1947.

Morris, Corbyn. *Observations on the Past Growth and Present State of the City of London.* London: s.n., 1751.

Mun, Thomas. *England's Treasure by Forraign Trade. Or, the Ballance of Our Forraign Trade Is the Rule of Our Treasure.* London: Printed by J.G. for Thomas Clark, 1664.

Neville, Henry. *Plato Redivivus: Or, a Dialogue Concerning Government.* London: Printed for S.I., 1681.

Nichols, John Gough, ed. *The Diary of Henry Machyn, Citizen and Merchant-Taylor of London, 1550–1563.* London: Camden Society, 1848.

Nicholls, William. *A Conference with a Theist.* London: Printed by T.W. for Francis Saunders and by Tho. Bennet, 1696.

Nicolay, Nicolas de. *The nauigations, peregrinations and voyages, made into Turkie by Nicholas Nicholay Daulphinois, Lord of Arfeuile, chamberlaine and geographer ordinarie to the King of Fraunce.* Trans. T. Washington. Ed. John Stell. London: Printed by Thomas Dawson, 1585.

Parker, Benjamin. *A Review of the State of the Antediluvian World.* London: Printed for W. Reeve, 1748.

Patrizi, Francesco. *De regno et regis institutione.* Milan, 1482.

Penn, William. *A Perswasive to Moderation to Dissenting Christians.* London: Printed by Andrew Sowle, 1685.

Perrott, James. *The Chronicle of Ireland, 1584–1608.* Dublin: Irish Manuscripts Commission, 1933.

Pett, Peter. *The Happy Future State of England.* London: s.n., 1688.

Petty, William. *The Petty Papers: Some Unpublished Writings of Sir William Petty.* Ed. *Marquis of Lansdowne,* 2 vols. London: Constable, 1927.

Petty, William. *The Economic Writings of Sir William Petty.* Ed. Charles Henry Hull, 2 vols. Cambridge: Cambridge University Press, 1899, vol. II, pp. 545–621.

Petty, William. *History of the Cromwellian Survey of Ireland, A.D. 1655–6, Commonly Called "the Down Survey."* Ed. Thomas A. Larcom. Dublin: Irish Archaeological Society, 1851.

Petty, William. *The Political Anatomy of Ireland.* London: Printed by D. Brown and W. Rogers, 1691.

Petty, William. *Political Arithmetick*. London: Printed for Robert Clavel and Henry Mortlock, 1690.

Petty, William. *Five Essays in Political Arithmetick*. London: Printed for Henry Mortlock, 1687.

Petty, William. *Two Essays in Political Arithmetick, Concerning the People, Housing, Hospitals, &c. Of London and Paris*. London: Printed for J. Lloyd, 1687.

Petty, William. *Another Essay in Political Arithmetick, Concerning the Growth of the City of London: With the Measures, Periods, Causes, and Consequences Thereof. 1682*. London: Printed by H.H. for Mark Pardoe, 1683.

Petty, William. *A Treatise of Taxes and Contributions*. London: Printed for N. Brooke, 1662.

Peyrère, Isaac la. *Men before Adam. Or a Discourse Upon the Twelfth, Thirteenth, and Fourteenth Verses of the Fifth Chapter of the Epistle of the Apostle Paul to the Romans. By Which Are Prov'd, that the First Men Were Created before Adam*. London: s.n., 1656.

Peyrère, Isaac la. *A Theological Systeme Upon That Presvpposition, That Men Were before Adam. The First Part*. London: s.n., 1655.

Plattes, Gabriel. *The Profitable Intelligencer, Communiating His Knowledge for the Generall Good of the Common-Wealth and All Posterity*. London: Printed for T. U., 1644.

Plattes, Gabriel. *A Description of the Famous Kingdome of Macaria; Shewing Its Excellent Government: Wherein the Inhabitants Live in Great Prosperity, Health, and Happinesse; the King Obeyed, the Nobles Honoured; and All Good Men Respected, Vice Punished, and Vertue Rewarded*. London: Printed for Francis Constable, 1641.

Plattes, Gabriel. *A Discovery of Infinite Treasvre, Hidden since the Worlds Beginning*. London: Printed by I.L. and are to be sold by George Hutton, 1639a.

Plattes, Gabriel. *A Discovery of Subterraneall Treasure*. London: Printed by J. Okes for Jasper Emery, 1639b.

Pound, John F., ed. *The Norwich Census of the Poor 1570*. Norwich: Norfolk Record Society, 1971.

Powell, Robert. *Depopulation Arraigned, Convicted and Condemned, by the Lawes of God and Man*. London: Printed by R. B., 1636.

Price, Richard. *An Essay on the Population of England, from the Revolution to the Present Time*. London: Printed for T. Cadell, 1780.

Salgado, Gamini, ed. *Cony-Catchers and Bawdy Baskets: An Anthology of Elizabethan Low Life*. Harmondsworth: Penguin, 1972.

Salter, Frank Reyner, ed. *Some Early Tracts on Poor Relief*. London: Methuen, 1926.

Secondat, Charles de and Baron de Montesquieu. *The Persian Letters*. Trans. George R. Healy. Indianapolis: Hackett, 1999.

Secondat, Charles de and Baron de Montesquieu. *Persian Letters*, 2 vols. Trans. John Ozell. London: Printed for J. Tonson, 1722.

Short, Thomas. *A Comparative History of the Increase and Decrease of Mankind in England, and Several Countries Abroad, According to the Different Soils, Situations, Business of Life, Use of the Non-Naturals, &c.* London: Printed for W. Nicoll, 1767.

Short, Thomas. *New Observations, Natural, Moral, Civil, Political, and Medical, on City, Town, and Country Bills of Mortality. To Which Are Added, Large and Clear Abstracts of the Best Authors Who Have Wrote on That Subject. With an Appendix on the Weather and Meteors.* London: Printed for T. Longman and A. Millar, 1750.

Short, Thomas. *A General Chronological History of the Air, Weather, Seasons, Meteors, &c. in Sundry Places and Different Times; More Particularly for the Space of 250 Years.* London: Printed for T. Longman and A. Millar, 1749.

Sidney, Philip. *The Complete Works of Sir Philip Sidney.* Ed. Albert Feuillerat, 4 vols. Cambridge: Cambridge University Press, 1923.

Smart, John and Charles Brand. *Tables of Interest, Discount, Annuities, &c. First Published in the Year 1724, by John Smart, and Now Revised, Enlarged, and Improved, by Charles Brand. To Which Is Added an Appendix, Containing Some Observations on the General Probability of Life.* London: Printed for T. Longman, T. Cadel, and N. Conant, 1730.

Smith, Adam. *Essays on Philosophical Subjects.* Eds. W. P. D. Wightman, J. C. Bryce and I. S. Ross. Oxford: Oxford University Press, 1980.

Smith, Adam. *An Inquiry into the Nature and Causes of the Wealth of Nations.* Eds. R. H. Campbell, A. S. Skinner, and W. B. Todd, 2 vols. Oxford: Oxford University Press, 1979.

Smith, Adam. *An Inquiry into the Nature and Causes of the Wealth of Nations.* Ed. Edwin Cannan, 2 vols. London: Methuen and Co., 1904.

Smith, John. *The Trade & Fishing of Great-Britain Displayed: With a Description of the Islands of Orkney and Shotland.* London: Printed by William Godbid, 1661.

Smith, Thomas. *A Discourse of the Common Weal of this Realm of England.* Ed. Elizabeth Lamond. Cambridge: Cambridge University Press, 1954.

Spenser, Edmund. *A View of the Present State of Ireland.* Eds. Andrew Hadfield and Willy Maley. Oxford: Blackwell, 1997.

Spenser, Edmund. *A View of the Present State of Ireland [A vewe of the Present State of Ireland Discoursed by Way of a Dialogue betwene Eudoxus and Irenius. 1596.] Edited, Principally from MS Rawlinson B 478 in the Bodleian Library and MS 188.221 in Caius College, Cambridge.* Ed. W. L. Renwick. London: Scholartis Press, 1934.

Sprengell, Conrad Joachim. *The Aphorisms of Hippocrates and the Sentences of Celsus.* London: Printed for R. Bonwick, W. Freeman, Tim. Goodwin, et al., 1708.

Standish, Arthur. *Nevv Directions of Experience.* London: s.n., 1613.

Standish, Arthur. *The Commons Complaint.* London: Printed by William Stansby, 1611.

Starkey, Thomas. *A Dialogue Between Pole and Lupset.* Ed. T. F. Mayer. Camden Fourth Series. London: Royal Historical Society, 1989.

Stiles, Ezra. *Extracts from the Itineraries and Other Miscellanies of Ezra Stiles, D.D., Ll.D., 1755–1794, with a Selection from His Correspondence.* Ed. Franklin Bowditch Dexter. New Haven: Yale University Press, 1916.

Stiles, Ezra. *A Discourse on the Christian Union: The Substance of Which Was Delivered before the Reverend Convention of the Congregational Clergy in the Colony of Rhode-Island; Assembled at Bristol, April 23, 1760*. Boston: Printed by Edes and Gill, 1761.

Stow, John. *A Survey of London Written in the Year 1598*. Stroud: Sutton, 1994.

Swift, Jonathan. *The Writings of Jonathan Swift*. Eds. Robert A. Greenberg and William B. Piper. New York: W. W. Norton, 1973.

Tawney, Richard Henry, and Eileen Power, eds. *Tudor Economic Documents: Being Select Documents Illustrating the Economic and Social History of Tudor England*, 3 vols. London: Longmans, Green and Co., 1951.

Temple, William. *A Vindication of Commerce and the Arts; Proving That They Are the Source of the Greatness, Power, Riches and Populousness of a State*. London: Printed for J. Nourse, 1758.

Temple, William. *An Essay Upon the Advancement of Trade in Ireland*. Dublin: s.n., 1673.

Temporarius, Johannes. *Chronologicarum demonstrationum libri tres*. Frankfurt, 1596.

Thirsk, Joan and J. P. Cooper, eds. *Seventeenth-Century Economic Documents*. Oxford: Oxford University Press, 1972.

Trigge, Francis. *The Humble Petition of Two Sisters; the Church and Common-Wealth: For the Restoring of their Ancient Commons and Liberties, which Late Inclosure with Depopulation Hath Uncharitably Taken Away*. London: Printed by George Bishop, 1604.

Wallace, Robert. *A Dissertation on the Numbers of Mankind in Antient and Modern Times: In Which the Superior Populousness of Antiquity Is Maintained*. Edinburgh: Printed for G. Hamilton and J. Balfour, 1753.

Walsh, Frances. *The Antediluvian World; or, a New Theory of the Earth*. Dublin: Printed by S. Powell, 1743.

Ware, James. *The Historie of Ireland, Collected by Three Learned Authors viz. Meredith Hanmer Doctor in Divinitie: Edmund Campion sometime fellow of St Iohns Colledge in Oxford: and Edmund Spenser Esq*. Dublin: Printed by the Society of Stationers, 1633.

Warrington, John, ed. *The Diary of Samuel Pepys*, 3 vols. London: J. M. Dent and Sons, 1953.

Whiston, William. *A New Theory of the Earth, from Its Original to the Consummation of All Things. Wherein the Creation of the World in Six Days, the Universal Deluge, and the General Conflagration, as Laid Down in the Holy Scriptures, Are Shewn to Be Perfectly Agreeable to Reason and Philosophy*. London: Printed by R. Roberts for Benj. Tooke, 1696.

Whiteman, Anne, ed. *The Compton Census of 1676: A Critical Edition*. London: Oxford University Press, 1986.

Wood, William. *Nevv Englands Prospect. A True, Lively and Experimentall Description of That Part of America, Commonly Called Nevv England: Discovering the State of That Countrie, Both As It Stands to Our New-Come English Planters; and to the Old Native Inhabitants*. London: Printed by Tho. Coates for Iohn Bellamie, 1634.

Wright, Louis B., ed. *A Voyage to Virginia in 1609: Two Narratives: Strachey's "True Reportory" and Jourdain's Discovery of the Bermudas*. Charlottesville: University Press of Virginia, 1964.

Xenophon. *Xenophons Treatise of Housholde*. Trans. Gentian Hervet. London: Printed by Thomas Berthelet, 1532.

Doctoral Dissertations

Deringer, William Peter. "Calculated Values: The Politics and Epistemology of Economic Numbers in Britain, 1688–1738." Unpublished Ph.D. dissertation. Princeton University, 2012.

Trace, Jamie. "Giovanni Botero and English Political Thought." Unpublished Ph.D. dissertation. University of Cambridge, 2018.

Published Secondary Works

Agnew, Jean-Christophe. *Worlds Apart: The Market and the Theater in Anglo-American Thought, 1550–1750*. Cambridge: Cambridge University Press, 1986.

Aiken, William Appleton and Basil Duke Henning, eds. *Conflict in Stuart England: Essays in Honour of Wallace Notestein*. London: Jonathan Cape, 1960.

Albritton Jonsson, Fredrik. "Island, Nation, Planet: Malthus in the Enlightenment," in *New Perspectives on Malthus*. Ed. Robert J. Mayhew. Cambridge: Cambridge University Press, 2016, pp. 128–52.

Allen, Don Cameron. *The Legend of Noah: Renaissance Rationalism in Art, Science, and Letters*. Urbana: University of Illinois Press, 1963.

Amussen, Susan Dwyer. *Caribbean Exchanges: Slavery and the Transformation of English Society, 1640–1700*. Chapel Hill: University of North Carolina Press, 2007.

Anderson, Benedict. *Imagined Communities: Reflections on the Origin and Spread of Nationalism*, revised edition. London: Verso, 2006.

Andrew, Donna T. *Philanthropy and Police: London Charity in the Eighteenth Century*. Princeton: Princeton University Press, 1989.

Andrews, John Harwood. *Shapes of Ireland: Maps and Their Makers 1564–1839*. Dublin: Geography Publications, 1997.

Applebaum, Robert and John Wood Sweet, eds. *Envisioning an English Empire: Jamestown and the Making of the North Atlantic World*. Philadelphia: University of Pennsylvania Press, 2005.

Armitage, David. *The Ideological Origins of the British Empire*. Cambridge: Cambridge University Press, 2000.

Armitage, David. "The Political Economy of Britain and Ireland after the Glorious Revolution," in *Political Thought in Seventeenth-Century Ireland: Kingdom or Colony*. Ed. Jane H. Ohlmeyer. Cambridge: Cambridge University Press, 2000, pp. 221–43.

Arnold, R. J. "'Learned Lumber': The Unlikely Survival of Sacred History in the Eighteenth Century," *English Historical Review* 125:516 (2010): 1139–72.

Ash, Eric H. *The Draining of the Fens: Projectors, Popular Politics, and State-Building in Early Modern England*. Baltimore: Johns Hopkins University Press, 2017.

Ashley, Maurice. *Financial and Commercial Policy under the Cromwellian Protectorate*. London: Frank Cass, 1962.

Aspromourgos, Tony. "Political Economy, Political Arithmetic and Political Medicine in the Thought of William Petty," in *Physicians and Political Economy: Six Studies of the Work of Doctor-Economists*. Ed. Peter D. Groenewegen. London: Routledge, 2001, pp. 10–25.

Attié, Katherine Bootle. "Enclosure Polemics and the Garden in the 1650s," *Studies in English Literature, 1500–1900* 51:1 (2011): 135–57.

Bailyn, Bernard. *The Peopling of British North America: An Introduction*. New York: Random House, 1988.

Bailyn, Bernard and Philip D. Morgan, eds. *Strangers within the Realm: Cultural Margins of the First British Empire*. Chapel Hill: University of North Carolina Press, 1991.

Ball, Terence. "Political Parties and the Legitimacy of Opposition," in *Discourses of Tolerance and Intolerance in the European Enlightenment*. Eds. Hans Erich Bödeker, Christina Donato, and Hanns Peter Reill. Toronto: University of Toronto Press, 2009, pp. 73–99.

Barber, Sarah. "Settlement, Transplantation and Expulsion: A Comparative Study of the Placement of Peoples," in *British Interventions in Early Modern Ireland*. Eds. Ciaran Brady and Jane H. Ohlmeyer. Cambridge: Cambridge University Press, 2005, pp. 280–98.

Barnard, Toby. "Interests in Ireland: The 'Fanatic Zeal and Irregular Ambition' of Richard Lawrence," in *British Interventions in Early Modern Ireland*. Eds. Ciaran Brady and Jane H. Ohlmeyer. Cambridge: Cambridge University Press, 2005, pp. 299–314.

Barnard, Toby. "Conclusion: Settling and Unsettling Ireland: The Cromwellian and Williamite Revolutions," in *Ireland from Independence to Occupation 1641–1660*. Ed. Jane H. Ohlmeyer. Cambridge: Cambridge University Press, 1995, pp. 265–91.

Barnard, Toby. "The Hartlib Circle and the Cult and Culture of Improvement in Ireland," in *Samuel Hartlib and Universal Reformation: Studies in Intellectual Communication*. Eds. Mark Greengrass, Michael Leslie, and Timothy Raylor. Cambridge: Cambridge University Press, 1994, pp. 281–97.

Barnard, Toby. "Miles Symner and the New Learning in Seventeenth-Century Ireland," *Journal of the Royal Society of Antiquaries of Ireland* 102:2 (1972): 129–42.

Barr, James. "Pre-Scientific Chronology: The Bible and the Origin of the World," *Proceedings of the American Philosophical Society* 143:3 (1999): 379–87.

Bartlett, Robert. *The Making of Europe: Conquest, Colonization and Cultural Change, 950–1350*. London: Penguin, 1994.

Bashford, Alison and Joyce E. Chaplin. "Malthus and the New World," in *New Perspectives on Malthus*. Ed. Robert J. Mayhew. Cambridge: Cambridge University Press, 2016a, pp. 105–27.

Bashford, Alison and Joyce E. Chaplin. *The New Worlds of Thomas Robert Malthus: Rereading the Principle of Population*. Princeton: Princeton University Press, 2016b.

Bauer, Ralph. *The Alchemy of Conquest: Science, Religion, and the Secrets of the New World*. Charlottesville: University of Virginia Press, 2019.

Beer, George Louis. *The Origins of the British Colonial System, 1578–1660*. Gloucester: Peter Smith, 1959.

Bender, John and Michael Marrinan, eds. *Regimes of Description: In the Archive of the Eighteenth Century*. Stanford: Stanford University Press, 2005.

Berry, Christopher J. *The Idea of Luxury: A Conceptual and Historical Investigation*. Cambridge: Cambridge University Press, 1994.

Berry, Helen. *Orphans of Empire: The Fate of London's Foundlings*. Oxford: Oxford University Press, 2019.

Biller, Peter. *The Measure of Multitude: Population in Medieval Thought*. Oxford: Oxford University Press, 2000.

Blackburn, Robin. *The Making of New World Slavery: From the Baroque to the Modern, 1492–1800*. London: Verso, 1997.

Bloch, Ruth H. *Gender and Morality in Anglo-American Culture, 1650–1800*. Berkeley: University of California Press, 2003.

Blum, Carol. *Strength in Numbers: Population, Reproduction, and Power in Eighteenth-Century France*. Baltimore: The Johns Hopkins University Press, 2002.

Bödeker, Hans Erich, Clorinda Donato, and Peter Hanns Reill, eds. *Discourses of Tolerance and Intolerance in the European Enlightenment*. Toronto: University of Toronto Press, 2009.

Bonar, James. *Theories of Population from Raleigh to Arthur Young*. London: George Allen and Unwin, 1982.

Bottigheimer, Karl. "The Restoration Land Settlement in Ireland: A Structural View," *Irish Historical Studies* 18:69 (1972): 1–21.

Bowker, Geoffrey C. and Susan Leigh Star. *Sorting Things Out: Classification and Its Consequences*. Cambridge: MIT Press, 1999.

Braddick, Michael. *State Formation in Early Modern England, c.1550–1700*. Cambridge: Cambridge University Press, 2000.

Bradshaw, Brendan. *The Irish Constitutional Revolution of the Sixteenth Century*. Cambridge: Cambridge University Press, 1979.

Brady, Ciaran. "From Policy to Power: The Evolution of Tudor Reform Strategies in Sixteenth-Century Ireland," in *Reshaping Ireland, 1550–1700: Colonisation and Its Consequences*. Ed. Brian Mac Cuarta, S. J. Dublin: Four Courts Press, 2011, pp. 21–42.

Brady, Ciaran. *The Chief Governors: The Rise and Fall of Reform Government in Tudor Ireland, 1536–1588*. Cambridge: Cambridge University Press, 1994.

Brady, Ciaran and Raymond Gillespie, eds. *Natives and Newcomers: Essays in the Making of Irish Colonial Society, 1534–1641*. Dublin: Irish Academic Press, 1986.

Brady, Ciaran and Jane H. Ohlmeyer, eds. *British Interventions in Early Modern Ireland*. Cambridge: Cambridge University Press, 2005.

Brewer, John. *The Sinews of Power: War, Money and the English State, 1688–1788*. Cambridge: Harvard University Press, 1988.

Briggs, Peter M. "John Graunt, Sir William Petty, and Swift's Modest Proposal," *Eighteenth-Century Life* 29:2 (2005): 3–24.

Brooks, Colin. "Projecting, Political Arithmetic, and the Act of 1695," *English Historical Review* 97:382 (1982): 31–53.

Brown, Vincent. *Tacky's Revolt: The Story of an Atlantic Slave War*. Cambridge: Harvard University Press, 2020.

Buchwald, Jed Z. and Mordechai Feingold. *Newton and the Origin of Civilization*. Princeton: Princeton University Press, 2013.

Buck, Peter. "People Who Counted: Political Arithmetic in the Eighteenth Century," *Isis* 73:1 (1982): 28–45.

Buck, Peter. "Seventeenth-Century Political Arithmetic: Civil Strife and Vital Statistics," *Isis* 68:1 (1977): 67–84.

Burchell, Graham, Colin Gordon, and Peter Miller, eds. *The Foucault Effect: Studies in Governmentality*. Chicago: University of Chicago Press, 1991.

Burke, Peter. *A Social History of Knowledge: From Gutenberg to Diderot*. Cambridge: Polity Press, 2000.

Burns, James Henderson and Mark Goldie, eds. *The Cambridge History of Political Thought, 1450–1700*. Cambridge: Cambridge University Press, 1991.

Burtt, Shelley. "The Societies for the Reformation of Manners: Between John Locke and the Devil in Augustan England," in *The Margins of Orthodoxy: Heterodox Writing and Cultural Response, 1660–1750*. Ed. Roger D. Lund. Cambridge: Cambridge University Press, 1995, pp. 149–69.

Burtt, Shelley. *Virtue Transformed: Political Argument in England, 1688–1740*. Cambridge: Cambridge University Press, 1992.

Campbell, Mildred. "'Of People either Too Few or Too Many': The Conflict of Opinion on Population and Its Relation to Emigration," in *Conflict in Stuart England: Essays in Honour of Wallace Notestein*. Eds. William Appleton Aiken and Basil Duke Henning. London: Jonathan Cape, 1960, pp. 169–201.

Canny, Nicholas. *Making Ireland British, 1580–1650*. Oxford: Oxford University Press, 2001.

Canny, Nicholas. "England's New World and the Old, 1480s–1630s," in *The Origins of Empire: British Overseas Enterprise to the Close of the Seventeenth Century*. Ed. Nicholas Canny. Oxford: Oxford University Press, 1998a, pp. 148–69.

Canny, Nicholas, ed. *The Origins of Empire: British Overseas Enterprise to the Close of the Seventeenth Century*. Oxford: Oxford University Press, 1998b.

Canny, Nicholas. "The Marginal Kingdom: Ireland as a Problem in the First British Empire," in *Strangers within the Realm: Cultural Margins of the First British Empire*. Eds. Bernard Bailyn and Philip D. Morgan. Chapel Hill: University of North Carolina Press, 1991, pp. 35–66.

Canny, Nicholas. *Kingdom and Colony: Ireland in the Atlantic World, 1560–1800*. Baltimore: Johns Hopkins University Press, 1988.

Canny, Nicholas. "Rowland White's 'Discors Touching Ireland' c. 1569," *Irish Historical Studies* 20:80 (1977): 439–63.

Canny, Nicholas. "The Ideology of English Colonization: From Ireland to America," *The William and Mary Quarterly* 30:4 (1973): 575–98.

Cantor, Leonard. *The Changing English Countryside, 1400–1700*. London: Routledge and Kegan Paul, 1987.

Carrette, Jeremy R., ed. *Religion and Culture: Michel Foucault*. New York: Routledge, 1999.

Carroll, Patrick. *Science, Culture, and Modern State Formation*. Berkeley: University of California Press, 2006.

Cassedy, James H. *Demography in America: Beginnings of the Statistical Mind, 1600–1800*. Cambridge: Harvard University Press, 1969.

Chaplin, Joyce E. *Benjamin Franklin's Political Arithmetic: A Materialist View of Humanity* [Dibner Library Lecture]. Washington: Smithsonian Institution Libraries, 2006.

Chaplin, Joyce E. *Subject Matter: Technology, the Body, and Science on the Anglo-American Frontier, 1500–1676*. Cambridge: Harvard University Press, 2001.

Chapman, Colin R. *Pre-1841 Censuses and Population Listings in the British Isles*, fifth edition. Baltimore: Genealogical Publishing, 2012.

Charbit, Yves. *The Classical Foundations of Population Thought*. Dordrecht: Springer, 2011.

Chartier, Roger. "Les élite et les gueux. Quelques représentations (XVIe-XVIIe siècles)," *Revue d'histoire moderne et contemporaine* 21:3 (1974): 376–88.

Christopher, Emma, Cassandra Pybus, and Markus Rediker, eds. *Many Middle Passages: Forced Migration and the Making of the Modern World*. Berkeley: University of California Press, 2007.

Clark, Elizabeth A. *History, Theory, Text: Historians and the Linguistic Turn*. Cambridge: Harvard University Press, 2004.

Clark, William, Jan Golinski, and Simon Schaffer, eds. *The Sciences in Enlightened Europe*. Chicago: University of Chicago Press, 1999.

Clarke, Aidan. *The Old English in Ireland, 1625–1642*. Dublin: MacGibbon and Kee, 1966.

Claydon, Tony. "Daily News and the Construction of Time in Late Stuart England, 1695–1714," *Journal of British Studies* 52:1 (2013): 55–78.

Cody, Lisa Forman. *Birthing the Nation: Sex, Science, and the Conception of Eighteenth-Century Britons*. Oxford: Oxford University Press, 2005.

Cohen, Patricia Cline. *A Calculating People: The Spread of Numeracy in Early America*. Chicago: University of Chicago Press, 1982.

Coleman, Donald Cuthbert, ed. *Revisions in Mercantilism*. London: Methuen, 1969.

Conforti, Joseph A. *Saints and Strangers: New England in British North America*. Baltimore: The Johns Hopkins University Press, 2006.

Connelly, Matthew. *Fatal Misconception: The Struggle to Control World Population*. Cambridge: Harvard University Press, 2008.

Cook, Harold J. *Matters of Exchange: Commerce, Medicine, and Science in the Dutch Golden Age*. New Haven: Yale University Press, 2007.

Corcoran, Irma. *Thomas Holme, 1624–1695: Surveyor General of Pennsylvania*. Philadelphia: American Philosophical Society, 1992.

Coughlan, Patricia. "Counter-Currents in Colonial Discourse: The Political Thought of Vincent and Daniel Gookin," in *Political Thought in Seventeenth-Century Ireland: Kingdom or Colony*. Ed. Jane H. Ohlmeyer. Cambridge: Cambridge University Press, 2000, pp. 56–82.

Creighton, Anne. "'Grace and Favour': The Cabal Ministry and Irish Catholic Politics, 1667–1673," in *Restoration Ireland: Always Settling and Never Settled*. Ed. Coleman A. Dennehy. Aldershot: Ashgate, 2008, pp. 141–60.

Cressy, David. *Gypsies: An English History*. New Haven: Yale University Press, 2018.

Cronin, Nessa. "Writing the 'New Geography': Cartographic Discourse and Colonial Governmentality in William Petty's The Political Anatomy of Ireland (1672)," *Historical Geography* 42 (2014): 58–71.

Crosby, Alfred W. *The Measure of Reality: Quantification and Western Society, 1250–1600*. Cambridge: Cambridge University Press, 1997.

Cunningham, Andrew and Roger French, eds. *The Medical Enlightenment of the Eighteenth Century*. Cambridge: Cambridge University Press, 1990.

Cunningham, Bernadette. "Representations of King, Parliament and the Irish People in Geoffrey Keating's Foras Feasa Ar Eirinn," in *Political Thought in Seventeenth-Century Ireland*. Ed. Jane H. Ohlmeyer. Cambridge: Cambridge University Press, 2000, pp. 131–54.

Cunningham, John. *Conquest and Land in Ireland: The Transplantation to Connacht, 1649–1680*. Woodbridge: Boydell Press, 2011.

Curran, Andrew. *The Anatomy of Blackness: Science and Slavery in the Age of Enlightenment*. Baltimore: Johns Hopkins University Press, 2011.

Darcy, Eamon. *The Irish Rebellion of 1641 and the Wars of the Three Kingdoms*. Woodbridge: Royal Historical Society/Boydell Press, 2013.

Daston, Lorraine. "Description by Omission: Nature Enlightened and Obscured," in *Regimes of Description: In the Archive of the Eighteenth Century*. Eds. John Bender and Michael Marrinan. Stanford: Stanford University Press, 2005, pp. 11–24.

Daston, Lorraine. "The Domestication of Risk: Mathematical Probability and Insurance, 1650–1830," in *The Probabilistic Revolution, Volume 1: Ideas in History*. Eds. Lorenz Krüger, Lorraine J. Daston, and Michael Heidelberger. Cambridge: MIT Press, 1987, pp. 237–60.

Daston, Lorraine. *Classical Probability in the Enlightenment*. Princeton: Princeton University Press, 1985.

Daston, Lorraine and Katharine Park. *Wonders and the Order of Nature, 1150–1750*. New York: Zone Books, 2001.

Dear, Peter. *Discipline and Experience: The Mathematical Way in the Scientific Revolution*. Chicago: University of Chicago Press, 1995.

Demos, John. *A Little Commonwealth: Family Life in Plymouth Colony*, second edition. New York: Oxford University Press, 2000.

Dennehy, Coleman A., ed. *Restoration Ireland: Always Settling and Never Settled*. Aldershot: Ashgate, 2008.

Deringer, William. *Calculated Values: Finance, Politics, and the Quantitative Age.* Cambridge: Harvard University Press, 2018.

Deringer, William. "Finding the Money: Public Accounting, Political Arithmetic, and Probability in the 1690s," *Journal of British Studies* 52:3 (2013): 638–68.

Descendre, Romain. *L'État du Monde: Giovanni Botero entre raison d'État et géopolitique.* Geneva: Librairie Droz S. A., 2009.

Dolan, Brian, ed. *Malthus, Medicine, and Morality: 'Malthusianism' after 1798.* Amsterdam: Rodopi, 2000.

Duffy, Eamon. *The Stripping of the Altars: Traditional Religion in England, c.1400–c.1580.* New Haven: Yale University Press, 1992.

Dunn, Richard S. *Sugar and Slaves: The Rise of the Planter Class in the English West Indies, 1624–1713.* New York: W. W. Norton, 1973.

Dupâquier, Jacques and Michel Dupâquier. *Histoire de la démographie: la statistique de la population des origines à 1914.* Paris: Librarie Académique Perrin, 1985.

Eamon, William. *Science and the Secrets of Nature: Books of Secrets in Medieval and Early Modern Culture.* Princeton: Princeton University Press, 1994.

Edwards, David. "Political Change and Social Transformation, 1603–1641," in *The Cambridge History of Ireland, Volume II: 1550–1730.* Ed. Jane H. Ohlmeyer. Cambridge: Cambridge University Press, 2018, pp. 48–71.

Edwards, David. "The Escalation of Violence in Sixteenth-Century Ireland," in *Age of Atrocity: Violence and Political Conflict in Early Modern Ireland.* Eds. David Edwards, Pádraig Lenihan, and Clodagh Tait. Dublin: Four Courts Press, 2007, pp. 34–78.

Edwards, David, Pádraig Lenihan, and Clodagh Tait, eds. *Age of Atrocity: Violence and Political Conflict in Early Modern Ireland.* Dublin: Four Courts Press, 2007.

Egerton III, Frank N. "The Longevity of the Patriarchs: A Topic in the History of Demography," *Journal of the History of Ideas* 27:4 (1966): 575–84.

Ellis, Steven G. *Ireland in the Age of the Tudors, 1447–1603: English Expansion and the End of Gaelic Rule.* London: Longman, 1998.

Elton, Geoffrey R. *The Tudor Revolution in Government: Administrative Changes in the Reign of Henry VIII.* Cambridge: Cambridge University Press, 1962.

Emigh, Rebecca Jean, Dylan Riley, and Patricia Ahmed. *Antecedents of Censuses from Medieval to Nation States: How Societies and States Count.* Basingstoke: Palgrave Macmillan, 2016.

Endres, Anthony M. "The Functions of Numerical Data in the Writings of Graunt, Petty, and Davenant," *History of Political Economy* 17:1 (1985): 245–64.

Farrell, Molly. *Counting Bodies: Population in Colonial American Writing.* Oxford: Oxford University Press, 2016.

Feingold, Mordechai. *The Mathematicians' Apprenticeship: Science, Universities and Society in England, 1560–1640.* Cambridge: Cambridge University Press, 1984.

Fields, Barbara Jeanne. "Slavery, Race, and Ideology in the United States of America," *New Left Review* 1:181 (1990): 95–118.

Finkelstein, Andrea. *Harmony and the Balance: An Intellectual History of Seventeenth-Century Economic Thought.* Ann Arbor: University of Michigan Press, 2000.

Fitzmaurice, Edmond. *The Life of Sir William Petty, 1623–1687.* London: John Murray, 1895.

Foucault, Michel. *Security, Territory, Population: Lectures at the Collège de France, 1977–1978.* Ed. Michel Senellart. Trans. Graham Burchell. Basingstoke: Palgrave Macmillan, 2007.

Foucault, Michel. "Omnes et Singulatim: Towards a Criticism of Political Reason," The Tanner Lectures on Human Values, Stanford University, 10 and 16 October 1979. Reprinted in *Religion and Culture: Michel Foucault.* Ed. Jeremy R. Carrette. New York: Routledge, 1999, pp. 134–52.

Foucault, Michel. *Discipline and Punish: The Birth of the Prison.* Trans. Alan Sheridan. New York: Vintage, 1995.

Foucault, Michel. *The Order of Things: An Archaeology of the Human Sciences.* New York: Random House, 1994.

Foucault, Michel. "Governmentality," in *The Foucault Effect: Studies in Governmentality.* Eds. Graham Burchell, Colin Gordon, and Peter Miller. Chicago: University of Chicago Press, 1991, pp. 87–104.

Foucault, Michel. *The Will to Knowledge: The History of Sexuality Volume 1.* Trans. Robert Hurley. London: Penguin, 1978.

Fowler, Elizabeth. "The Failure of Moral Philosophy in the Work of Edmund Spenser," *Representations* 51 (1995): 47–76.

Fox, Adam. "Printed Questionnaires, Research Networks, and the Discovery of the British Isles, 1650–1800," *The Historical Journal* 53:3 (2010): 593–621.

Fox, Alistair. "English Humanism and the Body Politic," in *Reassessing the Henrician Age: Humanism, Politics, and Reform, 1500–1550.* Eds. Alistair Fox and John Guy. Oxford: Blackwell, 1986, pp. 34–51.

Fox, Alistair and John Guy, eds. *Reassessing the Henrician Age: Humanism, Politics, and Reform, 1500–1550.* Oxford: Blackwell, 1986.

Fox, Christopher, Roy Porter, and Robert Wokler, eds. *Inventing Human Science: Eighteenth-Century Domains.* Berkeley: University of California Press, 1995.

Fradkin, Jeremy. "Protestant Unity and Anti-Catholicism: The Irenicism and Philo-Semitism of John Dury in Context," *Journal of British Studies* 56:2 (2017): 273–94.

Frängsmyr, Tore, John L. Heilbron, and Robin E. Rider, eds. *The Quantifying Spirit in the Eighteenth Century.* Berkeley: University of California Press, 1990.

Franklin, Julian H. *Jean Bodin and the Sixteenth-Century Revolution in the Methodology of Law and History.* New York: Columbia University Press, 1963.

Fumerton, Patricia. *Unsettled: The Culture of Mobility and the Working Poor in Early Modern England.* Chicago: University of Chicago Press, 2006.

Games, Alison. *Migration and the Origins of the English Atlantic World.* Cambridge: Harvard University Press, 1999.

Garner, Guillaume and Sandra Richter, eds. *"Eigennutz" und "gute Ordnung": Ökonomisierungen im 17. Jahrhundert.* Wiesbaden: Harrassowitz Verlag, 2016.

Gay, Peter. *The Enlightenment: An Interpretation*, vol. I, *The Rise of Modern Paganism*. New York: W. W. Norton, 1966.

Gibney, John. *The Shadow of a Year: The 1641 Rebellion in Irish History and Memory*. Madison: University of Wisconsin Press, 2013.

Gibson, Jeremy and Medlycott Mervyn. *Local Census Listings, 1522–1930: Holdings in the British Isles*, third edition. Bury: Federation of Family History Societies, 1992.

Glacken, Clarence W. *Traces on the Rhodian Shore: Nature and Culture in Western Thought from Ancient Times to the End of the Eighteenth Century*. Berkeley: University of California Press, 1967.

Glaisyer, Natasha. *The Culture of Commerce in England, 1660–1720*. Woodbridge: Boydell Press, 2006.

Glass, David V. *Numbering the People: The Eighteenth-Century Population Controversy and the Development of Census and Vital Statistics in Britain*. Farnborough: D. C. Heath, 1973.

Gleach, Frederic W. *Powhatan's World and Colonial Virginia: A Conflict of Cultures*. Lincoln: University of Nebraska Press, 1997.

Glimp, David. *Increase and Multiply: Governing Cultural Reproduction in Early Modern England*. Minneapolis: University of Minnesota Press, 2003.

Golinski, Jan. *British Weather and the Climate of Enlightenment*. Chicago: University of Chicago Press, 2007.

Golinski, Jan. *Making Natural Knowledge: Constructivism and the History of Science*. Chicago: University of Chicago Press, 2005.

Goodacre, Hugh. *The Economic Thought of William Petty: Exploring the Colonialist Roots of Economics*. Abingdon: Routledge, 2018.

Gorski, Philip S. *The Disciplinary Revolution: Calvinism and the Rise of the State in Early Modern Europe*. Chicago: University of Chicago Press, 2003.

Grafton, Anthony. *What Was History? The Art of History in Early Modern Europe*. Cambridge: Cambridge University Press, 2007.

Grafton, Anthony. "Joseph Scaliger and Historical Chronology: The Rise and Fall of a Discipline," *History and Theory* 14:2 (1975): 156–85.

Greenblatt, Stephen. *Shakespearean Negotiations: The Circulation of Social Energy in Renaissance England*. Berkeley: University of California Press, 1988.

Greene, Jack P. *Evaluating Empire and Confronting Colonialism in Eighteenth-Century Britain*. Baltimore: Johns Hopkins University, 2013.

Greengrass, Mark, Michael Leslie, and Timothy Raylor, eds. *Samuel Hartlib and the Universal Reformation: Studies in Intellectual Communication*. Cambridge: Cambridge University Press, 1994.

Greer, Margaret R., Walter D. Mignolo, and Maureen Quilligan. "Introduction," in *Rereading the Black Legend: The Discourses of Religious and Racial Difference in the Renaissance Empires*. Eds. Margaret R. Greer, Walter D. Mignolo, and Maureen Quilligan. Chicago: University of Chicago Press, 2007a, pp. 1–24.

Greer, Margaret R., Walter D. Mignolo, and Maureen Quilligan, eds. *Rereading the Black Legend: The Discourses of Religious and Racial Difference in the Renaissance Empires*. Chicago: University of Chicago Press, 2007b.

Gregory, Stephan. "The Tabulation of England: How the Social World Was Brought in Rows and Columns," *Distinktion: Scandinavian Journal of Social Theory* 14:3 (2013): 305–25.

Groebner, Valentin. *Who Are You? Identification, Deception, and Surveillance in Early Modern Europe.* New York: Zone Books, 2007.

Grove, Richard. "Cressey Dymock and the Draining of the Fens: An Early Agricultural Model," *The Geographical Journal* 147:1 (1981): 27–37.

Haakonssen, Lisbeth. *Medicine and Morals in the Enlightenment: John Gregory, Thomas Percival and Benjamin Rush.* Amsterdam: Rodopi, 1997.

Hacking, Ian. *The Emergence of Probability: A Philosophical Study of Early Ideas about Probability, Induction, and Statistical Inference*, second edition. Cambridge: Cambridge University Press, 2006.

Hacking, Ian. *The Taming of Chance.* Cambridge: Cambridge University Press, 1990.

Hadfield, Andrew. "Irish Colonies and the Americas," in *Envisioning an English Empire: Jamestown and the Making of the North Atlantic World.* Eds. Robert Applebaum and John Wood Sweet. Philadelphia: University of Pennsylvania Press, 2005, pp. 172–91.

Hadfield, Andrew. "Briton and Scythian: Tudor Representations of Irish Origins," *Irish Historical Studies* 28:112 (1993): 390–408.

Hadot, Pierre. *The Veil of Isis: An Essay on the History of the Idea of Nature.* Trans. Michael Chase. Cambridge: Harvard University Press, 2006.

Hannaford, Ivan. *Race: The History of an Idea in the West.* Baltimore: The Johns Hopkins University Press, 1996.

Harari, Yuval Noah. *Sapiens: A Brief History of Humankind.* New York: Harper, 2015.

Harkness, Deborah E. *The Jewel House: Elizabethan London and the Scientific Revolution.* New Haven: Yale University Press, 2007.

Harris, Frances. "Ireland as a Laboratory: The Archive of Sir William Petty," in *Archives of the Scientific Revolution: The Formation and Exchange of Ideas in Seventeenth-Century Europe.* Ed. Michael Hunter. Woodbridge: Boydell Press, 1998, pp. 73–90.

Harris, Jonathan Gil. *Foreign Bodies and the Body Politic: Discourses of Social Pathology in Early Modern England.* Cambridge: Cambridge University Press, 1998.

Harris, Tim. *Restoration: Charles II and His Kingdoms, 166–1685.* New York: Penguin, 2006.

Harris, Tim. *Revolution: The Great Crisis of the British Monarchy, 1685–1720.* New York: Penguin, 2006.

Harrison, Peter. *'Religion' and the Religions in the English Enlightenment.* Cambridge: Cambridge University Press, 1990.

Hartman, Saidiya V. *Scenes of Subjection: Terror, Slavery, and Self-Making in Nineteenth-Century America.* Oxford: Oxford University Press, 1997.

Hayton, David William. *Ruling Ireland, 1685–1742: Politics, Politicians and Parties.* Woodbridge: Boydell Press, 2004.

Headrick, Daniel. *When Information Came of Age: Technologies of Knowledge in the Age of Reason and Revolution, 1700–1850.* Oxford: Oxford University Press, 2000.

Hecksher, Eli F. *Mercantilism.* Trans. Mendel Shapiro, 2 vols. London: George Allen and Unwin, 1935.

Henry, Aaron James. "William Petty, the Down Survey, Territory and Population in the Seventeenth Century," *Territory, Politics, Governance* 2:2 (2014): 1–20.

Higgs, Edward. *The Information State in England: The Central Collection of Information on Citizens since 1500.* Basingstoke: Palgrave Macmillan, 2004.

Hill, George. *An Historical Account of the MacDonnells of Antrim.* Belfast: Archer and Sons, 1873.

Hindle, Steve. *On the Parish? The Micro-Politics of Poor Relief in Rural England, 1550–1750.* Oxford: Oxford University Press, 2004.

Hindle, Steve. *The State and Social Change in Early Modern England, 1550–1640.* Basingstoke: Palgrave, 2002.

Hitchcock, David. *Vagrancy in English Culture and Society, 1650–1750.* London: Bloomsbury Academic, 2016.

Hogarth, Rana. *Medicalizing Blackness: Making Racial Difference in the Atlantic World, 1780–1840.* Chapel Hill: University of North Carolina, 2017.

Hoppit, Julian. *Britain's Political Economies: Parliament and Economic Life, 1660–1800.* Cambridge: Cambridge University Press, 2017.

Hoppit, Julian. "Political Arithmetic in Eighteenth-Century England," *Economic History Review* 49:3 (1996): 516–40.

Horn, James. "Tobacco Colonies: The Shaping of English Society in the Seventeenth-Century Chesapeake," in *The Origins of Empire: British Overseas Enterprise to the Close of the Seventeenth Century.* Ed. Nicholas Canny. Oxford: Oxford University Press, 1998, pp. 170–92.

Horning, Audrey. *Ireland in the Virginian Sea: Colonialism in the British Atlantic.* Chapel Hill: University of North Carolina Press, 2013.

Houston, Alan. *Benjamin Franklin and the Politics of Improvement.* New Haven: Yale University Press, 2008.

Houston, Alan and Steve Pincus, eds. *A Nation Transformed: England After the Restoration.* Cambridge: Cambridge University Press, 2001.

Houston, Robert Allan. *The Population History of Britain and Ireland 1500–1700.* Cambridge: Cambridge University Press, 1992.

Hundert, Edward J. *The Enlightenment's Fable: Bernard Mandeville and the Discovery of Society.* Cambridge: Cambridge University Press, 1994.

Hunter, Michael. "Robert Boyle and the Early Royal Society: A Reciprocal Exchange in the Making of Early Modern Science," *British Journal for the History of Science* 40:1 (2007): 1–23.

Hunter, Michael, ed. *Archives of the Scientific Revolution: The Formation and Exchange of Ideas in Seventeenth-Century Europe.* Woodbridge: Boydell Press, 1998.

Hutchinson, Edward Prince. *The Population Debate: The Development of Conflicting Theories up to 1900.* New York: Houghton Mifflin, 1967.

Innes, Joanna. *Inferior Politics: Social Problems and Social Policies in Eighteenth-Century Britain*. Oxford: Oxford University Press, 2000.

Jackson, Patrick Wyse. *The Chronologers' Quest: Episodes in the Search for the Age of the Earth*. Cambridge: Cambridge University Press, 2006.

Jackson, Zakiyyah Iman. *Becoming Human: Matter and Meaning in an Antiblack World*. New York: New York University Press, 2020.

Jacob, Margaret C. *The Newtonians and the English Revolution, 1689–1720*. Ithaca: Cornell University Press, 1976.

James, Francis G. *Lords of the Ascendancy: The Irish House of Lords and Its Members, 1600–1800*. Washington: Catholic University of America Press, 1995.

Jenner, Mark S. R. "Plague on a Page: Lord Have Mercy Upon Us in Early Modern London," *The Seventeenth Century* 27:3 (2012): 255–86.

Jones, Ann Rosalind and Stallybrass Peter. *Renaissance Clothing and the Materials of Memory*. Cambridge: Cambridge University Press, 2000.

Jordan, Winthrop D. *White over Black: American Attitudes toward the Negro, 1550–1812*. Baltimore: Penguin, 1968.

Jütte, Robert. *Poverty and Deviance in Early Modern Europe*. Cambridge: Cambridge University Press, 1994.

Kane, Brendan. "Domesticating the Counter-Reformation: Bridging the Bardic and Catholic Traditions in Geoffrey Keating's 'The Three Shafts of Death'," *The Sixteenth-Century Journal* 40:4 (2009): 1029–44.

Keller, Vera. *Knowledge and the Public Interest, 1575–1725*. Cambridge: Cambridge University Press, 2015.

Keller, Vera. "Mining Tacitus: Secrets of Empire, Nature and Art in the Reason of State," *British Journal for the History of Science* 45:2 (2012): 189–212.

Keller, Vera and Ted McCormick. "Towards a History of Projects," *Early Science and Medicine* 21:5 (2016): 423–44.

Kidd, Colin. *The Forging of Races: Race and Scripture in the Protestant Atlantic World, 1600–2000*. Cambridge: Cambridge University Press, 2006.

Kiernan, Ben. *Blood and Soil: A World History of Genocide and Extermination from Sparta to Darfur*. New Haven: Yale University Press, 2007.

King, Rachel Scarborough. *Writing to the World: Letters and the Origins of Modern Print Genres*. Baltimore: Johns Hopkins University Press, 2018.

Kinsella, Eoin. "'Dividing the Bear's Skin before She Is Taken': Irish Catholics and Land in the Late Stuart Monarchy, 1683–91," in *Restoration Ireland: Always Settling and Never Settled*. Ed. Coleman A. Dennehy. Aldershot: Ashgate, 2008, pp. 161–78.

Kläger, Florian. *Forgone Nations: Constructions of National Identity in Elizabethan Historiography and Literature: Stanihurst, Spenser, Shakespeare*. Trier: Wissenschaftlicher Verlag Trier, 2006.

Klepp, Susan E. *Revolutionary Conceptions: Women, Fertility, and Family Limitation in America, 1760–1820*. Chapel Hill: University of North Carolina Press, 2009.

Klepp, Susan E. "Revolutionary Bodies: Women and the Fertility Transition in the Mid-Atlantic Region, 1760–1820," *Journal of American History* 85:3 (1998): 910–45.

Klepp, Susan E. *"The Swift Progress of Population": A Documentary Study of Philadelphia's Growth, 1642–1859.* Philadelphia: American Philosophical Society, 1991.

Krüger, Lorenz, Lorraine J. Daston, and Michael Heidelberger, eds. *The Probabilistic Revolution, Volume 1: Ideas in History.* Cambridge, MA: MIT Press, 1987.

Kuhn, Thomas S. *The Structure of Scientific Revolutions,* third edition. Chicago: University of Chicago Press, 1996.

Kupperman, Karen Ordahl. *The Jamestown Project.* Cambridge: Harvard University Press, 2009.

Kupperman, Karen Ordahl. "The Puzzle of the American Climate in the Early Colonial Period," *American Historical Review* 87:5 (1982): 1262–89.

Kussmaul, Ann. *A General View of the Rural Economy of England, 1538–1840.* Cambridge: Cambridge University Press, 1990.

Le Bras, Hervé. "Introduction: peuples et populations," in *L'Invention des populations: biologie, idéologie et politique.* Eds. HervéLe Bras and Sandrine Bertaux. Paris: Éditions Odile Jacob, 2000, pp. 9–54.

Le Goff, Jacques. *The Medieval Imagination.* Trans. Arthur Goldhammer. Chicago: University of Chicago Press, 1988.

Leng, Thomas. *Benjamin Worsley (1618–1677): Trade, Interest and the Spirit in Revolutionary England.* Woodbridge: Royal Historical Society/Boydell Press, 2008.

Lennon, Colm. *The Life of Richard Stanihurst the Dubliner, 1547–1618.* Dublin: Irish Academic Press, 1981.

Levene, Alyssa. *Childcare, Health and Mortality at the London Foundling Hospital, 1741–1800: 'Left to the Mercy of the World'.* Manchester: Manchester University Press, 2007.

Levin, Samuel M. "Malthus and the Idea of Progress," *Journal of the History of Ideas* 27:1 (January 1966): 92–108.

Levitan, Kathrin. *A Cultural History of the British Census: Envisioning the Multitude in the Nineteenth Century.* New York: Palgrave Macmillan, 2011.

Little, Patrick. *Lord Broghill and the Cromwellian Union with Ireland and Scotland.* Woodbridge: Boydell Press, 2004.

Livesay, Daniel. *Children of Uncertain Fortune: Mixed-Race Jamaicans in Britain and the Atlantic Family, 1733–1833.* Chapel Hill: University of North Carolina Press, 2018.

Livingstone, David N. *Adam's Ancestors: Race, Religion, and the Politics of Human Origins.* Baltimore: The Johns Hopkins University Press, 2008.

Lloyd, Genevieve. *Providence Lost.* Cambridge: Harvard University Press, 2008.

Lloyd, Sarah. *Charity and Poverty in England, c.1680–1820: Wild and Visionary Schemes.* Manchester: Manchester University Press, 2009.

Lobo, Francis M. "John Haygarth, Smallpox and Religious Dissent in Eighteenth-Century England," in *The Medical Enlightenment of the Eighteenth Century.* Eds. Andrew Cunningham and Roger French. Cambridge: Cambridge University Press, 1990, pp. 217–53.

Long, Pamela O. *Artisan/Practitioners and the Rise of the New Sciences, 1400–1600.* Corvallis: Oregon State University Press, 2011.

Lund, Roger D., ed. *The Margins of Orthodoxy: Heterodox Writing and Cultural Response, 1660–1750.* Cambridge: Cambridge University Press, 1995.

Mac Cuarta, Brian, S. J., ed. *Reshaping Ireland, 1550–1700: Colonization and Its Consequences.* Dublin: Four Courts Press, 2011.

MacCulloch, Diarmaid. *The Boy King: Edward VI and the Protestant Reformation.* Berkeley: University of California Press, 2002.

Maginn, Christopher. *William Cecil, Ireland, and the Tudor State.* Oxford: Oxford University Press, 2012.

Magnusson, Lars. *Mercantilism: The Shaping of an Economic Language.* Abingdon: Routledge, 1994.

Major, J. Russell. *From Renaissance Monarchy to Absolute Monarchy: French Kings, Nobles, and Estates.* Baltimore: The Johns Hopkins University Press, 1994.

Malcolmson, Cristina. *Studies of Skin Color in the Early Royal Society: Boyle, Cavendish, Swift.* London: Routledge, 2016.

Mancall, Peter. *Hakluyt's Promise: An Elizabethan's Obsession for an English America.* New Haven: Yale University Press, 2007.

Martin, Julian. *Francis Bacon, the State, and the Reform of Natural Philosophy.* Cambridge: Cambridge University Press, 1991.

Martin, Thierry, ed. *Arithmétique politique dans la France du 18e siècle.* Paris: INED, 2003.

Mayer, Thomas F. *Thomas Starkey and the Commonweal: Humanist Politics and Religion in the Reign of Henry VIII.* Cambridge: Cambridge University Press, 1989.

Mayhew, Robert J., ed. *New Perspectives on Malthus.* Cambridge: Cambridge University Press, 2016.

Mayhew, Robert J. *Malthus: The Life and Legacies of an Untimely Prophet.* Cambridge: Harvard University Press, 2014.

Mayr, Otto. *Authority, Liberty, and Automatic Machinery in Early Modern Europe.* Baltimore: Johns Hopkins University Press, 1986.

McConica, James Kelsey. *English Humanists and Reformation Politics under Henry VIII and Edward VI.* Oxford: Oxford University Press, 1965.

McCormick, Ted. "Improvement, Projecting, and Self-Interest in the Hartlib Circle, c. 1640–1660," in *Historicizing Self-Interest in the Modern Atlantic World: A Plea for Ego?* Ed. Christine Zabel. Abingdon: Routledge, 2021, pp. 25–43.

McCormick, Ted. "Food, Population, and Empire in the Hartlib Circle, 1639–1660," in *Critical Histories of Food and the Sciences.* Eds. Emma Spary and Anya Zilberstein, *Osiris* 35 (2020): pp. 60–83.

McCormick, Ted. "Alchemy into Economy: Material Transmutation and the Conceptualization of Utility in Gabriel Plattes (c.1600–1644) and William Petty (1623–1687)," in *"Eigennutz" und "gute Ordnung": Ökonomisierungen im 17. Jahrhundert,* Eds. Guillaume Garner and Sandra Richter. Wiesbaden: Harassowitz Verlag, 2016, pp. 339–52.

McCormick, Ted. "Statistics in the Hands of an Angry God? John Graunt's Observations in Cotton Mather's New England," *The William and Mary Quarterly* 72:4 (2015): 563–86.

McCormick, Ted. "Governing Model Populations: Queries, Quantification, and William Petty's 'Scale of Salubrity,'" *History of Science* 51:2 (2013): 179–97.

McCormick, Ted. "Political Arithmetic and Sacred History: Population Thought in the English Enlightenment, 1660–1750," *Journal of British Studies* 52:4 (2013): 829–57.

McCormick, Ted. *William Petty and the Ambitions of Political Arithmetic.* Oxford: Oxford University Press, 2009.

McCormick, Ted. "Alchemy in the Political Arithmetic of Sir William Petty (1623–1687)," *Studies in History and Philosophy of Science* 37:2 (2006): 290–307.

McCoy, Drew R. *The Elusive Republic: Political Economy in Jeffersonian America.* Chapel Hill: University of North Carolina Press, 1980.

McCurdy, John Gilbert. *Citizen Bachelors: Manhood and the Creation of the United States.* Ithaca: Cornell University Press, 2009.

McKenny, Kevin. "The Restoration Land Settlement in Ireland: A Statistical Interpretation," in *Restoration Ireland: Always Settling and Never Settled.* Ed. Coleman A. Dennehy. Aldershot: Ashgate, 2008, pp. 35–52.

McRae, Andrew. *God Speed the Plough: The Representation of Agrarian England, 1500–1660.* Cambridge: Cambridge University Press, 1996.

Meek, Ronald L. *Social Science and the Ignoble Savage.* Cambridge: Cambridge University Press, 1976.

Meinel, Christoph. "Early Seventeenth-Century Atomism: Theory, Epistemology, and the Insufficiency of Experiment," *Isis* 79:1 (1988): 68–103.

Merchant, Carolyn. *The Death of Nature: Women, Ecology, and the Scientific Revolution.* San Francisco: Harper and Row, 1990.

Miller, John. *James II.* New Haven: Yale University Press, 2000.

Miller, John. *Charles II.* London: Weidenfeld and Nicholson, 1991.

Miller, Peter. *Defining the Common Good: Empire, Religion, and Philosophy in Eighteenth-Century Britain.* Cambridge: Cambridge University Press, 1994.

Montaño, John Patrick. *The Roots of English Colonialism in Ireland.* Cambridge: Cambridge University Press, 2011.

Morgan, Jennifer L. *Laboring Women: Reproduction and Gender in New World Slavery.* Philadelphia: University of Pennsylvania Press, 2004.

Morgan, Philip D. "British Encounters with Africans and African-Americans, Circa 1600–1780," in *Strangers within the Realm: Cultural Margins of the First British Empire.* Eds. Bernard Bailyn and Philip D. Morgan. Chapel Hill: University of North Carolina Press, 1991, pp. 157–219.

Morrogh, Michael McCarthy. "The English Presence in Early Seventeenth Century Munster," in *Natives and Newcomers: Essays in the Making of Irish Colonial Society, 1534–1641.* Eds. Ciaran Brady and Raymond Gillespie. Dublin: Irish Academic Press, 1986, pp. 171–90.

Muller, Hannah Weiss. *Subjects and Sovereign: Bonds of Belonging in the Eighteenth-Century British Empire*. Oxford: Oxford University Press, 2017.

Newman, Brooke N. *A Dark Inheritance: Blood, Race, and Sex in Colonial Jamaica*. New Haven: Yale University Press, 2018.

Newman, William R. *Promethean Ambitions: Alchemy and the Quest to Perfect Nature*. Chicago: University of Chicago Press, 2004.

Nipperdey, Justus. "Johann Peter Süssmilch: From Divine Law to Human Intervention," *Population* 66:3 (2011): 611–36.

Novak, Maximilian, ed. *The Age of Projects*. Toronto: University of Toronto Press, 2008.

Nyquist, Mary. *Arbitrary Rule: Slavery, Tyranny, and the Power of Life and Death*. Chicago: University of Chicago Press, 2013.

Ogilvie, Brian W. *The Science of Describing: Natural History in Renaissance Europe*. Chicago: University of Chicago Press, 2006.

Ohlmeyer, Jane H., ed. *The Cambridge History of Ireland, Volume II: 1550–1730*. Cambridge: Cambridge University Press, 2018.

Ohlmeyer, Jane H. *Making Ireland English: The Irish Aristocracy in the Seventeenth Century*. New Haven: Yale University Press, 2012.

Ohlmeyer, Jane H., ed. *Political Thought in Seventeenth-Century Ireland: Kingdom or Colony*. Cambridge: Cambridge University Press, 2000.

Ohlmeyer, Jane H. "'Civilizinge of Those Rude Partes': Colonization within Britain and Ireland, 1580s-1640s," in *The Origins of Empire: British Overseas Enterprise to the Close of the Seventeenth Century*. Ed. Nicholas Canny. Oxford: Oxford University Press, 1998, pp. 124–46.

Ohlmeyer, Jane H. "Introduction: A Failed Revolution?" in *Ireland from Independence to Occupation, 1641–1660*. Ed. Jane H. Ohlmeyer. Cambridge: Cambridge University Press, 1995a, pp. 1–23.

Ohlmeyer, Jane H., ed. *Ireland from Independence to Occupation, 1641–1660*. Cambridge: Cambridge University Press, 1995b.

Ohlmeyer, Jane H. "Ireland Independent: Confederate Foreign Policy and International Relations During the Mid-Seventeenth Century," in *Ireland from Independence to Occupation, 1641–1660*. Ed. Jane H. Ohlmeyer. Cambridge: Cambridge University Press, 1995c, pp. 89–111.

Olson, Richard. *The Emergence of the Social Sciences, 1642–1792*. New York: Twayne Publishers, 1993.

Outram, Dorinda. *The Enlightenment*, second edition. Cambridge: Cambridge University Press, 2005.

Overbeek, Johannes. *History of Population Theories*. Rotterdam: Rotterdam University Press, 1974.

Overton, Mark. *Agricultural Revolution in England: The Transformation of the Agrarian Economy 1500–1850*. Cambridge: Cambridge University Press, 1996.

Pagden, Anthony. *Lords of All the World: Ideologies of Empire in Spain, Britain, and France, c.1500–c.1800*. New Haven: Yale University Press, 1995.

Park, Katharine and Lorraine Daston, eds. *The Cambridge History of Science, Volume 3: Early Modern Science*. Cambridge: Cambridge University Press, 2006.

Parrish, Susan Scott. *American Curiosity: Cultures of Natural History in the Colonial British Atlantic World*. Chapel Hill: University of North Carolina Press, 2006.

Pastorino, Cesare. "The Philosopher and the Craftsman: Francis Bacon's Notion of Experiment and Its Debt to Early Stuart Inventors," *Isis* 108:4 (2017): 749–68.

Pearson, Karl and Egon Sharpe Pearson. *The History of Statistics in the Seventeenth and Eighteenth Centuries: Against the Changing Background of Intellectual, Scientific, and Religious Thought*. High Wycombe: Charles Griffin, 1978.

Peltonen, Markku. "Politics and Science: Francis Bacon and the True Greatness of States," *Historical Journal* 35:2 (1992): 279–305.

Perry, Mary Elizabeth. *The Handless Maiden: Moriscos and the Politics of Religion in Early Modern Spain*. Princeton: Princeton University Press, 2005.

Pestana, Carla Gardina. *The English Conquest of Jamaica: Oliver Cromwell's Bid for Empire*. Cambridge: Harvard University Press, 2017.

Pettigrew, William A. *Freedom's Debt: The Royal African Company and the Politics of the Atlantic Slave Trade, 1672–1752*. Chapel Hill: University of North Carolina Press, 2013.

Pincus, Steve. "From Holy Cause to Economic Interest: The Study of Population and the Invention of the State," in *A Nation Transformed: England After the Restoration*. Eds. Alan Houston and Steve Pincus. Cambridge: Cambridge University Press, 2001, pp. 272–98.

Pincus, Steve. *Protestantism and Patriotism: Ideologies and the Making of English Foreign Policy, 1650–1668*. Cambridge: Cambridge University Press, 1996.

Pluymers, Keith. "Taming the Wilderness in Sixteenth- and Seventeenth-Century Ireland and Virginia," *Environmental History* 16:4 (2011): 610–32.

Pocock, John Greville Agard. *The Machiavellian Moment: Florentine Political Thought and the Atlantic Republican Tradition*. Princeton: Princeton University Press, 2003.

Poole, William. *The World Makers: Scientists of the Restoration and the Search for the Origins of the Earth*. Oxford: Peter Lang, 2010.

Poovey, Mary. *A History of the Modern Fact: Problems of Knowledge in the Sciences of Wealth and Society*. Chicago: University of Chicago Press, 1998.

Popkin, Richard H. *Isaac La Peyrère (1596–1676): His Life, Work, and Influence*. Leiden: E. J. Brill, 1987.

Popper, Nicholas. "An Information State for Elizabethan England," *Journal of Modern History*, 90:3 (2018): 503–35.

Popper, Nicholas. *Walter Ralegh's History of the World and the Historical Culture of the Late Renaissance*. Chicago: University of Chicago Press, 2012.

Porter, Theodore M. *Trust in Numbers: The Pursuit of Objectivity in Science and Public Life*. Princeton: Princeton University Press, 1995.

Raeff, Mark. "The Well-Ordered Police State and the Development of Modernity in Seventeenth- and Eighteenth-Century Europe: An Attempt at a Comparative Approach," *American Historical Review* 80:5 (1975): 1221–43.

Reungoat, Sabine. *William Petty: Observateur des Îles Britanniques*. Paris: Institut National d'Études Démographiques [INED], 2004.

Rheinberger, Hans-Jörg. *On Historicizing Epistemology: An Essay.* Stanford: Stanford University Press, 2010.

Robertson, James C. "Reckoning with London: Interpreting the Bills of Mortality before John Graunt," *Urban History* 23:3 (1996): 325–50.

Robertson, John. *The Case for Enlightenment: Scotland and Naples 1680–1760.* Cambridge: Cambridge University Press, 2005.

Robinson, Philip. *The Plantation of Ulster: British Settlement in an Irish Landscape, 1600–1670.* Belfast: Ulster Historical Foundation, 1994.

Rohrbasser, Jean-Marc and Jacques Véron, *Leibniz et les raisonnements sur la vie humaine.* Paris: INED, 2001.

Rosenberg, Daniel and Anthony Grafton. *Cartographies of Time: A History of the Timeline.* Princeton: Princeton University Press, 2010.

Rossi, Paolo. *The Dark Abyss of Time: The History of the Earth and the History of Nations from Hooke to Vico.* Trans. Lydia G. Cochrane. Chicago: University of Chicago Press, 1984.

Rubinstein, Nicolai. "Italian Political Thought, 1450–1530," in *The Cambridge History of Political Thought, 1450–1700.* Eds. J. H. Burns and Mark Goldie. Cambridge: Cambridge University Press, 1991, pp. 30–65.

Rusnock, Andrea A. *Vital Accounts: Quantifying Health and Population in Eighteenth-Century England and France.* Cambridge: Cambridge University Press, 2002.

Rusnock, Andrea A. "Biopolitics: Political Arithmetic in the Enlightenment," in *The Sciences in Enlightened Europe.* Eds. William Clark, Jan Golinski, and Simon Schaffer. Chicago: University of Chicago Press, 1999, pp. 49–68.

Rutkin, H. Darrel. "Astrology," in *The Cambridge History of Science, Volume 3: Early Modern Science.* Eds. Katharine Park and Lorraine Daston. Cambridge: Cambridge University Press, 2006, pp. 541–61.

Schaffer, Simon. "The Show That Never Ends: Perpetual Motion in the Early Eighteenth Century," *British Journal for the History of Science* 28:2 (1995): 157–89.

Schurer, Kevin and Tom Arkell, eds. *Surveying the People: The Interpretation and Use of Document Sources for the Study of Population in the Later Seventeenth Century.* Oxford: Leopard's Head Press, 1992.

Schweber, Libby. *Disciplining Statistics: Demography and Vital Statistics in France and England, 1830–1885.* Durham: Duke University Press, 2006.

Scott, James C. *Seeing Like a State: How Certain Schemes to Improve the Human Condition Have Failed.* New Haven: Yale University Press, 1998.

Seth, Suman. *Difference and Disease: Medicine, Race, and the Eighteenth-Century British Empire.* Cambridge: Cambridge University Press, 2018.

Shagan, Ethan. *The Rule of Moderation: Violence, Religion, and the Politics of Restraint in Early Modern England.* Cambridge: Cambridge University Press, 2011.

Shapin, Steven. *A Social History of Truth.* Chicago: University of Chicago Press, 1994.

Shapiro, Barbara J. *Political Communication and Political Culture in England, 1588–1688.* Stanford: Stanford University Press, 2012.

Shapiro, Barbara J. "Empiricism and English Political Thought, 1550–1720," *Eighteenth-Century Thought* 1 (2003): 3–35.

Shapiro, Barbara J. *A Culture of Fact: England, 1550–1720.* Ithaca: Cornell University Press, 2000.

Sharpe, Christina. *In the Wake: On Blackness and Being.* Durham: Duke University Press, 2016.

Shovlin, John. *The Political Economy of Virtue: Luxury, Patriotism, and the Origins of the French Revolution.* Ithaca: Cornell University Press, 2006.

Siena, Kevin. *Rotten Bodies: Class and Contagion in Eighteenth-Century Britain.* New Haven: Yale University Press, 2019.

Ó Siochrú, Micheál. *Confederate Ireland, 1642–1649: A Constitutional and Political Analysis.* Dublin: Four Courts Press, 1999.

Skinner, Quentin. *Visions of Politics I: Regarding Method.* Cambridge: Cambridge University Press, 2002.

Skinner, Quentin. *The Foundations of Modern Political Thought,* 2 vols. Cambridge: Cambridge University Press, 1978.

Slack, Paul. *The Invention of Improvement: Information and Material Progress in Seventeenth-Century England.* Oxford: Oxford University Press, 2015.

Slack, Paul. "Government and Information in Seventeenth-Century England," *Past and Present* 184 (2004): 33–68.

Slack, Paul. *From Reformation to Improvement.* Oxford: Oxford University Press, 1999.

Slack, Paul. *The English Poor Law, 1531–1782.* Cambridge: Cambridge University Press, 1995.

Slack, Paul. *Poverty and Policy in Tudor and Stuart England.* Harlow: Longman, 1988.

Slack, Paul. *The Impact of Plague in Tudor and Stuart England.* Oxford: Oxford University Press, 1985.

Smith, Abbot Emerson. *Colonists in Bondage: White Servitude and Convict Labor in America, 1607–1776.* New York: W. W. Norton, 1971.

Smith, Daniel Scott and J. David Hacker. "Cultural Demography: New England Deaths and the Puritan Perception of Risk," *Journal of Interdisciplinary History* 26:3 (1996): 367–92.

Smith, Leslie F. "Francesco Patrizi: Forgotten Political Scientist and Humanist," *Proceedings of the Oklahoma Academy of Science* 47 (1966): 348–51.

Smith, Pamela H. "Science on the Move: Recent Trends in the History of Early Modern Science," *Renaissance Quarterly* 62 (2009): 345–75.

Smith, Pamela H. *The Body of the Artisan: Art and Experience in the Scientific Revolution.* Chicago: University of Chicago Press, 2004.

Smyth, William J. *Map-Making, Landscapes and Memory: A Geography of Colonial and Early Modern Ireland c. 1530–1750.* Cork: Cork University Press, 2006.

Snyder, Jon. *Dissimulation and the Culture of Secrecy in Early Modern Europe.* Berkeley: University of California Press, 2009.

Soll, Jacob. *The Information Master: Jean-Baptiste Colbert's Secret State Intelligence System.* Ann Arbor: University of Michigan Press, 2009.

Soll, Jacob. *Publishing the Prince: History, Reading, and the Birth of Political Criticism.* Ann Arbor: University of Michigan Press, 2005.

Sommerville, C. John. *The News Revolution in England*. Oxford: Oxford University Press, 1996.

Sowerby, Scott. *Making Toleration: The Repealers and the Glorious Revolution*. Cambridge: Harvard University Press, 2013.

Spadafora, David. *The Idea of Progress in Eighteenth-Century Britain*. New Haven: Yale University Press, 1990.

Spengler, Joseph J. *French Predecessors of Malthus: A Study in Eighteenth-Century Wage and Population Theory*. Durham: Duke University Press, 1942.

Spierenburg, Pieter. *The Prison Experience: Disciplinary Institutions and Their Inmates in Early Modern Europe*. Amsterdam: Amsterdam University Press, 2007.

Stagl, Justin. *A History of Curiosity: The Theory of Travel, 1550–1800*. London: Routledge, 1995.

Stearns, Raymond Phineas. *Science in the British Colonies of America*. Urbana: University of Illinois Press, 1970.

Stern, Philip J. and Carl Wennerlind, eds. *Mercantilism Reimagined: Political Economy in Early Modern Britain and Its Empire*. Oxford: Oxford University Press, 2013.

Strangeland, Charles Emil. *Pre-Malthusian Doctrines of Population: A Study in the History of Economic Theory*. New York: Augustus M. Kelley, 1904.

Strasser, Ulrike. *State of Virginity: Gender, Religion, and Politics in an Early Modern Catholic State*. Ann Arbor: University of Michigan Press, 2004.

Strathmann, Ernest A. "Ralegh on the Problems of Chronology," *Huntington Library Quarterly* 11:2 (1948): 129–48.

Sussman, Charlotte. *Peopling the World: Representing Human Mobility from Milton to Malthus*. Philadelphia: University of Pennsylvania Press, 2020.

Sussman, Charlotte. "The Colonial Afterlife of Political Arithmetic: Swift, Demography, and Mobile Populations," *Cultural Critique* 56 (2004): 96–126.

Sweet, Timothy. *American Georgics: Economy and Environment in Early American Literature*. Philadelphia: University of Pennsylvania Press, 2002.

Swingen, Abigail L. *Competing Visions of Empire: Labor, Slavery, and the Origins of the British Atlantic Empire*. New Haven: Yale University Press, 2015.

Swingen, Abigail L. "Labor: Employment, Colonial Servitude, and Slavery in the Seventeenth-Century Atlantic," in *Mercantilism Reimagined: Political Economy in Early Modern Britain and Its Empire*. Eds. Philip J. Stern and Carl Wennerlind. Oxford: Oxford University Press, 2014, pp. 46–73.

Symcox, Geoffrey. "Toleration and Ragion Di Stato: Jews and Protestants in the Savoyard State, ca. 1650–1750," in *Discourses of Tolerance and Intolerance in the European Enlightenment*. Eds. Hans Erich Bödeker, Clorinda Donato, and Peter Hanns Reill. Toronto: University of Toronto Press, 2009, pp. 27–52.

Szreter, Simon. "Registration of Identities in Early Modern English Parishes and amongst the English Overseas," in *Registration and Recognition: Documenting the Person in World History: Proceedings of the British Academy*. Eds. Keith Breckinridge and Simon Szreter, 182 (2012): 67–92.

Taylor, Alan. *American Colonies: The Settling of North America*. New York: Penguin, 2001, pp. 118–23.

Taylor, John A. *British Empiricism and Early Political Economy: Gregory King's 1696 Estimates of National Wealth and Population*. Westport: Praeger, 2005.

Tazzara, Corey. *The Free Port of Livorno and the Transformation of the Mediterranean World, 1574–1790*. Oxford: Oxford University Press, 2017.

Terpstra, Nicholas. *Religious Refugees in the Early Modern World: An Alternative History of the Reformation*. Cambridge: Cambridge University Press, 2015.

Thirsk, Joan, ed. *Agricultural Change: Policy and Practice, 1500–1750 (Chapters from the Agrarian History of England and Wales, 1500–1750, volume 3)*. Cambridge: Cambridge University Press, 1990.

Thirsk, Joan, ed. "Enclosing and Engrossing, 1500–1640," in *Agricultural Change: Policy and Practice, 1500–1750 (Chapters from the Agrarian History of England and Wales, 1500–1750, volume 3)*. Cambridge: Cambridge University Press, 1990, pp. 54–109.

Thirsk, Joan. *Economic Policy and Projects: The Development of a Consumer Society in Early Modern England*. Oxford: Oxford University Press, 1978.

Thomas, David Oswald. *The Honest Mind: The Thought and Work of Richard Price*. Oxford: Oxford University Press, 1977.

Thornton, John. *Africa and Africans in the Making of the Atlantic World*. Cambridge: Cambridge University Press, 1998.

Todd, Margo. *Christian Humanism and the Puritan Social Order*. Cambridge: Cambridge University Press, 1987.

Tomaselli, Sylvana. "Political Economy: The Desire and Needs of Present and Future Generations," in *Inventing Human Science: Eighteenth-Century Domains*. Eds. Christopher Fox, Roy Porter, and Robert Wokler. Berkeley: University of California Press, 1995, pp. 292–322.

Tomaselli, Sylvana. "Moral Philosophy and Population Questions in Eighteenth-Century Europe," *Population and Development Review* 14:Supplement (1988): 7–29.

Trace, Jamie. "The Only Early English Translation of Giovanni Botero's Della ragion di stato: Richard Etherington and Sloane MS. 1065." *Electronic British Library Journal* (2016), article 4, www.bl.uk/eblj/2016articles/pdf/ebljarticle42016.pdf.

Tribe, Keith. *Land, Labour and Economic Discourse*. London: Routledge & Kegan Paul, 1978.

Tuck, Richard. *Philosophy and Government, 1572–1651*. Cambridge: Cambridge University Press, 1993.

Turner, Sasha. *Contested Bodies: Pregnancy, Childrearing, and Slavery in Jamaica*. Philadelphia: University of Pennsylvania Press, 2017.

Tuttle, Leslie. *Conceiving the Old Regime: Pronatalism and the Politics of Reproduction in Early Modern France*. Oxford: Oxford University Press, 2010.

Vogel, Brant. "The Letter from Dublin: Climate Change, Colonialism, and the Royal Society in the Seventeenth Century," *Osiris* 26 (2011): 111–28.

Walle, Etienne van de. "Fertility Transition, Conscious Choice, and Numeracy," *Demography* 29:4 (1992): 487–502.

Walsham, Alexandra. *The Reformation of the Landscape: Religion, Identity, and Memory in Early Modern Britain and Ireland*. Oxford: Oxford University Press, 2011.

Walsham, Alexandra. *Charitable Hatred: Tolerance and Intolerance in England, 1500–1700*. Manchester: Manchester University Press, 2006.

Walsham, Alexandra. *Providence in Early Modern England*. Oxford: Oxford University Press, 1999.

Waterman, Anthony Michael C. Waterman. *Revolution, Economics and Religion: Christian Political Economy 1798–1833*. Cambridge: Cambridge University Press, 1991.

Wear, Andrew. *Knowledge and Practice in English Medicine, 1550–1680*. Cambridge: Cambridge University Press, 2000.

Webster, Charles. *The Great Instauration: Science, Medicine and Reform 1626–1660*. London: Gerald Duckworth, 1975.

Webster, Charles. "The Authorship and Significance of Macaria," *Past and Present* 56 (1972): 34–48.

Weitz, Eric D. "From Vienna to the Paris System: International Politics and the Entangled Histories of Human Rights, Forced Deportations, and Civilizing Missions," *American Historical Review* 113:5 (2008): 1313–43.

Weitz, Eric D. "Racial Politics without the Concept of Race: Reevaluating Soviet Ethnic and National Purges," *Slavic Review* 61:1 (2002): 1–29.

Wennerlind, Carl. *Casualties of Credit: The English Financial Revolution, 1620–1720*. Cambridge: Harvard University Press, 2011.

Wennerlind, Carl. "Credit-Money as the Philosopher's Stone: Alchemy and the Coinage Problem in Seventeenth-Century England," *History of Political Economy* 35: Supplement (2003): 234–61.

Whiteman, Anne. "The Compton Census of 1676," in *Surveying the People: The Interpretation and Use of Document Sources for the Study of Population in the Later Seventeenth Century*. Eds. Kevin Schurer and Tom Arkell. Oxford: Leopard's Head Press, 1992, pp. 78–96.

Winch, Donald. *Riches and Poverty: An Intellectual History of Political Economy in Britain, 1750–1834*. Cambridge: Cambridge University Press, 1996.

Withers, Charles W. J. *Placing the Enlightenment: Thinking Geographically about the Age of Reason*. Chicago: University of Chicago Press, 2007.

Withington, Phil. *Society in Early Modern England: The Vernacular Origins of Some Powerful Ideas*. Cambridge: Polity Press, 2010.

Withington, Phil. *The Politics of Commonwealth: Citizens and Freemen in Early Modern England*. Cambridge: Cambridge University Press, 2005.

Wood, Andy. *The 1549 Rebellions and the Making of Early Modern England*. Cambridge: Cambridge University Press, 2007.

Wood, Diana. *Medieval Economic Thought*. Cambridge: Cambridge University Press, 2002.

Wood, Neal. *Foundations of Political Economy: Some Early Tudor View on State and Society*. Berkeley: University of California Press, 1994.

Wrightson, Keith. *Earthly Necessities: Economic Lives in Early Modern Britain*. New Haven: Yale University Press, 2000.

Wrigley, Edward Anthony and Roger S. Schofield. *The Population History of England, 1541–1871: A Reconstruction*. Cambridge: Cambridge University Press, 1989.

Yamamoto, Koji. *Taming Capitalism before Its Triumph: Public Service, Distrust, and 'Projecting' in Early Modern England*. Oxford: Oxford University Press, 2018.

Yamamoto, Koji. "Reformation and the Distrust of the Projector in the Hartlib Circle," *The Historical Journal* 55:2 (2012): 375–97.

Young, Brian. "Malthus Among the Theologians," in *Malthus, Medicine, and Morality: 'Malthusianism' after 1798*. Ed. Brian Dolan. Amsterdam: Rodopi, 2000, pp. 93–113.

Zabel, Christine, ed. *Historicizing Self-Interest in the Modern Atlantic World: A Plea for Ego?* Abingdon: Routledge, 2021.

Zagorin, Perez. *Francis Bacon*. Princeton: Princeton University Press, 1998.

Zilberstein, Anya. *A Temperate Empire: Making Climate Change in Early America*. Oxford: Oxford University Press, 2016.

Index

CPSIA information can be obtained
at www.ICGtesting.com
Printed in the USA
LVHW080735020522
717673LV00002B/61